Ordinations of
U.S. Catholic Bishops
1790-1989

A Chronological List
by Charles N. Bransom, Jr.

National Conference of Catholic Bishops
United States Catholic Conference

In August 1989, Most Reverend John L. May, Archbishop of Saint Louis and then-President of the National Conference of Catholic Bishops and the United States Catholic Conference, proposed that *Ordinations of U.S. Catholic Bishops, 1790-1989: A Chronological List* be considered for publication by the United States Catholic Conference, in order to fill a void in the availability of a volume that addresses chronologically the episcopal ordinations of the U.S. episcopate since its inception. In September 1989, after careful consideration and review, the present document was authorized for publication by the undersigned.

Monsignor Robert N. Lynch
General Secretary
NCCB/USCC

April 11, 1990

ISBN 1-55586-323-X

Contents

Foreword

Bishops are . . . shepherds of souls, who together with the Roman
Pontiff, the successor of Peter, and under his authority make
perennial the work of Christ, the eternal Shepherd. Christ gave
the apostles and their successors the command and the power to
teach all nations, to hallow them in the truth, and to feed them
(*Directory on the Pastoral Ministry of Bishops*, p. 14).

In this, the 200th year of the establishment of the first Roman Catholic See
in the city of Baltimore, Maryland, it is most fitting that *Ordinations of U.S.
Catholic Bishops, 1790–1989: A Chronological List* be made available to
Catholics throughout the country. From the consecration of John Carroll
on August 15, 1790 to the consecration of Sam Galip Jacobs on August 24,
1989, the tapestry woven by the Shepherds of the U.S. Church is splendid
indeed.

Framed within the historical context of a newborn nation, this volume's
chronological format follows the Church's evolution in the United States.
Each of the more than 1,000 entries provides a unique thread which, in
combination with all the others, helps form the fabric of the Church we
know today. By examining the threads of the tapestry, we learn about
ourselves and our Church. We discover who was ordained to the episcopate and when; who participated in the consecration and where; when
each diocese was erected; and who was named to that diocese. In addi-
tion, brief histories of the prelates are provided, detailing information
such as date and place of birth, date of ordination to the priesthood,
diocesan assignments, and so forth.

More than two decades of research went into producing *Ordinations of
U.S. Catholic Bishops, 1790–1989*. Nowhere else can one find a complete
chronological listing of the American episcopate nor such a rich lode of
information about bishops.

As we begin this third century of Catholicism in the United States, we
pause to remember those who came before us and reflect upon their con-
tributions to the tapestry yet being woven.

Most Reverend Daniel E. Pilarczyk, President
National Conference of Catholic Bishops
United States Catholic Conference

1

Introduction

On August 15, 1790, Fr. John Carroll of Upper Marlboro, Prince George's County, Maryland, bishop-elect of Baltimore, became a successor of the apostles through the imposition of the hands of Bishop Charles Walmesley, OSB, vicar apostolic of the Western District of England. Since that summer's day in 1790, more than one thousand men have received the fullness of the priesthood to serve as the shepherds of America's Catholics and dozens more have been called to the office of bishop in countries around the globe and in the service of the Holy See.

Since the erection of the Diocese of Baltimore on November 6, 1789, more than one hundred and eighty other dioceses have been established. This book chronicles the episcopal ordinations of the bishops of those dioceses.

By its very nature, the Roman Catholic Church is a hierarchical institution. The Fathers of the Second Vatican Council affirmed, in the decree *Christus Dominus,* that bishops are appointed by the Holy Spirit and are successors to the apostles through the Sacrament of Orders. A bishop is the chief priest in his diocese and it is from him that his priests receive their authority to celebrate the sacraments. It has been the constant teaching of the Roman Catholic Church that its bishops trace their orders back to the apostles through an unbroken sacramental and historical chain. This is also the belief of the Orthodox and Anglican Churches.

While this work has been prepared as part of the Bicentennial Celebration of the Establishment of the U.S. Hierarchy, it is the result of more than two decades of research by the author and is in the genre of works authored by members of the Wisques Group, to which its author belongs.

The Wisques Group is an informal association of researchers on the episcopate and draws its members—usually not more than a dozen—from around the world. The group originated in France in the 1950s and derives its name from the Abbey of Saint-Paul de Wisques, near Saint-Omer, where Dom André Chapeau, OSB, collects data submitted by members and disseminates it through a bimonthly publication, *Le Petit Episcopologe.* The present membership of the group includes researchers from Austria, Chile, England, France, Hungary, Spain, and the United States of America.

The present work is divided into two parts. The first part is a chronology

3

of the consecrations of all bishops who served as ordinaries, coadjutors, auxiliaries, and apostolic administrators of ecclesiastical territories found within the present-day limits of the fifty states, the District of Columbia, and the U.S. Virgin Islands. It also includes three bishops who have functioned as vicars general in American sees after being ordained for service in other countries and four bishops who were superiors general of Maryknoll.

This part has two appendices. Appendix A chronicles the consecrations of twelve American prelates who were consecrated bishops for service to the Holy See and who have not exercised episcopal ministry in the United States. Appendix B gives the details of the consecrations of the ten papal diplomats who served as apostolic delegates in the United States.

In preparing this work, it was decided to include only those American bishops who served a diocese within the present territorial limits of the United States of America or whose dioceses belonged to the National Conference of Catholic Bishops at the time of publication. For that reason, the Diocese of Saint Thomas in the U.S. Virgin Islands is included. The bishops of Puerto Rico are not included, since they form their own episcopal conference. Likewise, the Archdiocese of Agana and the Diocese of Carolines Marshalls are part of another bishops' conference and are not included herein. Using the same criteria, the dozens of Americans who have been consecrated for service in other countries have not been included.

Since this work is a chronology of bishops' ordinations, those priests who were named bishops but for one reason or another were not consecrated have not been included.

Each entry contains the date and place of consecration, including the church or other building in which it took place, as well as the names of the consecrator and two principal co-consecrators. A short *curriculum vitae* of the bishop consecrated is given, noting the date and place of his birth, the dates of his priestly ordination, nomination as bishop, and any subsequent transfers and/or resignation, and, where appropriate, the date and place of his death.

Some further explanation of the composition of these entries and the criteria used in determining the orthography of names will be helpful. The orthography of the names of the consecrators and co-consecrators in every case is that which they themselves employed. Every attempt has been made to give each name in full. The spelling of the names of non-American cities has been given in their common English equivalents when such exist.

The names of the bishops consecrated are given in English, with a few exceptions. The names of American bishops of French origin have been consistently given in their English equivalents, except in those few cases in which the bishops in question returned to France after consecration to occupy an episcopal see. Contemporary Hispanic bishops are listed using their proper Spanish names.

The name in parentheses after the birthplace of each bishop is that of the diocese or other ecclesiastical territory to which that city pertained at the time of the bishop's birth. Where no name is given in parentheses, the birthplace is synonymous with the episcopal see.

The proper term for the process of the nomination of a bishop is *election*. In the Roman Rite, it is the pope who elects each bishop. Nonetheless, I have chosen to use the colloquial "named" rather than "elected" in giving the appointment dates for priests as bishops.

Until 1970, all bishops who were not heads of dioceses were required to hold title to a defunct see. This class of bishops, known as titular bishops, included auxiliaries, coadjutors, apostolic administrators, vicars apostolic, territorial prelates, retired residential bishops, and members of the Roman Curia and Vatican diplomatic corps. Most of these titular dioceses were located in North Africa and the Middle East. However, in 1968 the Holy See, faced with a dwindling number of titular sees, added defunct European and American dioceses to the list of titular sees. In this work, the ancient titular sees are given in Latin, while the European and American titular sees are given in their respective vernacular languages. In 1970, it was decided that retired bishops would no longer be required to hold a titular see and could instead be called *emeriti* of their former dioceses. This decision had a retroactive effect and most retired American bishops at that time resigned from their titular sees. Beginning in July 1976, coadjutor bishops were no longer given titular sees, and in the following year, the same practice was instituted for territorial prelates.

Bishops who belong to religious orders and congregations have the traditional abbreviations of their orders given after their names. For the Sulpician bishops, the initials PSS have been employed, since that is the traditional usage everywhere except in the United States.

The second part of this work includes a diocesan overview of American consecrations and an index of all bishops whose consecrations are contained in Part I.

This overview is divided into two sections, one for the United States and one for foreign nations. The first section presents an alphabetical list of those American dioceses in which a consecration took place. Each diocesan list is subdivided, where necessary, between consecrations taking place in the episcopal city and those that took place elsewhere in the diocese. Within each subdivision, there is a chronological list of consecrations that took place in that city, listing the date, name of the bishop, and the see that he held at the time of his consecration.

The second part of the overview consists of an alphabetical list of foreign countries, subdivided by dioceses and then by cities, where necessary. The same information is given in each entry in this section as in the preceding one.

An alphabetical list of all bishops consecrated completes this section. The numbers after each name are keyed to the chronological list of consecrations, rather than to the pages on which the consecrations will be found.

In assembling the material for this book, difficulties in research and verification of data were numerous. The most common difficulties relate to dates, whether they be dates of birth, death, ordination, nomination, or consecration. In several cases, there have been discrepancies concerning dates of death, with incorrect dates being published in official publications and repeated in subsequent works. In other instances—happily very few—incorrect consecration dates have been published year after year without any correction being made.

An uncommon yet serious difficulty arises when a change in the participants of a ceremony is made after official programs are printed. Unless verification of the details are made independently of the program, incorrect information will be accepted as fact. Three recent instances, one in 1983 and two in 1988, where published co-consecrators were impeded by illness, illustrate the need for proper verification of details.

The most disheartening difficulty for any researcher is the lack of a response to an inquiry. While this has been a rare occurrence for domestic inquiries, foreign inquiries have a fairly high rate of nonresponse and, in both instances, the only remedies are diligence and the searching out of other possible sources. In the final analysis, one must realize that not everyone from whom information is requested has an interest in or the time for replying to an inquiry.

This book is not the first to treat the subject of American bishops, but it is the first to approach them from a chronological viewpoint. In 1888, Richard H. Clarke published his *Lives of the Deceased Bishops of the Catholic Church in the United States from the Earliest Period to the Present Time with Biographical Sketches of the Living Bishops.* In 1898, Francis Xavier Reuss published his *Biographical Cyclopedia of the Catholic Hierarchy of the United States (1798-1898)*. The late Joseph Bernard Code published two editions of his excellent *Dictionary of the American Hierarchy*, in 1939 and 1964. Over the years, numerous articles on the American hierarchy have appeared in the *Records of the American Catholic Historical Society* and in *The Catholic Historical Review*.

The episcopal lineage of the American hierarchy has been treated in *The Episcopal Lineage of the Catholic Hierarchy in the United States 1790-1963* (revised), by Jesse W. Lonsway and Aaron Pembleton, OFM. This study by Frs. Lonsway and Pembleton, as well as others by members of the Wisques Group, notably Monsieur Yves Guichart, have shown that more than ninety-six percent of the American hierarchy, past and present, and more than ninety-one percent of the current worldwide hierarchy, trace their apostolic succession back to one Italian bishop named in 1541, Scipione Rebiba, auxiliary bishop of Chieti. As of this date, no record of his consecration has been found.

The heraldry of the American hierarchy was to have been treated in two projects of Bro. Gerard Brassard, AA. The first, which was projected as a nine-volume work, began in 1956 with Volume III as *Armorial of the American Hierarchy* and continued with a second volume in 1964 as *Biographical and Heraldic Dictionary of Catholic Bishops in America*. In 1984, the first volume of a projected ten-volume *Encyclopedia of the Catholic Bishops in America 1789-1989* appeared, but no other volumes have been forthcoming.

This work began twenty-five years ago as part of my research project on the worldwide episcopate. The principal sources for this book can be divided into five areas. My correspondence and conversations over a period of twenty-five years with hundreds of bishops, archivists, diocesan historians, chancery officials, and members of the staff of the Apostolic Nunciature in Washington, D.C. make up the first and most important area. My extensive newspaper clippings file from both the Catholic and secular press, as well as those given to me by others, and news releases from Catholic News Service comprise the second category of sources. Also included in this category are dozens of commemorative issues of diocesan newspapers that have been published in conjunction with the ordinations or installations of bishops or to commemorate diocesan anniversaries. The third category encompasses information received from my colleagues over the years, including their research findings in the Vatican Archives and European diocesan archives. The fourth category is comprised of other works that I have utilized to fill in *lacunae* on a few early American bishops and some French-born American bishops. Francis X. Reuss's *Biographical Cyclopedia of the Catholic Hierarchy of United*

States (1798-1898) (Milwaukee, 1898) was consulted for details of the consecrations and biographies of several American bishops ordained prior to 1898. *Episcopologe Français des Temps Modernes 1592-1973,* by André Chapeau, OSB, and Fernand Combaluzier, CM (Paris, 1977) was of immense assistance in verifying and correcting information on the several dozen French bishops who served the early American Church. The fifth category is made up of several official and semiofficial publications of the Holy See. The *Acta Sanctae Sedis (1789-1908)* and the *Acta Apostolicae Sedis (1909 to the present)* were consulted for the official dates of appointment of many American bishops. The *Annuario Pontificio* from 1945 to the present was consulted for the biographical details of many American bishops when such details were not obtained elsewhere.

This work would not have been possible without the cooperation and assistance of the hundreds of bishops, archivists, and chancery officials who so patiently and painstakingly responded to my numerous inquiries over the years. Likewise, the staff of the Apostolic Nunciature and my colleagues in France, England, Austria, Spain, and Ireland have always responded so generously to my written and telephone requests. Not least of all, I must acknowledge the assistance of the staff of the Office of Media Relations, United States Catholic Conference, who have patiently answered my telephone inquiries every Tuesday for these many years. To all of them, I owe a great debt of gratitude.

I am grateful to Fr. Isidore Perraud, CSSp, of La Turballe, France, who has given me complete access to his extensive files on my visits to France and has supplied me with other invaluable assistance.

I must also acknowledge the continuing assistance of Msgr. Joseph M. Whalen of the Apostolic Nunciature and that of Fr. Thomas P. Doyle, OP, during his time of service at the Nunciature. They have both been extremely helpful in numerous ways, and their assistance is greatly appreciated.

I am particularly grateful to Msgr. Francis J. Weber, archivist of the Archdiocese of Los Angeles, and to Fr. Paul K. Thomas, archivist of the Archdiocese of Baltimore. Msgr. Weber presented me with an extensive amount of material concerning many American bishops, which he had amassed over a period of several years, and supplied additional material on several other bishops. Fr. Thomas meticulously reviewed many of the Baltimore-related entries of my manuscript. He corrected my errors, provided me with much additional information that I requested, and searched out information that I was unable to obtain from other dioceses. This work would not be nearly as complete or accurate had it not been for their generous assistance.

I wish to express my sincere thanks to Adam Joseph Voytek, who spent many hours reading over my manuscript, offering valuable suggestions, insights, and assistance. Finally, I am indebted in a most special way to Dom André Chapeau, OSB, for his advice, suggestions, generosity, support, and assistance for almost fifteen years. Dom Chapeau has always put himself and his archives at my disposition without reserve, and I am deeply grateful to him.

Charles N. Bransom, Jr.
Brandon, Florida

February 2, 1990
Feast of the Presentation of the Lord

Part I

Ordinations of U.S. Catholic Bishops by Chronological Order

1. 1790, August 15, at Lulworth Castle, Dorset, England. Charles Walmesley, OSB, Titular Bishop of Ramatha, assisted by Fr. Charles Plowden and Fr. James Porter, consecrated John Carroll, first Bishop of Baltimore, born at Upper Marlboro, Maryland (London District, England), January 8/19, 1736; priest February 14, 1761; Jesuit from September 8, 1753 until 1773; Prefect Apostolic of the United States June 9, 1784; named November 6, 1789; Apostolic Administrator of New Orleans from September 1, 1805 until 1815; first Archbishop of Baltimore April 8, 1808; died at Baltimore December 3, 1815.

2. 1795, April 26, at Havana, Cuba, Cathedral of the Immaculate Conception. Francisco de La Cuerda, Bishop of Puerto Rico, assisted by Felipe José de Trespalacios, Bishop of Havana, and by Cirilo Antonio Sieni, Titular Bishop of Tricala, consecrated Luis Ignacio Maria Peñalver y Cardenas, first Bishop of New Orleans, born at Havana, Cuba, April 3, 1749; priest April 4, 1772; named September 12, 1794; Archbishop of Guatemala July 20, 1801; resigned May 9, 1805; died at Havana July 17, 1810.

3. 1800, December 7, at Baltimore, Maryland, Saint Peter's Pro-cathedral. John Carroll, Bishop of Baltimore, assisted by Fr. Francis Charles Nagot, PSS, and Fr. Francis Beeston, consecrated Leonard Neale, Titular Bishop of Gortyna, Coadjutor of Baltimore, born at Port Tobacco, Maryland (London District, England), October 15, 1746; priest June 5, 1773; named April 17, 1795; succeeded to the metropolitan see of Baltimore December 3, 1815; died at Georgetown June 18, 1817.

4. 1801, November 15, at Rome, Italy, Church of Saints Vincent and Anastasius. Francesco Cardinal Lorenzana, assisted by Camillo Campanelli, Titular Archbishop of Athens, and by Simone de Magistris, Titular Bishop of Cyrene, consecrated Francisco Porro y Reinado, CC.RR.MM, Bishop of New Orleans, born at Gibraltar (Cadiz), Spain, October 15, 1739; named July 20, 1801; Bishop of Tarazona January 17, 1803; died at Tarazona January 3, 1814.

5. 1808, April 24, at Rome, Italy, Church of Saint Catherine of Siena. Michele Cardinal DiPietro, assisted by Tommaso Arezzo, Titular Archbishop of Seleucia, and Benedetto Sinibaldi, Titular Archbishop of Ephesus, consecrated Richard Luke Concanen, OP, first Bishop of New York, born at Kilbegnet (Elphin), Ireland, December 27, 1747; priest December 22, 1770; named April 8, 1808; died at Naples June 19, 1810.

6. 1810, October 28, at Baltimore, Maryland, Saint Peter's Pro-cathedral. John Carroll, Archbishop of Baltimore, assisted by Benedict Joseph Flaget, Bishop-elect of Bardstown, and Jean Louis de Cheverus, Bishop-elect of Boston, consecrated Michael Francis Egan, OFM.Rec, first Bishop of Philadelphia, born in Ireland, September 29, 1761; priest in 1785 or 1786; named April 8, 1808; died at Philadelphia July 22, 1815.

7. 1810, November 1, at Baltimore, Maryland, Saint Peter's Pro-cathedral. John Carroll, Archbishop of Baltimore, assisted by Leonard Neale, Titular Bishop of Gortyna, and Michael Francis Egan, Bishop of Philadelphia, consecrated Jean Louis Anne Madelain Lefebvre de Cheverus, first Bishop of Boston, born at Mayenne (Le Mans), France, January 28, 1768; priest December 18, 1790; named April 8, 1808; Apostolic Administrator of New York 1810 to 1815; Bishop of Montauban May 3, 1824; Archbishop of Bordeaux October 2, 1826; Cardinal February 1, 1836; died at Bordeaux July 19, 1836.

8. 1810, November 4, at Fell's Point, Maryland, Saint Patrick's Church. John Carroll, Archbishop of Baltimore, assisted by Jean de Cheverus, Bishop of Boston, and Michael Francis Egan, Bishop of Philadelphia, consecrated Benedict Joseph Flaget, PSS, first Bishop of Bardstown, born at Contournat (Clermont), France, November 7, 1763; priest June 1, 1788; named April 8, 1808; resigned May 7, 1832; renamed Bishop of Bardstown March 17, 1833; title of the see changed to Louisville February 13, 1841; died at Louisville February 11, 1850.

9. 1814, November 6, at Rome, Italy, Church of Saints Dominic and Sixtus. Cesare Cardinal Brancadoro, assisted by Giovanni Guerreri, Titular Archbishop of Athens, and Giovanni Marchetti, Titular Archbishop of Ancyra, consecrated John Connolly, OP, Bishop of New York, born at Monknewtown (Meath), Ireland, in 1751; priest September 24, 1774; named October 4, 1814; died at New York February 6, 1825.

10. 1815, September 24, at Rome, Italy, Church of Saint-Louis des Français. Giuseppe Cardinal Doria Pamphili, Bishop of Porto, assisted by Gabriel Cortois de Pressigny, Bishop emeritus of Saint Malo, and Francesco Saverio Pereira, Bishop of Terracina, Sezze e Priverno, consecrated Louis Guillaume Valentin DuBourg, PSS, Bishop of New Orleans, born at Cap Français (Santo Domingo), Hispaniola, January 10, 1766; priest March 20, 1790; named September 18, 1815; Apostolic Administrator of the Vicariate of the Two Floridas from July 14, 1823 to August 19, 1825; Vicar Apostolic of Mississippi August 19, 1825; resigned June 26, 1826; Bishop of Montauban October 2, 1826; Archbishop of Besançon July 29, 1833; died at Besançon December 12, 1833.

11. 1817, December 14, at Baltimore, Maryland, Saint Peter's Pro-cathedral. Jean de Cheverus, Bishop of Boston, assisted by John Connolly, Bishop of New York, and Fr. Louis de Barth of Philadelphia, consecrated Ambrose Maréchal, PSS, Archbishop of Baltimore, born at Ingré (Orléans), France, December 4, 1768; priest March 25, 1792; named Titular Archbishop of Stauropolis and Coadjutor of Baltimore July 4, 1817; succeeded to Baltimore July 4, 1817; Apostolic Administrator of the Vicariate of Alabama and Mississippi from 1823 to 1825; died at Baltimore January 29, 1828.

12. 1819, August 15, at Bardstown, Kentucky, Saint Joseph's Cathedral. Benedict Joseph Flaget, Bishop of Bardstown, assisted by Fr. Charles Nerinckx and Fr. Samuel Wilson, OP, consecrated John Baptist David, PSS, Titular Bishop of Mauricastro and Coadjutor of Bardstown, born at Couëron (Nantes), France, June 4, 1761; priest September 24, 1785; named July 4, 1817; succeeded to Bardstown August 25, 1832; Titular Bishop of Mauricastro March 17, 1833; died at Nazareth, Kentucky, July 12, 1841.

13. 1820, August 24, at Kilkenny, Ireland, Saint Mary's Church. John Troy, Archbishop of Dublin, assisted by Daniel Murray, Titular Archbishop of Hierapolis, and Kieran Marum, Bishop of Ossory, consecrated Patrick Kelly, first Bishop of Richmond, born at Kilkenny (Ossory), Ireland, April 16, 1779; priest July 18, 1802; named July 11, 1820; Bishop of Waterford and Leighlin February 22, 1822; died at Waterford October 8, 1829.

14. 1820, September 21, at Cork, Ireland, Saint Finbar's Cathedral. John Murphy, Bishop of Cork, assisted by Kieran Marum, Bishop of Ossory, and Patrick Kelly, Bishop of Richmond, consecrated John England, first Bishop of Charleston, born at Cork, Ireland, September 23, 1786; priest October 11, 1808; named July 11, 1820; died at Charleston April 11, 1842.

15. 1820, September 24, at London, England, Private chapel of Bishop Poynter. William Poynter, Titular Bishop of Alia, assisted by Fr. James Yorke Bramston and Fr. Joseph Carpue, consecrated Henry Conwell, Bishop of Philadelphia, born at Ballyriff (Armagh), Ireland, in 1748; priest in October or November 1776; named November 26, 1819; died at Philadelphia April 22, 1842.

16. 1822, January 13, at Springfield, Kentucky, Saint Rose's Church. Benedict Joseph Flaget, Bishop of Bardstown, assisted by Fr. Samuel Wilson, OP, and Fr. Augustine Hill, OP, consecrated Edward Dominic Fenwick, OP, first Bishop of Cincinnati, born at Saint Mary's County, Maryland (London District, England), August 19, 1768; priest February 23, 1793; named June 19, 1821; died at Wooster, Ohio, September 26, 1832.

17. 1824, March 25, at Donaldsonville, Louisiana, Church of the Ascension. Louis Guillaume Valentin DuBourg, Bishop of New Orleans, assisted by Fr. Louis Sibourg and Fr. Antonio Sedella, OFM.Cap., consecrated Joseph Rosati, CM, Titular Bishop of Tanagra and Coadjutor of New Orleans, born at Sora (Naples), Italy, January 12, 1789; priest February 10, 1811; named Titular Bishop of Tanagra and Vicar Apostolic of Alabama and Mississippi August 13, 1822, to which was added Florida on January 21, 1823; refused the Vicariate May 6, 1823; named Coadjutor of New Orleans July 14, 1823; did not succeed to New Orleans upon the resignation of Bishop DuBourg on June 26, 1826; first Bishop of Saint Louis March 20, 1827; died at Rome September 25, 1843.

18. 1825, November 1, at Baltimore, Maryland, Cathedral of the Assumption. Ambrose Maréchal, Archbishop of Baltimore, assisted by John England, Bishop of Charleston, and by Henry Conwell, Bishop of Philadelphia, consecrated Benedict Joseph Fenwick, SJ, Bishop of Boston, born at Leonard Town, Maryland (London District, England), September 3, 1782; Jesuit at Baltimore October 18, 1806; priest June 11, 1808; named May 10, 1825; died at Boston August 11, 1846.

19. 1826, October 29, at Baltimore, Maryland, Cathedral of the Assumption. Ambrose Maréchal, Archbishop of Baltimore, assisted by Henry Conwell, Bishop of Philadelphia, and Fr. John Power of New York, consecrated John Dubois, Bishop of New York, born at Paris, France, August 24, 1764; priest September 28, 1787; named May 26, 1826; died at New York December 20, 1842.

20. 1826, November 5, at Saint Louis, Missouri, Cathedral of Saint Louis King of France. Joseph Rosati, Titular Bishop of Tanagra, assisted by Fr. Donatien Olivier and Fr. Charles Van Quickenborne, SJ, consecrated Michael Portier, Titular Bishop of Olena and Vicar Apostolic of Florida and Alabama, born at Montbrison (Lyons), France, September 7, 1795; priest May 16, 1818; named August 26, 1825; first Bishop of Mobile May 15, 1829; died at Mobile May 14, 1859.

21. 1828, May 25, at Baltimore, Maryland, Cathedral of the Assumption. Benedict Joseph Flaget, Bishop of Bardstown, assisted by Henry Conwell, Bishop of Philadelphia, and John Dubois, Bishop of New York, consecrated James Whitfield, Archbishop of Baltimore, born at Liverpool (Northern District), England, November 3, 1770; priest July 24, 1809; named Titular Bishop of Apollonia January 8, 1828 and Coadjutor of Baltimore January 11, 1828; succeeded to Baltimore January 29, 1828; Apostolic Administrator of Richmond from 1828 to 1834; died at Baltimore October 19, 1834.

22. 1830, June 6, at Bardstown, Kentucky, Saint Joseph's Cathedral. Benedict Joseph Flaget, Bishop of Bardstown, assisted by Henry Conwell, Bishop of Philadelphia, and John Baptist David, Titular Bishop of Mauricastro, consecrated Francis Patrick Kenrick, Titular Bishop of Arathia, Coadjutor and Apostolic Administrator of Philadelphia, born at Dublin, Ireland, December 3, 1797; priest April 7, 1821; named February 25, 1830; succeeded to Philadelphia April 22, 1842; Archbishop of Baltimore August 19, 1851; died at Baltimore July 8, 1863.

23. 1830, June 24, at New Orleans, Louisiana, Saint Louis Cathedral. Joseph Rosati, Bishop of Saint Louis, assisted by Michael Portier, Bishop of Mobile, and Fr. Benedict Richard, Vicar General, consecrated Leo Raymond DeNeckère, CM, Bishop of New Orleans, born at Wevelghem (Ghent), Belgium, June 7, 1799; priest October 13, 1822; named August 4, 1829; died at New Orleans September 5, 1833.

24. 1833, October 6, at Cincinnati, Ohio, Saint Peter in Chains Cathedral, Sycamore Street. Joseph Rosati, Bishop of Saint Louis, assisted by Fr. Stephen Badin and Fr. Jerome Vogeler, consecrated Frederick John Conrad Résé, first Bishop of Detroit, born at Vienenberg (Hildesheim), Germany, February 6, 1791; priest March 15, 1823; named March 8, 1833; suspended from all episcopal functions August 20, 1840; died at Kloppenburg, Germany, December 29, 1871.

25. 1833, October 13, at Baltimore, Maryland, Cathedral of the Assumption. James Whitfield, Archbishop of Baltimore, assisted by John Dubois, Bishop of New York, and Francis Patrick Kenrick, Titular Bishop of Arathia, consecrated John Baptist Purcell, Bishop of Cincinnati, born at Mallow (Cloyne), Ireland, February 26, 1800; priest May 20, 1826; named March 8, 1833; first Archbishop of Cincinnati July 19, 1850; died at Saint Martin, Ohio, July 4, 1883.

26. 1834, July 20, at Bardstown, Kentucky, Saint Joseph's Cathedral. Benedict Joseph Flaget, Bishop of Bardstown, assisted by John Baptist David, Titular Bishop of Mauricastro, and Fr. Richard Pius Miles, OP, consecrated Guy Ignatius Chabrat, PSS, Titular Bishop of Bolina and Coadjutor of Bardstown, born at Chambres (Saint-Flour), France, December 27, 1787; priest December 21, 1811; named July 27, 1832, but refused; named again March 21, 1834; Apostolic Administrator of Bardstown from 1835 to 1839; resigned as coadjutor April 10, 1847; died at Mauriac, France, November 21, 1868.

27. 1834, September 14, at Baltimore, Maryland, Cathedral of the Assumption. James Whitfield, Archbishop of Baltimore, assisted by Benedict Joseph Flaget, Bishop of Bardstown, and Francis Patrick Kenrick, Titular Bishop of Arathia, consecrated Samuel Eccleston, PSS, Titular Bishop of Thermae and Coadjutor of Baltimore, born near Chestertown, Maryland (Baltimore), June 27, 1801; priest April 24, 1825; named Coadjutor March 4, 1834 and to the titular see of Thermae March 11, 1834; succeeded to Baltimore and the administration of Richmond October 19, 1834; resigned as Apostolic Administrator of Richmond November 22, 1840; died at Georgetown April 22, 1851.

28. 1834, October 28, at Saint Louis, Missouri, Cathedral of Saint Louis King of France.* Benedict Joseph Flaget, Bishop of Bardstown, assisted by Joseph Rosati, Bishop of Saint Louis, and John Baptist Purcell, Bishop of Cincinnati, consecrated Simon William Gabriel Bruté de Remur, first Bishop of Vincennes, born at Rennes, France, March 20, 1779; priest June 11, 1808; named May 6, 1834; died at Vincennes June 26, 1839.

This was the first consecration in the second cathedral.

29. 1834, December 21, at Carlow, Ireland, Cathedral of Our Lady of the Assumption. Edward Nolan, Bishop of Kildare, assisted by Michael Slattery, Archbishop of Cashel, and William Kinsella, Bishop of Ossory, consecrated William Clancy, Titular Bishop of Oreus and Coadjutor of Charleston, born at Cork, Ireland, February 12, 1802; priest May 24, 1823; named October 30, 1834; Vicar Apostolic of British Guyana April 12, 1837; resigned his vicariate September 3, 1843; died at Cork June 19, 1847.

30. 1835, November 22, at New Orleans, Louisiana, Saint Louis Cathedral. Joseph Rosati, Bishop of Saint Louis, assisted by Michael Portier, Bishop of Mobile, and John Baptist Purcell, Bishop of Cincinnati, consecrated Anthony Blanc, Bishop of New Orleans, born at Sury-le-Comtal (Lyons), France, October 11, 1792; priest July 22, 1816; named June 19, 1835; first Archbishop of New Orleans July 19, 1850; died at New Orleans June 20, 1860.

31. 1837, December 10, at Mobile, Alabama, Cathedral of the Immaculate Conception. Michael Portier, Bishop of Mobile, assisted by Anthony Blanc, Bishop of New Orleans, and Fr. Jean Stephen Bazin of Mobile, consecrated John Mathias Peter Loras, first Bishop of Dubuque, born at Lyons, France, August 30, 1792; priest November 12, 1815; named

July 28, 1837; died at Dubuque February 19, 1858.

32. 1838, January 7, at New York, New York, Saint Patrick's Cathedral on Mott Street. John Dubois, Bishop of New York, assisted by Benedict Joseph Fenwick, Bishop of Boston, and Francis Patrick Kenrick, Titular Bishop of Arathia, consecrated John Joseph Hughes, Titular Bishop of Basilinopolis, Coadjutor of New York, born at Annaloghan (Armagh), Ireland, June 24, 1797; priest October 15, 1826; named August 8, 1837; Apostolic Administrator of New York in August 1838; succeeded to New York December 20, 1842; first Archbishop of New York July 19, 1850; died at New York January 3, 1864.

33. 1838, September 16, at Bardstown, Kentucky, Saint Joseph's Cathedral. Joseph Rosati, Bishop of Saint Louis, assisted by Simon William Gabriel Bruté de Remur, Bishop of Vincennes, and Guy Ignatius Chabrat, Titular Bishop of Bolina, consecrated Richard Pius Miles, OP, first Bishop of Nashville, born at Prince George's County, Maryland (Baltimore), May 17, 1791; priest September 21, 1816; named July 28, 1837; died at Nashville February 21, 1860.

34. 1839, August 18, at Paris, France, Dames du Sacré-Coeur. Charles de Forbin-Janson, Bishop of Nancy, assisted by Louis Blanquart de Bailleul, Bishop of Versailles, and Jean Simon Lemercier, Bishop of Beauvais, consecrated Celestin René Laurent Guynemer de La Hailandière, Bishop of Vincennes, born at Triandin (Rennes), France, May 2, 1798; priest May 28, 1825; named Titular Bishop of Axiere and Coadjutor of Vincennes May 17, 1839; succeeded to Vincennes June 26, 1839; resigned February 7, 1847; died at Triandin May 1, 1882.

35. 1840, October 4, at Guadalupe, State of Zacatecas, Mexico, Franciscan Church. Antonio María de Jesús Campos, Titular Bishop of Rhesaina, assisted by José Belaunzarán, Bishop emeritus of Linares, and Joaquín Fernández Madrid y Canal, Titular Bishop of Tanagra, consecrated Francisco José Vicente Garcia Diego y Moreno, OFM.Obs, first Bishop of California, born at Lagos (Guadalajara), Mexico September 17, 1785; priest November 14, 1808; named April 27, 1840; died at Santa Barbara, California, April 30, 1846.

36. 1841, March 14, at Baltimore, Maryland, Cathedral of the Assumption. Samuel Eccleston, Archbishop of Baltimore, assisted by Benedict Joseph Fenwick, Bishop of Boston, and John Joseph Hughes, Titular Bishop of Basilinopolis, consecrated John Joseph Mary Benedict Chanche, PSS, first Bishop of Natchez, born at Baltimore, Maryland, October 4, 1795; priest June 5, 1819; named December 15, 1840; died at Frederick, Maryland, July 22, 1852.

37. 1841, March 21, at Baltimore, Maryland, Cathedral of the Assumption. Samuel Eccleston, Archbishop of Baltimore, assisted by Benedict Joseph Fenwick, Bishop of Boston, and John Joseph Hughes, Titular Bishop of Basilinopolis, consecrated Richard Vincent Whelan, Bishop of Richmond, born at Baltimore, Maryland, January 28, 1809; priest May 1, 1831; named December 15, 1840; first Bishop of Wheeling July 23, 1850; died at Baltimore July 7, 1874.

38. 1841, November 21, at Philadelphia, Pennsylvania, Saint John's Procathedral. Francis Patrick Kenrick, Titular Bishop of Arathia, assisted by John England, Bishop of Charleston, and John Joseph Hughes, Titular Bishop of Basilinopolis, consecrated Peter Paul Lefevère, Titular Bishop of Zela, Coadjutor and Apostolic Administrator of Detroit, born at Roulers (Bruges), Belgium, April 29, 1804; priest November 30, 1831; named July 23, 1841; died at Detroit March 4, 1869.

39. 1841, November 30, at Philadelphia, Pennsylvania, Saint Mary's Church. Joseph Rosati, Bishop of Saint Louis, assisted by Francis Patrick Kenrick, Titular Bishop of Arathia, and Peter Paul Lefevère, Titular Bishop of Zela, consecrated Peter Richard Kenrick, Titular Bishop of Drasus, Coadjutor of Saint Louis, born at Dublin, Ireland, August 17, 1806; priest March 6, 1832; named April 30, 1841; succeeded to Saint Louis September 25, 1843; first Archbishop of Saint Louis July 20, 1847; Titular Archbishop of Marcianopolis May 21, 1895; died at Saint Louis March 4, 1896.

40. 1842, March 6, at New Orleans, Louisiana, Saint Louis Cathedral. Anthony Blanc, Bishop of New Orleans, assisted by Michael Portier, Bishop of Mobile, and John Joseph Chanche, Bishop of Natchez, consecrated John Mary Odin, CM, Titular Bishop of Claudiopolis, Vicar Apostolic of Texas, born at Ambierle, hamlet of Hauteville (Lyons), France, February 25, 1800; priest May 4, 1823; named Titular Bishop of Claudiopolis and Coadjutor and Apostolic Administrator of Detroit December 15, 1840; refused the nomination May 7, 1841; confirmed in the see of Claudiopolis and appointed Vicar Apostolic of Texas July 16, 1841; first Bishop of Galveston May 21, 1847; Archbishop of New Orleans February 15, 1861; died at Ambierle May 25, 1870.

41. 1843, August 15, at Rome, Italy, Irish College, Saint Agatha's Chapel. Giacomo Filippo Cardinal Fransoni, assisted by Fabio Asquini, Titular Archbishop of Tarsus, and Giuseppe Castellani, Titular Bishop of Porphyreon, consecrated Michael O'Connor, first Bishop of Pittsburgh, born at Cobh (Cloyne), Ireland, September 27, 1810; priest June 1, 1833; named August 11, 1843; first Bishop of Erie July 29, 1853; Bishop of Pittsburgh December 20, 1853; resigned May 23, 1860; joined the Jesuits

December 22, 1860; died at Woodstock, Maryland, October 18, 1872.

42–44. 1844, March 10, at New York, New York, Saint Patrick's Cathedral on Mott Street. John Joseph Hughes, Bishop of New York, assisted by Benedict Joseph Fenwick, Bishop of Boston, and Richard Vincent Whelan, Bishop of Richmond, consecrated (1) John McCloskey, Titular Bishop of Axieri, Coadjutor of New York, born at Brooklyn, New York (New York), March 10, 1810; priest January 12, 1834; named November 21, 1843; first Bishop of Albany May 21, 1847; Archbishop of New York May 6, 1864; Cardinal March 15, 1875; died at New York October 10, 1885. Consecrated (2) William Quarter, first Bishop of Chicago, born at Killurine (Killaloe), Ireland, January 21, 1806; priest September 19, 1829; named November 28, 1843; died at Chicago April 10, 1848. Consecrated (3) Andrew Byrne, first Bishop of Little Rock, born at Navan (Meath), Ireland, December 3, 1802; priest November 11, 1827; named November 28, 1843; died at Helena, Arkansas, June 10, 1862.

45. 1844, March 17, at Baltimore, Maryland, Cathedral of the Assumption. Benedict Joseph Fenwick, Bishop of Boston, assisted by Richard Vincent Whelan, Bishop of Richmond, and Andrew Byrne, Bishop of Little Rock, consecrated William Barber Tyler, first Bishop of Hartford, born at Derby, Vermont (Baltimore), June 5, 1806; priest June 3, 1829; named November 28, 1843; died at Providence June 18, 1849.

46–47. 1844, March 19, at Cincinnati, Ohio, Saint Peter in Chains Cathedral, Sycamore Street. John Baptist Purcell, Bishop of Cincinnati, assisted by Michael O'Connor, Bishop of Pittsburgh, and Richard Pius Miles, Bishop of Nashville, consecrated (1) Ignatius Aloysius Reynolds, Bishop of Charleston, born at Bardstown, Kentucky (Baltimore), August 22, 1798; priest October 24, 1823; named November 18, 1843; died at Charleston March 6, 1855. Consecrated (2) John Martin Henni, first Bishop of Milwaukee, born at Misanenga (Chur), Switzerland, June 15, 1805; priest February 2, 1829; named November 28, 1843; first Archbishop of Milwaukee February 12, 1875; died at Milwaukee September 7, 1881.

48. 1844, March 24, at Georgetown, District of Columbia, Chapel of the Visitation Nuns, Georgetown University. Benedict Joseph Fenwick, Bishop of Boston, assisted by Richard Vincent Whelan, Bishop of Richmond, and William Barber Tyler, Bishop of Hartford, consecrated John Bernard Fitzpatrick, Titular Bishop of Callipolis, Coadjutor of Boston, born at Boston, Massachusetts, November 15, 1812; priest June 13, 1840; named November 21, 1843; succeeded to Boston August 11, 1846; died at Boston February 13, 1866.

49. 1845, July 25, at Montréal, Canada, Saint James Cathedral. Ignace

Bourget, Bishop of Montréal, assisted by Rémi Gaulin, Bishop of Kingston, and Patrick Phelan, Titular Bishop of Carrhe, consecrated Francis Norbert Blanchet, Titular Bishop of Drasus, Vicar Apostolic of Oregon, born at Saint-Pierre, Rivière du Sud (Québec), Canada, September 3, 1795; priest July 19, 1819; named Titular Bishop of Philadelphia and Vicar Apostolic of Oregon December 1, 1843; Titular Bishop of Drasus May 7, 1844; first Archbishop of Oregon City July 24, 1846; Apostolic Administrator of Walla Walla from May 31, 1850 until the suppression of that see on July 29, 1853; resigned December 12, 1880; Titular Archbishop of Amida February 4, 1881; died at Portland, Oregon, June 18, 1883.

50. 1846, September 27, at Montréal, Canada, Saint James Cathedral. Ignace Bourget, Bishop of Montréal, assisted by Rémi Gaulin, Bishop of Kingston, and Jean-Charles Prince, Titular Bishop of Martyropolis, consecrated Augustine Magloire Alexander Blanchet, first Bishop of Walla Walla, born at Saint-Pierre, Rivière du Sud (Québec), Canada, August 22, 1797; priest June 3, 1821; named July 28, 1846; first Bishop of Nesqually May 31, 1850; Titular Bishop of Ibora December 23, 1879; died at Vancouver February 25, 1887.

51. 1847, October 10, at Cincinnati, Ohio, Saint Peter in Chains Cathedral.* John Baptist Purcell, Bishop of Cincinnati, assisted by Richard Vincent Whelan, Bishop of Richmond, and Fr. Timothy Collins, Vicar General, consecrated Louis Amadeus Rappe, first Bishop of Cleveland, born at Audrehem (Arras), France, February 2, 1801; priest March 14, 1829; named April 23, 1847; resigned August 22, 1870; died at Saint Albans, Vermont, September 8, 1877.

This was the first consecration in the cathedral at Eighth and Plum Streets. This edifice served as the cathedral from 1845 to 1938 and from 1957 to the present.

52. 1847, October 17, at New York, New York, Saint Patrick's Cathedral, Mott Street. John Joseph Hughes, Bishop of New York, assisted by William Walsh, Bishop of Halifax, and John McCloskey, Bishop of Albany, consecrated John Timon, CM, first Bishop of Buffalo, born at Conewago, Pennsylvania (Baltimore), February 12, 1797; priest September 23, 1826; named April 23, 1847; died at Buffalo April 16, 1867.

53. 1847, October 24, at Vincennes, Indiana, Saint Francis Xavier Cathedral. Michael Portier, Bishop of Mobile, assisted by John Baptist Purcell, Bishop of Cincinnati, and Celestin de La Hailandière, Bishop emeritus of Vincennes, consecrated John Stephen Bazin, Bishop of Vincennes, born at Duerne (Lyons), France, October 15, 1796; priest July 22, 1822; named April 3, 1847; died at Vincennes April 23, 1848.

54. 1847, November 28, at Santiago, Chile, Cathedral of the Assumption. Hilarion Etrura, Titular Bishop of Augustopolis, assisted by Fr. José Alejo Eyzaguirre, Dean of the Cathedral Chapter, and Fr. Pedro de Reyes, Canon, consecrated Louis Désiré Maigret, SS.CC, Titular Bishop of Arathia, Vicar Apostolic of Hawaii, born at Maille (Poitiers), France, September 14, 1804; priest September 23, 1828; named September 11, 1846; died at Honolulu June 11, 1882.

55. 1848, September 10, at Louisville, Kentucky, Saint Louis Cathedral. Benedict Joseph Flaget, Bishop of Louisville, assisted by Francis Patrick Kenrick, Bishop of Philadelphia, and Richard Pius Miles, Bishop of Nashville, consecrated Martin John Spalding, Titular Bishop of Lengone, Coadjutor of Louisville, born at Rolling Fork (Bardstown), Kentucky, May 23, 1810; priest August 13, 1834; named April 18, 1848; succeeded to Louisville February 11, 1850; Archbishop of Baltimore May 6, 1864; died at Baltimore February 7, 1872.

56. 1849, January 14, at Vincennes, Indiana, Saint Francis Xavier Cathedral. Richard Pius Miles, Bishop of Nashville, assisted by Martin John Spalding, Titular Bishop of Lengone, and Fr. Hippolytus DuPontavice, Vicar General of Vincennes, consecrated James Mary Maurice Des Landes d'Aussac de Saint-Palais, Bishop of Vincennes, born at La Salvetat (Montpellier), France, November 15, 1811; priest May 28, 1836; named October 3, 1848; died at Saint Mary of the Woods, Indiana, June 28, 1877.

57. 1849, February 11, at Saint Louis, Missouri, Saint Francis Xavier Church. Peter Richard Kenrick, Archbishop of Saint Louis, assisted by John Mathias Loras, Bishop of Dubuque, and Richard Pius Miles, Bishop of Nashville, consecrated John Oliver Van de Velde, SJ, Bishop of Chicago, born at Lebbeke, near Termonde, (Mechelin), Belgium, April 3, 1795; priest September 16, 1827; named December 1, 1848; Bishop of Natchez July 29, 1853; died at Natchez November 13, 1855.

58. 1850, June 30, at Rome, Italy, Church of San Carlo al Corso. Giacomo Filippo Cardinal Fransoni, assisted by Giuseppe Valerga, Patriarch of Jerusalem, and Giovanni Domenico Stefanelli, Titular Archbishop of Trajanopolis, consecrated Joseph Sadoc Alemany, OP, Bishop of Monterey, born at Vich, Spain, July 13, 1814; priest March 11, 1837; named May 31, 1850; first Archbishop of San Francisco July 29, 1853; resigned December 21, 1884; Titular Archbishop of Pelusium March 20, 1885; died at Valencia, Spain, April 14, 1888.

59. 1850, November 10, at Rochester, New York, Saint Patrick's Church. John Timon, Bishop of Buffalo, assisted by John McCloskey, Bishop of

Albany, and John Bernard Fitzpatrick, Bishop of Boston, consecrated Bernard O'Reilly, Bishop of Hartford, born at Cunnareen (Ardagh), March 1, 1803; priest October 16, 1831; named Titular Bishop of Pompeiopolis and Coadjutor of Hartford July 23, 1850, his predecessor having died prior to this nomination; named Bishop of Hartford August 9, 1850; died at sea in the sinking of the Pacific, which departed from England on January 23, 1856.

60. 1850, November 10, at Philadelphia, Pennsylvania, Saint John's Procathedral. Samuel Eccleston, Archbishop of Baltimore, assisted by Francis Patrick Kenrick, Bishop of Philadelphia, and Michael O'Connor, Bishop of Pittsburgh, consecrated Francis Xavier Gartland, first Bishop of Savannah, born at Dublin, Ireland, January 19, 1808; priest August 5, 1832; named July 23, 1850; died at Savannah September 20, 1854.

61. 1850, November 10, at Bardstown, Kentucky, former Cathedral of Saint Joseph. Peter Richard Kenrick, Archbishop of Saint Louis, assisted by Richard Pius Miles, Bishop of Nashville, and Martin John Spalding, Bishop of Louisville, consecrated John McGill, Bishop of Richmond, born at Philadelphia, Pennsylvania, November 4, 1809; priest June 13, 1835; named July 23, 1850; died at Richmond January 14, 1872.

62. 1850, November 24, at Cincinnati, Ohio, Cathedral of Saint Peter in Chains. Martin John Spalding, Bishop of Louisville, assisted by James de Saint-Palais, Bishop of Vincennes, and Louis Amadeus Rappe, Bishop of Cleveland, consecrated John Baptist Lamy, Titular Bishop of Agathonice, Vicar Apostolic of New Mexico, born at Lempdes (Clermont), France, October 11, 1814; priest December 22, 1838; named July 23, 1850; first Bishop of Santa Fe July 29, 1853; first Archbishop of Santa Fe February 12, 1875; Titular Archbishop of Cyzicus August 18, 1885; died at Santa Fe February 13, 1888.

63. 1851, January 26, at Belley, France, Chapel of the Bishopric. Alexandre Raymond Devie, Bishop of Belley, assisted by Etienne Marilley, Bishop of Lausanne, and Georges Chalandon, Titular Bishop of Thaumacus, consecrated Joseph Cretin, first Bishop of Saint Paul, born at Montluel (Lyons), France, December 10, 1799; priest December 20, 1823; named July 23, 1850; died at Saint Paul February 22, 1857.

64. 1851, March 25, at Saint Louis, Missouri, Saint Francis Xavier Church. Peter Richard Kenrick, Archbishop of Saint Louis, assisted by James Oliver Van de Velde, Bishop of Chicago, and James de Saint-Palais, Bishop of Vincennes, consecrated John Baptist Miège, SJ, Titular Bishop of Messene, Vicar Apostolic of Kansas and the Indian Territory, born at Albertville (Annecy), France, September 18, 1815; priest September 12,

1844; named July 23, 1850; resigned his vicariate November 18, 1874; died at Woodstock, Maryland, July 21, 1884.

65. 1852, March 28, at Baltimore, Maryland, Saint Alphonsus Church. Francis Patrick Kenrick, Archbishop of Baltimore, assisted by Bernard O'Reilly, Bishop of Hartford, and Fr. Francis L'Homme, PSS, consecrated John Nepomucene Neumann, C.SS.R, Bishop of Philadelphia, born at Prachatitz (Budweis), Bohemia, Austria, March 28, 1811; priest June 25, 1836; named February 5, 1852; died at Philadelphia January 5, 1860; beatified October 13, 1963; canonized June 19, 1977.

66–68. 1853, October 30, at New York, New York, Saint Patrick's Cathedral, Mott Street. Gaetano Bedini, Titular Archbishop of Thebes, Apostolic Nuncio to Brazil and special envoy to the United States, assisted by John McCloskey, Bishop of Albany, and Louis Amadeus Rappe, Bishop of Cleveland, consecrated (1) James Roosevelt Bayley, first Bishop of Newark, born at Rye (New York), New York, August 23, 1814; priest March 2, 1844; named July 29, 1853; Archbishop of Baltimore July 30, 1872; died at Newark October 3, 1877. Consecrated (2) John Loughlin, first Bishop of Brooklyn, born at Drumboniff (Down and Connor), Ireland, December 20, 1817; priest October 18, 1840; named July 29, 1853; died at Brooklyn December 29, 1891. Consecrated (3) Louis Joseph Mary Theodore de Goesbriand, first Bishop of Burlington, born at Saint-Urbain (Quimper), France, August 4, 1816; priest July 13, 1840; named July 29, 1853; died at Burlington November 3, 1899.

69–70. 1853, November 1, at Cincinnati, Ohio, Cathedral of Saint Peter in Chains. John Baptist Purcell, Archbishop of Cincinnati, assisted by Peter Paul Lefevère, Titular Bishop of Zela and Coadjutor and Apostolic Administrator of Detroit, and John Martin Henni, Bishop of Milwaukee, consecrated (1) George Aloysius Carrell, SJ, first Bishop of Covington, born at Philadelphia, Pennsylvania, June 13, 1803; priest December 20, 1827; named July 23, 1853; died at Covington September 25, 1868. Consecrated (2) Ireneus Frederick Baraga, Titular Bishop of Amyzone, Vicar Apostolic of Upper Michigan, born at Mala Vas (Ljubljana), Austria, June 29, 1797; priest September 21, 1823; named July 29, 1853; first Bishop of Sault Sainte Marie January 9, 1857; title changed to Sault Sainte Marie and Marquette October 23, 1865; died at Marquette January 19, 1868.

71. 1853, November 30, at New Orleans, Louisiana, Saint Louis Cathedral. Anthony Blanc, Archbishop of New Orleans, assisted by Michael Portier, Bishop of Mobile, and James Oliver Van de Velde, Bishop of Natchez, consecrated Augustus Mary Martin, first Bishop of Natchitoches, born at Saint-Malo (Rennes), France, February 1, 1803;

priest May 31, 1828; named July 29, 1853; died at Natchitoches September 29, 1875.

72. 1854, March 12, at Rome, Italy, College of the Propaganda. Giacomo Filippo Cardinal Fransoni, assisted by Lettorio Turchi, Bishop of Citta di Castello, and William Keane, Bishop of Ross, consecrated Thaddeus Amat, CM, Bishop of Monterey, born at Barcelona, Spain, December 31, 1811; priest December 23, 1837; named July 29, 1853; title changed to Monterey-Los Angeles July 7, 1859; died at Los Angeles May 12, 1878.

73. 1854, April 23, at Cincinnati, Ohio, Cathedral of Saint Peter in Chains. John Baptist Purcell, Archbishop of Cincinnati, assisted by Martin John Spalding, Bishop of Louisville, and Louis Amadeus Rappe, Bishop of Cleveland, consecrated Joshua Mary Moody Young, Bishop of Erie, born at Shapleigh, Maine (Boston), October 29, 1808; priest April 1, 1838; named Bishop of Pittsburgh July 29, 1853; Bishop of Erie February 20, 1854; died at Erie September 18, 1866.

74. 1854, June 4, at Bombay, India, Our Lady of Hope Cathedral. Anastasius Hartmann, Titular Bishop of Derbe, assisted by Fr. Walter Steins, SJ, and Fr. Thomas of the Passion, OCD, consecrated Ignatius Camillus Mary William Peter Persico, OFM.Cap, Titular Bishop of Gratianopolis, Coadjutor of the Vicar Apostolic of Bombay, born at Naples, Italy, June 30, 1823; priest January 24, 1846; named March 8, 1854; Vicar Apostolic of Tibet December 19, 1856; resigned from his vicariate in 1860; Bishop of Savannah March 20, 1870; Titular Bishop of Bolina, Coadjutor of Aquino, Sora e Pontecorvo June 20, 1874; succeeded to Aquino, Sora e Pontecorvo March 26, 1879; Titular Archbishop of Tamiathis March 14, 1887; Secretary of the Congregation for Oriental Churches March 20, 1889; Secretary of the Congregation for the Propagation of the Faith June 16, 1891; Cardinal January 16, 1893; died at Rome December 7, 1895.

75. 1854, July 25, at Saint Louis, Missouri, Saint Louis Cathedral. Peter Richard Kenrick, Archbishop of Saint Louis, assisted by James Oliver Van de Velde, Bishop of Natchez, and John Martin Henni, Bishop of Milwaukee, consecrated Anthony O'Regan, Bishop of Chicago, born at Lavalleyroe (Tuam), Ireland, July 27, 1809; priest November 29, 1834; named December 9, 1853; Apostolic Administrator of Quincy from July 25, 1854 to January 9, 1857; Titular Bishop of Dora June 25, 1858; died at London November 13, 1866.

76. 1855, April 22, at New York, New York, Immaculate Conception Church. John Joseph Hughes, Archbishop of New York, assisted by John Bernard Fitzpatrick, Bishop of Boston, and John Loughlin, Bishop of

Brooklyn, consecrated David William Bacon, first Bishop of Portland, born at New York, New York, September 15, 1815; priest December 13, 1838; named January 23, 1855; died at New York November 5, 1874.

77–78. 1857, April 26, at Cincinnati, Ohio, Cathedral of Saint Peter in Chains. John Baptist Purcell, Archbishop of Cincinnati, assisted by John Nepomucene Neumann, Bishop of Philadelphia, and Richard Vincent Whelan, Bishop of Richmond, consecrated (1) James Frederick Bryan Wood, Titular Bishop of Antigonea, Coadjutor of Philadelphia, born at Philadelphia, Pennsylvania, April 27, 1813; priest March 25, 1844; named January 9, 1857; succeeded to Philadelphia January 5, 1860; first Archbishop of Philadelphia February 12, 1875; died at Philadelphia June 20, 1883. Assisted by John Martin Henni, Bishop of Milwaukee, and Joshua Mary Moody Young, Bishop of Erie, consecrated (2) Henry Damian Juncker, first Bishop of Alton, born at Fénétrange (Nancy), France, August 22, 1809; priest March 16, 1834; named January 9, 1857; died at Alton October 2, 1868.

79. 1857, May 3, at Baltimore, Maryland, Cathedral of the Assumption. Francis Patrick Kenrick, Archbishop of Baltimore, assisted by John McGill, Bishop of Richmond, and James Frederick Bryan Wood, Titular Bishop of Antigonea, consecrated William Henry Elder, Bishop of Natchez, born at Baltimore, Maryland, March 22, 1819; priest March 29, 1846; named January 9, 1857; Titular Bishop of Avara and Coadjutor of San Francisco July 4, 1878, but declined the coadjutorship of San Francisco; Apostolic Administrator of Natchez April 27, 1879; Coadjutor of Cincinnati January 30, 1880; succeeded to the Metropolitan see of Cincinnati July 4, 1883; died at Cincinnati October 31, 1904.

80–81. 1857, May 3, at Saint Louis, Missouri, Cathedral of Saint Louis, King of France. Peter Richard Kenrick, Archbishop of Saint Louis, assisted by John Martin Henni, Bishop of Milwaukee, and Anthony O'Regan, Bishop of Chicago, consecrated (1) Timothy Clement Smyth, OCSO, Titular Bishop of Thennesus, Coadjutor of Dubuque, born at Finlea (Killaloe), Ireland, January 24, 1810; priest May 29, 1841; named January 9, 1857; succeeded to Dubuque February 19, 1858; died at Dubuque September 22, 1865. Consecrated (2) James Duggan, Titular Bishop of Gabala, Coadjutor of Saint Louis, born at Maynooth (Dublin), Ireland, May 22, 1825; priest May 29, 1847; named January 9, 1857; Bishop of Chicago January 21, 1859; resigned September 10, 1880; died at Saint Louis March 27, 1899.

82. 1857, August 2, at Baltimore, Maryland, Cathedral of the Assumption. Francis Patrick Kenrick, Archbishop of Baltimore, assisted by Michael Portier, Bishop of Mobile, and John Nepomucene Neumann,

Bishop of Philadelphia, consecrated John Barry, Bishop of Savannah, born at Coolamain (Ferns), Ireland, July 16, 1799; priest September 24, 1825; named January 9, 1857; died at Paris November 19, 1859.

83. 1858, January 10, at Cincinnati, Ohio, Cathedral of Saint Peter in Chains. John Baptist Purcell, Archbishop of Cincinnati, assisted by James de Saint Palais, Bishop of Vincennes, and George Aloysius Carrell, Bishop of Covington, consecrated John Henry Luers, first Bishop of Fort Wayne, born at Lutten (Munster), Germany, September 29, 1819; priest November 11, 1846; named September 22, 1857; died at Cleveland June 29, 1871.

84. 1858, March 14, at Providence, Rhode Island, Saint Patrick's Church. John Joseph Hughes, Archbishop of New York, assisted by John Bernard Fitzpatrick, Bishop of Boston, and John Timon, Bishop of Buffalo, consecrated Francis Patrick MacFarland, Bishop of Hartford, born at Chambersburg Parish, Pennsylvania (Philadelphia), April 16, 1819; priest May 1, 1845; named Titular Bishop of Hermopolis and Vicar Apostolic of Florida January 9, 1857; resigned April 28, 1857; Bishop of Hartford January 8, 1858; died at Hartford October 12, 1874.

85. 1858, March 14, at Charleston, South Carolina, Cathedral of Saint Finbar. Francis Patrick Kenrick, Archbishop of Baltimore, assisted by Michael Portier, Bishop of Mobile, and John Barry, Bishop of Savannah, consecrated Patrick Neeson Lynch, Bishop of Charleston, born at Kilberidogue (Clogher), Ireland, March 10, 1817; priest April 5, 1840; named December 11, 1857; died at Charleston February 26, 1882.

86. 1858, April 25, at Baltimore, Maryland, Cathedral of the Assumption. Francis Patrick Kenrick, Archbishop of Baltimore, assisted by John McGill, Bishop of Richmond, and John Barry, Bishop of Savannah, consecrated John Marcel Peter Augustine Verot, Titular Bishop of Danaba, Vicar Apostolic of Florida, born at Le Puy, France, May 23, 1805; priest September 20, 1828; named December 21, 1857; Bishop of Savannah and Apostolic Administrator of the Vicariate of Florida July 14, 1861; first Bishop of Saint Augustine March 11, 1870; died at Saint Augustine June 10, 1876.

87–88. 1859, May 8, at Saint Louis, Missouri, Cathedral of Saint Louis, King of France. Peter Richard Kenrick, Archbishop of Saint Louis, assisted by John Baptist Miège, Titular Bishop of Messene, and Henry Damian Juncker, Bishop of Alton, consecrated (1) James Michael Myles O'Gorman, OCSO, Titular Bishop of Raphanea, Vicar Apostolic of Nebraska, born at Cranna (Killaloe), Ireland, October 4, 1814; priest December 23, 1843; named January 18, 1859; died at Omaha July 4, 1874. Consecrated (2) James Whelan, OP, Titular Bishop of Marcopolis,

Coadjutor of Nashville, born at Scaehan Windgap (Ossory), Ireland, June 8, 1822; priest August 2, 1846; named April 15, 1859; succeeded to Nashville February 20, 1860; Titular Bishop of Diocletianopolis February 12, 1864; died at Zanesville, Ohio, February 18, 1878.

89. 1859, July 24, at Saint Louis, Missouri, Cathedral of Saint Louis, King of France. Peter Richard Kenrick, Archbishop of Saint Louis, assisted by Richard Pius Miles, Bishop of Nashville, and James Duggan, Bishop of Chicago, consecrated Thomas Langton Grace, OP, Bishop of Saint Paul, born at Charleston, South Carolina (Baltimore) November 16, 1814; priest December 21, 1839; named January 21, 1859; Titular Bishop of Mennith August 12, 1884; Titular Archbishop of Siunia September 24, 1889; died at Saint Paul February 22, 1897.

90. 1859, December 4, at New Orleans, Louisiana, Saint Louis Cathedral. Anthony Blanc, Archbishop of New Orleans, assisted by William Henry Elder, Bishop of Natchez, and James Frederick Bryan Wood, Titular Bishop of Antigonea, consecrated John Quinlan, Bishop of Mobile, born at Cloyne, Ireland, October 19, 1826; priest August 30, 1852; named August 19, 1859; died at New Orleans March 9, 1883.

91. 1860, November 25, at Le Mans, France, Church of Sainte Croix. Joseph Hippolyte Guibert, Archbishop of Tours, assisted by Jean-Jacques Nanquette, Bishop of Le Mans, and Celestine René de la Hailandière, Bishop emeritus of Vincennes, consecrated Peter Dufal, CSC, Titular Bishop of Dercos, Vicar Apostolic of Eastern Bengal, born at Saint-Gervais d'Auvergne (Clermont), France, November 8, 1822; priest September 2, 1852; named July 3, 1860; Superior General of the Holy Cross Fathers from August 25, 1866 to July 18, 1868; Coadjutor of Galveston March 14, 1878; resigned the coadjutorship December 6, 1879; died at Neuilly, France, March 15, 1898.

92. 1860, December 9, at Pittsburgh, Pennsylvania, Saint Paul Cathedral. Francis Patrick Kenrick, Archbishop of Baltimore, assisted by Richard Vincent Whelan, Bishop of Wheeling, and Joshua Mary Moody Young, Bishop of Erie, consecrated Michael Domenec, CM, Bishop of Pittsburgh, born at Ruez (Tarragona), Spain, December 27, 1816; priest June 30, 1839; named September 28, 1860; first Bishop of Allegheny January 11, 1876; resigned July 29, 1877; died at Tarragona January 5, 1878.

93. 1861, February 3, at Dublin, Ireland, All Hallows College. Paul Cullen, Archbishop of Dublin, assisted by Edward Walsh, Bishop of Ossory, and James Walsh, Bishop of Kildare, consecrated Eugene O'Connell, Titular Bishop of Flaviopolis, Vicar Apostolic of Marysville, born at Kingscourt (Meath), Ireland, June 18, 1815; priest May 21, 1842;

named September 26, 1860; first Bishop of Grass Valley February 3, 1868; Titular Bishop of Joppe February 29, 1884; died at Los Angeles December 4, 1891.

94. 1862, March 25, at Cincinnati, Ohio, Cathedral of Saint Peter in Chains. John Baptist Purcell, Archbishop of Cincinnati, assisted by Martin John Spalding, Bishop of Louisville, and John Henry Luers, Bishop of Fort Wayne, consecrated Sylvester Horton Rosecrans, Titular Bishop of Pompeiopolis, Auxiliary of Cincinnati, born at Homer, Ohio (Cincinnati) February 5, 1827; priest June 5, 1853; named December 23, 1861; first Bishop of Columbus March 3, 1868; died at Columbus October 21, 1878.

95. 1862, November 23, at Lyons, France, Major Seminary. John Mary Odin, Archbishop of New Orleans, assisted by Armand de Charbonnel, Bishop emeritus of Toronto, and Jean-Paul Lyonnet, Bishop of Valence, consecrated Claude Mary Dubuis, Bishop of Galveston, born at Coutouvre (Lyons), France, March 10, 1817; priest June 1, 1844; named October 15, 1862; resigned December 4, 1892; Titular Bishop of Arca January 21, 1893; died at Vernaison, Rhone, France May 22, 1895.

96. 1865, September 24, at Louisville, Kentucky, Cathedral of the Assumption. John Baptist Purcell, Archbishop of Cincinnati, assisted by James de Saint Palais, Bishop of Vincennes, and John McGill, Bishop of Richmond, consecrated Peter Joseph Lavialle, Bishop of Louisville, born at Mauriac (Saint-Flour), France, July 15, 1819; priest February 12, 1844; named July 7, 1865; died at Nazareth, Kentucky May 11, 1867.

97. 1865, October 15, at Albany, New York, Cathedral of the Immaculate Conception. John McCloskey, Archbishop of New York, assisted by John Timon, Bishop of Buffalo, and John Loughlin, Bishop of Brooklyn, consecrated John Joseph Conroy, Bishop of Albany, born at Clonaslee (Kildare), Ireland, July 25, 1819; priest May 21, 1842; named July 7, 1865; Titular Bishop of Curium March 10, 1878; died at New York November 20, 1895.

98. 1865, November 1, at Saint Louis, Missouri, Cathedral of Saint Louis King of France. Peter Richard Kenrick, Archbishop of Saint Louis, assisted by John Baptist Miège, Titular Bishop of Messene, and Henry Damian Juncker, Bishop of Alton, consecrated Patrick Augustine Feehan, Bishop of Nashville, born at Killenaule (Cashel), Ireland, August 28, 1829; priest November 1, 1852; named July 7, 1865; first Archbishop of Chicago September 10, 1880; died at Chicago July 12, 1902.

99. 1866, March 11, at Boston, Massachusetts, Saint James Church. John McCloskey, Archbishop of New York, assisted by John Joseph Conroy, Bishop of Albany, and John Loughlin, Bishop of Brooklyn, consecrated

John Joseph Williams, Bishop of Boston, born at Boston, Massachusetts, April 27, 1822; priest May 17, 1845; named Titular Bishop of Tripolis and Coadjutor of Boston January 8, 1866; succeeded to Boston February 13, 1866; first Archbishop of Boston February 12, 1875; died at Boston August 30, 1907.

100. 1866, September 30, at Dubuque, Iowa, Saint Raphael's Cathedral. Peter Richard Kenrick, Archbishop of Saint Louis, assisted by John Martin Henni, Bishop of Milwaukee, and James Duggan, Bishop of Chicago, consecrated John Hennessy, Bishop of Dubuque, born at Bulgaden (Limerick), Ireland, August 29, 1825; priest November 1, 1850; named April 24, 1866; first Archbishop of Dubuque June 16, 1893; died at Dubuque March 4, 1900.

101. 1867, February 3, at Columbus, Ohio, Saint Patrick's Church. John Baptist Purcell, Archbishop of Cincinnati, assisted by John Joseph Lynch, Bishop of Toronto, and Sylvester Horton Rosecrans, Titular Bishop of Pompeiopolis, consecrated Edward Fitzgerald, Bishop of Little Rock, born at Limerick, Ireland, October 21, 1833; priest August 22, 1857; named April 24, 1866; died at Hot Springs, Arkansas February 21, 1907.

102. 1868, May 24, at Rome, Italy, Church of Santa Maria dell'Umilta. August Karl Cardinal von Reisach, Archbishop of Munich, assisted by François Xavier de Nerode, Titular Archbishop of Melitene, and Salvatore Nobili-Vitelleschi, Archbishop-Bishop of Osimo e Cingoli, consecrated William George McCloskey, Bishop of Louisville, born at Brooklyn, New York (New York) November 10, 1823; priest October 6, 1852; named March 3, 1868; died at Louisville September 17, 1909.

103. 1868, July 12, at New York, New York, Saint Patrick's Cathedral, Mott Street. John McCloskey, Archbishop of New York, assisted by James Roosevelt Bayley, Bishop of Newark, and Louis de Goesbriand, Bishop of Burlington, consecrated Bernard Joseph John McQuaid, first Bishop of Rochester, born at New York, New York, December 15, 1823; priest January 16, 1848; named March 3, 1868; died at Rochester January 18, 1909.

104. 1868, July 12, at Saint Louis, Missouri, Saint Mary of Victories Church. Peter Richard Kenrick, Archbishop of Saint Louis, assisted by John Martin Henni, Bishop of Milwaukee, and Henry Damian Juncker, Bishop of Alton, consecrated Joseph Melcher, first Bishop of Green Bay, born at Vienna, Austria, March 19, 1806; priest March 27, 1830; named first Bishop of Quincy and Apostolic Administrator of Chicago July 23, 1853, but refused the nomination; named first Bishop of Green Bay March 3, 1868; died at Green Bay December 20, 1873.

105–106. 1868, July 12, at Philadelphia, Pennsylvania, Cathedral of Saints Peter and Paul. James Frederick Bryan Wood, Bishop of Philadelphia, assisted by John McGill, Bishop of Richmond, and Michael Domenec, Bishop of Pittsburgh, consecrated (1) Jeremiah Francis Shanahan, first Bishop of Harrisburg, born at Silver Lake, Pennsylvania (Philadelphia), July 13, 1834; priest July 3, 1859; named March 3, 1868; died at Harrisburg September 24, 1886. Assisted by William Henry Elder, Bishop of Natchez, and Patrick Neeson Lynch, Bishop of Charleston, consecrated (2) William O'Hara, first Bishop of Scranton, born at Dungiven (Derry), Ireland, April 14, 1816; priest December 21, 1842; named March 3, 1868; died at Scranton February 3, 1899.

107. 1868, August 2, at Pittsburgh, Pennsylvania, Saint Paul Cathedral. Michael Domenec, Bishop of Pittsburgh, assisted by James Frederick Bryan Wood, Bishop of Philadelphia, and Louis Amadeus Rappe, Bishop of Cleveland, consecrated Tobias Mullen, Bishop of Erie, born at Urney (Derry), Ireland, March 4, 1818; priest September 1, 1844; named March 3, 1868; resigned September 15, 1899; Titular Bishop of Germanicopolis September 30, 1899; died at Erie April 22, 1900.

108. 1868, August 9, at San Francisco, California, Cathedral of Saint Mary. Joseph Sadoc Alemany, Archbishop of San Francisco, assisted by Thaddeus Amat, Bishop of Monterey-Los Angeles, and Eugene O'Connell, Bishop of Grass Valley, consecrated Louis Lootens, Titular Bishop of Castabala, Vicar Apostolic of Idaho and Montana, born at Bruges, Belgium, March 17, 1827; priest June 14, 1851; named March 3, 1868; resigned his vicariate February 27, 1876; functioned as Auxiliary of Vancouver Island; died at Victoria January 10, 1898.

109–110. 1868, August 16, at Baltimore, Maryland, Cathedral of the Assumption. Martin John Spalding, Archbishop of Baltimore, assisted by Patrick Neeson Lynch, Bishop of Charleston, and Michael Domenec, Bishop of Pittsburgh, consecrated (1) James Gibbons, Titular Bishop of Adramyttium, Vicar Apostolic of North Carolina, born at Baltimore, Maryland, July 23, 1834; priest June 30, 1861; named March 3, 1868; Bishop of Richmond July 30, 1872; Titular Bishop of Jonopolis, Coadjutor of Baltimore May 29, 1877; succeeded to the Metropolitan see of Baltimore October 3, 1877; Cardinal June 7, 1886; died at Baltimore March 24, 1921. Assisted by Richard Vincent Whelan, Bishop of Wheeling, and John McGill, Bishop of Richmond, consecrated (2) Thomas Albert Andrew Becker, first Bishop of Wilmington, born at Pittsburgh, Pennsylvania, (Philadelphia) December 20, 1832; priest June 18, 1859; named March 3, 1868; Bishop of Savannah March 26, 1886; died at Washington, Georgia July 29, 1899.

111. 1868, August 16, at Cincinnati, Ohio, Cathedral of Saint Peter in Chains. John Baptist Purcell, Archbishop of Cincinnati, assisted by Louis Amadeus Rappe, Bishop of Cleveland, and Louis de Goesbriand, Bishop of Burlington, consecrated Joseph Projectus Macheboeuf, Titular Bishop of Epiphania, Vicar Apostolic of Colorado and Utah, born at Riom (Clermont), France, August 11, 1812; priest December 17, 1836; named March 3, 1868; Vicar Apostolic of Colorado November 23, 1886; first Bishop of Denver August 7, 1887; died at Denver July 10, 1889.

112. 1868, September 6, at Milwaukee, Wisconsin, Cathedral of Saint John the Evangelist. John Martin Henni, Bishop of Milwaukee, assisted by Peter Paul Lefevère, Titular Bishop of Zela, and Thomas Langton Grace, Bishop of Saint Paul, consecrated Michael Heiss, first Bishop of La Crosse, born at Pfahldorf (Eichstatt), Germany, April 12, 1818; priest October 18, 1840; named March 3, 1868; Titular Archbishop of Hadrianopolis and Coadjutor of Milwaukee April 9, 1880; succeeded to Milwaukee September 7, 1881; died at La Crosse March 26, 1890.

113. 1868, September 13, at Saint Louis, Missouri, Saint John's Church. Peter Richard Kenrick, Archbishop of Saint Louis, assisted by John Baptist Miège, Titular Bishop of Messene, and Patrick Augustine Feehan, Bishop of Nashville, consecrated John Joseph Hogan, first Bishop of Saint Joseph, born at Bruff (Limerick), Ireland, May 10, 1829; priest April 10, 1852; named March 3, 1868; first Bishop of Kansas City September 10, 1880, becoming Apostolic Administrator of Saint Joseph, *sede vacante*, until 1893; died at Kansas City, Missouri February 21, 1913.

114. 1868, November 8, at Buffalo, New York, Saint Joseph's Cathedral. John McCloskey, Archbishop of New York, assisted by John Loughlin, Bishop of Brooklyn, and John Joseph Lynch, Bishop of Toronto, consecrated Stephen Michael Vincent Ryan, CM, Bishop of Buffalo, born at Almonte (Vicariate of Upper Canada), Canada, January 1, 1826; priest June 24, 1849; named March 3, 1868; died at Buffalo April 10, 1896.

115. 1869, February 7, at Cincinnati, Ohio, Cathedral of Saint Peter in Chains. John Baptist Purcell, Archbishop of Cincinnati, assisted by Peter Paul Lefevère, Titular Bishop of Zela, and John Martin Henni, Bishop of Milwaukee, consecrated Ignatius Mrak, Bishop of Sault Sainte Marie and Marquette, born at Polland (Ljubljana), Austria, October 17, 1810; priest July 31, 1837; named September 25, 1868; resigned April 28, 1879; Titular Bishop of Antinoe April 26, 1881; died at Eagletown, Michigan January 2, 1901.

116. 1869, June 20, at Clermont, France, Notre-Dame Cathedral. Louis-Charles Feron, Bishop of Clermont, assisted by Claude Mary Dubuis,

Bishop of Galveston, and Pierre-Marc LeBreton, Bishop of Le Puy, consecrated John Baptist Salpointe, Titular Bishop of Dorileum, Vicar Apostolic of Arizona, born at Saint Maurice Poinsat (Clermont), France, February 21, 1825; priest December 20, 1851; named September 25, 1868; Coadjutor of Santa Fe April 22, 1884; Titular Archbishop of Anazarbus October 3, 1884; Apostolic Administrator of the Vicariate of Arizona until May 1, 1885; succeeded to Santa Fe August 18, 1885; Titular Archbishop of Constantia January 21, 1894; died at Tucson July 15, 1898.

117.   1870, January 9, at Cincinnati, Ohio, Cathedral of Saint Peter in Chains. Sylvester Horton Rosecrans, Bishop of Columbus, assisted by John Henry Luers, Bishop of Fort Wayne, and William George McCloskey, Bishop of Louisville, consecrated Augustus Maria Bernard Anthony John Gebhard Toebbe, Bishop of Covington, born at Meppen (Osnabruck), Germany, January 17, 1829; priest September 14, 1854; named September 27, 1869; died at Covington May 2, 1884.

118.   1870, January 23, at Belleville, Illinois, Saint Peter's Church. John Henry Luers, Bishop of Fort Wayne, assisted by Augustus Maria Bernard Anthony John Gebhard Toebbe, Bishop of Covington, and Fr. Patrick John Ryan, Administrator of Saint Louis, consecrated Peter Joseph Baltes, Bishop of Alton, born at Ensheim (Speyer), Germany, April 7, 1827; priest May 31, 1852; named September 24, 1869; died at Alton February 15, 1886.

119.   1870, February 27, at Baltimore, Maryland, Cathedral of the Assumption. William George McCloskey, Bishop of Louisville, assisted by Sylvester Horton Rosecrans, Bishop of Columbus, and Thomas Albert Andrew Becker, Bishop of Wilmington, consecrated Thomas Patrick Roger Foley, Titular Bishop of Pergamum, Coadjutor and Apostolic Administrator of Chicago, born at Baltimore, Maryland, March 6, 1822; priest August 16, 1846; named November 19, 1869; died at Chicago February 19, 1879.

120.   1870, April 24, at Cincinnati, Ohio, Cathedral of Saint Peter in Chains. Sylvester Horton Rosecrans, Bishop of Columbus, assisted by John Henry Luers, Bishop of Fort Wayne, and Patrick Augustine Feehan, Bishop of Nashville, consecrated Caspar Henry Borgess, Titular Bishop of Calydonia, Coadjutor and Apostolic Administrator of Detroit, born at Addrup (Osnabruck), Germany, August 1, 1826; priest December 8, 1848; named February 14, 1870; succeeded to Detroit December 30, 1871; Titular Bishop of Phacusa April 16, 1887; died at Kalamazoo May 3, 1890.

121.   1870, May 1, at New Orleans, Louisiana, Saint Louis Cathedral. Sylvester Horton Rosecrans, Bishop of Columbus, assisted by Patrick Augustine Feehan, Bishop of Nashville, and Thomas Patrick Roger Foley,

Titular Bishop of Pergamum, consecrated Napoleon Joseph Perché, Titular Bishop of Abdera, Coadjutor of New Orleans, born at Angers, France, January 10, 1805; priest September 19, 1829; named February 8, 1870; succeeded to the metropolitan see of New Orleans May 25, 1870; died at New Orleans December 27, 1883.

122.   1870, September 25, at Springfield, Massachusetts, Saint Michael's Cathedral. John McCloskey, Archbishop of New York, assisted by John Joseph Williams, Bishop of Boston, and John Joseph Conroy, Bishop of Albany, consecrated Patrick Thomas O'Reilly, first Bishop of Springfield, born at Kilnaleck (Kilmore), Ireland, December 24, 1833; priest August 15, 1857; named June 23, 1870; died at Springfield May 28, 1892.

123.   1871, June 11, at Chicago, Illinois, Saint Joseph's Church. Thomas Patrick Roger Foley, Titular Bishop of Pergamum, assisted by John Baptist Miège, Titular Bishop of Messene, and Joseph Melcher, Bishop of Green Bay, consecrated Michael Louis Mary Fink, OSB, Titular Bishop of Eucarpia, Coadjutor of the Vicar Apostolic of Kansas and the Indian Territory, born at Triftersberg (Regensburg), Germany, July 12, 1834; priest May 28, 1857; named March 1, 1871; succeeded to the vicariate November 18, 1874; first Bishop of Leavenworth March 22, 1877; first Bishop of Kansas City in Kansas May 29, 1891; Bishop of Leavenworth March 5, 1897; died at Kansas City, Kansas March 17, 1904.

124.   1872, April 14, at Saint Louis, Missouri, Saint John's Church. Peter Richard Kenrick, Archbishop of Saint Louis, assisted by Patrick Augustine Feehan, Bishop of Nashville, and Joseph Melcher, Bishop of Green Bay, consecrated Patrick John Ryan, Titular Bishop of Tricomia, Coadjutor of Saint Louis, born at Cloneyharp (Cashel), Ireland, February 20, 1831; priest September 8, 1853; named February 15, 1872; Titular Archbishop of Salamis January 29, 1884; Archbishop of Philadelphia July 8, 1884; died at Philadelphia February 11, 1911.

125–126.   1872, April 14, at Cincinnati, Ohio, Cathedral of Saint Peter in Chains. John Baptist Purcell, Archbishop of Cincinnati, assisted by Augustus Bernard Toebbe, Bishop of Covington, and Caspar Henry Borgess, Bishop of Detroit, consecrated (1) Joseph Gregory Dwenger, C.PP.S, Bishop of Fort Wayne, born at Saint John's, Mercer County, Ohio (Cincinnati), April 7, 1837; priest September 4, 1859; named February 10, 1872; died at Fort Wayne January 22, 1893. Consecrated (2) Richard Gilmour, Bishop of Cleveland, born at Glasgow, Scotland, September 28, 1824; priest August 30, 1852; named February 15, 1872; died at Saint Augustine, Florida April 13, 1891.

127.   1872, April 21, at New York, New York, Saint Patrick's Cathedral,

Mott Street. John McCloskey, Archbishop of New York, assisted by John Loughlin, Bishop of Brooklyn, and David William Bacon, Bishop of Portland, consecrated Francis McNeirny, Titular Bishop of Rhesaina, Coadjutor of Albany, born at New York, New York, April 25, 1828; priest August 17, 1854; named December 22, 1871; Apostolic Administrator of Albany in 1874; succeeded to Albany October 12, 1877; died at Albany January 2, 1894.

128. 1872, April 28, at Providence, Rhode Island, Cathedral of Saints Peter and Paul. John McCloskey, Archbishop of New York, assisted by John Joseph Williams, Bishop of Boston, and David William Bacon, Bishop of Portland, consecrated Thomas Francis Hendricken, first Bishop of Providence, born at Kilkenny (Ossory), Ireland, May 5, 1827; priest April 25, 1853; named February 16, 1872; died at Providence June 11, 1886.

129. 1872, May 5, at Albany, New York, Cathedral of the Immaculate Conception. John McCloskey, Archbishop of New York, assisted by Louis de Goesbriand, Bishop of Burlington, and John Joseph Williams, Bishop of Boston, consecrated Edgar Philip Prindle Wadhams, first Bishop of Ogdensburg, born at Lewis, New York (New York) May 21, 1817; priest January 15, 1850; named February 12, 1872; died at Ogdensburg December 5, 1891.

130. 1873, April 17, at Baltimore, Maryland, Cathedral of the Assumption. James Roosevelt Bayley, Archbishop of Baltimore, assisted by Thomas Albert Andrew Becker, Bishop of Wilmington, and James Gibbons, Bishop of Richmond, consecrated William Hickley Gross, C.SS.R, Bishop of Savannah, born at Baltimore, Maryland, June 12, 1837; priest March 21, 1863; named February 14, 1873; Archbishop of Oregon City March 31, 1885; died at Baltimore November 14, 1898.

131. 1873, May 4, at Newark, New Jersey, Saint Patrick's Pro-cathedral. John McCloskey, Archbishop of New York, assisted by John Loughlin, Bishop of Brooklyn, and William George McCloskey, Bishop of Louisville, consecrated Michael Augustine Corrigan, Bishop of Newark, born at Newark, New Jersey (New York) August 13, 1839; priest September 19, 1863; named February 14, 1873; Titular Archbishop of Petra, Coadjutor of New York October 1, 1880; succeeded to New York October 10, 1885; died at New York May 5, 1902.

132. 1873, June 29, at Victoria, British Columbia, Canada, Saint Andrew's Cathedral. Francis Norbert Blanchet, Archbishop of Oregon City, assisted by Augustine Magloire Alexander Blanchet, Bishop of Nesqually, and Louis Joseph d'Herbomez, Titular Bishop of Miletopolis, consecrated Charles John Seghers, Bishop of Vancouver Island, born at Ghent, Belgium, December 26, 1839; priest May 31, 1863; named March 11, 1873; Titular Bishop of Cana, Coadjutor of Oregon City July 18, 1878; Titular Archbishop of Hemesa September 28, 1878; succeeded to Oregon City December 18, 1880; Archbishop-Bishop of Vancouver Island March 9, 1884; murdered November 28, 1886 at Nulato, Alaska.

133. 1873, August 3, at Los Angeles, California, Our Lady of the Angels Church. Thaddeus Amat, Bishop of Monterey-Los Angeles, assisted by Joseph Sadoc Alemany, Archbishop of San Francisco, and Eugene O'Connell, Bishop of Grass Valley, consecrated Francis Mora, Titular Bishop of Mosynopolis, Coadjutor of Monterey-Los Angeles, born at Gurb (Vich), Spain, November 25, 1827; priest March 19, 1856; named May 20, 1873; succeeded to Monterey-Los Angeles May 12, 1878; Titular Archbishop of Hierapolis May 2, 1896; died August 3, 1905 at Sarria, Spain.

134–135. 1874, December 8, at Mobile, Alabama, Cathedral of the Immaculate Conception. Napoleon Joseph Perché, Archbishop of New Orleans, assisted by Edward Fitzgerald, Bishop of Little Rock, and James Gibbons, Bishop of Richmond, consecrated (1) Anthony Dominic Ambrose Pellicer, first Bishop of San Antonio, born at Saint Augustine, Florida (New Orleans), December 7, 1824; priest August 15, 1850; named September 2, 1874; died at San Antonio April 14, 1880. Assisted by William Henry Elder, Bishop of Natchez, and Claude Mary Dubuis, Bishop of Galveston, consecrated (2) Dominic Manucy, Titular Bishop of Dulma, Vicar Apostolic of Brownsville, born at Saint Augustine, Florida (New Orleans), December 20, 1823; priest August 15, 1850; named September 17, 1874; Bishop of Mobile January 18, 1884; resigned from Mobile September 27, 1884; Vicar Apostolic of Brownsville February 7, 1885; Titular Bishop of Maronea February 10, 1885; died at Mobile December 4, 1885.

136. 1875, May 23, at Wheeling, West Virginia, Saint Joseph's Cathedral. James Roosevelt Bayley, Archbishop of Baltimore, assisted by Thomas Albert Andrew Becker, Bishop of Wilmington, and James Gibbons, Bishop of Richmond, consecrated John Joseph Kain, Bishop of Wheeling, born at Martinsburg, Virginia (Richmond), May 31, 1841; priest July 2, 1866; named February 12, 1875; Titular Archbishop of Oxyrynchus, Coadjutor of Saint Louis June 16, 1893; Apostolic Administrator of Saint Louis December 14, 1893; succeeded to Saint Louis May 21, 1895; died at Baltimore October 13, 1903.

137. 1875, May 30, at Saint Cloud, Minnesota, Saint Mary's Church. Michael Heiss, Bishop of La Crosse, assisted by Joseph Gregory Dwenger,

Bishop of Fort Wayne, and Michael Louis Mary Fink, Titular Bishop of Eucarpia, consecrated Rupert Seidenbusch, OSB, Titular Bishop of Halia, Vicar Apostolic of Northern Minnesota, born at Munich, Germany, October 13, 1830; priest June 22, 1853; named February 12, 1875; resigned his vicariate October 19, 1888; died at Richmond June 3, 1895.

138. 1875, June 2, at Portland, Maine, Cathedral of the Immaculate Conception. John Joseph Williams, Archbishop of Boston, assisted by Francis McNeirny, Bishop of Albany, and Patrick Thomas O'Reilly, Bishop of Springfield, consecrated James Augustine Healy, Bishop of Portland, born at Macon, Georgia (Charleston), April 6, 1830; priest June 10, 1854; named February 12, 1875; died at Portland August 5, 1900.

139. 1875, June 29, at Milwaukee, Wisconsin, Cathedral of Saint John the Evangelist. John Martin Henni, Archbishop of Milwaukee, assisted by Michael Heiss, Bishop of La Crosse, and Thomas Langton Grace, Bishop of Saint Paul, consecrated Francis Xavier Krautbauer, Bishop of Green Bay, born at Mappach (Regensburg), Germany, January 12, 1824; priest July 16, 1850; named February 22, 1875; died at Green Bay December 17, 1885.

140. 1875, December 21, at Saint Paul, Minnesota, Cathedral of Saint Paul. Thomas Langton Grace, Bishop of Saint Paul, assisted by Michael Heiss, Bishop of La Crosse, and Rupert Seidenbusch, Titular Bishop of Halia, consecrated John Ireland, Titular Bishop of Maronea, Coadjutor of Saint Paul, born at Burnchurch (Ossory), Ireland, September 11, 1838; priest December 21, 1861; named Titular Bishop of Maronea and Vicar Apostolic of Nebraska February 12, 1875; Coadjutor of Saint Paul July 28, 1875; succeeded to Saint Paul July 31, 1884; first Archbishop of Saint Paul May 15, 1888; died at Saint Paul September 25, 1918.

141. 1876, March 19, at Hartford, Connecticut, Saint Peter's Church. John Joseph Williams, Archbishop of Boston, assisted by Patrick Thomas O'Reilly, Bishop of Springfield, and Edgar Philip Prindle Wadhams, Bishop of Ogdensburg, consecrated Thomas Galberry, OSA, Bishop of Hartford, born at Naas (Kildare), Ireland, May 28, 1833; priest December 20, 1856; named February 12, 1875; died at New York October 10, 1878.

142. 1876, March 19, at Pittsburgh, Pennsylvania, Saint Paul Cathedral. James Frederick Bryan Wood, Archbishop of Philadelphia, assisted by Michael Domenec, Bishop of Allegheny, and Tobias Mullen, Bishop of Erie, consecrated John Tuigg, Bishop of Pittsburgh, born at Donoughmore (Cork), Ireland, February 19, 1820; priest May 14, 1850; named January 11, 1876; Apostolic Administrator of Allegheny, *sede vacante*, from 1877 until his death; died at Altoona December 7, 1889.

143. 1876, August 20, at Philadelphia, Pennsylvania, Chapel of Saint Charles Seminary. Patrick John Ryan, Titular Bishop of Tricomia, assisted by William O'Hara, Bishop of Scranton, and Jeremiah Francis Shanahan, Bishop of Harrisburg, consecrated James O'Connor, Titular Bishop of Dibon, Vicar Apostolic of Nebraska, born at Cobh (Cloyne), Ireland, September 10, 1823; priest March 25, 1848; named June 30, 1876; first Bishop of Omaha October 2, 1885; died at Omaha May 27, 1890.

144. 1877, April 22, at Rennes, France, Cathedral of Saint-Sauveur. Godefroid Cardinal Brossais-Saint-Marc, Archbishop of Rennes, assisted by Celestine René de La Hailandière, Bishop emeritus of Vincennes, and Anselme Nouvel de la Fleche, Bishop of Quimper, consecrated Francis Xavier Leray, Bishop of Natchitoches, born at Chateaugiron (Rennes), France, April 20, 1825; priest March 19, 1852; named December 19, 1876; Coadjutor of New Orleans September 23, 1879; Titular Bishop of Jonopolis September 26, 1879; succeeded to the metropolitan see of New Orleans December 27, 1883; died at Chateaugiron September 23, 1887.

145. 1877, May 1, at New York, New York, Saint Patrick's Cathedral, Mott Street. John Cardinal McCloskey, Archbishop of New York, assisted by James Gibbons, Bishop of Richmond, and Thomas Patrick Roger Foley, Titular Bishop of Pergamum, consecrated John Lancaster Spalding, first Bishop of Peoria, born at Lebanon, Kentucky (Bardstown), June 2, 1840; priest December 19, 1863; named November 17, 1876; Titular Archbishop of Scythopolis October 14, 1908; died at Peoria August 25, 1916.

146. 1877, May 13, at Charleston, South Carolina, Saint John the Baptist Pro-cathedral. Patrick Neeson Lynch, Bishop of Charleston, assisted by Thomas Albert Andrew Becker, Bishop of Wilmington, and William Hickley Gross, Bishop of Savannah, consecrated John Moore, Bishop of Saint Augustine, born at Castletown-Devlin (Meath), Ireland, June 27, 1835; priest April 9, 1860; named February 16, 1877; died at Saint Augustine July 30, 1901.

147. 1878, May 12, at Rome, Italy, North American College. Alessandro Cardinal Franchi, assisted by Camillo Santori, Bishop of Fano, and Eduardo Agnelli, Titular Bishop of Troas, consecrated Francis Silas Marean Chatard, Bishop of Vincennes, born at Baltimore, Maryland, December 13, 1834; priest June 14, 1862; named March 28, 1878; title changed to Bishop of Indianapolis March 23, 1898; died at Indianapolis September 7, 1918.

148. 1878, August 25, at Richmond, Virginia, Saint Peter's Cathedral. James Gibbons, Archbishop of Baltimore, assisted by John Joseph Kain, Bishop of Wheeling, and Thomas Patrick Roger Foley, Titular Bishop of

Pergamum, consecrated John Joseph Keane, Bishop of Richmond and Apostolic Administrator of the Vicariate of North Carolina, born at Killbarn, Ballyshannon (Raphoe), Ireland, September 12, 1839; priest July 2, 1866; named March 28, 1878; Rector of The Catholic University of America April 10, 1887; Titular Bishop of Jasus August 12, 1888; Titular Archbishop of Damascus January 29, 1897; Archbishop of Dubuque July 24, 1900; Titular Archbishop of Cius April 28, 1911; died at Dubuque June 22, 1918.

149.   1879, August 10, at Hartford, Connecticut, Cathedral of Saint Joseph. John Joseph Williams, Archbishop of Boston, assisted by John Loughlin, Bishop of Brooklyn, and Patrick Thomas O'Reilly, Bishop of Springfield, consecrated Lawrence Stephen McMahon, Bishop of Hartford, born at Saint John (Saint John, New Brunswick), Canada, December 26, 1835; priest March 25, 1860; named May 8, 1879; died at Lakeville, Connecticut August 21, 1893.

150.   1879, September 14, at Negaunee, Michigan, Saint Paul's Church. Michael Heiss, Bishop of La Crosse, assisted by Caspar Henry Borgess, Bishop of Detroit, and John Lancaster Spalding, Bishop of Peoria, consecrated John Vertin, Bishop of Sault Sainte Marie and Marquette, born at Doblice Parice (Ljubljana), Austria, July 17, 1844; priest August 31, 1866; named May 16, 1879; died at Marquette February 26, 1899.

151.   1879, October 28, at Vancouver, Washington, Saint James Cathedral. Francis Norbert Blanchet, Archbishop of Oregon City, assisted by Augustine Magloire Alexander Blanchet, Titular Bishop of Ibora, and Fr. John Francis Fierens, Vicar General of Oregon City, consecrated Egidius Junger, Bishop of Nesqually, born at Burtscheid (Cologne), Germany, April 6, 1833; priest June 27, 1862; named August 6, 1879; died at Vancouver December 26, 1895.

152.   1879, December 14, at Victoria, British Columbia, Canada, Saint Andrew's Cathedral. Charles John Seghers, Titular Archbishop of Hemesa, assisted by Egidius Junger, Bishop of Nesqually, and Louis Joseph d'Herbomez, Titular Bishop of Mitelopolis, consecrated John Baptist Brondel, Bishop of Vancouver Island, born at Bruges, Belgium, February 23, 1842; priest December 17, 1864; named September 26, 1879; Apostolic Administrator of the Vicariate of Montana April 17, 1883; first Bishop of Helena March 17, 1884; died at Helena November 3, 1903.

153.   1880, February 1, at Ferdinand, Indiana, Saint Ferdinand's Church. Francis Silas Marean Chatard, Bishop of Vincennes, assisted by Rupert Seidenbusch, Titular Bishop of Halia, and Abbot Innocent Wolf, OSB, of Saint Benedict's Abbey, Atchison, Kansas, consecrated Martin Marty,

OSB, Titular Bishop of Tiberias, Vicar Apostolic of Dakota, born at Schwyz (Chur), Switzerland, January 11, 1834; priest September 14, 1856; named August 11, 1879; first Bishop of Sioux Falls November 15, 1889; Bishop of Saint Cloud January 21, 1895; died at Saint Cloud September 19, 1896.

154. 1881, August 8, at Columbus, Ohio, Saint Joseph Cathedral. William Henry Elder, Titular Bishop of Avara, assisted by William George McCloskey, Bishop of Covington, and John Tuigg, Bishop of Pittsburgh, consecrated John Ambrose Watterson, Bishop of Columbus, born at Bairdstown, Pennsylvania (Pittsburgh) May 27, 1844; priest August 9, 1868; named April 6, 1880; died at Columbus April 17, 1899.

155. 1881, January 16, at San Francisco, California, Cathedral of Saint Mary. Joseph Sadoc Alemany, Archbishop of San Francisco, assisted by Francis Mora, Bishop of Monterey-Los Angeles, and Eugene O'Connell, Bishop of Grass Valley, consecrated Patrick Manogue, Titular Bishop of Ceramus, Coadjutor of Grass Valley, born at Desart (Ossory), Ireland, March 15, 1831; priest December 21, 1861; named July 27, 1880; succeeded to Grass Valley February 29, 1884; title changed to Bishop of Sacramento May 28, 1886; died at Sacramento February 27, 1895.

156. 1881, May 1, at Richmond, Virginia, Saint Peter's Cathedral. James Gibbons, Archbishop of Baltimore, assisted by Thomas Albert Andrew Becker, Bishop of Wilmington, and John Joseph Keane, Bishop of Richmond, consecrated Francis Augustus Anthony Joseph Janssens, Bishop of Natchez, born at Tilburg (Bois le Duc), Netherlands, October 17, 1843; priest December 21, 1867; named February 18, 1881; Archbishop of New Orleans August 7, 1888; died at sea June 10, 1897.

157. 1881, May 8, at San Antonio, Texas, Cathedral of San Fernando. Edward Fitzgerald, Bishop of Little Rock, assisted by Dominic Manucy, Titular Bishop of Dulma, and Claude Mary Dubuis, Bishop of Galveston, consecrated John Claude Neraz, Bishop of San Antonio, born at Anse (Lyons), France, January 12, 1828; priest March 19, 1853; named February 18, 1881; Apostolic Administrator of the Vicariate of Brownsville from 1887 to 1891; died at San Antonio November 15, 1894.

158. 1881, July 25, at Chicago, Illinois, Cathedral of the Holy Name. Patrick Augustine Feehan, Archbishop of Chicago, assisted by John Hennessy, Bishop of Dubuque, and John Lancaster Spalding, Bishop of Peoria, consecrated John McMullen, first Bishop of Davenport, born at Ballynahinch (Dromore), Ireland, January 8, 1832; priest June 20, 1858; named June 14, 1881; died at Davenport July 4, 1883.

159. 1881, August 21, at San Francisco, California, Cathedral of Saint Mary. Joseph Sadoc Alemany, Archbishop of San Francisco, assisted by Eugene O'Connell, Bishop of Grass Valley, and Timoleon Raimondi, Titular Bishop of Acanthus, consecrated Bernard Hermann Koeckemann, SS.CC, Titular Bishop of Olba, Coadjutor of the Vicar Apostolic of Hawaii, born at Ostbeven (Munster), Germany, January 10, 1828; priest May 31, 1862; named May 17, 1881; succeeded to the vicariate June 11, 1882; died at Honolulu February 22, 1892.

160. 1881, August 24, at Milwaukee, Wisconsin, Saint Francis Seminary. Michael Heiss, Archbishop of Milwaukee, assisted by Francis Xavier Krautbauer, Bishop of Green Bay, and Rupert Seidenbusch, Titular Bishop of Halia, consecrated Kilian Casper Flasch, Bishop of La Crosse, born at Retzstadt (Munster), Germany, July 16, 1831; priest December 16, 1859; named June 14, 1881; died at La Crosse August 3, 1891.

161. 1881, October 18, at Newark, New Jersey, Saint Patrick's Pro-cathedral. Michael Augustine Corrigan, Titular Archbishop of Petra, assisted by John Loughlin, Bishop of Brooklyn, and Bernard John Joseph McQuaid, Bishop of Rochester, consecrated Winand Michael Wigger, Bishop of Newark, born at New York, New York, December 9, 1841; priest June 10, 1865; named July 11, 1881; died at Newark January 5, 1901.

162. 1881, November 1, at New York, New York, Saint Patrick's Cathedral. John Cardinal McCloskey, Archbishop of New York, assisted by Michael Augustine Corrigan, Titular Archbishop of Petra, and John Loughlin, Bishop of Brooklyn, consecrated Michael Joseph O'Farrell, first Bishop of Trenton, born at Limerick, Ireland, December 2, 1832; priest August 18, 1855; named August 11, 1881; died at Trenton April 2, 1894.

163. 1882, January 8, at Baltimore, Maryland, Cathedral of the Assumption. James Gibbons, Archbishop of Baltimore, assisted by John Joseph Keane, Bishop of Richmond, and Thomas Albert Andrew Becker, Bishop of Wilmington, consecrated Henry Pinckney Northrop, Titular Bishop of Rosalia, Vicar Apostolic of North Carolina, born at Charleston, South Carolina, May 5, 1842; priest June 25, 1865; named September 16, 1881; Bishop of Charleston January 27, 1883, remaining Vicar Apostolic of North Carolina until February 4, 1888; died at Charleston June 7, 1916.

164. 1882, April 30, at Galveston, Texas, Saint Mary's Cathedral. Edward Fitzgerald, Bishop of Little Rock, assisted by John Claude Neraz, Bishop of San Antonio, and Dominic Manucy, Titular Bishop of Dulma, consecrated Nicholas Aloysius Gallagher, Titular Bishop of Canopus, Coadjutor and Apostolic Administrator of Galveston, born at Temperanceville, Ohio (Cincinnati), February 19, 1846; priest December

25, 1868; named January 10, 1882; succeeded to Galveston December 16, 1892; died at Galveston January 21, 1918.

165. 1883, April 22, at Grand Rapids, Michigan, Cathedral of Saint Andrew. William Henry Elder, Titular Bishop of Avara, assisted by Caspar Henry Borgess, Bishop of Detroit, and William George McCloskey, Bishop of Louisville, consecrated Henry Joseph Richter, Bishop of Grand Rapids, born at Neuenkirchen (Munster), Germany, April 9, 1838; priest June 10, 1865; named January 30, 1883; died at Grand Rapids December 26, 1916.

166. 1883, June 24, at Nashville, Tennessee, Saint Mary's Cathedral. Patrick Augustine Feehan, Archbishop of Chicago, assisted by Joseph Gregory Dwenger, Bishop of Fort Wayne, and John Ambrose Watterson, Bishop of Columbus, consecrated Joseph Rademacher, Bishop of Nashville, born at Westphalia, Michigan (Detroit) December 3, 1840; priest August 2, 1863; named April 3, 1883; Bishop of Fort Wayne July 15, 1893; died at Fort Wayne June 12, 1900.

167. 1883, September 16, at Chicago, Illinois, Saint James Church. Patrick Augustine Feehan, Archbishop of Chicago, assisted by William George McCloskey, Bishop of Louisville, and Francis Silas Marean Chatard, Bishop of Vincennes, consecrated Patrick William Riordan, Titular Archbishop of Cabasa, Coadjutor of San Francisco, born at Chatham, Canada August 27, 1841; priest June 10, 1865; named July 17, 1883; succeeded to San Francisco December 21, 1884; died at San Francisco December 27, 1914.

168. 1884, June 11, at Manchester, New Hampshire, Cathedral of Saint Joseph. John Joseph Williams, Archbishop of Boston, assisted by Louis de Goesbriand, Bishop of Burlington, and John Moore, Bishop of Saint Augustine, consecrated Denis Mary Bradley, first Bishop of Manchester, born at Castle Island (Kerry), Ireland, February 25, 1846; priest June 3, 1871; named April 18, 1884; died at Manchester December 13, 1903.

169. 1884, September 14, at Davenport, Iowa, Saint Margaret's Cathedral. Patrick Augustine Feehan, Archbishop of Chicago, assisted by John Hennessy, Bishop of Dubuque, and James O'Connor, Bishop of Omaha, consecrated Henry Cosgrove, Bishop of Davenport, born at Williamsport, Pennsylvania (Philadelphia) December 19, 1834; priest August 27, 1857; named July 11, 1884; died at Davenport December 22, 1906.

170. 1885, January 25, at Covington, Kentucky, Saint Mary's Cathedral. William Henry Elder, Archbishop of Cincinnati, assisted by William

George McCloskey, Bishop of Louisville, and Caspar Henry Borgess, Bishop of Detroit, consecrated Camillus Paul Maes, Bishop of Covington, born at Courtrai (Bruges), Belgium, March 13, 1846; priest December 19, 1868; named October 1, 1884; died at Covington May 11, 1915.

171. 1885, March 19, at New Orleans, Louisiana, Saint Louis Cathedral. Francis Xavier Leray, Archbishop of New Orleans, assisted by John Claude Neraz, Bishop of San Antonio, and Nicholas Aloysius Gallagher, Bishop of Galveston, consecrated Anthony Durier, Bishop of Natchitoches, born at Saint-Bonnet-des-Quarts (Lyons), France, January 3, 1833; priest October 28, 1856; named December 19, 1884; died at Natchitoches February 28, 1904.

172. 1885, April 19, at Baltimore, Maryland, Cathedral of the Assumption. James Gibbons, Archbishop of Baltimore, assisted by William Hickley Gross, Archbishop of Oregon City, and Camillus Paul Maes, Bishop of Covington, consecrated Alphonse Joseph Glorieux, Titular Bishop of Apollonia, Vicar Apostolic of Idaho, born at Dottingies (Bruges), Belgium, February 1, 1844; priest August 17, 1867; named March 3, 1885; first Bishop of Boise City August 25, 1893; died at Portland, Oregon August 25, 1917.

173. 1885, May 1, at Santa Fe, New Mexico, Cathedral of San Francisco de Asis. John Baptist Lamy, Archbishop of Santa Fe, assisted by John Baptist Salpointe, Titular Archbishop of Anazarbus, and Joseph Projectus Macheboeuf, Titular Bishop of Epiphania, consecrated Peter Bourgade, Titular Bishop of Thaumacus, Vicar Apostolic of Arizona, born at Vollore-Ville (Clermont), France, October 17, 1845; priest November 30, 1869; named February 7, 1885; first Bishop of Tucson May 10, 1897; Archbishop of Santa Fe January 7, 1899; died at Chicago May 17, 1908.

174. 1885, August 2, at Pittsburgh, Pennsylvania, Saint Paul Cathedral. Patrick John Ryan, Archbishop of Philadelphia, assisted by Tobias Mullen, Bishop of Erie, and Jeremiah Francis Shanahan, Bishop of Harrisburg, consecrated Richard Phelan, Titular Bishop of Cibyra, Coadjutor of Pittsburgh, born at Ballyragget (Ossory), Ireland, January 1, 1828; priest May 4, 1854; named May 12, 1885; succeeded to Pittsburgh December 7, 1889; died at Idlewood, Pennsylvania December 20, 1904.

175. 1885, September 20, at Washington, District of Columbia, Saint Peter's Church. James Gibbons, Archbishop of Baltimore, assisted by John Joseph Keane, Bishop of Richmond, and Henry Pinckney Northrop, Bishop of Charleston, consecrated Jeremiah O'Sullivan, Bishop of Mobile, born at Kanturk (Cloyne), Ireland, February 6, 1842; priest June 30, 1868; named June 16, 1885; died at Mobile August 10, 1896.

176. 1886, September 21, at Green Bay, Wisconsin, Saint Francis Xavier Cathedral. Michael Heiss, Archbishop of Milwaukee, assisted by John Vertin, Bishop of Sault Sainte Marie and Marquette, and John Ireland, Bishop of Saint Paul, consecrated Frederick Francis Xavier Katzer, Bishop of Green Bay, born at Ebensee (Linz), Austria, February 7, 1844; priest December 21, 1866; named July 13, 1886; Archbishop of Milwaukee January 30, 1891; died at Fond du Lac, Wisconsin July 20, 1903.

177. 1886, November 14, at Baltimore, Maryland, Cathedral of the Assumption. James Cardinal Gibbons, Archbishop of Baltimore, assisted by John Moore, Bishop of Saint Augustine, and John Joseph Kain, Bishop of Wheeling, consecrated Alfred Allen Paul Curtis, Bishop of Wilmington, born at Rehobeth, Delaware (Baltimore), July 4, 1831; priest December 19, 1874; named August 3, 1886; resigned May 23, 1896; Titular Bishop of Echinus June 2, 1896; died at Baltimore July 11, 1908.

178. 1887, April 14, at Providence, Rhode Island, Cathedral of Saints Peter and Paul. John Joseph Williams, Archbishop of Boston, assisted by Patrick Thomas O'Reilly, Bishop of Springfield, and Lawrence Stephen McMahon, Bishop of Hartford, consecrated Matthew Harkins, Bishop of Providence, born at Boston, Massachusetts, November 17, 1845; priest May 22, 1869; named February 11, 1887; died at Providence May 25, 1921.

179. 1887, May 1, at Syracuse, New York, Church of the Assumption. Michael Augustine Corrigan, Archbishop of New York, assisted by Bernard Joseph John McQuaid, Bishop of Rochester, and Francis McNeirny, Bishop of Albany, consecrated Patrick Anthony Ludden, first Bishop of Syracuse, born at Breaffy (Tuam), Ireland, February 4, 1836; priest May 21, 1865; named December 14, 1886; died at Syracuse August 6, 1912.

180. 1887, June 29, at San Francisco, California, Cathedral of Saint Mary. Patrick William Riordan, Archbishop of San Francisco, assisted by Eugene O'Connell, Titular Bishop of Joppe, and Patrick Manogue, Bishop of Sacramento, consecrated Lawrence Scanlan, Titular Bishop of Laranda, Vicar Apostolic of Utah, born at Ballytarsna (Cashel), Ireland, September 28, 1843; priest June 28, 1868; named January 25, 1887; first Bishop of Salt Lake January 30, 1891; died at Salt Lake City May 10, 1915.

181. 1887, October 28, at Chicago, Illinois, Cathedral of the Holy Name. Patrick Augustine Feehan, Archbishop of Chicago, assisted by William George McCloskey, Bishop of Louisville, and Henry Cosgrove, Bishop of Davenport, consecrated Maurice Francis Burke, first Bishop of Cheyenne, born at Kockainy (Cashel), Ireland, May 5, 1845; priest May 22, 1875;

named August 9, 1887; Bishop of Saint Joseph June 19, 1893; died at Saint Joseph March 17, 1923.

182.   1887, October 28, at Denver, Colorado, Cathedral of the Immaculate Conception. John Baptist Salpointe, Archbishop of Santa Fe, assisted by Joseph Projectus Macheboeuf, Bishop of Denver, and Abbot Frowenus Conrad, OSB, Abbot of Conception Abbey, Missouri consecrated Nicholas Chrysostom Matz, Titular Bishop of Telmissus, Coadjutor of Denver, born at Munster (Metz), France, April 6, 1850; priest May 31, 1874; named August 16, 1887; succeeded to Denver July 10, 1889; died at Denver August 9, 1917.

183.   1887, November 30, at Saint Louis, Missouri, Saint John's Church. Peter Richard Kenrick, Archbishop of Saint Louis, assisted by Michael Louis Mary Fink, Bishop of Leavenworth, and James O'Connor, Bishop of Omaha, consecrated Thomas Bonacum, first Bishop of Lincoln, born at Penane, Loughmore (Cashel), Ireland, January 29, 1847; priest June 18, 1870; named August 9, 1887; died at Lincoln February 4, 1911.

184.   1887, November 30, at Nashville, Tennessee, Saint Joseph's Church. Patrick Augustine Feehan, Archbishop of Chicago, assisted by William George McCloskey, Bishop of Louisville, and Joseph Rademacher, Bishop of Nashville, consecrated Richard Scannell, first Bishop of Concordia, born at Cloyne, Ireland, May 12, 1845; priest February 26, 1871; named August 9, 1887; Bishop of Omaha January 30, 1891; died at Omaha January 8, 1916.

185.   1888, March 11, at Harrisburg, Pennsylvania, Saint Patrick's Procathedral. William O'Hara, Bishop of Scranton, assisted by Richard Gilmour, Bishop of Cleveland, and John Ambrose Watterson, Bishop of Columbus, consecrated Thomas McGovern, Bishop of Harrisburg, born at Swanlinbar (Kilmore), Ireland, April 10, 1832; priest December 27, 1861; named December 6, 1887; died at Harrisburg July 25, 1898.

186.   1888, April 25, at Belleville, Illinois, Cathedral of Saint Peter. Patrick Augustine Feehan, Archbishop of Chicago, assisted by John Joseph Hogan, Bishop of Kansas City, and Michael Louis Mary Fink, Bishop of Leavenworth, consecrated John Janssen, first Bishop of Belleville, born at Keppeln (Munster), Germany, March 3, 1835; priest November 19, 1858; named February 28, 1888; died at Belleville July 2, 1913.

187.   1888, May 1, at Alton, Illinois, Cathedral of Saints Peter and Paul. John Lancaster Spalding, Bishop of Peoria, assisted by William George McCloskey, Bishop of Louisville, and John Janssen, Bishop of Belleville, consecrated James Ryan, Bishop of Alton, born at Farnaybridge, Thurles (Cashel), Ireland, June 17, 1848; priest December 24, 1871; named February 28, 1888; died at Alton July 2, 1923.

188.   1888, July 1, at Baltimore, Maryland, Cathedral of the Assumption. James Cardinal Gibbons, Archbishop of Baltimore, assisted by John Joseph Kain, Bishop of Wheeling, and Thomas Albert Andrew Becker, Bishop of Savannah, consecrated Leo Michael Haid, OSB, Titular Bishop of Messene, Vicar Apostolic of North Carolina, born at Latrobe, Pennsylvania (Pittsburgh), July 15, 1849; priest December 21, 1872; named February 4, 1888; Abbot Ordinary of Belmont June 8, 1910, remaining Vicar Apostolic of North Carolina; died at Belmont July 24, 1924.

189.   1888, November 4, at Baltimore, Maryland, Cathedral of the Assumption. James Cardinal Gibbons, Archbishop of Baltimore, assisted by John Loughlin, Bishop of Brooklyn, and Edgar Philip Prindle Wadhams, Bishop of Ogdensburg, consecrated John Samuel Foley, Bishop of Detroit, born at Baltimore, Maryland, November 5, 1833; priest December 20, 1856; named February 11, 1888; died at Detroit January 5, 1918.

190.   1888, November 30, at Saint Louis, Missouri, Saint John's Church. Peter Richard Kenrick, Archbishop of Saint Louis, assisted by John Hennessy, Bishop of Dubuque, and Michael Louis Mary Fink, Bishop of Leavenworth, consecrated John Joseph Hennessy, first Bishop of Wichita, born at Cloyne, Ireland, July 19, 1847; priest November 28, 1869; named February 11, 1888; Apostolic Administrator of Concordia from 1891 to May 1898; died at Wichita July 13, 1920.

191.   1889, June 18, at New Orleans, Louisiana, Saint Louis Cathedral. Francis Augustus Anthony Joseph Janssens, Archbishop of New Orleans, assisted by Edward Fitzgerald, Bishop of Little Rock, and Anthony Durier, Bishop of Natchitoches, consecrated Thomas Heslin, Bishop of Natchez, born at Killoe (Ardagh), Ireland, December 21, 1845; priest September 8, 1869; named March 29, 1889; died at Natchez February 22, 1911.

192.   1889, October 20, at Einsiedeln, Switzerland, Abbey Church. William Hickley Gross, Archbishop of Oregon City, assisted by Augustin Egger, Bishop of Sankt Gallen, and Leonard Haas, Bishop of Basel, consecrated John Joseph Frederick Otto Zardetti, first Bishop of Saint Cloud, born at Rohrsbach (Sankt Gallen), Switzerland, January 24, 1847; priest August 21, 1870; named September 22, 1889; Archbishop of Bucharest March 6, 1894; resigned May 25, 1895; Titular Archbishop of Mocissus June 11, 1895; died at Rome May 10, 1902.

193. 1889, October 20, at Richmond, Virginia, Saint Peter's Cathedral. James Cardinal Gibbons, Archbishop of Baltimore, assisted by John Joseph Kain, Bishop of Wheeling, and Leo Michael Haid, Titular Bishop of Messene, consecrated Augustine Van de Vyver, Bishop of Richmond, born at Haasdonk (Ghent), Belgium, December 1, 1844; priest July 24, 1870; named July 16, 1889; died at Richmond October 16, 1911.

194–196. 1889, December 27, at Saint Paul, Minnesota, Cathedral of Saint Paul. John Ireland, Archbishop of Saint Paul, assisted by Thomas Langton Grace, Titular Archbishop of Siunia, and Martin Marty, Bishop of Sioux Falls, consecrated (1) Joseph Bernard Cotter, first Bishop of Winona, born at Liverpool (Northern District), England, November 19, 1844; priest May 3, 1871; named November 15, 1889; died at Winona June 28, 1909. Consecrated (2) James McGolrick, first Bishop of Duluth, born at Borrisokane (Killaloe), Ireland, May 1, 1841; priest June 11, 1867; named November 15, 1889; died at Duluth January 23, 1918. Consecrated (3) John Shanley, first Bishop of Jamestown, born at Albion, New York (Buffalo), January 4, 1852; priest May 30, 1874; named November 15, 1889; title of see changed to Fargo April 6, 1897; died at Fargo July 16, 1909.

197. 1890, November 9, at Barcelona, Spain, probably in Holy Cross Cathedral. Santiago Catala y Albosa, Bishop of Barcelona, assisted by José Morgades y Gili, Bishop of Vich, and José Meseguer y Costa, Bishop of Lerida, consecrated Peter Verdaguer, Titular Bishop of Aulon, Vicar Apostolic of Brownsville, born at San Pedro de Torello (Vich), Spain, December 10, 1835; priest December 12, 1862; named July 25, 1890; died en route from Santa Maria, Texas to Mercedes, Texas October 26, 1911.

198. 1891, April 5, at Erie, Pennsylvania, Saint Patrick's Pro-cathedral. Tobias Mullen, Bishop of Erie, assisted by Richard Phelan, Bishop of Pittsburgh, and Thomas McGovern, Bishop of Harrisburg, consecrated Thomas Francis Brennan, first Bishop of Dallas, born at Ballycullen (Cashel), Ireland, October 6, 1853; priest July 14, 1880; named January 9, 1891; Titular Bishop of Usula and Auxiliary of Saint John's, Newfoundland, February 1, 1893; Titular Bishop of Caesarea in Mauritania October 7, 1905; died at Grottaferrata, Italy, March 20, 1916.

199. 1891, August 5, at Boston, Massachusetts, Cathedral of the Holy Cross. John Joseph Williams, Archbishop of Boston, assisted by Patrick Thomas O'Reilly, Bishop of Springfield, and Matthew Harkins, Bishop of Providence, consecrated John Brady, Titular Bishop of Alabanda, Auxiliary of Boston, born at Kilnaleck (Kilmore), Ireland, February 11, 1840; priest December 4, 1864; named June 19, 1891; died at Boston January 6, 1910.

200. 1891, September 8, at Natchez, Mississippi, Saint Mary's Cathedral. Francis Augustus Anthony Joseph Janssens, Archbishop of New Orleans, assisted by Edward Fitzgerald, Bishop of Little Rock, and Thomas Heslin, Bishop of Natchez, consecrated Theophile Meerschaert, Titular Bishop of Sidyma, Vicar Apostolic of Oklahoma and the Indian Territory, born at Russignies (Ghent), Belgium, August 24, 1847; priest December 23, 1871; named June 2, 1891; first Bishop of Oklahoma August 17, 1905; died at Oklahoma City February 21, 1924.

201. 1891, November 1, at Baltimore, Maryland, Cathedral of the Assumption. James Cardinal Gibbons, Archbishop of Baltimore, assisted by John Baptist Salpointe, Archbishop of Santa Fe, and John Joseph Kain, Bishop of Wheeling, consecrated Placide Louis Chapelle, Titular Bishop of Arabissus, Coadjutor of Santa Fe, born at Runes (Mende), France, August 28, 1842; priest June 26, 1865; named August 21, 1891; Titular Archbishop of Sebastea May 10, 1893; succeeded to Santa Fe January 7, 1894; Archbishop of New Orleans December 1, 1897; extraordinary Apostolic Delegate to Cuba and Puerto Rico September 16, 1898; extraordinary Apostolic Delegate to the Philippines September 28, 1899; died at New Orleans August 9, 1905.

202. 1892, February 25, at La Crosse, Wisconsin, Saint Joseph's Cathedral. Frederick Francis Xavier Katzer, Archbishop of Milwaukee, assisted by John Janssen, Bishop of Belleville, and Joseph Bernard Cotter, Bishop of Winona, consecrated James Schwebach, Bishop of La Crosse, born at Platen, Luxemburg (Luxembourg) August 15, 1847; priest June 16, 1870; named December 14, 1891; died at La Crosse June 6, 1921.

203. 1892, February 25, at Philadelphia, Pennsylvania, Cathedral of Saints Peter and Paul. William Henry Elder, Archbishop of Cincinnati, assisted by William O'Hara, Bishop of Scranton, and Francis Silas Marean Chatard, Bishop of Vincennes, consecrated John Frederick Ignatius Horstmann, Bishop of Cleveland, born at Philadelphia December 16, 1840; priest June 10, 1865; named December 14, 1891; died at Canton, Ohio May 13, 1908.

204. 1892, March 27, at Newark, New Jersey, Saint Peter's Church. John Joseph Frederick Otto Zardetti, Bishop of Saint Cloud, assisted by Winand Michael Wigger, Bishop of Newark, and John Joseph Keane, Titular Bishop of Jasus, consecrated Sebastian Gebhard Messmer, Bishop of Green Bay, born at Goldach (Sankt Gallen), Switzerland, August 29, 1847; priest July 23, 1871; named December 14, 1891; Archbishop of Milwaukee November 28, 1903; died at Goldach, Switzerland August 4, 1930.

205. 1892, April 25, at New York, New York, Saint Patrick's Cathedral. Michael Augustine Corrigan, Archbishop of New York, assisted by Bernard Joseph John McQuaid, Bishop of Rochester, and Francis Silas Marean Chatard, Bishop of Vincennes, consecrated Charles Edward McDonnell, Bishop of Brooklyn, born at New York, New York, February 1, 1854; priest May 19, 1878; named March 11, 1892; died at Brooklyn August 8, 1921.

206. 1892, May 5, at Albany, New York, Cathedral of the Immaculate Conception. Michael Augustine Corrigan, Archbishop of New York, assisted by Francis McNeirny, Bishop of Albany, and Patrick Anthony Ludden, Bishop of Syracuse, consecrated Henry Gabriels, Bishop of Ogdensburg, born at Wannegem-Lede (Ghent), Belgium, October 6, 1838; priest September 21, 1861; named December 20, 1891; died at Ogdensburg April 23, 1921.

207. 1892, June 29, at Burlington, Vermont, Cathedral of the Immaculate Conception. John Joseph Williams, Archbishop of Boston, assisted by Denis Mary Bradley, Bishop of Manchester, and Henry Gabriels, Bishop of Ogdensburg, consecrated John Stephen Michaud, Titular Bishop of Modra, Coadjutor of Burlington, born at Burlington, Vermont (Boston), November 24, 1843; priest June 7, 1873; named May 4, 1892; succeeded to Burlington November 3, 1899; died at New York December 22, 1908.

208. 1892, September 25, at San Francisco, California, Cathedral of Saint Mary. Patrick William Riordan, Archbishop of San Francisco, assisted by Francis Mora, Bishop of Monterey-Los Angeles, and Lawrence Scanlan, Bishop of Salt Lake, consecrated Francis Gulstan Ropert, SS.CC, Titular Bishop of Panopolis, Vicar Apostolic of Hawaii, born at Kerfago (Vannes), France, August 30, 1839; priest May 26, 1866; named June 3, 1892; died at Honolulu January 4, 1903.

209. 1892, October 18, at Springfield, Massachusetts, Saint Michael's Cathedral. John Joseph Williams, Archbishop of Boston, assisted by Denis Mary Bradley, Bishop of Manchester, and John Stephen Michaud, Titular Bishop of Modra, consecrated Thomas Daniel Beaven, Bishop of Springfield, born at Springfield, Massachusetts (Boston), March 1, 1851; priest December 18, 1875; named August 9, 1892; died at Springfield October 5, 1920.

210. 1893, November 30, at Chicago, Illinois, All Saints Church. Patrick Augustine Feehan, Archbishop of Chicago, assisted by James Ryan, Bishop of Alton, and John Samuel Foley, Bishop of Detroit, consecrated Edward Joseph Dunne, Bishop of Dallas, born at Gortnahoe (Cashel),

Ireland, April 23, 1848; priest June 29, 1871; named September 24, 1893; died at Green Bay August 5, 1910.

211.   1894, February 22, at Hartford, Connecticut, Cathedral of Saint Joseph. John Joseph Williams, Archbishop of Boston, assisted by Matthew Harkins, Bishop of Providence, and Thomas Daniel Beaven, Bishop of Springfield, consecrated Michael Tierney, Bishop of Hartford, born at Ballylooby (Waterford), Ireland, September 29, 1839; priest May 26, 1866; named December 2, 1893; died at Hartford October 5, 1908.

212.   1894, April 8, at San Francisco, California, Cathedral of Saint Mary. Patrick William Riordan, Archbishop of San Francisco, assisted by John Baptist Brondel, Bishop of Helena, and Lawrence Scanlan, Bishop of Salt Lake, consecrated George Thomas Montgomery, Titular Bishop of Thmuis, Coadjutor of Monterey-Los Angeles, born at Saint Lawrence Parish, Kentucky (Louisville) December 30, 1847; priest December 20, 1879; named January 26, 1894; succeeded to Monterey-Los Angeles May 6, 1896; Titular Archbishop of Axomis, Coadjutor of San Francisco September 17, 1902; died at San Francisco January 10, 1907.

213.   1894, April 8, at Baltimore, Maryland, Cathedral of the Assumption. James Cardinal Gibbons, Archbishop of Baltimore, assisted by John Samuel Foley, Bishop of Detroit, and Leo Michael Haid, Titular Bishop of Messene, consecrated Patrick James Donahue, Bishop of Wheeling, born at Little Malvern (Western District), England, April 14, 1849; priest December 19, 1885; named January 22, 1894; died at Wheeling October 4, 1922.

214.   1894, July 1, at Albany, New York, Cathedral of the Immaculate Conception. Michael Augustine Corrigan, Archbishop of New York, assisted by Bernard Joseph John McQuaid, Bishop of Rochester, and Patrick Anthony Ludden, Bishop of Syracuse, consecrated Thomas Martin Aloysius Burke, Bishop of Albany, born at Swinford (Achonry), Ireland, January 10, 1840; priest June 30, 1864; named May 18, 1894; died at Albany January 20, 1915.

215.   1894, July 25, at Nashville, Tennessee, Saint Joseph's Church. William Henry Elder, Archbishop of Cincinnati, assisted by John Ambrose Watterson, Bishop of Columbus, and Camillus Paul Maes, Bishop of Covington, consecrated Thomas Sebastian Byrne, Bishop of Nashville, born at Hamilton, Ohio (Cincinnati), July 28, 1841; priest May 22, 1869; named May 10, 1894; died at Nashville September 4, 1923.

216.   1894, October 18, at Trenton, New Jersey, Saint Mary's Cathedral. Michael Augustine Corrigan, Archbishop of New York, assisted by

Charles Edward McDonnell, Bishop of Brooklyn, and Bernard Joseph John McQuaid, Bishop of Rochester, consecrated James Augustine McFaul, Bishop of Trenton, born at Larne (Down and Connor), Ireland, June 6, 1850; priest May 26, 1877; named July 20, 1894; died at Trenton June 16, 1917.

217. 1895, October 28, at San Antonio, Texas, Cathedral of San Fernando. Francis Augustus Anthony Janssens, Archbishop of New Orleans, assisted by Edward Fitzgerald, Bishop of Little Rock, and Nicholas Aloysius Gallagher, Bishop of Galveston, consecrated John Anthony Forest, Bishop of San Antonio, born at Saint Martin la Sauveté (Lyons), France, December 26, 1838; priest April 12, 1863; named August 27, 1895; died at San Antonio March 11, 1911.

218. 1895, December 21, at New York, New York, Saint Patrick's Cathedral. Michael Augustine Corrigan, Archbishop of New York, assisted by Charles Edward McDonnell, Bishop of Brooklyn, and Henry Gabriels, Bishop of Ogdensburg, consecrated John Murphy Farley, Titular Bishop of Zeugma, Auxiliary of New York, born at Newton-Hamilton (Armagh), Ireland, April 20, 1842; priest June 11, 1870; named November 18, 1895; Archbishop of New York September 15, 1902; Cardinal November 27, 1911; died at New York September 17, 1918.

219. 1896, March 22, at Scranton, Pennsylvania, Saint Peter's Cathedral. Francesco Satolli, Titular Archbishop of Naupactus, Apostolic Delegate to the United States, assisted by Thomas McGovern, Bishop of Harrisburg, and Thomas Daniel Beaven, Bishop of Springfield consecrated Michael John Hoban, Titular Bishop of Alali, Coadjutor of Scranton, born at Waterloo, New Jersey (New York), June 6, 1853; priest May 22, 1880; named February 1, 1896; succeeded to Scranton February 3, 1899; died at Scranton November 13, 1926.

220. 1896, April 19, at Washington, District of Columbia, Saint Patrick's Church. Francesco Satolli, Titular Archbishop of Naupactus, Apostolic Delegate to the United States, assisted by John Joseph Keane, Titular Bishop of Jasus, and Martin Marty, Bishop of Saint Cloud, consecrated Thomas O'Gorman, Bishop of Sioux Falls, born at Boston, Massachusetts, May 1, 1843; priest November 5, 1865; named January 24, 1896; died at Sioux Falls September 18, 1921.

221. 1896, June 16, at Sacramento, California, Cathedral of the Blessed Sacrament. Patrick William Riordan, Archbishop of San Francisco, assisted by Lawrence Scanlan, Bishop of Salt Lake, and George Montgomery, Bishop of Monterey-Los Angeles, consecrated Thomas Grace, Bishop of Sacramento, born at Wexford (Ferns), Ireland, August 2,

1841; priest June 24, 1867; named March 20, 1896; died at Sacramento December 27, 1921.

222. 1896, June 29, at Kansas City, Missouri, Cathedral of the Immaculate Conception. John Joseph Kain, Archbishop of Saint Louis, assisted by Maurice Francis Burke, Bishop of Saint Joseph, and John Joseph Hennessy, Bishop of Wichita, consecrated John Joseph Glennon, Titular Bishop of Pinara, Coadjutor of Kansas City, born at Kinnegad (Meath), Ireland, June 14, 1862; priest December 20, 1884; named March 14, 1896; Coadjutor and Apostolic Administrator of Saint Louis April 27, 1903; succeeded to the metropolitan see of Saint Louis October 13, 1903; Cardinal February 18, 1946; died at Dublin March 9, 1946.

223. 1896, September 8, at Vancouver, Washington, Saint James Cathedral. William Hickley Gross, Archbishop of Oregon City, assisted by John Nicholas Lemmens, Bishop of Victoria, and Alphonse Joseph Glorieux, Bishop of Boise City, consecrated Edward John O'Dea, Bishop of Nesqually, born at Dorchester, Massachusetts (Boston), November 23, 1856; priest December 23, 1882; named June 18, 1896; first Bishop of Seattle September 11, 1907; died at Seattle December 25, 1932.

224. 1897, February 24, at Philadelphia, Pennsylvania, Cathedral of Saints Peter and Paul. Patrick John Ryan, Archbishop of Philadelphia, assisted by John Frederick Ignatius Horstmann, Bishop of Cleveland, and Michael John Hoban, Titular Bishop of Alali, consecrated Edmond Francis Prendergast, Titular Bishop of Scilium, Auxiliary of Philadelphia, born at Clonmel (Waterford), Ireland, May 3, 1843; priest November 17, 1865; named November 27, 1896; Archbishop of Philadelphia May 27, 1911; died at Philadelphia February 27, 1918.

225. 1897, February 24, at Buffalo, New York, Saint Joseph's Cathedral. Michael Augustine Corrigan, Archbishop of New York, assisted by Bernard Joseph John McQuaid, Bishop of Rochester, and Charles Edward McDonnell, Bishop of Brooklyn, consecrated James Edward Quigley, Bishop of Buffalo, born at Oshawa, Ontario (Bytown), Canada, October 15, 1855; priest April 13, 1879; named November 30, 1896; Archbishop of Chicago June 12, 1903; died at Buffalo July 10, 1915.

226. 1897, February 24, at Dubuque, Iowa, Saint Raphael's Cathedral. John Hennessy, Archbishop of Dubuque, assisted by Henry Cosgrove, Bishop of Davenport, and Thomas Bonacum, Bishop of Lincoln, consecrated Thomas Mathias Lenihan, Bishop of Cheyenne, born at Mallow (Cloyne), Ireland, August 12, 1844; priest November 19, 1868; named November 30, 1896; died at Dubuque December 15, 1901.

227. 1897, May 9, at Wilmington, Delaware, Saint Peter's Pro-cathedral. James Cardinal Gibbons, Archbishop of Baltimore, assisted by Alfred Allen Paul Curtis, Titular Bishop of Echinus, and Henry Pinckney Northrop, Bishop of Charleston, consecrated John James Joseph Monaghan, Bishop of Wilmington, born at Sumter, South Carolina (Charleston), May 23, 1856; priest December 18, 1880; named January 26, 1897; Titular Bishop of Lydda July 10, 1925; died at Wilmington January 7, 1935.

228. 1897, May 16, at Baltimore, Maryland, Cathedral of the Assumption. James Cardinal Gibbons, Archbishop of Baltimore, assisted by Edward Fitzgerald, Bishop of Little Rock, and Matthew Harkins, Bishop of Providence, consecrated Edward Patrick Allen, Bishop of Mobile, born at Lowell, Massachusetts (Boston), March 17, 1853; priest December 17, 1881; named January 26, 1897; died at Mobile October 21, 1926.

229. 1897, September 21, at Saint Paul, Minnesota, Cathedral of Saint Paul. John Ireland, Archbishop of Saint Paul, assisted by Frederick Francis Xavier Katzer, Archbishop of Milwaukee, and John Vertin, Bishop of Sault Sainte Marie and Marquette, consecrated James Trobec, Bishop of Saint Cloud, born at Billichgratz (Ljubljana), Austria, July 10, 1838; priest September 8, 1865; named July 5, 1897; Titular Bishop of Lycopolis May 28, 1914; died at Saint Cloud December 15, 1921.

230. 1898, February 24, at Philadelphia, Pennsylvania, Cathedral of Saints Peter and Paul. Patrick John Ryan, Archbishop of Philadelphia, assisted by John Frederick Ignatius Horstmann, Bishop of Cleveland, and Edmond Francis Prendergast, Titular Bishop of Scilium, consecrated John Edmund Fitzmaurice, Titular Bishop of Amissus, Coadjutor of Erie, born at Moyvane, Newtownsandes (Kerry), Ireland, January 9, 1837; priest December 21, 1862; named December 14, 1897; succeeded to Erie September 15, 1899; died at Erie June 18, 1920.

231. 1898, June 29, at Saint Paul, Minnesota, Cathedral of Saint Paul. John Ireland, Archbishop of Saint Paul, assisted by John Baptist Brondel, Bishop of Helena, and John Shanley, Bishop of Fargo, consecrated Alexander Christie, Bishop of Vancouver Island, born at Highgate, Vermont (Boston) May 28, 1848; priest December 22, 1877; named March 26, 1898; Archbishop of Oregon City February 12, 1899; died at Portland, Oregon April 6, 1925.

232. 1898, September 21, at Leavenworth, Kansas, Cathedral of the Immaculate Conception. John Joseph Kain, Archbishop of Saint Louis, assisted by John Hennessy, Bishop of Wichita, and Thomas Bonacum,

Bishop of Lincoln, consecrated John Francis Cunningham, Bishop of Concordia, born at Irremore (Kerry), Ireland, June 20, 1842; priest August 8, 1865; named May 14, 1898; died at Concordia June 23, 1919.

233. 1899, April 9, at New Orleans, Louisiana, Saint Louis Cathedral. Placide Louis Chapelle, Archbishop of New Orleans, assisted by Thomas Heslin, Bishop of Natchez, and Jose Montes de Oca, Bishop of San Luis Potosi, consecrated Gustave Augustin Rouxel, Titular Bishop of Curium, Auxiliary of New Orleans, born at Redon (Rennes), France, February 2, 1840; priest November 4, 1863; named February 10, 1899; died at New Orleans March 16, 1908.

234. 1899, May 1, at Philadelphia, Pennsylvania, Cathedral of Saints Peter and Paul. Patrick John Ryan, Archbishop of Philadelphia, assisted by John Frederick Ignatius Horstmann, Bishop of Cleveland, and Edmond Francis Prendergast, Titular Bishop of Scilium, consecrated John Walter Shanahan, Bishop of Harrisburg, born at Silver Lake, Pennsylvania (Philadelphia) January 3, 1846; priest January 2, 1869; named January 2, 1899; died at Harrisburg February 19, 1916.

235. 1899, May 1, at Chicago, Illinois, Cathedral of the Holy Name. Patrick Augustine Feehan, Archbishop of Chicago, assisted by Edward Joseph Dunne, Bishop of Dallas, and Maurice Francis Burke, Bishop of Saint Joseph, consecrated Alexander Joseph McGavick, Titular Bishop of Marcopolis, Auxiliary of Chicago, born at Fox Lake, Illinois (Chicago), August 21, 1863; priest June 11, 1887; named November 2, 1898; Bishop of La Crosse November 21, 1921; died at La Crosse August 25, 1948.

236. 1899, July 2, at New Orleans, Louisiana, Saint Louis Cathedral. Placide Louis Chapelle, Archbishop of New Orleans, assisted by Gustave Augustin Rouxel, Titular Bishop of Curium, and Theophile Meerschaert, Titular Bishop of Sidyma, consecrated James Hubert Blenk, SM, Bishop of Puerto Rico, born at Neustadt (Speyer), Germany, August 6, 1856; priest August 16, 1885; named June 2, 1899; Archbishop of New Orleans April 20, 1906; died at New Orleans April 20, 1917.

237. 1899, August 24, at Marquette, Michigan, Saint Peter's Cathedral. Frederick Francis Xavier Katzer, Archbishop of Milwaukee, assisted by James Schwebach, Bishop of La Crosse, and Sebastian Gebhard Messmer, Bishop of Green Bay, consecrated Frederick Eis, Bishop of Sault Sainte Marie and Marquette, born at Arbach (Trier), Germany, January 20, 1843; priest October 30, 1870; named June 7, 1899; Titular Bishop of Bida July 8, 1922; died at Marquette May 5, 1926.

238. 1900, April 25, at Indianapolis, Indiana, Saint John's Church.

William Henry Elder, Archbishop of Cincinnati, assisted by John Samuel Foley, Bishop of Detroit, and Thomas Sebastian Byrne, Bishop of Nashville, consecrated Denis O'Donaghue, Titular Bishop of Pomaria, Auxiliary of Indianapolis, born at Daviess County, Indiana (Vincennes), November 30, 1848; priest September 6, 1874; named February 10, 1900; Bishop of Louisville February 7, 1910; Titular Bishop of Lesbus July 26, 1924; died at Louisville November 7, 1925.

239. 1900, June 3, at Richmond, Virginia, Saint Peter's Cathedral. James Cardinal Gibbons, Archbishop of Baltimore, assisted by Henry Pinckney Northrop, Bishop of Charleston, and John James Joseph Monaghan, Bishop of Wilmington, consecrated Benjamin Joseph Keiley, Bishop of Savannah, born at Petersburg, Virginia (Richmond), October 13, 1847; priest December 31, 1873; named April 2, 1900; Titular Bishop of Scilium March 18, 1922; died at Atlanta June 17, 1925.

240. 1900, June 17, at Baltimore, Maryland, Cathedral of the Assumption. James Cardinal Gibbons, Archbishop of Baltimore, assisted by John James Joseph Monaghan, Bishop of Wilmington, and Edward Patrick Allen, Bishop of Mobile, consecrated Henry Granjon, Bishop of Tucson, born at Saint-Etienne (Lyons), France, June 15, 1863; priest December 17, 1887; named April 19, 1900; died at Brignais, France November 9, 1922.

241. 1900, August 25, at Cincinnati, Ohio, Cathedral of Saint Peter in Chains. William Henry Elder, Archbishop of Cincinnati, assisted by Henry Joseph Richter, Bishop of Grand Rapids, and Thomas Sebastian Byrne, Bishop of Nashville, consecrated Henry Moeller, Bishop of Columbus, born at Cincinnati, Ohio, December 11, 1849; priest June 10, 1876; named April 6, 1900; Titular Archbishop of Areopolis, Coadjutor of Cincinnati April 27, 1903; succeeded to Cincinnati October 31, 1904; died at Cincinnati January 5, 1925.

242. 1900, September 21, at Peoria, Illinois, Saint Mary's Cathedral. Sebastiano Martinelli, Titular Archbishop of Ephesus, Apostolic Delegate to the United States, assisted by Henry Cosgrove, Bishop of Davenport, and James Ryan, Bishop of Alton, consecrated Peter Joseph O'Reilly, Titular Bishop of Lebedus, Auxiliary of Peoria, born at Moynalty (Meath), Ireland, April 14, 1850; priest June 24, 1877; named June 20, 1900; died at Dublin December 18, 1924.

243. 1900, November 30, at Fort Wayne, Indiana, Cathedral of the Immaculate Conception. William Henry Elder, Archbishop of Cincinnati, assisted by Denis O'Donaghue, Titular Bishop of Pomaria, and Henry Moeller, Bishop of Columbus, consecrated Herman Joseph Alerding,

Bishop of Fort Wayne, born at Westphalia (Munster), Germany, April 13, 1845; priest September 22, 1869; named August 30, 1900; died at Fort Wayne December 6, 1924.

244. 1901, May 19, at Rome, Italy, Basilica of Saint John Lateran, Corsini Chapel. Francesco Cardinal Satolli, assisted by Edmond Stonor, Titular Archbishop of Trapezus, and Raffaele Merry del Val, Titular Archbishop of Nicaea, consecrated William Henry O'Connell, Bishop of Portland, Maine, born at Lowell, Massachusetts (Boston), December 8, 1859; priest June 7, 1884; named February 8, 1901; Titular Archbishop of Constantia, Coadjutor of Boston February 21, 1906; succeeded to Boston August 30, 1907; Cardinal November 27, 1911; died at Boston April 22, 1944.

245. 1901, July 25, at Chicago, Illinois, Cathedral of the Holy Name. Sebastiano Cardinal Martinelli, Apostolic Delegate to the United States, assisted by Henry Cosgrove, Bishop of Davenport, and James Ryan, Bishop of Alton, consecrated Peter James Muldoon, Titular Bishop of Tamasus, Auxiliary of Chicago, born at Columbia, California (San Francisco), October 10, 1862; priest December 18, 1886; named June 10, 1901; first Bishop of Rockford September 28, 1908; Bishop of Monterey-Los Angeles March 22, 1917, but refused the nomination; died at Rockford October 8, 1927.

246. 1901, July 25, at Newark, New Jersey, Saint Patrick's Pro-cathedral. Michael Augustine Corrigan, Archbishop of New York, assisted by Charles Edward O'Donnell, Bishop of Brooklyn, and James Augustine McFaul, Bishop of Trenton, consecrated John Joseph O'Connor, Bishop of Newark, born at Newark, New Jersey, June 11, 1855; priest December 22, 1877; named May 24, 1901; died at South Orange, New Jersey May 20, 1927.

247. 1901, September 8, at Scranton, Pennsylvania, Saint Peter's Cathedral. Sebastiano Cardinal Martinelli, Apostolic Delegate to the United States, assisted by Michael John Hoban, Bishop of Scranton, and John Edmund Fitzmaurice, Bishop of Erie, consecrated Eugene Augustine Garvey, first Bishop of Altoona, born at Carbondale, Pennsylvania (Philadelphia), October 5, 1845; priest September 22, 1869; named May 31, 1901; died at Altoona October 22, 1920.

248. 1901, November 24, at Baltimore, Maryland, Cathedral of the Assumption. James Cardinal Gibbons, Archbishop of Baltimore, assisted by Camillus Paul Maes, Bishop of Covington, and Thomas Daniel Beaven, Bishop of Springfield, consecrated Thomas James Conaty, Titular Bishop of Samos, Rector of The Catholic University of America, born at Kilnaleck (Kilmore), Ireland, August 1, 1847; priest December 21, 1872;

Rector of The Catholic University of America November 23, 1896; named August 21, 1901; Bishop of Monterey-Los Angeles March 27, 1903; died at Coronado, California September 18, 1915.

249. 1902, May 18, at Saint Augustine, Florida, Cathedral of Saint Augustine. James Cardinal Gibbons, Archbishop of Baltimore, assisted by Benjamin Joseph Keiley, Bishop of Savannah, and Leo Michael Haid, Titular Bishop of Messene, consecrated William John Kenny, Bishop of Saint Augustine, born at Delhi, New York (Albany), October 14, 1853; priest January 15, 1879; named March 25, 1902; died at Baltimore October 24, 1913.

250. 1902, May 25, at Springfield, Massachusetts, Saint Michael's Cathedral. Thomas Daniel Beaven, Bishop of Springfield, assisted by Edward Patrick Allen, Bishop of Mobile, and Thomas Joseph Conaty, Titular Bishop of Samos, consecrated Philip Joseph Garrigan, first Bishop of Sioux City, born at Whitegate (Kilmore), Ireland, September 8, 1840; priest June 11, 1870; named March 21, 1902; died at Sioux City October 14, 1919.

251. 1902, July 25, at Santa Fe, New Mexico, Cathedral of San Francisco de Asis. Peter Bourgade, Archbishop of Santa Fe, assisted by Nicholas Chrysostom Matz, Bishop of Denver, and Henry Granjon, Bishop of Tucson, consecrated John Baptist Pitaval, Titular Bishop of Sora, Auxiliary of Santa Fe, born at Saint Genis-Terrenoire (Lyons), France, February 10, 1858; priest December 24, 1881; named May 15, 1902; Archbishop of Santa Fe January 3, 1909; Titular Archbishop of Amida January 29, 1918; died at Denver May 23, 1928.

252–253. 1902, October 28, at Saint Paul, Minnesota, Cathedral of Saint Paul. John Ireland, Archbishop of Saint Paul, assisted by Joseph Bernard Cotter, Bishop of Winona, and James McGolrick, Bishop of Duluth, consecrated (1) John Stariha, first Bishop of Lead, born at Semic (Ljubljana), Austria, May 12, 1845; priest September 19, 1869; named September 2, 1902; Titular Bishop of Antipatris November 8, 1909; died at Ljubljana December 15, 1915. Consecrated (2) James John Keane, Bishop of Cheyenne, born at Joliet, Illinois (Chicago), August 26, 1856; priest December 23, 1882; named June 10, 1902; Archbishop of Dubuque August 11, 1911; died at Dubuque August 2, 1929.

254. 1903, February 24, at Pittsburgh, Pennsylvania, Saint Paul Cathedral. Patrick John Ryan, Archbishop of Philadelphia, assisted by John Walter Shanahan, Bishop of Harrisburg, and Leo Michael Haid, Titular Bishop of Messene, consecrated John Francis Regis Canevin, Titular Bishop of Sabrata, Coadjutor of Pittsburgh, born at Beatty,

Pennsylvania (Pittsburgh), June 5, 1853; priest June 4, 1879; named January 16, 1903; succeeded to Pittsburgh December 20, 1904; Titular Archbishop of Pelusium January 9, 1921; died at Pittsburgh March 22, 1927.

255. 1903, June 14, at Rome, Italy, Church of Saints John and Paul. Francesco Cardinal Satolli, assisted by Pietro Gasparri, Titular Archbishop of Caesarea in Palestina, and Enrico Grazioli, Titular Archbishop of Nicopolis, consecrated Dennis Joseph Dougherty, Bishop of Nueva Segovia, born at Homesville, Pennsylvania (Philadelphia), August 16, 1865; priest May 31, 1890; named June 10, 1903; Bishop of Jaro June 21, 1908; Bishop of Buffalo December 9, 1915; Archbishop of Philadelphia May 1, 1918; Cardinal March 7, 1921; died at Philadelphia May 31, 1951.

256. 1903, July 25, at San Francisco, California, Cathedral of Saint Mary. George Thomas Montgomery, Titular Archbishop of Axium, assisted by Thomas Grace, Bishop of Sacramento, and Thomas James Conaty, Bishop of Monterey-Los Angeles, consecrated Libert Hubert John Louis Boeynaems, SS.CC, Titular Bishop of Zeugma, Vicar Apostolic of Hawaii, born at Antwerp, Belgium, August 18, 1857; priest September 11, 1881; named April 8, 1903; died at Honolulu May 13, 1926.

257. 1903, August 15, at Rome, Italy, Church of Saint Anthony. Francesco Cardinal Satolli, assisted by Diomede Panici, Titular Archbishop of Laodicea in Phrygia, and Amilcare Tonietti, Titular Archbishop of Tyana, consecrated Jeremiah James Harty, Archbishop of Manila, born at Saint Louis, Missouri, November 1, 1853; priest April 28, 1878; named June 6, 1903; Archbishop-Bishop of Omaha May 16, 1916; died at Los Angeles October 29, 1927.

258. 1903, August 24, at New York, New York, Saint Patrick's Cathedral. John Murphy Farley, Archbishop of New York, assisted by Bernard Joseph John McQuaid, Bishop of Rochester, and Charles Edward McDonnell, Bishop of Brooklyn, consecrated Charles Henry Colton, Bishop of Buffalo, born at New York, New York, October 15, 1848; priest June 10, 1876; named June 10, 1903; died at Buffalo May 9, 1915.

259. 1903, August 25, at Portland, Oregon, Cathedral of the Immaculate Conception. Alexander Christie, Archbishop of Oregon City, assisted by Alphonse Joseph Glorieux, Bishop of Boise City, and Edward John O'Dea, Bishop of Seattle, consecrated Charles Joseph O'Reilly, first Bishop of Baker City, born at Carleton (Saint John's, New Brunswick), Canada, January 4, 1860; priest June 29, 1890; named June 10, 1903; Bishop of Lincoln March 20, 1918; died at Lincoln February 4, 1923.

260. 1903, October 28, at Havana, Cuba, Cathedral of the Immaculate Conception. Placide Louis Chapelle, Archbishop of New Orleans, Apostolic Delegate to Cuba and Puerto Rico, assisted by Francisco Barnaba, Archbishop of Santiago de Cuba, and Fr. Manuel Espinosa of Havana, consecrated Bonaventure Finbarr Francis Broderick, Titular Bishop of Juliopolis, born at Hartford, Connecticut, December 25, 1868; priest July 26, 1896; named September 7, 1903; Auxiliary of Havana November 9, 1903; resigned as Auxiliary March 1, 1905; Vicar General of New York March 26, 1942; died at New York November 17, 1943.

261. 1904, February 25, at Steubenville, Ohio, Holy Name Church. Henry Moeller, Titular Archbishop of Areopolis, assisted by Denis O'Donaghue, Titular Bishop of Pomaria, and Herman Joseph Alerding, Bishop of Fort Wayne, consecrated James Joseph Hartley, Bishop of Columbus, born at Columbus, Ohio (Cincinnati), June 6, 1858; priest July 10, 1882; named December 23, 1903; died at Columbus January 12, 1944.

262. 1904, April 25, at New York, New York, Saint Patrick's Cathedral. John Murphy Farley, Archbishop of New York, assisted by Charles Henry Colton, Bishop of Buffalo, and James Augustine McFaul, Bishop of Trenton, consecrated Thomas Francis Cusack, Titular Bishop of Temiscyra, Auxiliary of New York, born at New York, New York, February 22, 1862; priest May 30, 1885; named March 11, 1904; Bishop of Albany July 5, 1915; died at Albany July 12, 1918.

263. 1904, May 1, at Providence, Rhode Island, Cathedral of Saints Peter and Paul. Matthew Harkins, Bishop of Providence, assisted by Michael Tierney, Bishop of Hartford, and John Brady, Titular Bishop of Alabanda, consecrated William Stang, first Bishop of Fall River, born at Langenbrucken (Freiburg im Brisgau), Germany, April 21, 1854; priest June 15, 1878; named March 12, 1904; died at Rochester, Minnesota February 2, 1907.

264. 1904, July 25, at Green Bay, Wisconsin, Saint Francis Xavier Cathedral. Sebastian Gebhard Messmer, Archbishop of Milwaukee, assisted by William Stang, Bishop of Fall River, and Frederick Eis, Bishop of Sault Sainte Marie and Marquette, consecrated Joseph John Fox, Bishop of Green Bay, born at Green Bay, Wisconsin (Milwaukee), August 2, 1855; priest June 7, 1879; named May 27, 1904; Titular Bishop of Jonopolis November 7, 1914; died at Chicago March 14, 1915.

265. 1904, September 8, at Manchester, New Hampshire, Saint Joseph Cathedral. Diomede Angelo Raffaele Gennaro Falconio, Titular assisted by William Henry O'Connell, Bishop of Portland, and Edward Patrick Allen, Bishop of Mobile, consecrated John Bernard Delaney, Bishop of

Manchester, born at Lowell, Massachusetts (Boston), August 9, 1864; priest May 23, 1891; named April 18, 1904; died at Manchester June 11, 1906.

266. 1904, September 21, at Dubuque, Iowa, Saint Raphael's Cathedral. John Joseph Keane, Archbishop of Dubuque, assisted by James John Keane, Bishop of Cheyenne, and Joseph Bernard Cotter, Bishop of Winona, consecrated Mathias Clement Lenihan, first Bishop of Great Falls, born at Dubuque, Iowa, October 6, 1854; priest December 20, 1879; named August 26, 1904; Titular Archbishop of Preslavus January 18, 1930; died at Dubuque August 19/20, 1943.

267. 1904, November 30, at Davenport, Iowa, Sacred Heart Cathedral. John Joseph Keane, Archbishop of Dubuque, assisted by Henry Cosgrove, Bishop of Davenport, and Mathias Clement Lenihan, Bishop of Great Falls, consecrated James Davis, Titular Bishop of Milopotamus, Coadjutor of Davenport, born at Tinvaun, Dunawaggen (Ossory), Ireland, August 31, 1851; priest June 21, 1878; named October 7, 1904; succeeded to Davenport December 22, 1906; died at Davenport December 2, 1926.

268. 1904, November 30, at New Orleans, Louisiana, Saint Louis Cathedral. Placide Louis Chapelle, Archbishop of New Orleans, assisted by Thomas Heslin, Bishop of Natchez, and Gustave Augustin Rouxel, Titular Bishop of Curium, consecrated Cornelius Van de Ven, Bishop of Natchitoches, born at Oirschot (Bois le Duc), Netherlands, June 16, 1865; priest May 31, 1890; named October 24, 1904; title of see changed to Alexandria August 6, 1910; died at Shreveport May 8, 1932.

269. 1904, December 21, at Dubuque, Iowa, Saint Raphael's Cathedral. John Joseph Keane, Archbishop of Dubuque, assisted by Richard Scannell, Bishop of Omaha, and Charles Joseph O'Reilly, Bishop of Baker City, consecrated John Patrick Carroll, Bishop of Helena, born at Dubuque, Iowa, February 22, 1864; priest July 7, 1886; named September 12, 1904; died at Fribourg, Switzerland, November 4, 1925.

270. 1904, December 27, at Kansas City, Missouri, Cathedral of the Immaculate Conception. John Joseph Glennon, Archbishop of Saint Louis, assisted by John Joseph Hogan, Bishop of Kansas City, and John Francis Cunningham, Bishop of Concordia, consecrated Thomas Francis Lillis, Bishop of Leavenworth, born at Lexington, Missouri (Saint Louis), March 3, 1861; priest August 15, 1885; named October 25, 1904; Titular Bishop of Cibyra, Coadjutor of Kansas City March 22, 1910; succeeded to Kansas City February 21, 1913; died at Kansas City, Missouri, December 29, 1938.

271. 1905, May 24, at Rochester, New York, Saint Patrick's Cathedral. John Murphy Farley, Archbishop of New York, assisted by Bernard Joseph John McQuaid, Bishop of Rochester, and Patrick Anthony Ludden, Bishop of Syracuse, consecrated Thomas Francis Hickey, Titular Bishop of Berenice, Coadjutor of Rochester, born at Rochester, New York (Buffalo), February 4, 1861; priest March 25, 1884; named February 18, 1905; succeeded to Rochester January 18, 1909; Titular Archbishop of Viminacium October 30, 1928; died at Rochester December 10, 1940.

272. 1905, July 25, at Milwaukee, Wisconsin, Cathedral of Saint John the Evangelist. Diomede Angelo Raffaele Gennaro Falconio, Titular Archbishop of Larissa, Apostolic Delegate to the United States, assisted by James Schwebach, Bishop of La Crosse, and James McGolrick, Bishop of Duluth, consecrated Augustine Francis Schinner, first Bishop of Superior, born at Milwaukee, Wisconsin, May 1, 1863; priest March 7, 1886; named May 13, 1905; first Bishop of Spokane March 18, 1914; Titular Bishop of Sala December 19, 1925; died at Milwaukee February 7, 1937.

273. 1906, June 11, at Nashville, Tennessee, Saint Mary's Cathedral. Thomas Sebastian Byrne, Bishop of Nashville, assisted by Edward Patrick Allen, Bishop of Mobile, and Nicholas Aloysius Gallagher, Bishop of Galveston, consecrated John Baptist Morris, Titular Bishop of Acmonia, Coadjutor of Little Rock, born at Hendersonville, Tennessee (Nashville), June 29, 1866; priest June 11, 1892; named April 6, 1906; succeeded to Little Rock February 21, 1907; died at Little Rock October 22, 1946.

274. 1906, October 18, at Portland, Maine, Cathedral of the Immaculate Conception. John Joseph Williams, Archbishop of Boston, assisted by Matthew Harkins, Bishop of Providence, and Thomas Daniel Beaven, Bishop of Springfield, consecrated Louis Sebastian Walsh, Bishop of Portland, born at Salem, Massachusetts (Boston), January 22, 1858; priest December 23, 1882; named August 3, 1906; died at Portland, Maine, May 12, 1924.

275. 1907, March 19, at Manchester, New Hampshire, Saint Joseph Cathedral. Diomede Angelo Raffaele Gennaro Falconio, Titular Archbishop of Larissa, Apostolic Delegate to the United States, assisted by Matthew Harkins, Bishop of Providence, and Michael Tierney, Bishop of Hartford, consecrated George Albert Guertin, Bishop of Manchester, born at Nashua, New Hampshire (Boston), February 17, 1869; priest December 17, 1892; named January 2, 1907; died at Morristown, New Jersey, August 6, 1931.

276. 1907, May 12, at Lviv, Ukraine, Saint George's Cathedral. Andrew Alexander Szeptyckyj, Archbishop of Lviv of the Ukrainians, assisted by

Constantine Czechowicz, Bishop of Przemysl of the Ukrainians, and Gregor Chomyszyn, Bishop of Stanislaviv of the Ukrainians, consecrated Soter Stephen Ortynsky de Labetz, OSBM, Titular Bishop of Daulia, Apostolic Exarch for Ukrainian and Ruthenian, born at Ortynychy (Przemysl of the Ukrainians), Ukraine January 29, 1866; priest July 18, 1891; named February 28, 1907; died at Philadelphia March 24, 1916.

277. 1907, September 19, at Fall River, Massachusetts, Cathedral of Saint Mary of the Assumption. Thomas Daniel Beaven, Bishop of Springfield, assisted by Matthew Harkins, Bishop of Providence, and Michael Tierney, Bishop of Hartford, consecrated Daniel Francis Feehan, Bishop of Fall River, born at Athol, Massachusetts (Boston), September 24, 1855; priest December 29, 1879; named July 2, 1907; died at Pocasset, Massachusetts, July 19, 1934.

278. 1907, December 29, at Rome, Italy, Chapel of the North American College. Girolamo Maria Cardinal Gotti, assisted by Patrick William Riordan, Archbishop of San Francisco, and William Giles, Titular Bishop of Philadelphia in Lydia, consecrated Thomas Francis Kennedy, Titular Bishop of Hadrianopolis, Rector of the North American College, Rome, born at Conshohocken, Pennsylvania (Philadelphia), March 23, 1858; priest July 24, 1887; Rector of the North American College, Rome June 14, 1901; named December 15, 1907; Titular Archbishop of Seleucia in Isauria June 17, 1915; died at Castelgandolfo, Italy, August 28, 1917.

279. 1908, February 25, at Cleveland, Ohio, Saint Michael's Church. John Frederick Ignatius Horstmann, Bishop of Cleveland, assisted by James Joseph Hartley, Bishop of Columbus, and Joseph John Fox, Bishop of Green Bay, consecrated Joseph Maria Koudelka, Titular Bishop of Germanicopolis, Auxiliary of Cleveland, born at Chlistova (Ceske Budejovice), Bohemia, Austria, December 8, 1852; priest October 8, 1875; named November 29, 1907; Bishop of Superior August 6, 1915; died at Superior June 24, 1921.

280. 1908, May 3, at Baltimore, Maryland, Cathedral of the Assumption James Cardinal Gibbons, Archbishop of Baltimore, assisted by Henry Moeller, Archbishop of Cincinnati, and Henry Pinckney Northrop, Bishop of Charleston, consecrated Denis Joseph O'Connell, Titular Bishop of Sebaste, Rector of The Catholic University of America, born at Donoughmore (Cloyne), Ireland, January 24, 1849; priest May 26, 1877; Rector of The Catholic University of America in 1903; named December 16, 1907; Auxiliary of San Francisco December 24, 1908; Bishop of Richmond January 19, 1912; Titular Archbishop of Mariamme January 15, 1926; died at Richmond January 1, 1927.

281. 1908, July 29, at Chicago, Illinois, Cathedral of the Holy Name. James Edward Quigley, Archbishop of Chicago, assisted by Peter James Muldoon, Titular Bishop of Tamasus, and Joseph Maria Koudelka, Titular Bishop of Germanicopolis, consecrated Paul Peter Rhode, Titular Bishop of Barca, Auxiliary of Chicago, born at Wejherowo Neustadt (Culm), Poland, September 16, 1871; priest June 17, 1894; named May 22, 1908; Bishop of Green Bay July 5, 1915; died at Green Bay March 3, 1945.

282. 1909, January 10, at Baltimore, Maryland, Cathedral of the Assumption. James Cardinal Gibbons, Archbishop of Baltimore, assisted by Maurice Francis Burke, Bishop of Saint Joseph, and Benjamin Joseph Keiley, Bishop of Savannah, consecrated Owen Patrick Bernard Corrigan, Titular Bishop of Macri, Auxiliary of Baltimore, born at Baltimore, Maryland, March 5, 1849; priest June 7, 1873; named September 29, 1908; died at Baltimore April 8, 1929.

283. 1909, May 1, at Rome, Italy, Chapel of the North American College. Girolamo Maria Caridnal Gotti, assisted by John Baptist Morris, Bishop of Little Rock, and Thomas Francis Kennedy, Titular Bishop of Hadrianopolis, consecrated John Patrick Farrelly, Bishop of Cleveland, born at Memphis, Tennessee (Nashville), March 15, 1856; priest March 22, 1880; named March 18, 1909; died at Cleveland February 12, 1921.

284. 1909, May 16, at Syracuse, New York, Cathedral of the Immaculate Conception. John Murphy Farley, Archbishop of New York, assisted by Patrick Anthony Ludden, Bishop of Syracuse, and Thomas Martin Aloysius Burke, Bishop of Albany, consecrated John Grimes, Titular Bishop of Hemeria, Coadjutor of Syracuse, born at Brooklawn (Limerick), Ireland, December 18, 1852; priest February 19, 1882; named February 1, 1909; succeeded to Syracuse August 6, 1912; died at Syracuse July 26, 1922.

285. 1909, July 25, at Boston, Massachusetts, Cathedral of the Holy Cross. William Henry O'Connell, Archbishop of Boston, assisted by George Albert Guertin, Bishop of Manchester, and Daniel Francis Feehan, Bishop of Fall River, consecrated Joseph Gaudentius Anderson, Titular Bishop of Myrina, Auxiliary of Boston, born at Boston, Massachusetts, September 30, 1865; priest May 20, 1892; named April 29, 1909; died at Boston July 2, 1927.

286. 1909, September 1, at Chicago, Illinois, Cathedral of the Holy Name. Diomede Angelo Raffaele Gennaro Falconio, Titular Archbishop of Larissa, Apostolic Delegate to the United States, assisted by John Janssen, Bishop of Belleville, and Peter James Muldoon, Bishop of Rockford, consecrated Edmund Michael Dunne, Bishop of Peoria, born at

Chicago, Illinois, February 2, 1864; priest June 24, 1887; named June 30, 1909; died at Peoria October 17/18, 1929.

287. 1909, September 21, at Brooklyn, New York, Saint James Pro-cathedral. Charles Edward McDonnell, Bishop of Brooklyn, assisted by Charles Henry Colton, Bishop of Buffalo, and John Joseph O'Connor, Bishop of Loryma, Auxiliary of Brooklyn, born at New York, New York, July 2, 1872; priest June 8, 1895; named June 30, 1909; Archbishop of Chicago December 9, 1915; Cardinal March 24, 1924; died at Mundelein, Illinois, October 2, 1939.

288. 1910, April 10, at Hartford, Connecticut, Cathedral of Saint Joseph. William Henry Cardinal O'Connell, Archbishop of Boston, assisted by Louis Sebastian Walsh, Bishop of Portland, and Daniel Francis Feehan, Bishop of Fall River, consecrated John Joseph Nilan, Bishop of Hartford, born at Newburyport, Massachusetts (Boston), August 1, 1855; priest December 2, 1878; named February 14, 1910; died at Hartford April 13, 1934.

289. 1910, April 14, at Burlington, Vermont, Cathedral of the Immaculate Conception. Thomas Daniel Beaven, Bishop of Springfield, assisted by Matthew Harkins, Bishop of Providence, and Louis Sebastian Walsh, Bishop of Portland, consecrated Joseph John Rice, Bishop of Burlington, born at Leicester, Massachusetts (Springfield), December 6, 1871; priest September 29, 1894; named January 8, 1910; died at Burlington March 31, 1938.

290. 1910, April 14, at Mobile, Alabama, Cathedral of the Immaculate Conception. James Hubert Blenk, Archbishop of New Orleans, assisted by Edward Patrick Allen, Bishop of Mobile, and Cornelius Van de Ven, Bishop of Natchitoches, consecrated John William Shaw, Titular Bishop of Castabala, Coadjutor of San Antonio, born at Mobile, Alabama, December 12, 1863; priest May 26, 1888; named February 7, 1910; Apostolic Administrator of San Antonio May 10, 1910; succeeded to San Antonio March 11, 1911; Archbishop of New Orleans January 25, 1918; died at New Orleans November 2, 1934.

291. 1910, May 10, at Philadelphia, Pennsylvania, Cathedral of Saints Peter and Paul. Diomede Angelo Raffaele Gennaro Falconio, Titular Archbishop of Larissa, Apostolic Delegate to the United States, assisted by John Edmund Fitzmaurice, Bishop of Erie, and Edmond Francis Prendergast, Titular Bishop of Scilium, consecrated John Bernard MacGinley, Bishop of Caceres, born at Croagh (Raphoe), Ireland, August 19, 1871; priest June 8, 1895; named April 2, 1910; Bishop of Monterey-Fresno March 24, 1924; Titular Bishop of Croae September 26, 1932; dean of age of the worldwide Catholic episcopate October 27, 1968; died at Killybegs, Ireland, October 18, 1969.

292–297. 1910, May 19, at Saint Paul, Minnesota, Saint Mary's Chapel of Saint Paul Seminary. John Ireland, Archbishop of Saint Paul, assisted by James McGolrick, Bishop of Duluth, and James Trobec, Bishop of Saint Cloud, consecrated (1) James O'Reilly, Bishop of Fargo, born at Lisgrea (Kilmore), Ireland, October 10, 1855; priest June 24, 1880; named December 18, 1909; died at Fargo December 19, 1934. Consecrated (2) John Jeremiah Lawler, Titular Bishop of Hermopolis, Auxiliary of Saint Paul, born at Rochester, Minnesota (Saint Paul), August 4, 1862; priest December 19, 1885; named February 8, 1910; Bishop of Lead January 29, 1916; title of see changed to Rapid City August 1, 1930; died at Rapid City March 11, 1948. Consecrated (3) Patrick Richard Heffron, Bishop of Winona, born at New York, New York, June 1, 1860; priest December 22, 1884; named March 4, 1910; died at Winona November 23, 1927. Consecrated (4) Joseph Francis Busch, Bishop of Lead, born at Red Wing, Minnesota (Saint Cloud), April 18, 1866; priest July 28, 1889; named April 9, 1910; Bishop of Saint Cloud January 19, 1915; died at St. Cloud May 31, 1953. Consecrated (5) John Baptist Vincent de Paul Wehrle, OSB, first Bishop of Bismarck, born at Berg (Sankt Gallen), Switzerland, December 19, 1855; priest April 23, 1882; named April 9, 1910; Titular Bishop of Teos December 11, 1939; died at Bismarck November 1, 1941. Consecrated (6) Timothy Corbett, first Bishop of Crookston, born at Mendota, Minnesota (Saint Paul), July 10, 1858; priest June 12, 1886; named April 9, 1910; Titular Bishop of Vita June 25, 1938; died at Crookston July 20, 1939.

298. 1910, September 15, at Indianapolis, Indiana, Cathedral of Saints Peter and Paul. Diomede Angelo Raffaele Gennaro Falconio, Titular Archbishop of Larissa, Apostolic Delegate to the United States, assisted by Denis O'Donaghue, Bishop of Louisville, and Herman Joseph Alerding, Bishop of Fort Wayne, consecrated Joseph Chartrand, Titular Bishop of Flavias, Coadjutor of Indianapolis, born at Saint Louis, Missouri, May 11, 1870; priest September 24, 1892; named July 27, 1910; succeeded to Indianapolis September 7, 1918; Archbishop of Cincinnati May 18, 1925, but refused the nomination; Bishop of Indianapolis July 3, 1925; died at Indianapolis December 8, 1933.

299. 1911, January 26, at Ann Arbor, Michigan, Saint Thomas the Apostle Church. James Cardinal Gibbons, Archbishop of Baltimore, assisted by Henry Joseph Richter, Bishop of Grand Rapids, and Camillus Paul Maes, Bishop of Covington, consecrated Edward Denis Kelly, Titular Bishop of Cestrus, Auxiliary of Detroit, born at Hartford, Michigan (Detroit), December 30, 1860; priest June 16, 1886; named December 9,

1910; Bishop of Grand Rapids January 16, 1919; died at Grand Rapids March 26, 1926.

300. 1911, February 22, at Grand Rapids, Michigan, Saint Andrew's Cathedral. Henry Joseph Richter, Bishop of Grand Rapids, assisted by Camillus Paul Maes, Bishop of Covington, and John Samuel Foley, Bishop of Detroit, consecrated Joseph Schrembs, Titular Bishop of Sophene, Auxiliary of Grand Rapids, born at Wutzelhofen (Regensburg), Germany, March 12, 1866; priest June 29, 1889; named January 8, 1911; first Bishop of Toledo August 11, 1911; Bishop of Cleveland June 16, 1921; Archbishop *ad personam* March 25, 1939; died at Cleveland November 2, 1945.

301. 1911, February 22, at Leavenworth, Kansas, Cathedral of the Immaculate Conception. Diomede Angelo Raffaele Gennaro Falconio, Titular Archbishop of Larissa, Apostolic Delegate to the United States, assisted by Thomas Francis Lillis, Titular Bishop of Cibyra, and John Joseph Hennessy, Bishop of Wichita, consecrated John Ward, Bishop of Leavenworth, born at West View, Ohio (Cleveland), May 25, 1857; priest July 17, 1884; named November 24, 1910; died at Kansas City, Kansas, April 20, 1929.

302. 1911, July 6, at Wichita, Kansas, Saint Aloysius Pro-cathedral. John Joseph Hennessy, Bishop of Wichita, assisted by Nicholas Chrysostom Matz, Bishop of Denver, and Richard Scannell, Bishop of Omaha, consecrated John Henry Tihen, Bishop of Lincoln, born at Oldenburg, Indiana (Vincennes), July 14, 1861; priest April 26, 1886; named May 12, 1911; Bishop of Denver September 21, 1917; Titular Bishop of Bosana January 6, 1931; died at Wichita January 14, 1940.

303. 1911, July 12, at Dallas, Texas, Sacred Heart Cathedral. James Hubert Blenk, Archbishop of New Orleans, assisted by Nicholas Aloysius Gallagher, Bishop of Galveston, and John Baptist Morris, Bishop of Little Rock, consecrated Joseph Patrick Lynch, Bishop of Dallas, born at Saint Joseph, Michigan (Detroit), November 16, 1872; priest June 9, 1900; named June 8, 1911; title of see changed to Dallas-Fort Worth December 8, 1953; died at Dallas August 19, 1954.

304. 1911, August 29, at Atlanta, Georgia, Sacred Heart Church. James Hubert Blenk, Archbishop of New Orleans, assisted by Edward Patrick Allen, Bishop of Mobile, and John Baptist Morris, Bishop of Little Rock, consecrated John Edward Gunn, SM, Bishop of Natchez, born at Fivemiletown (Armagh), Ireland, March 15, 1863; priest February 2, 1890; named July 1, 1911; died at New Orleans February 19, 1924.

65

305. 1911, November 29, at New Orleans, Louisiana, Saint Louis Cathedral. James Hubert Blenk, Archbishop of New Orleans, assisted by Cornelius Van de Ven, Bishop of Alexandria, and John William Shaw, Bishop of San Antonio, consecrated John Marius Laval, Titular Bishop of Hierocesarea, Auxiliary of New Orleans, born at Saint-Etienne (Lyons), France, September 21, 1854; priest November 10, 1877; named September 7, 1911; died at San Francisco June 4, 1937.

306. 1912, April 11, at Omaha, Nebraska, Saint Cecilia's Cathedral. James John Keane, Archbishop of Dubuque, assisted by Richard Scannell, Bishop of Omaha, and Philip Joseph Garrigan, Bishop of Sioux City, consecrated Patrick Aloysius Alphonsus McGovern, Bishop of Cheyenne, born at Omaha, Nebraska, October 14, 1872; priest August 18, 1895; named January 19, 1912; died at Cheyenne November 7, 1951.

307. 1912, April 25, at Providence, Rhode Island, Cathedral of Saints Peter and Paul. Matthew Harkins, Bishop of Providence, assisted by James Davis, Bishop of Davenport, and Louis Sebastian Walsh, Bishop of Portland, consecrated Austin Dowling, first Bishop of Des Moines, born at New York, New York, April 6, 1868; priest June 24, 1891; named January 31, 1912; Archbishop of Saint Paul March 10, 1919; died at Saint Paul November 28/29, 1930.

308. 1912, May 1, at Ogdensburg, New York, Saint Mary's Cathedral. John Murphy Cardinal Farley, Archbishop of New York, assisted by Henry Gabriels, Bishop of Ogdensburg, and Charles Henry Colton, Bishop of Buffalo, consecrated Joseph Henry Conroy, Titular Bishop of Arindela, Auxiliary of Ogdensburg, born at Watertown, New York (Albany), November 8, 1858; priest June 11, 1881; named March 11, 1912; Bishop of Ogdensburg November 21, 1921; died at Ogdensburg March 20, 1939.

309. 1912, September 17, at Philadelphia, Pennsylvania, Cathedral of Saints Peter and Paul. Edmond Francis Prendergast, Archbishop of Philadelphia, assisted by John Walter Shanahan, Bishop of Harrisburg, and John Edmund Fitzmaurice, Bishop of Erie, consecrated John Joseph McCort, Titular Bishop of Azotus, Auxiliary of Philadelphia, born at Philadelphia, Pennsylvania, February 16, 1860; priest October 14, 1883; named June 28, 1912; Coadjutor of Altoona January 27, 1920; succeeded to Altoona October 22, 1920; died at Altoona April 21, 1936.

310. 1912, December 4, at Rochester, New York, Saint Patrick's Cathedral. Giovanni Vincenzo Bonzano, Titular Archbishop of Melitene, Apostolic Delegate to the United States, assisted by James Edward Quigley, Archbishop of Chicago, and Denis Joseph O'Connell, Bishop of

Richmond, consecrated Edward Joseph Hanna, Titular Bishop of Titiopolis, Auxiliary of San Francisco, born at Rochester, New York (Buffalo), July 21, 1860; priest May 30, 1885; named October 22, 1912; Archbishop of San Francisco June 1, 1915; Titular Archbishop of Gortyna March 2, 1935; died at Rome July 10, 1944.

311. 1913, April 16, at Cheyenne, Wyoming, Saint Mary's Cathedral. James John Keane, Archbishop of Dubuque, assisted by Richard Scannell, Bishop of Omaha, and Patrick Aloysius Alphonsus McGovern, Bishop of Cheyenne, consecrated James Albert Duffy, first Bishop of Kearney, born at Saint Paul, Minnesota, September 13, 1873; priest May 27, 1899; named January 27, 1913; title of see changed to Grand Island April 11, 1917; Titular Bishop of Silandus June 5, 1931; died at Hot Springs, Arkansas, February 12, 1968.

312. 1913, May 20, at Union City, New Jersey, Saint Michael's Monastery. Giovanni Vincenzo Bonzano, Titular Archbishop of Melitene, assisted by John Joseph O'Connor, Bishop of Newark, and Charles Edward McDonnell, Bishop of Brooklyn, consecrated Henry Paul John Nussbaum, CP, first Bishop of Corpus Christi, born at Philadelphia, Pennsylvania, September 7, 1870; priest May 20, 1894; named April 4, 1913; Titular Bishop of Gerasa April 22, 1920; Bishop of Sault Sainte Marie and Marquette November 14, 1922; died at Marquette June 24, 1935.

313. 1914, January 14, at Milwaukee, Wisconsin, Cathedral of Saint John the Evangelist. Sebastian Gebhard Messmer, Archbishop of Milwaukee, assisted by Joseph Weber, Titular Archbishop of Darnis, and Joseph Henry Richter, Bishop of Grand Rapids, consecrated Edward Kozlowski, Titular Bishop of Germia, Auxiliary of Milwaukee, born at Tarnow, Poland, November 21, 1860; priest June 29, 1887; named November 12, 1913; died at Milwaukee August 6, 1915.

314. 1914, February 24, at Belleville, Illinois, Cathedral of Saint Peter. James Edward Quigley, Archbishop of Chicago, assisted by Peter James Muldoon, Bishop of Rockford, and Paul Peter Rhode, Titular Bishop of Barca, consecrated Henry Althoff, Bishop of Belleville, born at Aviston, Illinois (Alton), August 28, 1873; priest July 26, 1902; named December 4, 1913; died at Belleville July 3, 1947.

315. 1914, June 30, at Saint Augustine, Florida, Cathedral of Saint Augustine. Benjamin Joseph Keiley, Bishop of Savannah, assisted by Patrick James Donahue, Bishop of Wheeling, and Owen Patrick Bernard Corrigan, Titular Bishop of Macri, consecrated Michael Joseph Curley, Bishop of Saint Augustine, born at Athlone (Elphin), Ireland, October 12, 1879; priest March 19, 1904; named April 3, 1914; Archbishop of Baltimore

August 10, 1921; Archbishop of Baltimore and Washington July 22, 1939; died at Baltimore May 16, 1947.

316. 1914, October 28, at New York, New York, Saint Patrick's Cathedral. John Murphy Cardinal Farley, Archbishop of New York, assisted by Henry Gabriels, Bishop of Ogdensburg, and Thomas Francis Cusack, Bishop of Albany, consecrated Patrick Joseph Hayes, Titular Bishop of Thagaste, Auxiliary of New York, born at New York, New York, November 20, 1867; priest September 8, 1892; named July 3, 1914; Bishop ordinary of the U.S. armed forces November 24, 1917; Archbishop of New York March 10, 1919; Cardinal March 24, 1924; died at New York September 4, 1938.

317. 1914, November 15, at Baltimore, Maryland, Cathedral of the Assumption. James Cardinal Gibbons, Archbishop of Baltimore, assisted by Denis Joseph O'Connell, Bishop of Richmond, and John Joseph Nilan, Bishop of Hartford, consecrated Thomas Joseph Shahan, Titular Bishop of Germanicopolis, Rector of The Catholic University of America, born at Manchester, New Hampshire (Boston), September 11, 1857; priest June 3, 1882; Rector of The Catholic University of America from 1909 to 1927; named July 24, 1914; died at Washington March 9, 1932.

318. 1915, April 28, at Providence, Rhode Island, Cathedral of Saints Peter and Paul. Matthew Harkins, Bishop of Providence, assisted by Louis Sebastian Walsh, Bishop of Portland, and Austin Dowling, Bishop of Des Moines, consecrated Thomas Francis Doran, Titular Bishop of Halicarnassus, Auxiliary of Providence, born at Barrington, Rhode Island (Hartford), October 4, 1856; priest July 4, 1880; named February 26, 1915; died at Providence January 3, 1916.

319. 1915, August 24, at Los Angeles, California, Saint Vincent's Church. Edward Joseph Hanna, Archbishop of San Francisco, assisted by Thomas Francis Lillis, Bishop of Kansas City, and Thomas Grace, Bishop of Sacramento, consecrated Joseph Sarsfield Glass, CM, Bishop of Salt Lake, born at Bushnell, Illinois (Chicago), March 13, 1874; priest August 15, 1897; named June 1, 1915; died at Los Angeles January 26, 1926.

320. 1915, September 8, at Grand Rapids, Michigan, Saint Andrew's Cathedral. Henry Joseph Richter, Bishop of Grand Rapids, assisted by Joseph Schrembs, Bishop of Toledo, and Edward Denis Kelly, Titular Bishop of Cestrus, consecrated Michael James Gallagher, Titular Bishop of Tipasa in Mauretania, Coadjutor of Grand Rapids, born at Auburn, Michigan (Detroit), November 18, 1866; priest March 19, 1893; named July 5, 1915; succeeded to Grand Rapids December 26, 1916; Bishop of Detroit July 18, 1918; died at Detroit January 20, 1937.

321. 1915, October 28, at Denver, Colorado, Cathedral of the Immaculate Conception. John Baptist Pitaval, Archbishop of Santa Fe, assisted by Patrick Aloysius Alphonsus McGovern, Bishop of Cheyenne, and Henry Granjon, Bishop of Tucson, consecrated Anthony Joseph Schuler, SJ, first Bishop of El Paso, born at Saint Mary's, Pennsylvania (Erie), September 20, 1869; priest June 27, 1901; named June 17, 1915; Titular Bishop of Aradus November 29, 1942; died at Denver June 3, 1944.

322. 1916, January 25, at Covington, Kentucky, Saint Mary Cathedral. Henry Moeller, Archbishop of Cincinnati, assisted by Theophile Meerschaert, Bishop of Oklahoma, and James Joseph Hartley, Bishop of Columbus, consecrated Ferdinand Brossart, Bishop of Covington, born at Buechelberg (Speyer), Germany, October 14, 1849; priest September 1, 1892; named December 5, 1915; Titular Bishop of Vallis March 2, 1923; died at Fort Melbourne, Kentucky, August 6, 1930.

323. 1916, September 21, at Philadelphia, Pennsylvania, Cathedral of Saints Peter and Paul. Edmond Francis Prendergast, Archbishop of Philadelphia, assisted by John Joseph McCort, Titular Bishop of Azotus, and John Edmund Fitzmaurice, Bishop of Erie, consecrated Philip Richard McDevitt, Bishop of Harrisburg, born at Philadelphia, Pennsylvania, July 12, 1858; priest July 14, 1885; named July 10, 1916; died at Harrisburg November 11, 1935.

324. 1917, March 15, at Baltimore, Maryland, Cathedral of the Assumption. James Cardinal Gibbons, Archbishop of Baltimore, assisted by John James Joseph Monaghan, Bishop of Wilmington, and Owen Patrick Bernard Corrigan, Titular Bishop of Macri, consecrated William Thomas Russell, Bishop of Charleston, born at Baltimore, Maryland, October 20, 1863; priest June 21, 1889; named December 7, 1916; died at Charleston March 18, 1927.

325. 1917, July 25, at Seattle, Washington, Saint James Cathedral. Alexander Christie, Archbishop of Oregon City, assisted by Edward John O'Dea, Bishop of Seattle, and Augustine Francis Schinner, Bishop of Spokane, consecrated Joseph Raphael John Crimont, SJ, Titular Bishop of Ammaedara, Vicar Apostolic of Alaska, born at Ferrieres (Amiens), France, February 2, 1858; priest August 26, 1888; Prefect Apostolic of Alaska March 28, 1904; named March 22, 1917; died at Juneau May 20, 1945.

326. 1917, October 23, at Providence, Rhode Island, Cathedral of Saints Peter and Paul. Thomas Daniel Beaven, Bishop of Springfield, assisted by Daniel Francis Feehan, Bishop of Fall River, and John Joseph Nilan, Bishop of Hartford, consecrated Denis Matthew Lowney, Titular Bishop of Hadrianopolis, Auxiliary of Providence, born at Castletown-Bar Haven (Cloyne), Ireland, June 1, 1863; priest December 17, 1887; named August 24, 1917; died at Providence August 13, 1918.

327. 1917, December 5, at San Francisco, California, Cathedral of Saint Mary. Edward Joseph Hanna, Archbishop of San Francisco, assisted by Thomas Grace, Bishop of Sacramento, and Joseph Sarsfield Glass, Bishop of Salt Lake, consecrated John Joseph Cantwell, Bishop of Monterey-Los Angeles, born at Limerick, Ireland, December 1, 1874; priest June 18, 1899; named September 21, 1917; title of see changed to Los Angeles-San Diego June 1, 1922; first Archbishop of Los Angeles July 11, 1936; died at Los Angeles October 30, 1947.

328. 1918, February 6, at Erie, Pennsylvania, Saint Peter's Cathedral. Michael John Hoban, Bishop of Scranton, assisted by Philip Richard McDevitt, Bishop of Harrisburg, and John Joseph McCort, Bishop of Altoona, consecrated John Mark Gannon, Titular Bishop of Nilopolis, Auxiliary of Erie, born at Erie, Pennsylvania, June 12, 1877; priest December 21, 1901; named November 13, 1917; Bishop of Erie August 26, 1920; Archbishop *ad personam* November 25, 1953; Titular Archbishop of Tacarata December 9, 1966; died at Erie September 5, 1968.

329. 1918, May 1, at Dubuque, Iowa, Saint Raphael's Cathedral. Giovanni Vincenzo Bonzano, Titular Archbishop of Melitene, Apostolic Delegate to the United States, assisted by Mathias Clement Lenihan, Bishop of Great Falls, and Joseph Sarsfield Glass, Bishop of Salt Lake, consecrated Daniel Mary Gorman, Bishop of Boise City, born at Wyoming, Iowa (Dubuque), April 12, 1861; priest June 24, 1893; named February 8, 1918; died at Lewiston, Idaho, June 9, 1927.

330. 1918, July 25, at Buffalo, New York, Saint Joseph Cathedral.* Giovanni Vincenzo Bonzano, Titular Archbishop of Melitene, Apostolic Delegate to the United States, assisted by Denis Joseph Dougherty, Archbishop of Philadelphia, and John Joseph O'Connor, Bishop of Newark, consecrated Thomas Joseph Walsh, Bishop of Trenton, born at Parker's Landing, Pennsylvania (Pittsburgh), December 6, 1873; priest January 27, 1900; named May 10, 1918; Bishop of Newark March 2, 1928; first Archbishop of Newark December 10, 1937; died at South Orange, New Jersey, June 6, 1952.

---

*Note: This was the first consecration performed in the new Saint Joseph Cathedral. In 1976, due to major structural problems, this cathedral was closed and the old Saint Joseph Cathedral again became the cathedral of the diocese.

331. 1918, September 8, at Rome, Italy, Church of Santa Maria sopra

Minerva. Tommaso Pio Cardinal Boggiani, OP, assisted by Bonaventura Cerretti, Titular Archbishop of Corinth, and Thomas Esser, Titular Bishop of Sinita, consecrated John Timothy McNicholas, OP, Bishop of Duluth, born at Kilmaugh (Achonry), Ireland, December 15, 1877; priest October 10, 1901; named July 18, 1918; Bishop of Indianapolis May 18, 1925, but did not take possession of the see; Archbishop of Cincinnati July 8, 1925; died at Cincinnati April 22, 1950.

332. 1918, November 10, at Saint Louis, Missouri, Cathedral of Saint Louis.* John Joseph Glennon, Archbishop of Saint Louis, assisted by Thomas Francis Lillis, Bishop of Kansas City, and John Baptist Morris, Bishop of Little Rock, consecrated Christopher Edward Byrne, Bishop of Galveston, born at Byrnesville, Missouri (Saint Louis), April 21, 1867; priest September 23, 1891; named July 18, 1918; died at Galveston April 1, 1950.

Note: This was the first consecration performed in the new Cathedral of Saint Louis.

333–334. 1918, December 8, at New Orleans, Louisiana, Saint Louis Cathedral. Giovanni Vincenzo Bonzano, Titular Archbishop of Melitene, Apostolic Delegate to the United States, assisted by Theophile Meerschaert, Bishop of Oklahoma, and John Marius Laval, Titular Bishop of Hierocesarea, consecrated (1) Arthur Jerome Drossaerts, Bishop of San Antonio, born at Breda, Netherlands, September 11, 1862; priest June 15, 1889; named July 18, 1918; first Archbishop of San Antonio August 3, 1926; died at San Antonio September 8, 1940. Consecrated (2) Jules Benjamin Jeanmard, first Bishop of Lafayette, born at Pont-Breaux, Louisiana (New Orleans), August 15, 1879; priest June 10, 1903; named July 18, 1918; Titular Bishop of Bareta March 13, 1956; died at Lake Charles February 23, 1957.

335. 1919, March 25, at Buffalo, New York, Saint Joseph Cathedral. Giovanni Vincenzo Bonzano, Titular Archbishop of Melitene, Apostolic Delegate to the United States, assisted by John Grimes, Bishop of Syracuse, and Thomas Joseph Walsh, Bishop of Trenton, consecrated Edmund Francis Gibbons, Bishop of Albany, born at White Plains, New York (New York), September 16, 1868; priest May 27, 1893; named March 10, 1919; Titular Bishop of Verbe November 10, 1954; became dean of age of the worldwide episcopate December 6, 1963; died at Albany June 19, 1964.

336. 1919, March 25, at Seattle, Washington, Saint James Cathedral. Edward John O'Dea, Bishop of Seattle, assisted by Mathias Clement Lenihan, Bishop of Great Falls, and John Patrick Carroll, Bishop of

Helena, consecrated Joseph Francis McGrath, Bishop of Baker City, born at Kilmacow (Ossory), Ireland, March 1, 1871; priest December 21, 1895; named December 21, 1918; died at Baker April 12, 1950.

337. 1919, March 30, at Washington, District of Columbia, Church of the Franciscan Monastery of Mt. St. Sepulchre. James Cardinal Gibbons, Archbishop of Baltimore, assisted by Denis Joseph O'Connell, Bishop of Richmond, and Michael Joseph Curley, Bishop of Saint Augustine, consecrated William Turner, Bishop of Buffalo, born at Kilmallock (Cashel), Ireland, April 8, 1871; priest August 13, 1893; named March 10, 1919; died at New York July 10, 1936.

338. 1919, April 8, at Sioux City, Iowa, Cathedral of the Epiphany. James John Keane, Archbishop of Dubuque, assisted by James Davis, Bishop of Davenport, and Patrick Aloysius Alphonsus McGovern, Bishop of Cheyenne, consecrated Edmond Heelan, Titular Bishop of Gerasa, Auxiliary of Sioux City, born at Knockaney (Cashel), Ireland, February 4, 1868; priest June 24, 1890; named December 21, 1918; Bishop of Sioux City March 8, 1920; died at Sioux City September 20, 1948.

339. 1919, April 10, at Providence, Rhode Island, Cathedral of Saints Peter and Paul. Thomas Daniel Beaven, Bishop of Springfield, assisted by Louis Sebastian Walsh, Bishop of Portland, and Daniel Francis Feehan, Bishop of Fall River, consecrated William Augustine Hickey, Titular Bishop of Claudiopolis in Isauria, Coadjutor of Providence, born at Worcester, Massachusetts (Boston), May 13, 1869; priest December 22, 1893; named March 10, 1919; succeeded to Providence May 25, 1921; died at Providence October 4, 1933.

340. 1919, May 7, at Santa Fe, New Mexico, Cathedral of San Francisco de Asis. John Baptist Pitaval, Titular Archbishop of Amida, assisted by John Henry Tihen, Bishop of Denver, and Anthony Joseph Schuler, Bishop of El Paso, consecrated Albert Thomas Daeger, OFM, Archbishop of Santa Fe, born at Saint Ann, Indiana (Vincennes), March 5, 1872; priest July 25, 1896; named March 10, 1919; died at Santa Fe December 2, 1932.

341. 1919, May 21, at Dubuque, Iowa, Saint Raphael's Cathedral. James John Keane, Archbishop of Dubuque, assisted by James Davis, Bishop of Davenport, and Edmond Heelan, Titular Bishop of Gerasa, consecrated Thomas William Drumm, Bishop of Des Moines, born at Fore (Meath), Ireland, July 12, 1871; priest December 21, 1901; named March 28, 1919; died at Des Moines October 24, 1933.

342. 1920, April 28, at Hartford, Connecticut, Cathedral of Saint Joseph. Giovanni Vincenzo Bonzano, Titular Archbishop of Melitene, Apostolic

Delegate to the United States, assisted by John Joseph Nilan, Bishop of Hartford, and Thomas Joseph Shahan, Titular Bishop of Germanicopolis, consecrated John Gregory Murray, Titular Bishop of Flavias, Auxiliary of Hartford, born at Waterbury, Connecticut (Hartford), February 26, 1877; priest April 14, 1900; named November 15, 1919; Bishop of Portland May 29, 1925; Archbishop of Saint Paul October 29, 1931; died at Saint Paul October 11, 1936.

343. 1920, October 3, at Brooklyn, New York, Saint James Pro-cathedral. Charles Edward McDonnell, Bishop of Brooklyn, assisted by Edmund Francis Gibbons, Bishop of Albany, and Thomas Joseph Walsh, Bishop of Trenton, consecrated Thomas Edmund Molloy, Titular Bishop of Lorea, Auxiliary of Brooklyn, born at Nashua, New Hampshire (Manchester), September 8, 1884; priest September 19, 1908; named June 28, 1920; Bishop of Brooklyn November 21, 1921; Archbishop *ad personam* April 7, 1951; died at Brooklyn November 26, 1956.

344. 1920, December 4, at San Francisco, California, Cathedral of Saint Mary. Edward Joseph Hanna, Archbishop of San Francisco, assisted by John Joseph Cantwell, Bishop of Monterey-Los Angeles, and Thomas Grace, Bishop of Sacramento, consecrated Patrick Joseph James Keane, Titular Bishop of Sebastea in Palestina, Auxiliary of Sacramento, born at Ballybunnion (Kerry), Ireland, January 6, 1872; priest June 20, 1895; named September 10, 1920; Bishop of Sacramento March 17, 1922; died at Sacramento September 1, 1928.

345. 1921, March 30, at Kansas City, Missouri, Cathedral of the Immaculate Conception. Thomas Francis Lillis, Bishop of Kansas City, assisted by Peter James Muldoon, Bishop of Rockford, and John Henry Tihen, Bishop of Denver, consecrated Francis Joseph Tief, Bishop of Concordia, born at Greenwich, Connecticut (Hartford), March 7, 1881; priest June 11, 1908; named December 16, 1920; Titular Bishop of Nisa in Lycia June 11, 1938; died September 22, 1965.

346. 1921, June 10, at Toledo, Ohio, Saint Francis de Sales Cathedral. Joseph Schrembs, Bishop of Toledo, assisted by Michael James Gallagher, Bishop of Detroit, and John Henry Tihen, Bishop of Denver, consecrated August John Schwertner, Bishop of Wichita, born at Canton, Ohio (Cleveland), December 23, 1870; priest June 12, 1897; named March 10, 1921; died at Wichita October 2, 1939.

347. 1921, June 14, at Saint Mary of the Woods, Indiana, Saint Mary's Church. Joseph Chartrand, Bishop of Indianapolis, assisted by Cornelius Van de Ven, Bishop of Alexandria, and Joseph Patrick Lynch, Bishop of Dallas, consecrated Emmanuel Boleslaus Ledvina, Bishop of Corpus

Christi, born at Evansville, Indiana (Vincennes), October 28, 1868; priest March 14, 1893; named April 30, 1921; Titular Bishop of Pitanae March 15, 1949; died at Corpus Christi December 15, 1952.

348. 1921, June 29, at Pittsburgh, Pennsylvania, Saint Paul Cathedral. John Francis Canevin, Titular Archbishop of Pelusium, assisted by Philip Richard McDevitt, Bishop of Harrisburg, and John Joseph McCort, Bishop of Altoona, consecrated Hugh Charles Boyle, Bishop of Pittsburgh, born at Johnstown, Pennsylvania (Pittsburgh), October 8, 1873; priest July 2, 1898; named June 16, 1921; died at Pittsburgh December 22, 1950.

349. 1921, September 8, at Springfield, Massachusetts, Saint Michael's Cathedral. Alfred Arthur Sinnott, Archbishop of Winnipeg, assisted by Michael Joseph Curley, Archbishop of Baltimore, and George Albert Guertin, Bishop of Manchester, consecrated Thomas Mary O'Leary, Bishop of Springfield, born at Dover, New Hampshire (Boston), August 16, 1875; priest December 18, 1897; named June 16, 1921; died at Springfield October 10, 1949.

350. 1921, September 19, at Philadelphia, Pennsylvania, Cathedral of Saints Peter and Paul. Dennis Joseph Cardinal Dougherty, Archbishop of Philadelphia, assisted by John Joseph McCort, Bishop of Altoona, and Thomas Joseph Walsh, Bishop of Trenton, consecrated Michael Joseph Crane, Titular Bishop of Curium, Auxiliary of Philadelphia, born at Ashland, Pennsylvania (Philadelphia), September 8, 1863; priest June 15, 1889; named August 20, 1921; died at Philadelphia December 26, 1928.

351. 1921, October 28, at New York, New York, Saint Patrick's Cathedral. Patrick Joseph Hayes, Archbishop of New York, assisted by Joseph Henry Conroy, Bishop of Ogdensburg, and John Joseph O'Connor, Bishop of Newark, consecrated John Joseph Dunn, Titular Bishop of Camuliana, Auxiliary of New York, born at New York, New York, August 31, 1869; priest May 30, 1896; named August 19, 1921; died at New York August 31, 1933.

352. 1921, November 30, at Toledo, Ohio, Saint Francis De Sales Cathedral. Henry Moeller, Archbishop of Cincinnati, assisted by John Baptist Morris, Bishop of Little Rock, and Thomas Edmund Molloy, Bishop of Brooklyn, consecrated Samuel Alphonsus Stritch, Bishop of Toledo, born at Nashville, Tennessee, August 17, 1887; priest May 21, 1910; named August 10, 1921; Archbishop of Milwaukee August 26, 1930; Archbishop of Chicago December 27, 1939; Cardinal February 18, 1946; Proprefect of the Congregation for the Propagation of the Faith March 1, 1958; died at Rome May 26, 1958.

353. 1921, December 21, at Chicago, Illinois, Cathedral of the Holy Name. George William Mundelein, Archbishop of Chicago, assisted by Alexander Joseph McGavick, Bishop of La Crosse, and Thomas Edmund Molloy, Bishop of Brooklyn, consecrated Edward Francis Hoban, Titular Bishop of Colonia in Cappadocia, Auxiliary of Chicago, born at Chicago, Illinois, June 27, 1878; priest July 11, 1903; named November 21, 1921; Bishop of Rockford February 10, 1928; Titular Bishop of Lystra, Coadjutor of Cleveland November 14, 1942; succeeded to Cleveland November 2, 1945; Archbishop *ad personam* July 13, 1951; died at Cleveland September 22, 1966.

354. 1922, May 3, at Marquette, Michigan, Saint Peter's Cathedral. Sebastian Gebhard Messmer, Archbishop of Milwaukee, assisted by Paul Peter Rhode, Bishop of Green Bay, and John Timothy McNicholas, Bishop of Duluth, consecrated Joseph Gabriel Pinten, Bishop of Superior, born at Rockland, Michigan (Sault Sainte Marie and Marquette), October 3, 1867; priest November 1, 1890; named November 30, 1921; Bishop of Grand Rapids June 25, 1926; Titular Bishop of Sela November 1, 1940; died at Marquette November 6, 1945.

355. 1922, May 3, at Saint Augustine, Florida, Cathedral of Saint Augustine. Michael Joseph Curley, Archbishop of Baltimore, assisted by John James Monaghan, Bishop of Wilmington, and William Turner, Bishop of Buffalo, consecrated Patrick Joseph Barry, Bishop of Saint Augustine, born at Lauragh (Killaloe), Ireland, November 15, 1868; priest June 9, 1895; named February 22, 1922; died at Jacksonville August 13, 1940.

356. 1922, May 11, at Wheeling, West Virginia, Saint Joseph Cathedral. Michael Joseph Curley, Archbishop of Baltimore, assisted by Denis Joseph O'Connell, Bishop of Richmond, and Hugh Charles Boyle, Bishop of Pittsburgh, consecrated John Joseph Swint, Titular Bishop of Sura, Auxiliary of Wheeling, born at Pickens, West Virginia (Wheeling), December 15, 1879; priest June 23, 1904; named February 22, 1922; Bishop of Wheeling December 11, 1922; Archbishop *ad personam* March 12, 1954; died at Wheeling November 23, 1962.

357. 1922, June 29, at Rome, Italy, Chapel of the North American College. Gaetano Cardinal DeLai, Bishop of Sabina, assisted by Giovanni Maria Zonghi, Titular Archbishop of Colossae, and Giuseppe Sinibaldi, Titular Bishop of Tiberias, consecrated Bernard Joseph Mahoney, Bishop of Sioux Falls, born at Albany, New York, July 24, 1875; priest February 27, 1904; named May 24, 1922; died at Rochester, Minnesota, March 20, 1939.

358. 1922, October 18, at Savannah, Georgia, Cathedral of Saint John the Baptist. Michael Joseph Curley, Archbishop of Baltimore, assisted by Denis Joseph O'Connell, Bishop of Richmond, and Patrick Joseph Barry, Bishop of Saint Augustine, consecrated Michael Joseph Keyes, SM, Bishop of Savannah, born at Dingle (Kerry), Ireland, February 28, 1876; priest June 21, 1907; named June 27, 1922; Titular Bishop of Areopolis September 23, 1935; died at Washington July 31, 1959.

359. 1922, November 8, at Saint Louis, Missouri, Cathedral of Saint Louis. John Joseph Glennon, Archbishop of Saint Louis, assisted by Christopher Edward Byrne, Bishop of Galveston, and Thomas Francis Lillis, Bishop of Kansas City, consecrated Francis Gilfillan, Titular Bishop of Spiga, Coadjutor of Saint Joseph, born at Aghavas (Kilmore), Ireland, February 16, 1872; priest June 24, 1895; named July 8, 1922; succeeded to Saint Joseph March 17, 1923; died at Saint Joseph January 13, 1933.

360. 1923, April 8, at Rome, Italy, Urban College de Propaganda Fide. Giovanni Vincenzo Cardinal Bonzano, assisted by Francesco Marchetti-Selvaggiani, Titular Archbishop of Seleucia in Isauria, and Michele Cerrati, Titular Bishop of Lydda, consecrated John Alexander Floersh, Titular Bishop of Lycopolis, Coadjutor of Louisville, born at Nashville, Tennessee, October 5, 1886; priest June 10, 1911; named February 6, 1923; succeeded to Louisville July 26, 1924; first Archbishop of Louisville December 10, 1937; Titular Archbishop of Sistroniana February 25, 1967; died at Louisville June 11, 1968.

361. 1923, April 15, at Scranton, Pennsylvania, Saint Peter's Cathedral. Michael John Hoban, Bishop of Scranton, assisted by Bernard Joseph Mahoney, Bishop of Sioux Falls, and John Gregory Murray, Titular Bishop of Flavias, consecrated Andrew James Louis Brennan, Titular Bishop of Thapsus, Auxiliary of Scranton, born at Towanda, Pennsylvania (Scranton), December 14, 1877; priest December 17, 1904; named February 23, 1923; Bishop of Richmond May 28, 1926; Titular Bishop of Telmissus April 14, 1845; died at Norfolk, Virginia, May 23, 1956.

362. 1923, May 1, at New York, New York, Saint Patrick's Cathedral. Patrick Joseph Hayes, Archbishop of New York, assisted by Edmund Francis Gibbons, Bishop of Albany, and William Turner, Bishop of Buffalo, consecrated Daniel Joseph Curley, Bishop of Syracuse, born at New York, New York, June 16, 1869; priest May 19, 1894; named February 19, 1923; died at Syracuse August 3, 1932.

363. 1923, July 25, at Covington, Kentucky, Cathedral of Saint Mary. Henry Moeller, Archbishop of Cincinnati, assisted by James Joseph Hartley, Bishop of Columbus, and John Alexander Floersh, Titular Bishop of Lycopolis, consecrated Francis William Howard, Bishop of Covington, born at Columbus, Ohio (Cincinnati), June 21, 1867; priest June 16, 1891; named March 26, 1923; died at Covington January 18, 1944.

364. 1923, November 6, at Philadelphia, Pennsylvania, Cathedral of Saints Peter and Paul. Dennis Joseph Cardinal Dougherty, Archbishop of Philadelphia, assisted by John Bernard MacGinley, Bishop of Caceres, and James Paul McCloskey, Bishop of Jaro, consecrated Daniel James Gercke, Bishop of Tucson, born at Holmesburg, Pennsylvania (Philadelphia), October 9, 1874; priest June 1, 1901; named June 21, 1923; Titular Archbishop of Cotyaeum September 28, 1960; died at Tucson March 19, 1964.

365. 1924, February 25, at Chicago, Illinois, Cathedral of the Holy Name. George William Mundelein, Archbishop of Chicago, assisted by Samuel Alphonsus Stritch, Bishop of Toledo, and Edward Francis Hoban, Titular Bishop of Colonia in Cappadocia, consecrated James Aloysius Griffin, Bishop of Springfield in Illinois, born at Chicago, Illinois, February 27, 1883; priest July 4, 1909; named November 10, 1923; died at Springfield, Illinois, August 5, 1948.

366. 1924, March 25, at Indianapolis, Indiana, Cathedral of Saints Peter and Paul. Joseph Chartrand, Bishop of Indianapolis, assisted by Emmanuel Boleslaus Ledvina, Bishop of Corpus Christi, and Samuel Alphonsus Stritch, Bishop of Toledo, consecrated Alphonse John Smith, Bishop of Nashville, born at Madison, Indiana (Vincennes), November 14, 1883; priest April 18, 1908; named December 23, 1923; died at Nashville December 16, 1935.

367. 1924, April 8, at Dubuque, Iowa, Saint Raphael's Cathedral. Austin Dowling, Archbishop of Saint Paul, assisted by Daniel Mary Gorman, Bishop of Boise City, and Thomas William Drumm, Bishop of Des Moines, consecrated Edward Daniel Howard, Titular Bishop of Isauropolis, Auxiliary of Davenport, born at Cresco, Iowa (Dubuque), November 5, 1877; priest June 12, 1906; named December 23, 1923; Archbishop of Oregon City April 30, 1926; title of see changed to Portland in Oregon September 26, 1928; Titular Archbishop of Albulae December 9, 1966; died at Beaverton, Oregon, January 2, 1983, dean of age, nomination, and consecration of the worldwide episcopate.

368. 1924, May 1, at Cincinnati, Ohio, Cathedral of Saint Peter in Chains. Henry Moeller, Archbishop of Cincinnati, assisted by Joseph Schrembs, Bishop of Cleveland, and Joseph Chartrand, Bishop of Indianapolis, consecrated Francis Joseph Beckman, Bishop of Lincoln, born at Cincinnati, Ohio, October 25, 1875; priest June 20, 1902; named

December 23, 1923; Apostolic Administrator of Omaha, *sede vacante*, from 1926 to 1928; Archbishop of Dubuque January 17, 1930; Titular Archbishop of Phulli November 9, 1946; died at Chicago October 17, 1948.

369–370. 1924, June 15, at Rome, Italy, Church of Saint Athanasius. Josaphat Joseph Kocylovskyj, Bishop of Przemysl of the Ukrainians, assisted by Dionisius Nyaradi, Bishop of Krizevci, and Giovanni Mele, Bishop of Lungro, consecrated (1) Constantine Bohachevskyj, Titular Bishop of Amisus, Apostolic Exarch of Philadelphia for Ukrainian Byzantine Rite Catholics in the United States, born at Manajiw (Lviv of the Ukrainians), Ukraine, June 17, 1884; priest January 31, 1909; named May 20, 1924; Titular Archbishop of Beroe April 5, 1954; first Archbishop of Philadelphia of the Ukrainians August 6, 1958; died at Philadelphia January 6, 1961. Consecrated (2) Basil Takacs, Titular Bishop of Zela, Apostolic Exarch of Pittsburgh for Ruthenian Byzantine Rite Catholics in the United States, born at Vuckovoje (Mukachevo), Austria-Hungary, October 27, 1879; priest December 12, 1902; named May 20, 1924; died at Pittsburgh May 13, 1948.

371. 1924, August 24, at Los Angeles, California, Saint Vibiana's Cathedral. John Joseph Cantwell, Bishop of Los Angeles-San Diego, assisted by Joseph Sarsfield Glass, Bishop of Salt Lake, and Patrick Joseph James Keane, Bishop of Sacramento, consecrated Stephen Peter Alencastre, SS.CC, Titular Bishop of Arabissus, Coadjutor of the Vicar Apostolic of Hawaii, born at Porto Santo (Funchal), Azores, Portugal, November 3, 1876; priest April 5, 1902; named April 29, 1924; succeeded to the vicariate May 13, 1926; died at sea November 9, 1940.

372. 1924, September 30, at Detroit, Michigan, Cathedral of Saints Peter and Paul. Michael James Gallagher, Bishop of Detroit, assisted by Paul Peter Rhode, Bishop of Green Bay, and Edward Francis Hoban, Titular Bishop of Colonia in Cappadocia, consecrated Joseph Casimir Plagens, Titular Bishop of Rhodiapolis, Auxiliary of Detroit, born at Czeszewo (Poznan), Poland, January 29, 1880; priest July 5, 1903; named May 22, 1924; Bishop of Sault Sainte Marie and Marquette November 13, 1935; title of see changed to Marquette January 3, 1937; Bishop of Grand Rapids December 6, 1940; died at Grand Rapids March 31, 1943.

373. 1924, October 2, at Chicago, Illinois, Cathedral of the Holy Name. George William Cardinal Mundelein, Archbishop of Chicago, assisted by Alfred Arthur Sinnott, Archbishop of Winnipeg, and Leopoldo Ruiz y Flores, Archbishop of Morelia, consecrated Francis Clement Kelley, Bishop of Oklahoma, born at Vernon River, Prince Edward Island (Charlottetown), Canada, October 23, 1870; priest August 23, 1893; named

June 25, 1924; title of see changed to Oklahoma City and Tulsa November 14, 1930; died at Oklahoma City February 1, 1948.

374. 1924, October 15, at Mobile, Alabama, Cathedral of the Immaculate Conception. Edward Patrick Allen, Bishop of Mobile, assisted by Jules Benjamin Jeanmard, Bishop of Lafayette, and James Aloysius Griffin, Bishop of Springfield in Illinois, consecrated Richard Oliver Gerow, Bishop of Natchez, born at Mobile, Alabama, May 3, 1885; priest June 5, 1909; named June 25, 1924; title of see changed to Natchez-Jackson December 18, 1956; Titular Bishop of Vageata December 2, 1967; Bishop emeritus of Natchez-Jackson January 5, 1971; died at Jackson December 20, 1976.

375. 1925, June 24, at Baltimore, Maryland, Cathedral of the Assumption. Michael Joseph Curley, Archbishop of Baltimore, assisted by Thomas Mary O'Leary, Bishop of Springfield-in-Massachusetts, and Michael Joseph Keyes, Bishop of Savannah, consecrated William Joseph Hafey, first Bishop of Raleigh, born at Springfield, Massachusetts, March 19, 1888; priest June 16, 1914; named April 6, 1925; Titular Bishop of Appia, Coadjutor and Apostolic Administrator of Scranton September 22, 1937; succeeded to Scranton March 25, 1938; died at Scranton May 12, 1954.

376. 1925, June 30, at Fort Wayne, Indiana, Cathedral of the Immaculate Conception. George William Cardinal Mundelein, Archbishop of Chicago, assisted by Alphonse John Smith, Bishop of Nashville, and Emmanuel Boleslaus Ledvina, Bishop of Corpus Christi, consecrated John Francis Noll, Bishop of Fort Wayne, born at Fort Wayne, Indiana, January 25, 1875; priest June 4, 1898; named May 12, 1925; Archbishop *ad personam* September 2, 1953; died at Fort Wayne July 31, 1956.

377–378. 1925, November 30, at Philadelphia, Pennsylvania, Cathedral of Saints Peter and Paul. Dennis Joseph Cardinal Dougherty, Archbishop of Philadelphia, assisted by John Joseph Swint, Bishop of Wheeling, and Andrew James Louis Brennan, Titular Bishop of Thapsus, consecrated (1) Edmond John Fitzmaurice, Bishop of Wilmington, born at Tarbert (Kerry), Ireland, June 24, 1881; priest May 28, 1904; named July 24, 1925; Titular Archbishop of Tomi March 1, 1960; died at Wilmington July 25, 1962. Consecrated (2) Edwin Vincent Byrne, first Bishop of Ponce, born at Philadelphia, Pennsylvania, August 9, 1891; priest May 22, 1915; named June 23, 1925; Bishop of San Juan de Puerto Rico March 8, 1929; Archbishop of Santa Fe June 12, 1943; died at Santa Fe July 25, 1963.

379. 1926, January 31, at Rome, Italy, Chapel of the North American College. Willem Cardinal Van Rossum, C.SS.R, assisted by Francesco

Marchetti-Selvaggiani, Titular Archbishop of Seleucia in Isauria, and Giulio Serafini, Titular Bishop of Lampsacus, consecrated Edward Aloysius Mooney, Titular Archbishop of Irenopolis in Isauria, Apostolic Delegate to India, born at Mount Savage, Maryland (Baltimore), May 9, 1882; priest April 10, 1909; named January 18, 1926; Apostolic Delegate to Japan February 25, 1931; Archbishop-Bishop of Rochester August 28, 1933; Archbishop of Detroit May 26, 1937; Cardinal February 18, 1946; died at Rome October 25, 1958.

380. 1926, February 3, at Saint Paul, Minnesota, Cathedral of Saint Paul. Austin Dowling, Archbishop of Saint Paul, assisted by James O'Reilly, Bishop of Fargo, and Joseph Francis Busch, Bishop of Saint Cloud, consecrated Thomas Anthony Welch, Bishop of Duluth, born at Faribault, Minnesota (Saint Paul), November 2, 1884; priest June 11, 1909; named December 14, 1925; died at Duluth September 9, 1959.

381. 1926, April 28, at Hartford, Connecticut, Cathedral of Saint Joseph. John Joseph Nilan, Bishop of Hartford, assisted by John Gregory Murray, Bishop of Portland, and William Augustine Hickey, Bishop of Providence, consecrated Maurice Francis McAuliffe, Titular Bishop of Dercos, Auxiliary of Hartford, born at Hartford, Connecticut, June 17, 1875; priest July 29, 1900; named December 17, 1925; Bishop of Hartford April 23, 1934; died at Hartford December 15, 1944.

382. 1926, June 9, at Winona, Minnesota, Chapel of Saint Mary at the College of Saint Theresa. Patrick Richard Heffron, Bishop of Winona, assisted by Joseph Francis Busch, Bishop of Saint Cloud, and Thomas Anthony Welch, Bishop of Duluth, consecrated Francis Martin Kelly, Titular Bishop of Mylasa, Auxiliary of Winona, born at Houston, Minnesota (Saint Paul), November 15, 1886; priest November 1, 1912; named March 22, 1926; Bishop of Winona February 10, 1928; Titular Bishop of Nasai October 17, 1949; died at Rochester, Minnesota, June 24, 1950.

383. 1926, September 8, at New York, New York, Saint Patrick's Cathedral. Patrick Joseph Cardinal Hayes, Archbishop of New York, assisted by John Joseph Dunn, Titular Bishop of Camuliana, and Daniel Joseph Curley, Bishop of Syracuse, consecrated John Joseph Mitty, Bishop of Salt Lake, born at New York, New York, January 20, 1884; priest December 22, 1906; named June 21, 1926; Titular Archbishop of Aegina, Coadjutor of San Francisco January 29, 1932; succeeded to San Francisco March 2, 1935; died at Menlo Park, California, October 15, 1961.

384. 1926, November 30, at Louisville, Kentucky, Cathedral of the Assumption. John Alexander Floersh, Bishop of Louisville, assisted by

Joseph Gabriel Pinten, Bishop of Grand Rapids, and Henry Althoff, Bishop of Belleville, consecrated Theodore Mary Reverman, Bishop of Superior, born at Louisville, Kentucky, August 9, 1877; priest July 26, 1901; named July 2, 1926; died at Superior July 18, 1941.

385. 1927, February 24, at Grand Rapids, Michigan, Saint Andrew's Cathedral. Joseph Gabriel Pinten, Bishop of Grand Rapids, assisted by Samuel Alphonsus Stritch, Bishop of Toledo, and Alphonse John Smith, Bishop of Nashville, consecrated Charles Daniel White, Bishop of Spokane, born at Grand Rapids, Michigan (Detroit), January 5, 1879; priest September 24, 1910; named December 20, 1926; died at Spokane September 25, 1955.

386. 1927, April 26, at Dallas, Texas, Sacred Heart Cathedral. Joseph Patrick Lynch, Bishop of Dallas, assisted by Christopher Edward Byrne, Bishop of Galveston, and Francis Clement Kelley, Bishop of Oklahoma, consecrated Rudolph Aloysius Gerken, first Bishop of Amarillo, born at Dyersville, Iowa (Dubuque), March 7, 1887; priest June 10, 1917; named August 25, 1926; Archbishop of Santa Fe June 2, 1933; died at Santa Fe March 2, 1943.

387. 1927, May 4, at Baltimore, Maryland, Cathedral of the Assumption Michael Joseph Curley, Archbishop of Baltimore, assisted by Michael Joseph Keyes, Bishop of Savannah, and Richard Oliver Gerow, Bishop of Natchez, consecrated Thomas Joseph Toolen, Bishop of Mobile, born at Baltimore, Maryland, February 28, 1886; priest September 27, 1910; named February 28, 1927; title of see changed to Mobile-Birmingham April 30, 1954; Archbishop *ad personam* May 27, 1954; Titular Archbishop of Glastonia September 29, 1969; died at Mobile December 4, 1976.

388. 1927, May 22, at Sancian Island, China, Sanctuary. Antoine Pierre Fourquet, Titular Bishop of Themisonium, assisted by Jose da Costa Nunes, Bishop of Macao, and Manuel Prat, Titular Bishop of Mactaris, consecrated James Edward Walsh, MM, Titular Bishop of Sata, Vicar Apostolic of Kongmoon, born at Cumberland, Maryland (Baltimore), April 30, 1891; priest December 7, 1915; named February 1, 1927; Superior General of Maryknoll from July 1936 until August 7, 1946; imprisoned in China from December 15, 1958 to July 10, 1970; died at Maryknoll, New York, July 29, 1981.

389. 1927, July 25, at Dubuque, Iowa, Saint Raphael's Cathedral. James John Keane, Archbishop of Dubuque, assisted by Edmond Heelan, Bishop of Sioux City, and Thomas William Drumm, Bishop of Des Moines, consecrated Henry Patrick Rohlman, Bishop of Davenport, born at Appelhausen (Munster), Germany, March 17, 1876; priest December 21,

1901; named May 20, 1927; Titular Archbishop of Macra, Coadjutor and Apostolic Administrator of Dubuque June 15, 1944; succeeded to Dubuque November 11, 1946; Titular Archbishop of Cotrada December 2, 1954; died at Dubuque September 13, 1957.

390. 1927, August 1, at Notre Dame, Indiana, University Church of the Sacred Heart. Peter Joseph Hurth, Titular Archbishop of Bostra, assisted by John Francis Noll, Bishop of Fort Wayne, and Edward Francis Hoban, Titular Bishop of Colonia in Cappadocia, consecrated George Joseph Finnegan, CSC, Bishop of Helena, born at Potsdam, New York (Ogdensburg), February 22, 1885; priest June 13, 1915; named May 20, 1927; died at Helena August 14, 1932.

391. 1927, September 8, at Savannah, Georgia, Cathedral of Saint John the Baptist. Michael Joseph Keyes, Bishop of Savannah, assisted by Patrick Joseph Barry, Bishop of Saint Augustine, and William Joseph Hafey, Bishop of Raleigh, consecrated Emmet Michael Walsh, Bishop of Charleston, born at Beaufort, South Carolina (Charleston), March 6, 1892; priest January 15, 1916; named June 20, 1927; Titular Bishop of Rhaedustus, Coadjutor of Youngstown September 8, 1929; succeeded to Youngstown November 16, 1952; died at Youngstown March 16, 1968.

392. 1927, November 10, at Boston, Massachusetts, Cathedral of the Holy Cross. William Henry Cardinal O'Connell, Archbishop of Boston, assisted by George Albert Guertin, Bishop of Manchester, and John Gregory Murray, Bishop of Portland, consecrated John Bertram Peterson, Titular Bishop of Hippos, Auxiliary of Boston, born at Salem, Massachusetts (Boston), July 15, 1871; priest September 15, 1899; named October 7, 1927; Bishop of Manchester May 13, 1937; died at Manchester March 15, 1944.

393. 1928, February 16, at Cleveland, Ohio, Cathedral of Saint John the Evangelist. Dennis Joseph Cardinal Dougherty, Archbishop of Philadelphia, assisted by Joseph Schrembs, Bishop of Cleveland, and Bernard Joseph Mahoney, Bishop of Sioux Falls, consecrated Thomas Charles O'Reilly, Bishop of Scranton, born at Cleveland, Ohio, February 22, 1873; priest June 4, 1898; named December 19, 1927; died at Miami Beach, Florida, March 25, 1938.

394. 1928, March 6, at Baker, Oregon, Saint Francis Cathedral. Joseph Francis McGrath, Bishop of Baker City, assisted by Mathias Clement Lenihan, Bishop of Great Falls, and Charles Daniel White, Bishop of Spokane, consecrated Edward Joseph Kelly, Bishop of Boise City, born at The Dalles, Oregon (Oregon City), February 26, 1890; priest June 2, 1917; named December 19, 1927; died at Boise April 21, 1956.

395. 1928, March 29, at Baltimore, Maryland, Cathedral of the Assumption. Michael Joseph Curley, Archbishop of Baltimore, assisted by William Joseph Hafey, Bishop of Raleigh, and Thomas Joseph Toolen, Bishop of Mobile, consecrated John Michael McNamara, Titular Bishop of Eumenia, Auxiliary of Baltimore, born at Baltimore, Maryland, August 12, 1878; priest June 21, 1902; named December 19, 1927; Auxiliary of Baltimore and Washington July 22, 1939; Auxiliary of Washington November 15, 1947; died at Washington November 26, 1960.

396. 1928, April 26, at Buffalo, New York, Saint Joseph Cathedral. William Turner, Bishop of Buffalo, assisted by Thomas Joseph Walsh, Bishop of Newark, and Edmund Francis Gibbons, Bishop of Albany, consecrated John Joseph McMahon, Bishop of Trenton, born at Hinsdale, New York (Buffalo), September 27, 1875; priest May 20, 1900; named March 2, 1928; died at Buffalo December 31, 1932.

397. 1928, May 1, at Saint Joseph, Missouri, Cathedral of Saint Joseph. Francis Gilfillan, Bishop of Saint Joseph, assisted by Francis Joseph Tief, Bishop of Concordia, and Augustus John Schwertner, Bishop of Wichita, consecrated Francis Johannes, Titular Bishop of Thasus, Coadjutor of Leavenworth, born at Mittelstreu (Wurzburg), Germany, February 17, 1874; priest January 3, 1897; named December 19, 1927; succeeded to Leavenworth April 20, 1929; died at Denver March 13, 1937.

398. 1928, May 1, at Chicago, Illinois, Cathedral of the Holy Name. George William Cardinal Mundelein, Archbishop of Chicago, assisted by Edward Francis Hoban, Bishop of Rockford, and Edmund Michael Dunne, Bishop of Peoria, consecrated Bernard James Sheil, Titular Bishop of Pegae, Auxiliary of Chicago, born at Chicago, Illinois, February 18, 1886; priest May 21, 1910; named March 25, 1928; Titular Archbishop of Selge, remaining Auxiliary of Chicago, June 5, 1959; died at Tucson September 13, 1969.

399. 1928, May 29, at New York, New York, Saint Patrick's Cathedral. Patrick Joseph Cardinal Hayes, Archbishop of New York, assisted by Thomas Edmund Molloy, Bishop of Brooklyn, and John Joseph Dunn, Titular Bishop of Camuliana, consecrated Joseph Francis Rummel, Bishop of Omaha, born at Steinmauern (Freiburg im Brisgau), Germany, October 14, 1876; priest May 24, 1902; named March 30, 1928; Archbishop of New Orleans March 9, 1935; died at New Orleans November 8, 1964.

400. 1929, March 12, at Seattle, Washington, Saint James Cathedral. Edward John O'Dea, Bishop of Seattle, assisted by Mathias Clement Lenihan, Bishop of Great Falls, and Joseph Francis McGrath, Bishop of Baker City, consecrated Robert John Armstrong, Bishop of Sacramento, born at San Francisco, California, December 17, 1884; priest December 10, 1910; named January 4, 1929; died at Sacramento January 14, 1957.

401. 1929, March 19, at Rochester, New York, Saint Patrick's Cathedral. Patrick Joseph Cardinal Hayes, Archbishop of New York, assisted by Edward Joseph Hanna, Archbishop of San Francisco, and Thomas Charles O'Reilly, Bishop of Scranton, consecrated John Francis O'Hern, Bishop of Rochester, born at Olean, New York (Buffalo), June 8, 1874; priest February 17, 1901; named January 4, 1929; died at Rochester May 22, 1933.

402. 1929, May 20, at Philadelphia, Pennsylvania, Cathedral of Saints Peter and Paul. Dennis Joseph Cardinal Dougherty, Archbishop of Philadelphia, assisted by John Bernard MacGinley, Bishop of Monterey-Fresno, and Thomas Charles O'Reilly, Bishop of Scranton, consecrated Gerald Patrick Aloysius O'Hara, Titular Bishop of Heliopolis, Auxiliary of Philadelphia, born at Green Ridge, Pennsylvania (Scranton), May 4, 1895; priest April 3, 1920; named April 26, 1929; Bishop of Savannah November 16, 1935; title of diocese changed to Savannah-Atlanta January 5, 1937; Regent *ad interim* of the Nunciature in Rumania May 21, 1946; expelled from Rumania July 4, 1950; Archbishop *ad personam* July 12, 1950; Nuncio to Ireland November 27, 1951; Apostolic Delegate to Great Britain June 8, 1954; Titular Archbishop of Pessinonte November 12, 1959; died at London July 16, 1963.

403. 1929, October 20, at Rome, Italy, Church of Saints Sergius and Bacchus. Andrij Alexander Szeptyckyj, Archbishop of Lviv of the Ukrainians, assisted by Gregor Chomyszyn, Bishop of Stanislaviv of the Ukrainians, and Josaphat Kocylovskyj, Bishop of Przemysl of the Ukrainians, consecrated Ivan Bucko, Titular Bishop of Cadi, Auxiliary of Lviv of the Ukrainians, born at Hermaniw (Lviv of the Ukrainians), Ukraine, October 1, 1891; priest February 21, 1915; named September 16, 1929; Apostolic Visitor for the Ukrainians in South America June 5, 1939; Auxiliary of the Exarch of Philadelphia of the Ukrainians April 17, 1940; Apostolic Visitor for the Ukrainians in Western Europe July 28, 1945; Titular Archbishop of Leucas April 27, 1953; resigned as Apostolic Visitor November 29, 1971; died at Rome September 27, 1974.

404. 1929, October 28, at Brooklyn, New York, Our Lady of Perpetual Help Church. Thomas Edmund Molloy, Bishop of Brooklyn, assisted by John Mark Gannon, Bishop of Erie, and John Joseph Dunn, Titular Bishop of Camuliana, consecrated Aloysius Joseph Willinger, C.SS.R, Bishop of Ponce, born at Baltimore, Maryland, April 19, 1886; priest July 2, 1911; named March 8, 1929; Titular Bishop of Bida, Coadjutor of Monterey-Fresno, December 12, 1946; succeeded to Monterey-Fresno January 3,

1953; Titular Bishop of Tiguala October 16, 1967; died at Fresno July 25, 1973.

405. 1929, December 27, at Cincinnati, Ohio, Cathedral of Saint Peter in Chains. John Timothy McNicholas, Archbishop of Cincinnati, assisted by Francis William Howard, Bishop of Covington, and Francis Joseph Beckman, Bishop of Lincoln, consecrated Joseph Henry Albers, Titular Bishop of Lunda, Auxiliary of Cincinnati, born at Cincinnati, Ohio, March 18, 1891; priest June 17, 1916; named December 16, 1929; first Bishop of Lansing May 26, 1937; died at Lansing December 1, 1965.

406. 1930, May 27, at Fall River, Massachusetts, Cathedral of Saint Mary of the Assumption. Pietro Fumasoni-Biondi, Titular Archbishop of Dioclea, Apostolic Delegate to the United States, assisted by John Joseph Rice, Bishop of Burlington, and George Albert Guertin, Bishop of Manchester, consecrated James Edwin Cassidy, Titular Bishop of Ibora, Auxiliary of Fall River, born at Woonsocket, Rhode Island (Hartford), August 1, 1869; priest September 8, 1898; named March 21, 1930; Apostolic Administrator of Fall River October 3, 1950; Coadjutor of Fall River July 13, 1934, but without effect; Bishop of Fall River July 28, 1934; died at Fall River May 17, 1951.

407. 1930, June 17, at Belleville, Illinois, Cathedral of Saint Peter. George William Cardinal Mundelein, Archbishop of Chicago, assisted by Henry Althoff, Bishop of Alton, and Edward Francis Hoban, Bishop of Rockford, consecrated Joseph Henry Leo Schlarman, Bishop of Peoria, born at Breese Township, Illinois (Alton), February 23, 1879; priest June 29, 1904; named April 16, 1930; Archbishop *ad personam* June 17, 1951; died at Peoria November 10, 1951.

408. 1930, October 28, at Dubuque, Iowa, Saint Raphael's Cathedral. Francis Joseph Beckman, Archbishop of Dubuque, assisted by Thomas William Drumm, Bishop of Des Moines, and Henry Patrick Rohlman, Bishop of Davenport, consecrated Louis Benedict Kucera, Bishop of Lincoln, born at Wheatland, Minnesota (Saint Paul), August 24, 1888; priest June 8, 1915; named June 30, 1930; died at Lincoln May 9, 1957.

409. 1930, October 28, at Portland, Oregon, Cathedral of the Immaculate Conception. Edward Daniel Howard, Archbishop of Portland in Oregon, assisted by Charles Daniel White, Bishop of Spokane, and Joseph Raphael John Crimont, Titular Bishop of Ammaedara, consecrated Edwin Vincent O'Hara, Bishop of Great Falls, born at Lanesboro, Minnesota (Winona), September 6, 1881; priest June 9, 1905; named August 1, 1930; Bishop of Kansas City April 15, 1939; Archbishop *ad personam* June 29, 1954;

Archbishop-Bishop of Kansas City-Saint Joseph July 2, 1956; died at Milan, Italy, September 11, 1956.

410. 1931, June 10, at Cincinnati, Ohio, Cathedral of Saint Peter in Chains. John Timothy McNicholas, Archbishop of Cincinnati, assisted by Francis Joseph Beckman, Archbishop of Dubuque, and Joseph Henry Albers, Titular Bishop of Lunda, consecrated Urban John Vehr, Bishop of Denver, born at Cincinnati, Ohio, May 30, 1891; priest May 29, 1915; named April 17, 1931; first Archbishop of Denver November 15, 1941; Titular Archbishop of Masuccaba February 18, 1967; Archbishop emeritus of Denver December 31, 1970; died at Denver September 19, 1973.

411. 1931, June 17, at Toledo, Ohio, Cathedral of Saint Francis de Sales. John Timothy McNicholas, Archbishop of Cincinnati, assisted by Augustus John Schwertner, Bishop of Wichita, and Joseph Henry Albers, Titular Bishop of Lunda, consecrated Karl Joseph Alter, Bishop of Toledo, born at Toledo, Ohio (Cleveland), August 18, 1885; priest June 4, 1910; named April 17, 1931; Archbishop of Cincinnati June 21, 1950; Titular Archbishop of Minori July 19, 1969; Archbishop emeritus of Cincinnati December 31, 1970; died at Cincinnati August 23, 1977.

412. 1931, July 22, at Los Angeles, California, Saint Vibiana's Cathedral. John Joseph Cantwell, Bishop of Los Angeles-San Diego, assisted by John Joseph Mitty, Bishop of Salt Lake, and Robert John Armstrong, Bishop of Sacramento, consecrated Thomas Kiely Gorman, first Bishop of Reno, born at Pasadena, California (Monterey-Los Angeles), August 30, 1892; priest June 23, 1917; named April 14, 1931; Titular Bishop of Rhasus, Coadjutor of Dallas February 1, 1952; title of see changed to Dallas-Fort Worth October 20, 1953; succeeded to Dallas-Fort Worth August 19, 1954; Titular Bishop of Pinhel August 22, 1969; Bishop emeritus of Dallas-Fort Worth January 21, 1971; died at Dallas August 16, 1980.

413. 1932, February 25, at Chicago, Illinois, Cathedral of the Holy Name. George William Cardinal Mundelein, Archbishop of Chicago, assisted by Paul Peter Rhode, Bishop of Green Bay, and Francis Martin Kelly, Bishop of Winona, consecrated Stanislaus Vincent Bona, Bishop of Grand Island, born at Chicago, Illinois, October 1, 1888; priest November 1, 1912; named December 18, 1931; Titular Bishop of Mela, Coadjutor of Green Bay December 2, 1944; succeeded to Green Bay March 3, 1945; died at Green Bay December 1, 1967.

414. 1932, August 24, at Portland, Maine, Cathedral of the Immaculate Conception. Maurice Francis McAuliffe, Titular Bishop of Dercos, assisted by John Joseph Nilan, Bishop of Hartford, and John Bertram Peterson, Bishop of Manchester, consecrated Joseph Edward McCarthy, Bishop of

Portland, born at Waterbury, Connecticut (Hartford), November 14, 1876; priest July 4, 1903; named May 13, 1932; died at Portland September 8, 1955.

415. 1932, September 8, at Rome, Vatican City, Saint Peter's Basilica. Eugenio Cardinal Pacelli, assisted by Giuseppe Pizzardo, Titular Archbishop of Nicaea, and Francesco Borgongini-Duca, Titular Archbishop of Heraclea in Europa, consecrated Francis Joseph Spellman, Titular Bishop of Sila, Auxiliary of Boston, born at Whitman, Massachusetts (Boston), May 4, 1889; priest May 14, 1916; named July 30, 1932; Archbishop of New York April 15, 1939; Military Vicar of the U.S. Armed Forces December 11, 1939; Cardinal February 18, 1946; first Military Vicar of the Military Vicariate for the United States September 8, 1957; died at New York December 2, 1967.

416. 1932, September 8, at Cleveland, Ohio, Cathedral of Saint John the Evangelist. Joseph Schrembs, Bishop of Cleveland, assisted by Michael James Gallagher, Bishop of Detroit, and Thomas Charles O'Reilly, Bishop of Scranton, consecrated James Augustine McFadden, Titular Bishop of Bida, Auxiliary of Cleveland, born at Cleveland, Ohio, December 24, 1880; priest June 17, 1905; named May 13, 1932; first Bishop of Youngstown July 2, 1943; died at Youngstown November 15, 1952.

417. 1932, October 28, at New York, New York, Saint Patrick's Cathedral. Patrick Joseph Cardinal Hayes, Archbishop of New York, assisted by John Joseph Mitty, Titular Archbishop of Aegina, and John Joseph Dunn, Titular Bishop of Camuliana, consecrated James Edward Kearney, Bishop of Salt Lake, born at Red Oak, Iowa (Davenport), October 28, 1884; priest September 19, 1908; named July 1, 1932; Bishop of Rochester July 31, 1937; Titular Bishop of Tabaicara October 21, 1966; Bishop emeritus of Rochester January 18, 1971; died at Rochester January 12, 1977.

418. 1933, January 5, at Boston, Massachusetts, Cathedral of the Holy Cross. John Bertram Peterson, Bishop of Manchester, assisted by Joseph Edward McCarthy, Bishop of Portland, and Francis Joseph Spellman, Titular Bishop of Sila, consecrated Daniel Francis Desmond, Bishop of Alexandria, born at Haverhill, Massachusetts (Boston), April 4, 1884; priest June 9, 1911; named December 16, 1932; died at Magnolia, Massachusetts, September 11, 1945.

419. 1933, March 28, at Indianapolis, Indiana, Cathedral of Saints Peter and Paul. Joseph Chartrand, Bishop of Indianapolis, assisted by Alphonse John Smith, Bishop of Nashville, and Emmanuel Boleslaus Ledvina, Bishop of Corpus Christi, consecrated Joseph Elmer Ritter, Titular Bishop of Hippos, Auxiliary of Indianapolis, born at New Albany, Indiana (Vincennes), July 20, 1892; priest May 30, 1917; named February 3, 1933; Bishop of Indianapolis March 24, 1934; first Archbishop of Indianapolis November 11, 1944; Archbishop of Saint Louis July 20, 1946; Cardinal January 16, 1961; died at Saint Louis June 10, 1967.

420. 1933, June 29, at Fresno, California, Saint John's Cathedral. Edward Joseph Hanna, Archbishop of San Francisco, assisted by John Joseph Cantwell, Bishop of Los Angeles-San Diego, and Thomas Kiely Gorman, Bishop of Reno, consecrated Philip George Scher, Bishop of Monterey-Fresno, born at Belleville, Illinois (Alton), February 22, 1880; priest June 6, 1903; named April 28, 1933; died at Fresno January 3, 1953.

421. 1933, June 29, at Newark, New Jersey, Sacred Heart Cathedral. Thomas Joseph Walsh, Bishop of Newark, assisted by James Aloysius Griffin, Bishop of Springfield in Illinois, and Alphonse John Smith, Bishop of Nashville, consecrated John Aloysius Duffy, Bishop of Syracuse, born at Jersey City, New Jersey (Newark), October 29, 1884; priest June 13, 1908; named April 21, 1933; Bishop of Buffalo January 5, 1937; died at Buffalo September 27, 1944.

422. 1933, June 29, at Rome, Italy, College de Propaganda Fide. Pietro Cardinal Fumasoni-Biondi, assisted by John Timothy McNicholas, Archbishop of Cincinnati, and John Joseph Dunn, Titular Bishop of Camuliana, consecrated James Anthony Walsh, MM, Titular Bishop of Syene, Superior General of Maryknoll, born at Cambridge, Massachusetts (Boston), February 24, 1867; priest May 20, 1892; helped found the Maryknoll Fathers June 29, 1911 and elected first Superior General, 1911; named April 20, 1933; died at Maryknoll April 14, 1936.

423. 1933, September 19, at Washington, District of Columbia, National Shrine of the Immaculate Conception. Amleto Giovanni Cicognani, Titular Archbishop of Laodicea in Phrygia, Apostolic Delegate to the United States, assisted by Michael Joseph Keyes, Bishop of Savannah, and Charles Daniel White, Bishop of Spokane, consecrated Gerald Shaughnessy, SM, Bishop of Seattle, born at Everett, Massachusetts (Boston), May 19, 1887; priest June 20, 1920; named July 1, 1933; died at Seattle May 18, 1950.

424. 1933, September 21, at Cleveland, Ohio, Cathedral of Saint John the Evangelist. Joseph Schrembs, Bishop of Cleveland, assisted by James Augustine McFadden, Titular Bishop of Bida, and Thomas Charles O'Reilly, Bishop of Scranton, consecrated Charles Hubert LeBlond, Bishop of Saint Joseph, born at Celina, Ohio (Cincinnati), November 21, 1883; priest June 29, 1909; named July 21, 1933; Titular Bishop of Orcistus

August 24, 1956; died at Saint Joseph December 30, 1958.

425. 1933, September 21, at Pittsburgh, Pennsylvania, Saint Paul Cathedral. Hugh Charles Boyle, Bishop of Pittsburgh, assisted by James Aloysius Griffin, Bishop of Springfield in Illinois, and Alphonse John Smith, Bishop of Nashville, consecrated Ralph Leo Hayes, Bishop of Helena, born at Pittsburgh, Pennsylvania, September 21, 1884; priest September 18, 1909; named June 23, 1933; Titular Bishop of Hierapolis, Rector of the North American College, Rome October 26, 1935; Bishop of Davenport November 11, 1944; Titular Bishop of Naraggara October 29, 1966; died at Davenport July 4, 1970.

426. 1933, October 25, at Washington, District of Columbia, National Shrine of the Immaculate Conception. Joseph Chartrand, Bishop of Indianapolis, assisted by Thomas Edmund Molloy, Bishop of Brooklyn, and Joseph Elmer Ritter, Titular Bishop of Hippos, consecrated James Hugh Ryan, Titular Bishop of Modra, Rector of The Catholic University of America, born at Indianapolis, Indiana (Vincennes), December 15, 1886; priest June 5, 1909; Rector of The Catholic University of America, July 12, 1928; named August 3, 1933; Bishop of Omaha August 6, 1935; first Archbishop of Omaha August 7, 1945; died at Omaha November 23, 1947.

427. 1933, November 30, at Saint Louis, Missouri, Cathedral of Saint Louis. John Joseph Glennon, Archbishop of Saint Louis, assisted by Thomas Francis Lillis, Bishop of Kansas City, and Francis Johannes, Bishop of Leavenworth, consecrated Christian Winkelmann, Titular Bishop of Sita, Auxiliary of Saint Louis, born at Saint Louis, Missouri, September 12, 1883; priest June 11, 1907; named September 13, 1933; Bishop of Wichita December 27, 1939; died at Wichita November 18, 1946.

428. 1934, March 17, at Rome, Italy, Church of Santa Susanna. Raffaele Carlo Cardinal Rossi, OCD, assisted by Carlo Salotti, Titular Archbishop of Philippopolis in Thrace, and Thomas Joseph Walsh, Bishop of Newark, consecrated Moses Elias Kiley, Bishop of Trenton, born at Margaree, Cape Breton, Nova Scotia (Antigonish), Canada, November 13, 1876; priest June 10, 1911; named February 10, 1934; Archbishop of Milwaukee January 1, 1940; died at Milwaukee April 15, 1953.

429. 1934, April 25, at Chicago, Illinois, Cathedral of the Holy Name. George William Cardinal Mundelein, Archbishop of Chicago, assisted by Joseph Patrick Lynch, Bishop of Dallas, and Bernard James Sheil, Titular Bishop of Pegae, consecrated William David O'Brien, Titular Bishop of Calynda, Auxiliary of Chicago, born at Chicago, Illinois, August 3, 1878; priest July 11, 1903; named February 10, 1934; Titular Archbishop of

Calynda, remaining Auxiliary of Chicago, November 18, 1953; died at San Pierre, Indiana, February 19, 1962.

430. 1934, May 1, at New York, New York, Saint Patrick's Cathedral. Patrick Joseph Cardinal Hayes, Archbishop of New York, assisted by Edward Aloysius Mooney, Archbishop-Bishop of Rochester, and John Joseph Mitty, Titular Archbishop of Aegina, consecrated Stephen Joseph Donahue, Titular Bishop of Medea, Auxiliary of New York, born at New York, New York, December 10, 1893; priest May 25, 1918; named March 5, 1934; resigned as Auxiliary of New York May 3, 1972; died at New York August 17, 1982.

431. 1934, May 1, at Los Angeles, California, Saint Vibiana's Cathedral. Amleto Giovanni Cicognani, Titular Archbishop of Laodicea in Phrygia, Apostolic Delegate to the United States, assisted by John Joseph Cantwell, Bishop of Los Angeles-San Diego, and Thomas Kiely Gorman, Bishop of Reno, consecrated Robert Emmet Lucey, Bishop of Amarillo, born at Los Angeles, California (Monterey-Los Angeles), March 16, 1891; priest May 14, 1916; named February 10, 1934; Archbishop of San Antonio January 21, 1941; Titular Archbishop of Taormina May 23, 1969; Archbishop emeritus of San Antonio December 31, 1970; died at San Antonio August 2, 1977.

432. 1934, May 22, at Providence, Rhode Island, Cathedral of Saints Peter and Paul. Amleto Giovanni Cicognani, Titular Archbishop of Laodicea in Phrygia, Apostolic Delegate to the United States, assisted by John Gregory Murray, Archbishop of Saint Paul, and James Edwin Cassidy, Titular Bishop of Ibora, consecrated Francis Patrick Keough, Bishop of Providence, born at New Britain, Connecticut (Hartford), December 30, 1889; priest June 10, 1916; named February 10, 1934; Archbishop of Baltimore November 29, 1947; died at Baltimore December 8, 1961.

433. 1934, June 13, at Peoria, Illinois, Saint Mary's Cathedral. George William Cardinal Mundelein, Archbishop of Chicago, assisted by Joseph Henry Leo Schlarman, Bishop of Peoria, and Henry Patrick Rohlman, Bishop of Davenport, consecrated Gerald Thomas Bergan, Bishop of Des Moines, born at Peoria, Illinois, January 26, 1892; priest October 28, 1915; named March 24, 1934; Archbishop of Omaha February 7, 1948; Titular Archbishop of Tacarata June 11, 1969; Archbishop emeritus of Omaha January 28, 1971; died at Omaha July 12, 1972.

434. 1935, February 25, at Brooklyn, New York, Our Lady of Perpetual Help Church. Thomas Edmund Molloy, Bishop of Brooklyn, assisted by Moses Elias Kiley, Bishop of Trenton, and Stephen Joseph Donahue,

Titular Bishop of Medea, consecrated Raymond Augustine Kearney, Titular Bishop of Lysinia, Auxiliary of Brooklyn, born at Jersey City, New Jersey (Newark), September 25, 1902; priest March 12, 1927; named December 22, 1934; died at Brooklyn October 1, 1956.

435. 1935, May 1, at Chicago, Illinois, Cathedral of the Holy Name. George William Cardinal Mundelein, Archbishop of Chicago, assisted by Christian Herman Winkelman, Titular Bishop of Sita, and William David O'Brien, Titular Bishop of Calynda, consecrated William Richard Griffin, Titular Bishop of Lydda, Auxiliary of La Crosse, born at Chicago, Illinois, September 1, 1883; priest May 25, 1907; named March 9, 1935; died at La Crosse March 18, 1944.

436. 1935, July 25, at Newark, New Jersey, Sacred Heart Cathedral. Thomas Joseph Walsh, Bishop of Newark, assisted by John Aloysius Duffy, Bishop of Syracuse, and Joseph Henry Leo Schlarman, Bishop of Peoria, consecrated Thomas Henry McLaughlin, Titular Bishop of Nisa in Lycia, Auxiliary of Newark, born at New York, New York, July 15, 1881; priest July 26, 1904; named May 18, 1935; first Bishop of Paterson December 16, 1937; died at Paterson March 17, 1947.

437. 1935, October 15, at Milwaukee, Wisconsin, Church of the Gesu. Amleto Giovanni Cicognani, Titular Archbishop of Laodicea in Phrygia, Apostolic Delegate to the United States, assisted by Christian Herman Winkelman, Titular Bishop of Sita, and William Richard Griffin, Titular Bishop of Lydda, consecrated Aloisius Joseph Muench, Bishop of Fargo, born at Milwaukee, Wisconsin, February 18, 1889; priest June 8, 1913; named August 10, 1935; Apostolic Visitor to Germany in May 1946; Regent of the Nunciature in Germany in November 1949; Archbishop *ad personam* October 28, 1950; Nuncio to Germany March 10, 1951; Titular Archbishop of Selymbria December 9, 1959; Cardinal December 14, 1959; died at Rome February 15, 1962.

438. 1935, October 17, at Philadelphia, Pennsylvania, Cathedral of Saints Peter and Paul. Dennis Joseph Cardinal Dougherty, Archbishop of Philadelphia, assisted by Thomas Charles O'Reilly, Bishop of Scranton, and James Hugh Ryan, Bishop of Omaha, consecrated George Leo Leech, Titular Bishop of Mela, Auxiliary of Harrisburg, born at Ashley, Pennsylvania (Scranton), May 21, 1890; priest May 29, 1920; named July 6, 1935; Bishop of Harrisburg December 19, 1935; Titular Bishop of Allegheny October 29, 1971; died at Harrisburg March 12, 1985.

439. 1935, October 23, at Baltimore, Maryland, Cathedral of the Assumption. Michael Joseph Curley, Archbishop of Baltimore, assisted by Thomas Charles O'Reilly, Bishop of Scranton, and James Hugh Ryan,

Bishop of Omaha, consecrated Peter Leo Ireton, Titular Bishop of Cyme, Coadjutor and Apostolic Administrator of Richmond, born at Baltimore, Maryland, September 21, 1882; priest June 20, 1906; named August 3, 1935; succeeded to Richmond April 14, 1945; died at Washington April 27, 1958.

440. 1936, February 19, at Helena, Montana, Cathedral of Saint Helena. Amleto Giovanni Cicognani, Titular Archbishop of Laodicea in Phrygia, Apostolic Delegate to the United States, assisted by Edwin Vincent O'Hara, Bishop of Great Falls, and Joseph Michael McGrath, Bishop of Baker City, consecrated Joseph Michael Gilmore, Bishop of Helena, born at New York, New York, March 22, 1893; priest July 25, 1915; named December 16, 1935; died at San Francisco April 2, 1962.

441. 1936, March 19, at Philadelphia, Pennsylvania, Cathedral of Saints Peter and Paul. Dennis Joseph Cardinal Dougherty, Archbishop of Philadelphia, assisted by Gerald Patrick Aloysius O'Hara, Bishop of Savannah, and George Leo Leech, Bishop of Harrisburg, consecrated Hugh Louis Lamb, Titular Bishop of Helos, Auxiliary of Philadelphia, born at Modena, Pennsylvania (Philadelphia), October 6, 1890; priest May 29, 1915; named December 19, 1935; first Bishop of Greensburg May 28, 1951; died at Jeannette, Pennsylvania, December 8, 1959.

442. 1936, April 16, at Davenport, Iowa, Sacred Heart Cathedral. Amleto Giovanni Cicognani, Titular Archbishop of Laodicea in Phrygia, Apostolic Delegate to the United States, assisted by Henry Patrick Rohlman, Bishop of Davenport, and Moses Elias Kiley, Bishop of Trenton, consecrated William Lawrence Adrian, Bishop of Nashville, born at Sigourney, Iowa (Davenport), April 16, 1883; priest April 15, 1911; named February 6, 1936; Titular Bishop of Elo September 4, 1969 (the official announcement gave his titular see as Lanelvia); Bishop emeritus of Nashville January 13, 1971; died at Nashville February 13, 1972.

443. 1936, June 29, at Newark, New Jersey, Sacred Heart Cathedral. Thomas Joseph Walsh, Bishop of Newark, assisted by Joseph Henry Conroy, Bishop of Ogdensburg, and Thomas Henry McLaughlin, Titular Bishop of Nisa in Lycia, consecrated Francis Joseph Monaghan, Titular Bishop of Mela, Coadjutor of Ogdensburg, born at Newark, New Jersey, October 30, 1890; priest May 29, 1915; named April 17, 1936; succeeded to Ogdensburg March 20, 1939; died at Watertown, New York, November 13, 1942.

444. 1936, September 21, at San Antonio, Texas, Cathedral of San Fernando. Arthur Jerome Drossaerts, Archbishop of San Antonio, assisted by Emmanuel Boleslaus Ledvina, Bishop of Corpus Christi, and Aloisius

Joseph Muench, Bishop of Fargo, consecrated Mariano Simon Garriga, Titular Bishop of Syene, Coadjutor of Corpus Christi, born at Port Isabel, Texas (Corpus Christi), May 31, 1886; priest July 2, 1911; named June 20, 1936; succeeded to Corpus Christi March 15, 1949; died at Corpus Christi February 21, 1965.

445. 1936, November 30, at Erie, Pennsylvania, Saint Peter Cathedral. John Mark Gannon, Bishop of Erie, assisted by Thomas Joseph Walsh, Bishop of Newark, and Francis Joseph Tief, Bishop of Concordia, consecrated Richard Thomas Guilfoyle, Bishop of Altoona, born at Adrian, Pennsylvania (Erie), December 22, 1892; priest June 2, 1917; named August 8, 1936; died at Altoona June 10, 1957.

446. 1936, December 21, at Saint Joseph, Missouri, Cathedral of Saint Joseph. Charles Hubert LeBlond, Bishop of Saint Joseph, assisted by Gerald Thomas Bergan, Bishop of Des Moines, and Francis Joseph Monaghan, Titular Bishop of Mela, consecrated Charles Francis Buddy, first Bishop of San Diego, born at Saint Joseph, Missouri, October 4, 1887; priest September 19, 1914; named October 31, 1936; died at San Diego March 5, 1966.

447. 1937, August 18, at Rochester, New York, Saint Patrick's Cathedral. Edward Aloysius Mooney, Archbishop of Detroit, assisted by Emmet Michael Walsh, Bishop of Charleston, and Francis Patrick Keough, Bishop of Providence, consecrated Walter Andrew Foery, Bishop of Syracuse, born at Rochester, New York, July 6, 1890; priest June 10, 1916; named May 26, 1937; Titular Bishop of Miseno August 4, 1970; Bishop emeritus of Syracuse December 31, 1970; died at Syracuse May 9, 1978.

448. 1937, September 21, at Saint Louis, Missouri, Cathedral of Saint Louis. John Joseph Glennon, Archbishop of Saint Louis, assisted by Christopher Edward Byrne, Bishop of Galveston, and Christian Herman Winkelmann, Titular Bishop of Sita, consecrated Paul Clarence Schulte, Bishop of Leavenworth, born at Fredericktown, Missouri (Saint Louis), March 18, 1890; priest June 11, 1915; named May 20, 1937; Archbishop of Indianapolis July 20, 1946; Titular Archbishop of Elicroca January 3, 1970; died at Indianapolis February 17, 1984.

449. 1937, October 7, at Cincinnati, Ohio, Cathedral of Saint Peter in Chains. John Timothy McNicholas, Archbishop of Cincinnati, assisted by John Henry Albers, Bishop of Lansing, and Urban John Vehr, Bishop of Denver, consecrated George John Rehring, Titular Bishop of Lunda, Auxiliary of Cincinnati, born at Cincinnati, Ohio, June 10, 1890; priest March 28, 1914; named August 6, 1937; Bishop of Toledo July 18, 1950; Titular Bishop of Tunnuna February 25, 1967; Bishop emeritus of Toledo

December 31, 1970; died at Toledo February 29, 1976.

450. 1937, October 28, at Salt Lake City, Utah, Cathedral of the Madeleine. John Joseph Mitty, Archbishop of San Francisco, assisted by Robert John Armstrong, Bishop of Sacramento, and Thomas Kiely Gorman, Bishop of Reno, consecrated Duane Garrison Hunt, Bishop of Salt Lake, born at Reynolds, Nebraska (Omaha), September 19, 1884; priest June 27, 1920; named August 6, 1937; title of see changed to Salt Lake City March 31, 1951; died at Salt Lake City March 31, 1960.

451. 1937, December 21, at Philadelphia, Pennsylvania, Cathedral of Saints Peter and Paul. Dennis Joseph Cardinal Dougherty, Archbishop of Philadelphia, assisted by William David O'Brien, Titular Bishop of Calynda, and Hugh Louis Lamb, Titular Bishop of Helos, consecrated Eugene Joseph McGuinness, Bishop of Raleigh, born at Hallertown, Pennsylvania (Philadelphia), September 6, 1889; priest May 22, 1915; named October 13, 1937; Titular Bishop of Ilium, Coadjutor of Oklahoma City and Tulsa November 11, 1944; succeeded to Oklahoma City and Tulsa February 1, 1948; died at Oklahoma City December 24, 1957.

452. 1938, January 25, at Detroit, Michigan, Cathedral of Saints Peter and Paul. Edward Aloysius Mooney, Archbishop of Detroit, assisted by Joseph Casimir Plagens, Bishop of Sault Sainte Marie and Marquette, and William Joseph Hafey, Titular Bishop of Appia, consecrated Stephen Stanislaus Woznicki, Titular Bishop of Peltae, Auxiliary of Detroit, born at Miners Mills, Pennsylvania (Scranton), August 17, 1894; priest December 22, 1917; named December 13, 1937; Bishop of Saginaw March 29, 1950; Titular Bishop of Thiava October 28, 1968; died at Saginaw December 10, 1968.

453. 1938, February 24, at Louisville, Kentucky, Cathedral of the Assumption. John Alexander Floersh, Archbishop of Louisville, assisted by Theodore Mary Reverman, Bishop of Superior, and Moses Elias Kiley, Bishop of Trenton, consecrated Francis Ridgley Cotton, first Bishop of Owensboro, born at Bardstown, Kentucky (Louisville), September 19, 1895; priest June 17, 1920; named December 16, 1937; died at Owensboro September 25, 1960.

454. 1938, March 25, at New York, New York, Saint Patrick's Cathedral. Patrick Joseph Cardinal Hayes, Archbishop of New York, assisted by Edward Joseph Kelly, Bishop of Boise City, and Stephen Joseph Donahue, Titular Bishop of Medea, consecrated Bartholomew Joseph Eustace, first Bishop of Camden, born at New York, New York, October 9, 1887; priest November 1, 1914; named December 16, 1937; died at Haddonfield, New Jersey, December 11/12, 1956.

455. 1938, May 1, at Newark, New Jersey, Sacred Heart Cathedral. Thomas Joseph Walsh, Archbishop of Newark, assisted by John Aloysius Duffy, Bishop of Buffalo, and Moses Elias Kiley, Bishop of Trenton, consecrated William Aloysius Griffin, Titular Bishop of Sanavus, Auxiliary of Newark, born at Elizabeth, New Jersey (Newark), November 20, 1885; priest August 15, 1910; named March 3, 1938; Bishop of Trenton May 18, 1940; died at Elizabeth, New Jersey, January 1, 1950.

456. 1938, May 17, at Saginaw, Michigan, Saint Mary Cathedral. Edward Aloysius Mooney, Archbishop of Detroit, assisted by John Aloysius Duffy, Bishop of Buffalo, and Joseph Casimir Plagens, Bishop of Sault Sainte Marie and Marquette, consecrated William Francis Murphy, first Bishop of Saginaw, born at Kalamazoo, Michigan (Detroit), May 11, 1885; priest June 13, 1908; named March 17, 1938; died at Saginaw February 7, 1950.

457. 1938, October 26, at Burlington, Vermont, Cathedral of the Immaculate Conception. Amleto Giovanni Cicognani, Titular Archbishop of Laodicea in Phrygia, Apostolic Delegate to the United States, assisted by Maurice Francis McAuliffe, Bishop of Hartford, and Joseph Edward McCarthy, Bishop of Portland, consecrated Matthew Francis Brady, Bishop of Burlington, born at Waterbury, Connecticut (Hartford), January 15, 1893; priest June 10, 1916; named July 30, 1938; Bishop of Manchester November 11, 1944; died at Burlington September 20, 1959.

458. 1938, October 28, at Cincinnati, Ohio, Saint Monica's Cathedral.* John Timothy McNicholas, Archbishop of Cincinnati, assisted by Francis Joseph Beckman, Archbishop of Dubuque, and Urban John Vehr, Bishop of Denver, consecrated Francis Augustine Thill, Bishop of Concordia, born at Dayton, Ohio (Cincinnati), October 12, 1893; priest February 28, 1920; named August 24, 1938; title of see changed to Salina December 23, 1944; died at Salina May 21, 1957.

---

*Note: This was the first consecration performed in the newly designated Saint Monica's Cathedral. In 1957, Saint Peter in Chains again became the cathedral of the archdiocese.

459. 1938, November 9, at Winona, Minnesota, Chapel of Saint Mary at the College of Saint Theresa. Francis Martin Kelly, Bishop of Winona, assisted by Joseph Francis Busch, Bishop of Saint Cloud, and Edwin Vincent O'Hara, Bishop of Great Falls, consecrated John Hubert Peschges, Bishop of Crookston, born at West Newton, Minnesota (Saint Paul), May 11, 1881; priest April 15, 1905; named August 30, 1938; died at Crookston October 30, 1944.

460. 1939, February 24, at Spokane, Washington, Saint Aloysius Church. Joseph Raphael Crimont, Titular Bishop of Ammaedara, assisted by Charles Daniel White, Bishop of Spokane, and Robert John Armstrong, Bishop of Sacramento, consecrated Walter James Fitzgerald, SJ, Titular Bishop of Tymbrias, Coadjutor to the Vicar Apostolic of Alaska, born at Peola, Washington (Nesqually), November 17, 1883; priest May 16, 1918; named December 14, 1938; succeeded to the Vicariate of Alaska May 20, 1945; died at Seattle July 19, 1947.

461. 1939, June 29, at Boston, Massachusetts, Cathedral of the Holy Cross. William Henry Cardinal O'Connell, Archbishop of Boston, assisted by John Bertram Peterson, Bishop of Manchester, and Thomas Addis Emmet, Titular Bishop of Tuscamia, consecrated Richard James Cushing, Titular Bishop of Mela, Auxiliary of Boston, born at South Boston, Massachusetts (Boston), August 24, 1895; priest May 26, 1921; named June 10, 1939; Archbishop of Boston September 25, 1944; Cardinal December 15, 1958; resigned September 8, 1970; died at Boston November 2, 1970.

462. 1939, August 24, at San Francisco, California, Cathedral of Saint Mary. John Joseph Mitty, Archbishop of San Francisco, assisted by Robert John Armstrong, Bishop of Sacramento, and Thomas Kiely Gorman, Bishop of Reno, consecrated Thomas Arthur Connolly, Titular Bishop of Sila, Auxiliary of San Francisco, born at San Francisco, California, October 5, 1899; priest June 11, 1926; named June 10, 1939; Coadjutor of Seattle February 28, 1948; succeeded to Seattle May 18, 1950; first Archbishop of Seattle June 23, 1951; resigned February 13, 1975.

463. 1939, August 24, at Saint Paul, Minnesota, Cathedral of Saint Paul. John Gregory Murray, Archbishop of Saint Paul, assisted by James Edwin Cassidy, Bishop of Fall River, and Urban John Vehr, Bishop of Denver, consecrated William Otterwell Brady, Bishop of Sioux Falls, born at Fall River, Massachusetts (Providence), February 1, 1899; priest December 21, 1923; named June 10, 1939; Titular Archbishop of Selymbria, Coadjutor of Saint Paul June 16, 1956; succeeded to Saint Paul October 11, 1956; died at Rome October 1, 1961.

464. 1939, October 18, at Spokane, Washington, Cathedral of Our Lady of Lourdes. Charles Daniel White, Bishop of Spokane, assisted by Joseph Francis McGrath, Bishop of Baker City, and Edward Joseph Kelly, Bishop of Boise City, consecrated William Joseph Condon, Bishop of Great Falls, born at Colton, Washington (Nesqually), April 7, 1895; priest October 14, 1917; named August 5, 1939; died at Great Falls August 17, 1967.

465. 1940, January 15, at Notre Dame, Indiana, University Church of the

Sacred Heart. Francis Joseph Spellman, Archbishop of New York, assisted by John Francis Noll, Bishop of Fort Wayne, and Joseph Elmer Ritter, Bishop of Indianapolis, consecrated John Francis O'Hara, CSC, Titular Bishop of Mylasa, Auxiliary of the Military Vicar of the United States, born at Ann Arbor, Michigan (Detroit), May 1, 1888; priest September 9, 1916; named December 11, 1939; Bishop of Buffalo March 10, 1945; Archbishop of Philadelphia November 28, 1951; Cardinal December 15, 1958; died at Philadelphia August 20, 1960.

466. 1940, April 2, at Washington, District of Columbia, National Shrine of the Immaculate Conception. Dennis Joseph Cardinal Dougherty, Archbishop of Philadelphia, assisted by Michael Joseph Curley, Archbishop of Baltimore and Washington and Edward Aloysius Mooney, Archbishop of Detroit, consecrated Joseph Moran Corrigan, Titular Bishop of Bilta, Rector of The Catholic University of America, born at Philadelphia, Pennsylvania, May 18, 1879; priest June 6, 1903; Rector of The Catholic University of America March 27, 1936; named February 3, 1940; died at Washington June 9, 1942.

467. 1940, April 10, at San Antonio, Texas, Cathedral of San Fernando. Arthur Jerome Drossaerts, Archbishop of San Antonio, assisted by Rudolph Aloysius Gerken, Archbishop of Santa Fe, and Mariano Simon Garriga, Titular Bishop of Syene, consecrated Sidney Matthew Metzger, Titular Bishop of Birtha, Auxiliary of Santa Fe, born at Fredericksburg, Texas (San Antonio), July 11, 1902; priest April 3, 1926; named December 27, 1939; Coadjutor of El Paso December 26, 1941; succeeded to El Paso November 29, 1942; resigned March 17, 1978; died at El Paso April 12, 1986.

468. 1940, April 23, at Saint Louis, Missouri, Cathedral of Saint Louis. John Joseph Glennon, Archbishop of Saint Louis, assisted by Christian Herman Winkelmann, Bishop of Wichita, and Paul Clarence Schulte, Bishop of Leavenworth, consecrated George Joseph Donnelly, Titular Bishop of Coela, Auxiliary of Saint Louis, born at Maplewood, Missouri (Saint Louis), April 23, 1889; priest June 12, 1921; named March 19, 1940; Bishop of Leavenworth November 9, 1946; title of see changed to Kansas City in Kansas May 10, 1947; died at Kansas City, Kansas, December 13, 1950.

469. 1940, April 25, at Little Rock, Arkansas, Cathedral of Saint Andrew. Amleto Giovanni Cicognani, Titular Archbishop of Laodicea in Phrygia, Apostolic Delegate to the United States, assisted by Jules Benjamin Jeanmard, Bishop of Lafayette, and William David O'Brien, Titular Bishop of Calynda, consecrated Albert Lewis Fletcher, Titular Bishop of Samos, Auxiliary of Little Rock, born at Little Rock, Arkansas, October 28,

1896; priest June 4, 1920; named December 11, 1939; Bishop of Little Rock December 7, 1946; resigned July 4, 1972; died at Little Rock December 6, 1979.

470. 1940, May 14, at Hartford, Connecticut, Cathedral of Saint Joseph. Amleto Giovanni Cicognani, Titular Archbishop of Laodicea in Phrygia, Apostolic Delegate to the United States, assisted by Maurice Francis McAuliffe, Bishop of Hartford, and Joseph Edward McCarthy, Bishop of Portland, consecrated Henry Joseph O'Brien, Titular Bishop of Sita, Auxiliary of Hartford, born at New Haven, Connecticut (Hartford), July 21, 1896; priest July 8, 1923; named March 19, 1940; Bishop of Hartford April 1, 1945; first Archbishop of Hartford August 6, 1953; Titular Archbishop of Uthina November 20, 1968; Archbishop emeritus of Hartford January 5, 1971; died at Hartford July 23, 1976.

471. 1940, May 28, at Fargo, North Dakota, Saint Mary's Cathedral. Aloisius Joseph Muench, Bishop of Fargo, assisted by Joseph Francis Busch, Bishop of Saint Cloud, and Thomas Anthony Welch, Bishop of Duluth, consecrated Vincent James Ryan, Bishop of Bismarck, born at Arlington, Wisconsin (Milwaukee), July 1, 1884; priest June 7, 1912; named March 19, 1940; died at Bismarck November 10, 1951.

472. 1940, June 11, at Lawrence, Massachusetts, Saint Mary's Church. James Edward Walsh, Titular Bishop of Sata, assisted by Joseph Edward McCarthy, Bishop of Portland, and Richard James Cushing, Titular Bishop of Mela, consecrated Raymond Aloysius Lane, MM, Titular Bishop of Hypaepa, Vicar Apostolic of Fushun, China, born at Lawrence, Massachusetts (Boston), January 2, 1894; priest February 8, 1920; Prefect Apostolic of Fushun in 1932; named February 13, 1940; first Bishop of Fushun April 11, 1946; Superior General of Maryknoll August 7, 1946; did not take possession of the Diocese of Fushun and remained Titular Bishop of Hypaepa; term as Superior General of Maryknoll ended August 6, 1956; died at San Francisco July 31, 1974.

473. 1940, July 25, at Newark, New Jersey, Sacred Heart Cathedral. Thomas Joseph Walsh, Archbishop of Newark, assisted by William Aloysius Griffin, Bishop of Trenton, and Bartholomew Joseph Eustace, Bishop of Camden, consecrated Thomas Aloysius Boland, Titular Bishop of Hirina, Auxiliary of Newark, born at Orange, New Jersey (Newark), February 17, 1896; priest December 23, 1922; named May 21, 1940; Bishop of Paterson June 21, 1947; Archbishop of Newark November 15, 1952; resigned March 25, 1974; died at Newark March 16, 1979.

474. 1940, October 6, at Rome, Italy, College de Propaganda Fide. Luigi Cardinal Maglione, assisted by Clemente Micara, Titular Archbishop of

Apamea in Syria, and Celso Costantini, Titular Archbishop of Theodosia, consecrated Joseph Patrick Hurley, Bishop of Saint Augustine, born at Cleveland, Ohio, January 21, 1894; priest May 29, 1919; named August 16, 1940; Regent *ad interim* of the Nunciature in Yugoslavia October 22, 1945; Archbishop *ad personam* August 20, 1949; died at Orlando, Florida, October 30, 1967.

475. 1940, October 9, at Cincinnati, Ohio, Saint Monica's Cathedral. John Timothy McNicholas, Archbishop of Cincinnati, assisted by John Henry Albers, Bishop of Lansing, and Joseph Elmer Ritter, Bishop of Indianapolis, consecrated Bernard Theodore Espelage, OFM, first Bishop of Gallup, born at Cincinnati, Ohio, February 16, 1892; priest May 16, 1918; named July 20, 1940; Titular Bishop of Penafiel August 25, 1969; died at Gallup February 19, 1971.

476. 1941, January 8, at New York, New York, Saint Patrick's Cathedral. Francis Joseph Spellman, Archbishop of New York, assisted by Stephen Joseph Donahue, Titular Bishop of Medea, and John Francis O'Hara, Titular Bishop of Mylasa, consecrated James Francis Aloysius McIntyre, Titular Bishop of Cyrene, Auxiliary of New York, born at New York, New York, June 25, 1886; priest May 21, 1921; named November 16, 1940; Titular Archbishop of Paltus, Coadjutor *sedi datus* of New York July 20, 1946; Archbishop of Los Angeles February 7, 1948; Cardinal January 12, 1953; resigned January 21, 1970; died at Los Angeles July 16, 1979.

477. 1941, February 24, at Chicago, Illinois, Cathedral of the Holy Name. Samuel Alphonsus Stritch, Archbishop of Chicago, assisted by Eugene Joseph McGuinness, Bishop of Raleigh, and William David O'Brien, Titular Bishop of Calynda, consecrated Francis Joseph Magner, Bishop of Marquette, born at Wilmington, Illinois (Chicago), March 18, 1887; priest May 17, 1913; named December 21, 1940; died at Marquette June 13, 1947.

478. 1941, March 19, at Los Angeles, California, Saint Vibiana's Cathedral. John Joseph Cantwell, Archbishop of Los Angeles, assisted by Daniel James Gercke, Bishop of Tucson, and Philip George Scher, Bishop of Monterey-Fresno, consecrated Joseph Thomas McGucken, Titular Bishop of Sanavus, Auxiliary of Los Angeles, born at Los Angeles, California (Monterey-Los Angeles), March 13, 1902; priest January 15, 1928; named February 4, 1941; Coadjutor of Sacramento October 26, 1955; succeeded to Sacramento January 14, 1957; Archbishop of San Francisco February 19, 1962; resigned February 16, 1977; died at San Francisco October 26, 1983.

479. 1941, July 25, at San Francisco, California, Cathedral of Saint Mary.

John Joseph Mitty, Archbishop of San Francisco, assisted by Eugene Joseph McGuinness, Bishop of Raleigh, and Thomas Arthur Connolly, Titular Bishop of Sila, consecrated James Joseph Sweeney, first Bishop of Honolulu, born at San Francisco, California, June 19, 1898; priest June 20, 1925; named May 17, 1941; Titular Bishop of Vicus Aterii March 6, 1968; died at San Francisco June 20, 1968.

480. 1941, October 22, at San Antonio, Texas, Cathedral of San Fernando. Amleto Giovanni Cicognani, Titular Archbishop of Laodicea in Phrygia, Apostolic Delegate to the United States, assisted by Mariano Simon Garriga, Titular Bishop of Syene, and Sydney Matthew Metzger, Titular Bishop of Birtha, consecrated Lawrence Julius FitzSimon, Bishop of Amarillo, born at San Antonio, Texas, January 31, 1895; priest May 17, 1921; named August 2, 1941; died at Amarillo July 2, 1958.

481. 1942, February 24, at Helena, Montana, Cathedral of Saint Helena. Amleto Giovanni Cicognani, Titular Archbishop of Laodicea in Phrygia, Apostolic Delegate to the United States, assisted by Henry Patrick Rohlman, Bishop of Davenport, and Joseph Michael Gilmore, Bishop of Helena, consecrated Joseph Clement Willging, first Bishop of Pueblo, born at Dubuque, Iowa, September 6, 1884; priest June 20, 1908; named December 6, 1941; died at Denver March 3, 1959.

482. 1942, February 24, at Columbus, Ohio, Saint Joseph Cathedral. James Joseph Hartley, Bishop of Columbus, assisted by Francis William Howard, Bishop of Covington, and George John Rehring, Titular Bishop of Lunda, consecrated Edward Gerhard Hettinger, Titular Bishop of Teos, Auxiliary of Columbus, born at Lancaster, Ohio (Columbus), October 14, 1902; priest June 2, 1928; named December 6, 1941; resigned as Auxiliary of Columbus October 18, 1977.

483. 1942, March 3, at Rochester, Minnesota, Chapel of Saint Mary's Hospital. Amleto Giovanni Cicognani, Titular Archbishop of Laodicea in Phrygia, Apostolic Delegate to the United States, assisted by Joseph Francis Busch, Bishop of Saint Cloud, and John Hubert Peschges, Bishop of Crookston, consecrated Peter William Bartholome, Titular Bishop of Lete, Coadjutor of Saint Cloud, born at Bellechester, Minnesota (Winona), April 2, 1893; priest June 12, 1917; named December 6, 1941; succeeded to Saint Cloud May 31, 1953; Titular Bishop of Tanaramusa January 31, 1968; Bishop emeritus of Saint Cloud January 13, 1971; died near Ward Springs, Minnesota, June 17, 1982.

484. 1942, March 7, at Milwaukee, Wisconsin, Cathedral of Saint John the Evangelist. Moses Elias Kiley, Archbishop of Milwaukee, assisted by Aloisius Joseph Muench, Bishop of Fargo, and Vincent James Ryan,

Bishop of Bismarck, consecrated William Patrick O'Connor, Bishop of Superior, born at Milwaukee, Wisconsin, October 18, 1886; priest March 10, 1912; named December 27, 1941; first Bishop of Madison February 22, 1946; Titular Bishop of Siccesi February 18, 1967; Bishop emeritus of Madison December 31, 1970; died at Madison July 13, 1973.

485. 1942, October 7, at Dallas, Texas, Sacred Heart Cathedral. Amleto Giovanni Cicognani, Titular Archbishop of Laodicea in Phrygia, Apostolic Delegate to the United States, assisted by Joseph Patrick Lynch, Bishop of Dallas, and William David O'Brien, Titular Bishop of Calynda, consecrated Augustine Danglmayr, Titular Bishop of Olba, Auxiliary of Dallas, born at Muenster, Texas (Dallas), December 11, 1898; priest June 10, 1922; named April 24, 1942; title of see changed to Dallas-Fort Worth December 8, 1953; resigned as Auxiliary of Dallas-Fort Worth August 22, 1969.

486. 1942, October 22, at Chicago, Illinois, Saint Nicholas Ukrainian Catholic Church. Constantine Bohachevsky, Titular Bishop of Amisus, assisted by Basil Takach, Titular Bishop of Zela, and Vladimir Ladyka, Titular Bishop of Abydus, consecrated Ambrose Andrew Senyshyn, OSBM, Titular Bishop of Maina, Auxiliary of the Ukrainian Exarch of Philadelphia, born at Stary Sambor (Przemysl of the Ukrainians), Ukraine, February 23, 1903; priest August 23, 1931; named July 6, 1942; first Bishop of Stamford of the Ukrainians July 10, 1958; Archbishop of Philadelphia of the Ukrainians August 14, 1961; died at Philadelphia September 11, 1976.

487. 1942, December 21, at Rockford, Illinois, Saint James Pro-cathedral. Amleto Giovanni Cicognani, Titular Archbishop of Laodicea in Phrygia, Apostolic Delegate to the United States, assisted by Edward Francis Hoban, Titular Bishop of Lystra, and Henry Patrick Rohlman, Bishop of Davenport, consecrated Leo Binz, Titular Bishop of Pinara, Coadjutor and Apostolic Administrator of Winona, born at Stockton, Illinois (Chicago), October 31, 1900; priest March 15, 1924; named November 21, 1942; Titular Archbishop of Silyum, Coadjutor of Dubuque October 15, 1949; succeeded to Dubuque December 2, 1954; Archbishop of Saint Paul December 16, 1961; title of see changed to Saint Paul and Minneapolis July 11, 1966; resigned May 21, 1975; died at Maywood, Illinois, October 9, 1979.

488. 1943, January 25, at New York, New York, Saint Patrick's Cathedral. Francis Joseph Spellman, Archbishop of New York, assisted by Thomas Edmund Molloy, Bishop of Brooklyn, and John Francis O'Hara, Titular Bishop of Mylasa, consecrated William Tiburtius McCarty, C.SS.R, Titular Bishop of Anaea, Auxiliary of the Military Vicar of the United

States, born at Crossingville, Pennsylvania (Erie), August 11, 1889; priest June 10, 1915; named January 2, 1943; Coadjutor of Rapid City April 10, 1947; succeeded to Rapid City March 11, 1948; Titular Bishop of Rotdon September 11, 1969; Bishop emeritus of Rapid City January 15, 1971; died at Rapid City September 14, 1972.

489. 1943, January 27, at Scranton, Pennsylvania, Saint Peter's Cathedral. William Joseph Hafey, Bishop of Scranton, assisted by Gerald Patrick Aloysius O'Hara, Bishop of Savannah-Atlanta, and George Leo Leech, Bishop of Harrisburg, consecrated Martin John O'Connor, Titular Bishop of Thespiae, Auxiliary of Scranton, born at Scranton, Pennsylvania, May 18, 1900; priest March 15, 1924; named November 14, 1942; Rector of the North American College, Rome, November 26, 1946; President of the Pontifical Commission for Social Communications in January 1948; Titular Archbishop of Laodicea in Syria September 5, 1959; Nuncio to Malta December 15, 1965; resigned as Nuncio to Malta in May 1969; resigned as President of the Pontifical Commission for Social Communications September 8, 1971; died at Wilkes-Barre, Pennsylvania, December 1, 1986.

490. 1943, February 17, at Des Moines, Iowa, Saint Ambrose Cathedral. Gerald Thomas Bergan, Bishop of Des Moines, assisted by Edmond Heelan, Bishop of Sioux City, and Henry Patrick Rohlman, Bishop of Davenport, consecrated John Joseph Boylan, Bishop of Rockford, born at New York, New York, October 7, 1889; priest July 28, 1915; named November 21, 1942; died at Narragansett, Rhode Island, July 19, 1953.

491. 1943, June 29, at Buffalo, New York, Saint Joseph Cathedral. Amleto Giovanni Cicognani, Titular Archbishop of Laodicea in Phrygia, Apostolic Delegate to the United States, assisted by Thomas Joseph Walsh, Archbishop of Newark, and Edmund Francis Gibbons, Bishop of Albany, consecrated Joseph Aloysius Burke, Titular Bishop of Vita, Auxiliary of Buffalo, born at Buffalo, New York, August 27, 1886; priest August 3, 1912; named April 17, 1943; Bishop of Buffalo February 7, 1952; died at Rome October 16, 1962, the first bishop to die at Rome during the Second Vatican Council.

492. 1943, August 3, at New York, New York, Saint Patrick's Cathedral. Amleto Giovanni Cicognani, Titular Archbishop of Laodicea in Phrygia, Apostolic Delegate to the United States, assisted by Edmund Francis Gibbons, Bishop of Albany, and Stephen Joseph Donahue, Titular Bishop of Medea, consecrated Bryan Joseph McEntegart, Bishop of Ogdensburg, born at New York, New York, January 5, 1893; priest September 8, 1917; named June 5, 1943; Rector of The Catholic University of America June 26, 1953; Titular Bishop of Aradi August 19, 1953; Bishop of Brooklyn

April 16, 1957; Archbishop *ad personam* May 12, 1966; Titular Archbishop of Gabi July 15, 1968; died at Brooklyn September 30, 1968.

493. 1943, October 6, at Tucson, Arizona, Cathedral of Saint Augustine. Daniel James Gercke, Bishop of Tucson, assisted by Thomas Arthur Connolly, Titular Bishop of Sila, and Joseph Thomas McGucken, Titular Bishop of Sanavus, consecrated James Peter Davis, Bishop of San Juan, born at Houghton, Michigan (Sault Sainte Marie and Marquette), June 9, 1904; priest May 19, 1929; named July 3, 1943; first Archbishop of San Juan April 30, 1960; Archbishop of Santa Fe January 3, 1964; resigned June 1, 1974; died at Albuquerque, New Mexico, March 4, 1988.

494. 1943, November 18, at Grand Rapids, Michigan, Saint Andrew's Cathedral. Amleto Giovanni Cicognani, Titular Archbishop of Laodicea in Phrygia, Apostolic Delegate to the United States, assisted by Edward Aloysius Mooney, Archbishop of Detroit, and Moses Elias Kiley, Archbishop of Milwaukee, consecrated Francis Joseph Haas, Bishop of Grand Rapids, born at Racine, Wisconsin (Milwaukee), March 18, 1889; priest June 11, 1913; named September 26, 1943; died at Grand Rapids August 29, 1953.

495. 1944, December 14, at Washington, District of Columbia, Saint Matthew's Cathedral. Amleto Giovanni Cicognani, Titular Archbishop of Laodicea in Phrygia, Apostolic Delegate to the United States, assisted by John Timothy McNicholas, Archbishop of Cincinnati, and Edward Francis Hoban, Titular Bishop of Lystra, consecrated Michael Joseph Ready, Bishop of Columbus, born at New Haven, Connecticut (Hartford), April 9, 1893; priest September 14, 1918; named November 11, 1944; Apostolic Administrator of Steubenville from March 10, 1945 to May 1, 1945; died at Columbus May 2, 1957.

496. 1944, December 21, at Worthington, Ohio, Pontifical College Josephinum. Amleto Giovanni Cicognani, Titular Archbishop of Laodicea in Phrygia, Apostolic Delegate to the United States, assisted by Urban John Vehr, Archbishop of Denver, and George John Rehring, Titular Bishop of Lunda, consecrated Henry Joseph Grimmelsman, first Bishop of Evansville, born at Cincinnati, Ohio, December 22, 1890; priest August 15, 1915; named November 11, 1944; Titular Bishop of Tabla October 18, 1965; died at Evansville June 26, 1972.

497. 1945, January 3, at Boston, Massachusetts, Cathedral of the Holy Cross. Richard James Cushing, Archbishop of Boston, assisted by Francis Joseph Spellman, Archbishop of New York, and Francis Patrick Keough, Bishop of Providence, consecrated Edward Francis Ryan, Bishop of Burlington, born at Lynn, Massachusetts (Boston), March 10, 1879; priest

August 10, 1905; named November 11, 1944; died at Burlington November 3, 1956.

498. 1945, January 10, at Fargo, North Dakota, Saint Mary's Cathedral. Aloisius Joseph Muench, Bishop of Fargo, assisted by Vincent James Ryan, Bishop of Bismarck, and Peter William Bartholome, Titular Bishop of Lete, consecrated William Theodore Mulloy, Bishop of Covington, born at Ardoch (Jamestown), November 9, 1892; priest June 7, 1916; named November 11, 1944; died at Covington June 1, 1959.

499. 1945, January 10, at Fort Wayne, Indiana, Cathedral of the Immaculate Conception. John Francis Noll, Bishop of Fort Wayne, assisted by Francis Ridgely Cotton, Bishop of Owensboro, and John Francis O'Hara, Titular Bishop of Mylasa, consecrated John George Bennett, first Bishop of Lafayette in Indiana, born at Dinnington, Indiana (Fort Wayne), January 20, 1891; priest June 27, 1914; named November 11, 1944; died at Lafayette November 20, 1957.

500. 1945, March 19, at New York, New York, Saint Patrick's Cathedral. Francis Joseph Spellman, Archbishop of New York, assisted by John Francis O'Hara, Bishop of Buffalo, and James Francis Aloysius McIntyre, Titular Bishop of Cyrene, consecrated Joseph Patrick Donahue, Titular Bishop of Emmaus, Auxiliary of New York, born at New York, New York, November 6, 1870; priest June 8, 1895; named January 27, 1945; died at New York April 26, 1959.

501. 1945, May 1, at Omaha, Nebraska, Saint Cecilia's Cathedral. Amleto Giovanni Cicognani, Titular Archbishop of Laodicea in Phrygia, Apostolic Delegate to the United States, assisted by James Hugh Ryan, Bishop of Omaha, and Stanislaus Vincent Bona, Bishop of Green Bay, consecrated Edward Joseph Hunkeler, Bishop of Grand Island, born at Medicine Lodge, Kansas (Wichita), January 1, 1894; priest June 14, 1919; named March 10, 1945; Bishop of Kansas City in Kansas March 28, 1951; first Archbishop of Kansas City in Kansas August 9, 1952; Titular Archbishop of Selsea September 4, 1969; died at Kansas City, Kansas, October 1, 1970.

502. 1945, May 1, at Cincinnati, Ohio, Saint Monica's Cathedral. John Timothy McNicholas, Archbishop of Cincinnati, assisted by Michael Joseph Ready, Bishop of Columbus, and George John Rehring, Titular Bishop of Lunda, consecrated John Anthony King Mussio, first Bishop of Steubenville, born at Cincinnati, Ohio, June 13, 1902; priest August 15, 1935; named March 10, 1945; resigned September 27, 1977; died at Steubenville April 15, 1978.

503. 1945, May 15, at Richmond, Virginia, Cathedral of the Sacred Heart. Peter Leo Ireton, Bishop of Richmond, assisted by Gerald Patrick Aloysius O'Hara, Bishop of Savannah-Atlanta, and Emmet Michael Walsh, Bishop of Charleston, consecrated Vincent Stanislaus Waters, Bishop of Raleigh, born at Roanoke, Virginia (Richmond), August 15, 1904; priest December 8, 1931; named March 10, 1945; died at Raleigh December 3, 1974.

504–505. 1945, May 24, at Saint Paul, Minnesota, Cathedral of Saint Paul. John Gregory Murray, Archbishop of Saint Paul, assisted by William Otterwell Brady, Bishop of Sioux Falls, and Leo Binz, Titular Bishop of Pinara, consecrated (1) James Louis Connolly, Titular Bishop of Mylasa, Coadjutor of Fall River, born at Fall River, Massachusetts (Providence), November 15, 1894; priest December 21, 1923; named April 7, 1945; succeeded to Fall River May 17, 1951; Titular Bishop of Thibuzabetum October 30, 1970; Bishop emeritus of Fall River December 31, 1970; died at Fall River September 12, 1986. Assisted by Thomas Anthony Welch, Bishop of Duluth, and Aloisius Joseph Muench, Bishop of Fargo, consecrated (2) Francis Joseph Schenk, Bishop of Crookston, born at Superior, Wisconsin (La Crosse), April 1, 1901; priest June 13, 1926; named March 10, 1945; Bishop of Duluth January 19, 1960; Titular Bishop of Scardona April 30, 1969; died at Duluth October 28, 1969.

506. 1945, June 8, at Boston, Massachusetts, Cathedral of the Holy Cross. Richard James Cushing, Archbishop of Boston, assisted by Francis Joseph Spellman, Archbishop of New York, and Edward Francis Ryan, Bishop of Burlington, consecrated Louis Francis Kelleher, Titular Bishop of Thenae, Auxiliary of Boston, born at Cambridge, Massachusetts (Boston), August 4, 1889; priest April 3, 1915; named April 21, 1945; died at Sommerville, Massachusetts, November 26, 1946.

507. 1945, October 2, at Cleveland, Ohio, Cathedral of Saint John the Evangelist. Amleto Giovanni Cicognani, Titular Archbishop of Laodicea in Phrygia, Apostolic Delegate to the United States, assisted by Edward Francis Hoban, Bishop of Cleveland, and William David O'Brien, Titular Bishop of Calynda, consecrated John Patrick Treacy, Titular Bishop of Metelis, Coadjutor of La Crosse, born at Marlboro, Massachusetts (Boston), July 23, 1890; priest December 8, 1918; named August 21, 1945; succeeded to La Crosse August 25, 1948; died October 11, 1964.

508. 1945, October 11, at New York, New York, Saint Patrick's Cathedral. Francis Joseph Spellman, Archbishop of New York, assisted by John Francis Noll, Bishop of Fort Wayne, and John Francis O'Hara, Bishop of Buffalo, consecrated William Richard Arnold, Titular Bishop of Phocaea, Auxiliary of the Military Vicar of the United States, born at

Wooster, Ohio (Cleveland), June 10, 1881; priest June 13, 1908; named May 5, 1945; died at New York January 7, 1965.

509. 1945, October 24, at New York, New York, Saint Patrick's Cathedral. Edmund Francis Gibbons, Bishop of Albany, assisted by Thomas Edmund Molloy, Bishop of Brooklyn, and Bryan Joseph McEntegart, Bishop of Ogdensburg, consecrated William Aloysius Scully, Titular Bishop of Pharsalus, Coadjutor of Albany, born at New York, New York, August 6, 1894; priest September 20, 1919; named August 21, 1945; succeeded to Albany November 10, 1954; died at Albany January 5, 1969.

510. 1945, December 12, at Washington, District of Columbia, Saint Patrick's Church. Amleto Giovanni Cicognani, Titular Archbishop of Laodicea in Phrygia, Apostolic Delegate to the United States, assisted by Peter Leo Ireton, Bishop of Richmond, and John Michael McNamara, Titular Bishop of Eumenia, consecrated Lawrence Joseph Shehan, Titular Bishop of Lydda, Auxiliary of Baltimore and Washington, born at Baltimore, Maryland, March 18, 1898; priest December 23, 1922; named November 17, 1945; Auxiliary of Baltimore November 15, 1947; first Bishop of Bridgeport August 25, 1953; Titular Archbishop of Nicopolis ad Nestum, Coadjutor of Baltimore July 10, 1961; succeeded to Baltimore December 8, 1961; Cardinal February 22, 1965; resigned March 25, 1974; died at Baltimore August 26, 1984.

511. 1946, February 25, at New Orleans, Louisiana, Saint Louis Cathedral. Joseph Francis Rummel, Archbishop of New Orleans, assisted by Richard Oliver Gerow, Bishop of Natchez, and Thomas Joseph Toolen, Bishop of Mobile, consecrated Charles Pascal Greco, Bishop of Alexandria, born at Rodney, Mississippi (Natchez), October 29, 1894; priest July 25, 1918; named January 15, 1946; resigned May 10, 1973; died at Alexandria January 20, 1987.

512. 1946, March 19, at Grand Rapids, Michigan, Saint Andrew's Cathedral. Edward Aloysius Cardinal Mooney, Archbishop of Detroit, assisted by Charles Daniel White, Bishop of Spokane, and Joseph Henry Albers, Bishop of Lansing, consecrated Thomas Lawrence Noa, Titular Bishop of Salona, Coadjutor of Sioux City, born at Iron Mountain, Michigan (Sault Sainte Marie and Marquette), December 18, 1892; priest December 23, 1916; named February 22, 1946; Bishop of Marquette August 20, 1947; Titular Bishop of Talaptula January 5, 1968; Bishop emeritus of Marquette December 31, 1970; died at Marquette March 13, 1977.

513. 1946, April 11, at Milwaukee, Wisconsin, Saint John Cathedral. Moses Elias Kiley, Archbishop of Milwaukee, assisted by Aloisius Joseph Muench, Bishop of Fargo, and William Patrick O'Connor, Bishop of

Madison, consecrated Albert Gregory Meyer, Bishop of Superior, born at Milwaukee, Wisconsin, March 9, 1903; priest July 11, 1926; named February 18, 1946; Archbishop of Milwaukee July 21, 1953; Archbishop of Chicago September 19, 1958; Cardinal December 14, 1959; died at Chicago April 9, 1965.

514. 1946, May 28, at Cleveland, Ohio, Saint Agnes Church. Edward Francis Hoban, Bishop of Cleveland, assisted by James Augustine McFadden, Bishop of Youngstown, and John Patrick Treacy, Titular Bishop of Metelis, consecrated John Raphael Hagan, Titular Bishop of Limata, Auxiliary of Cleveland, born at Pittsburgh, Pennsylvania, February 26, 1890; priest March 7, 1914; named April 27, 1946; died at Cleveland September 28, 1946.

515. 1946, August 22, at Fargo, North Dakota, Saint Mary's Cathedral. Amleto Giovanni Cicognani, Titular Archbishop of Laodicea in Phrygia, Apostolic Delegate to the United States, assisted by Vincent James Ryan, Bishop of Bismarck, and William Theodore Mulloy, Bishop of Covington, consecrated Leo Ferdinand Dworschak, Titular Bishop of Tium, Coadjutor of Rapid City, born at Independence, Wisconsin (La Crosse), April 6, 1900; priest May 29, 1926; named June 22, 1946; Auxiliary of Fargo April 10, 1947; Apostolic Administrator of Fargo December 4, 1959; Bishop of Fargo May 10, 1960; Titular Bishop of Meta September 8, 1970; Bishop emeritus of Fargo January 13, 1971; died at Fargo November 5, 1976.

516. 1946, September 12, at Portland, Maine, Cathedral of the Immaculate Conception. Amleto Giovanni Cicognani, Titular Archbishop of Laodicea in Phrygia, Apostolic Delegate to the United States, assisted by Matthew Francis Brady, Bishop of Manchester, and Louis Francis Kelleher, Titular Bishop of Thenae, consecrated Daniel Joseph Feeney, Titular Bishop of Sita, Auxiliary of Portland, born at Portland, Maine, September 12, 1894; priest May 21, 1921; named June 22, 1946; Coadjutor of Portland March 4, 1952; succeeded to Portland September 8, 1955; died at Portland September 15, 1969.

517. 1946, September 12, at Dubuque, Iowa, Saint Raphael's Cathedral. Henry Patrick Rohlman, Titular Archbishop of Macra, assisted by Louis Benedict Kucera, Bishop of Lincoln, and Leo Binz, Titular Bishop of Pinara, consecrated Edward Aloysius Fitzgerald, Titular Bishop of Cantanus, Auxiliary of Dubuque, born at Cresco, Iowa (Dubuque), February 13, 1893; priest July 25, 1916; named August 3, 1946; Bishop of Winona October 20, 1949; Titular Bishop of Zerta January 8, 1969; Bishop emeritus of Winona December 31, 1970; died at Winona March 31, 1972.

518. 1946, October 15, at Los Angeles, California, Saint Vibiana's Cathedral. Joseph Thomas McGucken, Titular Bishop of Sanavus, assisted by James Edward Walsh, Titular Bishop of Sata, and Thomas Arthur Connolly, Titular Bishop of Sila, consecrated Timothy Manning, Titular Bishop of Lesvi, Auxiliary of Los Angeles, born at Ballingeary (Cork), Ireland, November 15, 1909; priest June 16, 1934; named August 3, 1946; first Bishop of Fresno October 16, 1967; Titular Archbishop of Capri, Coadjutor of Los Angeles May 26, 1969; succeeded to Los Angeles January 21, 1970; Cardinal March 5, 1973; resigned July 12, 1985; died at Los Angeles June 23, 1989.

519. 1946, November 5, at Pittsburgh, Pennsylvania, Saint Paul Cathedral. Constantine Bohachevsky, Titular Bishop of Amisus, assisted by Ambrose Andrew Senyshyn, Titular Bishop of Maina, and Nile Nicholas Savaryn, Titular Bishop of Jos, consecrated Daniel Ivancho, Titular Bishop of Europus, Coadjutor of the Exarch of Pittsburgh of the Ruthenians, born at Jasina (Mukachevo), Austria-Hungary, March 30, 1908; priest September 30, 1934; named July 30, 1946; Apostolic Administrator of the Exarchate of Pittsburgh of the Ruthenians November 26, 1946; succeeded to the Exarchate of Pittsburgh of the Ruthenians May 13, 1948; resigned as Exarch December 2, 1954; resigned from his titular see, laicized, and married in 1957; died at Saint Petersburg August 2, 1972.

520. 1947, March 25, at Detroit, Michigan, Cathedral of the Most Blessed Sacrament. Edward Aloysius Cardinal Mooney, Archbishop of Detroit, assisted by William Francis Murphy, Bishop of Saginaw, and Stephen Stanislaus Woznicki, Titular Bishop of Peltae, consecrated Allen James Babcock, Titular Bishop of Irenopolis, Auxiliary of Detroit, born at Bad Axe, Michigan (Detroit), June 17, 1898; priest March 7, 1925; named February 15, 1947; Bishop of Grand Rapids March 23, 1954; died June 27, 1969.

521. 1947, April 23, at Philadelphia, Pennsylvania, Cathedral of Saints Peter and Paul. Dennis Joseph Cardinal Dougherty, Archbishop of Philadelphia, assisted by Hugh Louis Lamb, Titular Bishop of Helos, and Eugene Joseph McGuinness, Titular Bishop of Ilium, consecrated Joseph Carroll McCormick, Titular Bishop of Ruspae, Auxiliary of Philadelphia, born at Philadelphia, Pennsylvania, December 15, 1907; priest July 10, 1932; named January 11, 1947; Bishop of Altoona-Johnstown June 26, 1960; Bishop of Scranton March 4, 1966; resigned February 15, 1983.

522. 1947, April 23, at Saint Louis, Missouri, Saint Louis Cathedral. Joseph Elmer Ritter, Archbishop of Saint Louis, assisted by Paul Clarence Schulte, Archbishop of Indianapolis, and George Joseph Donnelly, Bishop of Leavenworth, consecrated Mark Kenny Carroll, Bishop of Wichita, born at Saint Louis, Missouri, November 19, 1896; priest June 10, 1922; named February 15, 1947; Titular Bishop of Taparura September 27, 1967; Bishop emeritus of Wichita January 16, 1976; died at Wichita January 12, 1985.

523.   1947, April 30, at Saint Augustine, Florida, Cathedral of Saint Augustine. Dennis Joseph Cardinal Dougherty, Archbishop of Philadelphia, assisted by Emmet Michael Walsh, Bishop of Charleston, and Joseph Carroll McCormick, Titular Bishop of Ruspae, consecrated Thomas Joseph McDonough, Titular Bishop of Thenae, Auxiliary of Saint Augustine, born at Philadelphia, Pennsylvania, December 5, 1911; priest May 26, 1938; named March 10, 1947; Auxiliary of Savannah January 2, 1957; Bishop of Savannah February 23, 1960; Archbishop of Louisville February 25, 1967; resigned September 29, 1981.

524.   1947, May 1, at Cleveland, Ohio, Saint Agnes Church. Edward Francis Hoban, Bishop of Cleveland, assisted by James Augustine McFadden, Bishop of Youngstown, and Joseph Thomas McGucken, Titular Bishop of Sanavus, consecrated Floyd Lawrence Begin, Titular Bishop of Sala, Auxiliary of Cleveland, born at Cleveland, Ohio, February 5, 1902; priest July 31, 1927; named March 22, 1947; first Bishop of Oakland January 27, 1962; died April 26, 1977.

525.   1947, June 30, at Boston, Massachusetts, Cathedral of the Holy Cross. Richard James Cushing, Archbishop of Boston, assisted by Ralph Leo Hayes, Bishop of Davenport, and James Louis Connolly, Titular Bishop of Mylasa, consecrated John Joseph Wright, Titular Bishop of Aegeae, Auxiliary of Boston, born at Dorchester, Massachusetts (Boston), July 18, 1909; priest December 8, 1935; named May 10, 1947; first Bishop of Worcester January 28, 1950; Bishop of Pittsburgh January 23, 1959; Prefect of the Sacred Congregation for the Clergy April 23, 1969; Cardinal April 28, 1969; resigned from Pittsburgh June 1, 1969; died at Cambridge, Massachusetts, August 10, 1979.

526.   1947, July 1, at Brooklyn, New York, Our Lady of Perpetual Help Church. William Tiburtius McCarty, Titular Bishop of Anaea, assisted by Aloysius Joseph Willinger, Titular Bishop of Bida, and William David O'Brien, Titular Bishop of Calynda, consecrated James Edward McManus, C.SS.R, Bishop of Ponce, born at Brooklyn, New York, October 10, 1900; priest June 19, 1927; named May 10, 1947; Titular Bishop of Benda, Auxiliary of New York November 18, 1963; resigned as Auxiliary of New York in 1970; died at Long Branch, New Jersey, July 3, 1976.

527.   1947, July 2, at Saint Louis, Missouri, Saint Louis Cathedral.

Joseph Elmer Ritter, Archbishop of Saint Louis, assisted by George Joseph Donnelly, Bishop of Leavenworth, and Vincent Stanislaus Waters, Bishop of Raleigh, consecrated John Patrick Cody, Titular Bishop of Apollonia, Auxiliary of Saint Louis, born at Saint Louis, Missouri, December 24, 1907; priest December 8, 1931; named May 14, 1947; Coadjutor of Saint Joseph January 21, 1954; Apostolic Administrator of Saint Joseph May 9, 1955; Coadjutor of Kansas City-Saint Joseph August 24, 1956; succeeded to Kansas City-Saint Joseph September 11, 1956; Titular Archbishop of Bostra, Coadjutor of New Orleans August 10, 1961; Apostolic Administrator of New Orleans June 1, 1962; succeeded to New Orleans November 8, 1964; Archbishop of Chicago June 14, 1965; Cardinal June 26, 1967; died at Chicago April 25, 1982.

528.   1947, July 2, at Saint Paul, Minnesota, Cathedral of Saint Paul. Amleto Giovanni Cicognani, Titular Archbishop of Laodicea in Phrygia, Apostolic Delegate to the United States, assisted by Thomas Anthony Welch, Bishop of Duluth, and Francis Joseph Schenk, Bishop of Crookston, consecrated James Joseph Byrne, Titular Bishop of Etenna, Auxiliary of Saint Paul, born at Saint Paul, Minnesota, July 28, 1908; priest June 3, 1933; named May 10, 1947; Bishop of Boise City June 16, 1956; Archbishop of Dubuque March 19, 1962; resigned August 23, 1983.

529.   1947, July 2, at Scranton, Pennsylvania, Saint Peter's Cathedral. William Joseph Hafey, Bishop of Scranton, assisted by George Leo Leech, Bishop of Harrisburg, and Stephen Stanislaus Woznicki, Titular Bishop of Peltae, consecrated Henry Theophilus Klonowski, Titular Bishop of Daldis, Auxiliary of Scranton, born at Scranton, Pennsylvania, March 8, 1898; priest August 8, 1920; named May 10, 1947; resigned as Auxiliary of Scranton May 15, 1973; died at Scranton May 6, 1977.

530.   1947, August 6, at Cincinnati, Ohio, Saint Monica's Cathedral. Edwin Vincent O'Hara, Bishop of Kansas City, assisted by Joseph Henry Albers, Bishop of Lansing, and John George Bennett, Bishop of Lafayette in Indiana, consecrated Joseph Mary Marling, C.PP.S, Titular Bishop of Thasus, Auxiliary of Kansas City, born at Centralia, West Virginia (Wheeling), August 31, 1904; priest February 21, 1929; named June 7, 1947; first Bishop of Jefferson City August 24, 1956; Titular Bishop of Lesina July 2, 1969; Bishop emeritus of Jefferson City January 16, 1976; died at Kansas City, Missouri, October 2, 1979.

531.   1947, August 28, at Milwaukee, Wisconsin, Saint John Cathedral. Moses Elias Kiley, Archbishop of Milwaukee, assisted by Stanislaus Vincent Bona, Bishop of Green Bay, and William Patrick O'Connor, Bishop of Madison, consecrated Roman Richard Atkielski, Titular Bishop of Stobi, Auxiliary of Milwaukee, born at Milwaukee, Wisconsin, August

5, 1898; priest May 30, 1931; named August 2, 1947; died at Milwaukee June 30, 1969.

532. 1947, September 15, at New York, New York, Saint Patrick's Cathedral. Francis Joseph Cardinal Spellman, Archbishop of New York, assisted by Richard James Cushing, Archbishop of Boston, and James Francis Aloysius McIntyre, Titular Archbishop of Paltus, consecrated Thomas John McDonnell, Titular Bishop of Sela, Auxiliary of New York, born at New York, New York, August 18, 1894; priest September 20, 1919; named June 21, 1947; Coadjutor of Wheeling March 7, 1951; died at Huntington, West Virginia, February 25, 1961.

533. 1947, September 24, at Denver, Colorado, Cathedral of the Immaculate Conception. Urban John Vehr, Archbishop of Denver, assisted by Joseph Michael Gilmore, Bishop of Helena, and Joseph Clement Willging, Bishop of Pueblo, consecrated Hubert Michael Newell, Titular Bishop of Zapara, Coadjutor of Cheyenne, born at Denver, Colorado, February 16, 1904; priest June 15, 1930; named August 2, 1947; succeeded to Cheyenne November 8, 1951; resigned January 3, 1978; died at Denver September 8, 1987.

534. 1947, October 7, at Newark, New Jersey, Sacred Heart Cathedral. Thomas Joseph Walsh, Archbishop of Newark, assisted by William Aloysius Griffin, Bishop of Trenton, and Henry Joseph O'Brien, Bishop of Hartford, consecrated James Aloysius McNulty, Titular Bishop of Methone, Auxiliary of Newark, born at New York, New York, January 16, 1900; priest July 12, 1925; named August 2, 1947; Bishop of Paterson April 9, 1953; Bishop of Buffalo February 12, 1963; died at Montclair, New Jersey, September 4, 1972.

535. 1947, October 7, at San Francisco, California, Cathedral of Saint Mary. John Joseph Mitty, Archbishop of San Francisco, assisted by James Joseph Sweeney, Bishop of Honolulu, and Thomas Arthur Connolly, Titular Bishop of Sita, consecrated Hugh Aloysius Donohoe, Titular Bishop of Taium, Auxiliary of San Francisco, born at San Francisco, California, June 28, 1905; priest June 14, 1930; named August 2, 1947; first Bishop of Stockton February 21, 1962; Bishop of Fresno August 22, 1969; resigned July 1, 1980; died at Fresno October 26, 1987.

536. 1947, October 16, at Belleville, Illinois, Cathedral of Saint Peter. Amleto Giovanni Cicognani, Titular Archbishop of Laodicea in Phrygia, Apostolic Delegate to the United States, assisted by Joseph Henry Leo Schlarman, Bishop of Peoria, and Edward Joseph Hunkeler, Bishop of Grand Island, consecrated Joseph Maximilian Mueller, Titular Bishop of Sinda, Coadjutor of Sioux City, born at Saint Louis, Missouri, December 1,

1894; priest June 14, 1919; named August 20, 1947; succeeded to Sioux City September 20, 1948; Titular Bishop of Simittu October 15, 1970; Bishop emeritus of Sioux City January 13, 1971; died at Sioux City August 9, 1981.

537. 1947, October 28, at New Orleans, Louisiana, Saint Louis Cathedral. Francis Joseph Rummel, Archbishop of New Orleans, assisted by Jules Benjamin Jeanmard, Bishop of Lafayette, and Charles Pascal Greco, Bishop of Alexandria, consecrated Louis Abel Caillouet, Titular Bishop of Setea, Auxiliary of New Orleans, born at Thibodaux, Louisiana (New Orleans), August 2, 1900; priest March 7, 1925; named August 2, 1947; resigned as Auxiliary of New Orleans July 7, 1976; died at New Orleans September 16, 1984.

538. 1948, January 14, at New York, New York, Saint Patrick's Cathedral. Francis Joseph Cardinal Spellman, Archbishop of New York, assisted by John Michael McNamara, Titular Bishop of Eumenia, and Henry Theophilus Klonowski, Titular Bishop of Daldis, consecrated Patrick Aloysius O'Boyle, first Archbishop of Washington, born at Scranton, Pennsylvania, July 18, 1896; priest May 21, 1921; named November 29, 1947; Metropolitan Archbishop of Washington October 12, 1965; Cardinal June 26, 1967; resigned March 3, 1973; died at Washington August 10, 1987.

539. 1948, January 29, at Belleville, Illinois, Cathedral of Saint Peter. Joseph Henry Leo Schlarman, Bishop of Peoria, assisted by John Patrick Cody, Titular Bishop of Apollonia, and Joseph Maximilian Mueller, Titular Bishop of Sinda, consecrated Albert Rudolph Zuroweste, Bishop of Belleville, born at East Saint Louis, Illinois (Belleville), April 26, 1901; priest June 8, 1924; named November 29, 1947; resigned August 30, 1976; died at Belleville March 28, 1987.

540. 1948, February 25, at Dallas, Texas, Sacred Heart Cathedral. Joseph Patrick Lynch, Bishop of Dallas, assisted by Christopher Edward Byrne, Bishop of Galveston, and Augustine Danglmayr, Titular Bishop of Olba, consecrated Wendelin Joseph Nold, Titular Bishop of Sasima, Coadjutor of Galveston, born at Bonham, Texas (Dallas), January 18, 1900; priest April 11, 1925; named November 29, 1947; succeeded to Galveston April 1, 1950; title of see changed to Galveston-Houston July 25, 1959; resigned April 22, 1975; died at Houston October 1, 1981.

541. 1948, April 5, at Spokane, Washington, Saint Aloysius Church. Edward Daniel Howard, Archbishop of Portland in Oregon, assisted by Charles Daniel White, Bishop of Spokane, and Martin Michael Johnson, Bishop of Nelson, consecrated Francis Doyle Gleeson, SJ, Titular Bishop of Cotenna, Vicar Apostolic of Alaska, born at Carrollton, Missouri (Saint Joseph), January 17, 1895; priest January 29, 1926; named January 8, 1948; first Bishop of Fairbanks August 8, 1962; Titular Bishop of Cuicul November 15, 1968; Bishop emeritus of Fairbanks January 13, 1971; died at Fairbanks April 30, 1983.

542.   1948, April 14, at Galveston, Texas, Saint Mary's Cathedral. Christopher Edward Byrne, Bishop of Galveston, assisted by Joseph Henry Albers, Bishop of Lansing, and Mariano Simon Garriga, Titular Bishop of Syene, consecrated Louis Joseph Reicher, first Bishop of Austin, born at Piqua, Ohio (Cincinnati), June 14, 1890; priest December 6, 1918; named November 29, 1947; resigned November 15, 1971; died near Austin February 23, 1984.

543.   1948, May 13, at Des Moines, Iowa, Saint Ambrose Cathedral. Amleto Giovanni Cicognani, Titular Archbishop of Laodicea in Phrygia, Apostolic Delegate in the United States, assisted by Henry Patrick Rohlman, Archbishop of Dubuque, and Leo Binz, Titular Bishop of Pinara, consecrated Edward Celestine Daly, OP, Bishop of Des Moines, born at Cambridge, Massachusetts (Boston), October 24, 1894; priest June 12, 1921; named March 13, 1948; died in a plane crash upon departure from Rome November 23, 1964.

544.   1948, May 18, at Cleveland, Ohio, Saint Agnes Church. Amleto Giovanni Cicognani, Titular Archbishop of Laodicea in Phrygia, Apostolic Delegate to the United States, assisted by Edward Francis Hoban, Bishop of Cleveland, and Floyd Lawrence Begin, Titular Bishop of Sala, consecrated John Francis Dearden, Titular Bishop of Sarepta, Coadjutor of Pittsburgh, born at Valley Falls, Rhode Island (Providence), October 15, 1907; priest December 8, 1932; named March 13, 1948; succeeded to Pittsburgh December 22, 1950; Archbishop of Detroit December 18, 1958; Cardinal April 28, 1969; resigned July 16, 1980; died at Southfield, Michigan, August 2, 1988.

545.   1948, May 20, at Saint Louis, Missouri, Saint Louis Cathedral. Joseph Elmer Ritter, Archbishop of Saint Louis, assisted by Mark Kenny Carroll, Bishop of Wichita, and John Patrick Cody, Titular Bishop of Apollonia, consecrated Leo John Steck, Titular Bishop of Ilium, Auxiliary of Salt Lake, born at Saint Louis, Missouri, August 30, 1898; priest June 8, 1924; named March 13, 1948; died at Saint Louis June 19, 1950.

546.   1948, May 26, at Bay Saint Louis, Mississippi, Our Lady of the Gulf Church. Richard Oliver Gerow, Bishop of Natchez, assisted by Leo Binz, Titular Bishop of Pinara, and Louis Abel Caillouet, Titular Bishop of Setea, consecrated Leo Fabian Fahey, Titular Bishop of Ipsus, Coadjutor of

Baker City, born at Bay Saint Louis, Mississippi (Natchez), July 21, 1898; priest May 29, 1926; named March 13, 1948; died at Baker March 31, 1950, 12 days before the death of the Bishop of Baker City.

547. 1948, June 29, at San Francisco, California, Cathedral of Saint Mary. John Joseph Mitty, Archbishop of San Francisco, assisted by Thomas Arthur Connolly, Titular Bishop of Sila, and Hugh Aloysius Donohoe, Titular Bishop of Taium, consecrated James Thomas O'Dowd, Titular Bishop of Cea, Auxiliary of San Francisco, born at San Francisco, California, August 4, 1907; priest June 4, 1932; named May 22, 1948; died at midnight February 4/5, 1950 in an automobile accident.

548. 1948, July 14, at Providence, Rhode Island, Cathedral of Saints Peter and Paul. Amleto Giovanni Cicognani, Titular Archbishop of Laodicea in Phrygia, Apostolic Delegate to the United States, assisted by Henry Joseph O'Brien, Bishop of Hartford, and James Louis Connolly, Titular Bishop of Mylasa, consecrated Russell Joseph McVinney, Bishop of Providence, born at Warren, Rhode Island (Providence), November 25, 1898; priest July 13, 1924; named May 29, 1948; died at Providence August 10, 1971.

549. 1948, October 28, at Erie, Pennsylvania, Saint Peter Cathedral. John Mark Gannon, Bishop of Erie, assisted by William Joseph Hafey, Bishop of Scranton, and William Tiburtius McCarty, Bishop of Rapid City, consecrated Edward Peter McManaman, Titular Bishop of Floriana, Auxiliary of Erie, born at Wilkes-Barre, Pennsylvania (Scranton), May 3, 1900; priest March 12, 1927; named July 24, 1948; died July 18, 1964.

550. 1948, December 16, at New York, New York, Saint Patrick's Cathedral. Francis Joseph Cardinal Spellman, Archbishop of New York, assisted by Joseph Patrick Donahue, Titular Bishop of Emmaus, and Stephen Joseph Donahue, Titular Bishop of Medea, consecrated Joseph Francis Flannelly, Titular Bishop of Metelis, Auxiliary of New York, born at New York, New York, October 22, 1894; priest September 1, 1918; named November 9, 1948; resigned as Auxiliary of New York November 8, 1969; died at New York May 23, 1973.

551–553. 1949, March 7, at Chicago, Illinois, Cathedral of the Holy Name. Samuel Alphonsus Cardinal Stritch, Archbishop of Chicago, assisted by John Joseph Boylan, Bishop of Rockford, and Albert Rudolph Zuroweste, Bishop of Belleville, consecrated (1) Martin Dewey McNamara, first Bishop of Joliet, born at Chicago, Illinois, May 12, 1898; priest December 23, 1922; named December 17, 1948; died at Rochester, Minnesota, May 23, 1966. Consecrated (2) William Edward Cousins, Titular Bishop of Forma, Auxiliary of Chicago, born at Chicago, Illinois,

August 20, 1902; priest April 23, 1927; named December 17, 1948; Bishop of Peoria May 19, 1952; Archbishop of Milwaukee December 18, 1958; resigned September 17, 1977; died at Milwaukee September 14, 1988. Consecrated (3) William Aloysius O'Connor, Bishop of Springfield in Illinois, born at Chicago, Illinois, December 27, 1903; priest September 24, 1927; named December 17, 1948; resigned July 22, 1975; died at Springfield, Illinois, November 14, 1983.

554. 1949, April 19, at Saint Louis, Missouri, Saint Louis Cathedral. Joseph Elmer Ritter, Archbishop of Saint Louis, assisted by John Patrick Cody, Titular Bishop of Apollonia, and Leo John Steck, Titular Bishop of Ilium, consecrated Charles Herman Helmsing, Titular Bishop of Axomis, Auxiliary of Saint Louis, born at Shrewsbury, Missouri (Saint Louis), March 23, 1908; priest June 10, 1933; named March 17, 1949; first Bishop of Springfield-Cape Girardeau August 24, 1956; Bishop of Kansas City-Saint Joseph January 27, 1962; resigned June 21, 1977.

555. 1949, July 14, at Milwaukee, Wisconsin, Saint John Cathedral. Moses Elias Kiley, Archbishop of Milwaukee, assisted by Stanislaus Vincent Bona, Bishop of Green Bay, and Albert Gregory Meyer, Bishop of Superior, consecrated John Benjamin Grellinger, Titular Bishop of Syene, Auxiliary of Green Bay, born at Milwaukee, Wisconsin, November 5, 1899; priest July 14, 1929; named May 16, 1949; resigned as Auxiliary of Green Bay September 21, 1974; died April 13, 1984.

556. 1949, December 21, at Philadelphia, Pennsylvania, Cathedral of Saints Peter and Paul. Dennis Joseph Cardinal Dougherty, Archbishop of Philadelphia, assisted by Hugh Louis Lamb, Titular Bishop of Helos, and Joseph Carroll McCormick, Titular Bishop of Ruspae, consecrated Francis Edward Hyland, Titular Bishop of Gomphi, Auxiliary of Savannah-Atlanta, born at Philadelphia, Pennsylvania, October 9, 1901; priest June 11, 1927; named October 15, 1949; first Bishop of Atlanta July 17, 1957; Titular Bishop of Bisica October 11, 1961; died at Philadelphia January 31, 1968.

557. 1950, January 18, at New York, New York, Saint Patrick's Cathedral. Francis Joseph Cardinal Spellman, Archbishop of New York, assisted by Thomas Edmund Molloy, Bishop of Brooklyn, and William Richard Arnold, Titular Bishop of Phocaea, consecrated James Henry Ambrose Griffiths, Titular Bishop of Gaza, Auxiliary of the Military Vicar of the United States, born at Brooklyn, New York, July 16, 1903; priest March 12, 1927; named October 15, 1949; Auxiliary of New York in September 1955; died at New York February 25, 1964.

558. 1950, March 14, at Washington, District of Columbia, Saint

Matthew's Cathedral. Amleto Giovanni Cicognani, Titular Archbishop of Laodicea in Phrygia, Apostolic Delegate to the United States, assisted by Patrick Aloysius O'Boyle, Archbishop of Washington, and John Michael McNamara, Titular Bishop of Eumenia, consecrated John Joyce Russell, Bishop of Charleston, born at Baltimore, Maryland, December 1, 1897; priest July 8, 1923; named January 28, 1950; Bishop of Richmond July 3, 1958; resigned April 3, 1973.

559. 1950, March 20, at Trenton, New Jersey, Saint Mary's Cathedral. Thomas Joseph Walsh, Archbishop of Newark, assisted by Bartholomew Joseph Eustace, Bishop of Camden, and Thomas Aloysius Boland, Bishop of Paterson, consecrated George William Ahr, Bishop of Trenton, born at Newark, New Jersey, June 23, 1904; priest July 29, 1928; named January 28, 1950; resigned June 23, 1979.

560. 1950, March 24, at New York, New York, Saint Patrick's Cathedral. Francis Joseph Cardinal Spellman, Archbishop of New York, assisted by Richard James Cushing, Archbishop of Boston, and Stephen Joseph Donahue, Titular Bishop of Medea, consecrated Christopher Joseph Weldon, Bishop of Springfield, Massachusetts, born at New York, New York, September 6, 1905; priest September 21, 1929; named January 28, 1950; resigned October 15, 1977; died at Springfield, Massachusetts, March 19, 1982.

561. 1950, May 23, at Detroit, Michigan, Cathedral of the Most Blessed Sacrament. Edward Aloysius Cardinal Mooney, Archbishop of Detroit, assisted by Stephen Stanislaus Woznicki, Bishop of Saginaw, and Allen James Babcock, Titular Bishop of Irenopolis, consecrated Alexander Mieceslaus Zaleski, Titular Bishop of Lyrbe, Auxiliary of Detroit, born at Laurel, New York (Brooklyn), June 24, 1906; priest July 12, 1931; named March 28, 1950; Coadjutor of Lansing October 7, 1964; succeeded to Lansing December 1, 1965; died at Miami, Florida, May 16, 1975.

562. 1950, June 8, at Syracuse, New York, Cathedral of the Immaculate Conception. Francis Joseph Cardinal Spellman, Archbishop of New York, assisted by Walter Andrew Foery, Bishop of Syracuse, and Bryan Joseph McEntegart, Bishop of Ogdensburg, consecrated David Frederick Cunningham, Titular Bishop of Lampsacus, Auxiliary of Syracuse, born at Walkerville, Montana (Helena), December 3, 1900; priest June 12, 1926; named April 5, 1950; Coadjutor of Syracuse June 16, 1967; succeeded to Syracuse August 4, 1970; resigned November 9, 1976; died at Syracuse February 22, 1979.

563. 1950, September 12, at Portland, Oregon, Cathedral of the Immaculate Conception. Edward Daniel Howard, Archbishop of

Portland in Oregon, assisted by Edwin Vincent O'Hara, Bishop of Kansas City, and Edward Joseph Kelly, Bishop of Boise City, consecrated Francis Peter Leipzig, Bishop of Baker City, born at Chilton, Wisconsin (Green Bay), June 29, 1895; priest April 14, 1920; named July 18, 1950; title of see changed to Baker February 16, 1952; resigned April 26, 1971; died at Beaverton, Oregon, January 17, 1981.

564–565. 1950, September 14, at Boston, Massachusetts, Cathedral of the Holy Cross. Richard James Cushing, Archbishop of Boston, assisted by Patrick Aloysius O'Boyle, Archbishop of Washington, and Thomas Kiely Gorman, Bishop of Reno, consecrated (1) Eric Francis MacKenzie, Titular Bishop of Alba, Auxiliary of Boston, born at Boston, Massachusetts, December 6, 1893; priest October 20, 1918; named July 11, 1950; died at Boston August 20, 1969. Consecrated (2) Thomas Francis Markham, Titular Bishop of Acalissus, Auxiliary of Boston, born at Lowell, Massachusetts (Boston), March 22, 1891; priest June 2, 1917; named July 18, 1950; died at Lowell July 9, 1952.

566. 1950, September 19, at Fort Wayne, Indiana, Cathedral of the Immaculate Conception. Amleto Giovanni Cicognani, Titular Archbishop of Laodicea in Phrygia, Apostolic Delegate to the United States, assisted by John Francis Noll, Bishop of Fort Wayne, and Joseph Mary Marling, Titular Bishop of Thasus, consecrated Leo Aloysius Pursley, Titular Bishop of Hadrianopolis in Pisidia, Auxiliary of Fort Wayne, born at Hartford City, Indiana (Fort Wayne), March 12, 1902; priest June 11, 1927; named July 18, 1950; Apostolic Administrator of Fort Wayne March 9, 1955; Bishop of Fort Wayne December 29, 1956; title of see changed to Fort Wayne-South Bend May 28, 1960; resigned August 24, 1976.

567. 1950, September 21, at San Francisco, California, Cathedral of Saint Mary. John Joseph Mitty, Archbishop of San Francisco, assisted by James Joseph Sweeney, Bishop of Honolulu, and Hugh Aloysius Donohoe, Titular Bishop of Taium, consecrated Merlin Joseph Guilfoyle, Titular Bishop of Bulla, Auxiliary of San Francisco, born at San Francisco, California, July 15, 1908; priest June 10, 1933; named August 24, 1950; Bishop of Stockton November 12, 1969; resigned September 4, 1979; died at Stockton November 20, 1981.

568. 1950, September 21, at Washington, District of Columbia, National Shrine of the Immaculate Conception. Amleto Giovanni Cicognani, Titular Archbishop of Laodicea in Phrygia, Apostolic Delegate to the United States, assisted by Patrick Aloysius O'Boyle, Archbishop of Washington, and Henry Joseph O'Brien, Bishop of Hartford, consecrated Patrick Joseph McCormick, Titular Bishop of Atenia, Auxiliary of Washington, Rector of The Catholic University of America, born at

Norwich, Connecticut (Hartford), December 10, 1880; priest July 6, 1904; Rector of The Catholic University of America in 1943; named June 14, 1950; died at Washington May 18, 1953.

569. 1951, February 22, at New Orleans, Louisiana, Saint Louis Cathedral. Amleto Giovanni Cicognani, Titular Archbishop of Laodicea in Phrygia, Apostolic Delegate to the United States, assisted by Jules Benjamin Jeanmard, Bishop of Lafayette, and Louis Abel Caillouet, Titular Bishop of Setea, consecrated Maurice Schexnayder, Titular Bishop of Tuscamia, Auxiliary of Lafayette, born at Wallace, Louisiana (New Orleans), August 13, 1895; priest April 11, 1925; named December 11, 1950; Bishop of Lafayette March 13, 1956; resigned November 7, 1972; died at Lafayette January 12, 1981.

570. 1951, April 11, at Raleigh, North Carolina, Cathedral of the Sacred Heart. Amleto Giovanni Cicognani, Titular Archbishop of Laodicea in Phrygia, Apostolic Delegate to the United States, assisted by Eugene Joseph McGuinness, Bishop of Oklahoma City and Tulsa, and Vincent Stanislaus Waters, Bishop of Raleigh, consecrated Joseph Lennox Federal, Titular Bishop of Appiaria, Auxiliary of Salt Lake City, born at Greensboro, North Carolina (Raleigh), January 3, 1910; priest December 8, 1934; named February 5, 1951 as Auxiliary of Salt Lake; title changed to Salt Lake City March 31, 1951; Coadjutor of Salt Lake City May 8, 1958; succeeded to Salt Lake City March 31, 1960; resigned April 22, 1980.

571. 1951, June 11, at Rome, Italy, Church of Saints John and Paul. Adeodato Cardinal Piazza, Bishop of Sabina e Poggio Mirteto, assisted by Leone di Nigris, Titular Archbishop of Philippi, and Martin John O'Connor, Titular Bishop of Thespiae, consecrated Fulton John Sheen, Titular Bishop of Caesariana, Auxiliary of New York, born at El Paso, Illinois (Peoria), May 8, 1895; priest September 20, 1919; named May 28, 1951; Bishop of Rochester October 21, 1966; Titular Archbishop of Newport October 15, 1969; died at New York December 9, 1979.

572. 1951, August 20, at Dubuque, Iowa, Saint Raphael's Cathedral. Leo Binz, Titular Archbishop of Silyum, assisted by Joseph Clement Willging, Bishop of Pueblo, and Edward Aloysius Fitzgerald, Bishop of Winona, consecrated Loras Thomas Lane, Titular Bishop of Bencenna, Auxiliary of Dubuque, born at Cascade, Iowa (Dubuque), October 19, 1910; priest March 19, 1937; named May 29, 1951; Bishop of Rockford October 11, 1956; died at Chicago July 22, 1968.

573. 1951, August 29, at Springfield, Illinois, Cathedral of the Immaculate Conception. Samuel Alphonsus Cardinal Stritch, Archbishop of Chicago, assisted by Mark Kenny Carroll, Bishop of Wichita, and

William Aloysius O'Connor, Bishop of Springfield in Illinois, consecrated John Baptist Franz, first Bishop of Dodge City, born at Springfield, Illinois (Alton), October 29, 1896; priest June 13, 1920; named May 27, 1951; Bishop of Peoria August 8, 1959; resigned May 24, 1971.

574. 1951, September 26, at Seattle, Washington, Saint James Cathedral. Thomas Arthur Connolly, Archbishop of Seattle, assisted by Charles Daniel White, Bishop of Spokane, and Hugh Aloysius Donohoe, Titular Bishop of Taium, consecrated Joseph Patrick Dougherty, first Bishop of Yakima, born at Kansas City, Kansas (Leavenworth), January 11, 1905; priest June 14, 1930; named July 9, 1951; Titular Bishop of Altinum February 5, 1969; Auxiliary of Los Angeles April 16, 1969; died at Washington July 10, 1970.

575. 1951, October 3, at Anchorage, Alaska, Holy Family Church. Francis Doyle Gleeson, Titular Bishop of Cotenna, assisted by Charles Daniel White, Bishop of Spokane, and Joseph Patrick Dougherty, Bishop of Yakima, consecrated Dermot Robert O'Flanagan, first Bishop of Juneau, born at Lahinch (Killaloe), Ireland, March 9, 1901; priest August 27, 1929; named July 9, 1951; Titular Bishop of Tricala June 19, 1968; Bishop emeritus of Juneau January 13, 1971; died at San Diego December 31, 1972.

576. 1951, October 9, at Omaha, Nebraska, Saint Cecilia's Cathedral. Gerald Thomas Bergan, Archbishop of Omaha, assisted by Louis Benedict Kucera, Bishop of Lincoln, and Edward Joseph Hunkeler, Bishop of Kansas City in Kansas, consecrated John Linus Paschang, Bishop of Grand Island, born at Hemingford, Nebraska (Omaha), October 5, 1895; priest June 12, 1921; named July 28, 1951; resigned July 25, 1972.

577. 1952, March 19, at Philadelphia, Pennsylvania, Cathedral of Saints Peter and Paul. Amleto Giovanni Cicognani, Titular Archbishop of Laodicea in Phrygia, Apostolic Delegate to the United States, assisted by Eugene Joseph McGuinness, Bishop of Oklahoma City and Tulsa, and William David O'Brien, Titular Bishop of Calynda, consecrated Joseph McShea, Titular Bishop of Mina, Auxiliary of Philadelphia, born at Lattimer, Pennsylvania (Scranton), February 22, 1907; priest December 6, 1931; named February 8, 1952; first Bishop of Allentown February 11, 1961; resigned February 3, 1983.

578. 1952, March 25, at Sioux Falls, South Dakota, Saint Joseph Cathedral. Amleto Giovanni Cicognani, Titular Archbishop of Laodicea in Phrygia, Apostolic Delegate to the United States, assisted by William Otterwell Brady, Bishop of Sioux Falls, and Francis Joseph Schenk, Bishop of Crookston, consecrated Lambert Anthony Hoch, Bishop of Bismarck, born at Elkton, South Dakota (Sioux Falls), February 6, 1903; priest May 30, 1928; named January 23, 1952; Bishop of Sioux Falls November 27, 1956; resigned June 13, 1978.

579. 1952, June 11, at Brooklyn, New York, Our Lady of the Angels Church. Thomas Edmund Molloy, Archbishop-Bishop of Brooklyn, assisted by Raymond Augustine Kearney, Titular Bishop of Lisinia, and Thomas John McDonnell, Titular Bishop of Sela, consecrated John Joseph Boardman, Titular Bishop of Gunela, Auxiliary of Brooklyn, born at Brooklyn, New York, November 7, 1894; priest May 21, 1921; named March 28, 1952; resigned as Auxiliary of Brooklyn in October 1977; died at Brooklyn July 17, 1978.

580. 1952, August 5, at Salt Lake City, Utah, Cathedral of the Madeleine. John Joseph Mitty, Archbishop of San Francisco, assisted by Thomas Kiely Gorman, Titular Bishop of Rhasus, and Joseph Lennox Federal, Titular Bishop of Appiaria, consecrated Robert Joseph Dwyer, Bishop of Reno, born at Salt Lake City, August 1, 1908; priest June 11, 1902; named May 19, 1952; Archbishop of Portland in Oregon December 9, 1966; resigned January 15, 1974; died at Oakland, California, March 24, 1976.

581–582. 1952, September 24, at Buffalo, New York, Saint Joseph's Cathedral. Amleto Giovanni Cicognani, Titular Archbishop of Laodicea in Phrygia, Apostolic Delegate to the United States, assisted by Raymond Augustine Kearney, Titular Bishop of Lysinia, and James Henry Ambrose Griffiths, Titular Bishop of Gaza, consecrated (1) James Johnston Navagh, Titular Bishop of Ombi, Auxiliary of Raleigh, born at Buffalo, New York, April 4, 1901; priest December 21, 1929; named July 29, 1952; Bishop of Ogdensburg May 2, 1957; Bishop of Paterson February 12, 1963; died at Rome October 2, 1965. Consecrated (2) Leo Richard Smith, Titular Bishop of Marida, Auxiliary of Buffalo, born at Attica, New York (Buffalo), August 31, 1905; priest December 21, 1929; named June 30, 1952; Bishop of Ogdensburg February 12, 1963; died at Rome October 9, 1963.

583. 1952, October 15, at Richmond, Virginia, Cathedral of the Sacred Heart. Peter Leo Ireton, Bishop of Richmond, assisted by Vincent Stanislaus Waters, Bishop of Raleigh, and John Francis Dearden, Bishop of Pittsburgh, consecrated Joseph Howard Hodges, Titular Bishop of Rusadus, Auxiliary of Richmond, born at Harpers Ferry, West Virginia (Richmond), October 8, 1911; priest December 8, 1935; named August 8, 1952; Coadjutor of Wheeling May 24, 1961; succeeded to Wheeling November 23, 1962; died at Wheeling January 27, 1985.

584. 1953, February 11, at Buffalo, New York, Saint Joseph's Cathedral. Joseph Aloysius Burke, Bishop of Buffalo, assisted by John Francis

O'Hara, Archbishop of Philadelphia, and Leo Richard Smith, Titular Bishop of Marida, consecrated Celestine Joseph Damiano, Titular Archbishop of Nicopolis in Epiro, Apostolic Delegate to South Africa, born at Dunkirk, New York (Buffalo), November 1, 1911; priest December 21, 1935; named November 27, 1952; Archbishop-Bishop of Camden January 24, 1960; died October 2, 1967.

585. 1953, March 19, at Hartford, Connecticut, Cathedral of Saint Joseph. Henry Joseph O'Brien, Bishop of Hartford, assisted by Francis Patrick Keough, Archbishop of Baltimore, and Matthew Francis Brady, Bishop of Manchester, consecrated John Francis Hackett, Titular Bishop of Helenopolis in Palestina, Auxiliary of Hartford, born at New Haven, Connecticut (Hartford), December 7, 1911; priest June 29, 1936; named December 10, 1952; resigned as Auxiliary of Hartford December 16, 1986.

586. 1953, May 5, at Rochester, New York, Sacred Heart Cathedral. Francis Joseph Cardinal Spellman, Archbishop of New York, assisted by Walter Andrew Foery, Bishop of Syracuse, and Alexander Mieceslaus Zaleski, Titular Bishop of Lyrbe, consecrated Lawrence Bernard Brennan Casey, Titular Bishop of Cea, Auxiliary of Rochester, born at Rochester, New York, September 6, 1905; priest June 7, 1930; named February 10, 1953; Bishop of Paterson March 4, 1966; resigned June 13, 1977; died at Paterson June 15, 1977.

587. 1953, September 2, at Cleveland, Ohio, Cathedral of Saint John the Evangelist. Amleto Giovanni Cicognani, Titular Archbishop of Laodicea in Phrygia, Apostolic Delegate to the United States, assisted by Edward Francis Hoban, Archbishop-Bishop of Cleveland, and Floyd Lawrence Begin, Titular Bishop of Sala, consecrated John Joseph Krol, Titular Bishop of Cadi, Auxiliary of Cleveland, born at Cleveland, Ohio, October 26, 1910; priest February 20, 1937; named July 11, 1953; Archbishop of Philadelphia February 11, 1961; Cardinal June 26, 1967; resigned February 11, 1988.

588. 1953, September 17, at Tucson, Arizona, Saint Augustine Cathedral. Daniel James Gercke, Bishop of Tucson, assisted by James Peter Davis, Bishop of San Juan, and Hugh Aloysius Donohoe, Titular Bishop of Taium, consecrated Francis Joseph Green, Titular Bishop of Serra, Auxiliary of Tucson, born at Corning, New York (Rochester), July 7, 1906; priest May 15, 1932; named May 29, 1953; Coadjutor of Tucson May 11, 1960; succeeded to Tucson September 28, 1960; resigned July 28, 1981.

589–590. 1953, October 5, at New York, New York, Saint Patrick's Cathedral. James Francis Aloysius Cardinal McIntyre, Archbishop of Los Angeles, assisted by William Aloysius Scully, Titular Bishop of Pharsalus, and Joseph Francis Flannelly, Titular Bishop of Metelis, consecrated (1) Walter Philip Kellenberg, Titular Bishop of Joannina, Auxiliary of New York, born at New York, New York, June 3, 1901; priest June 2, 1928; named August 25, 1953; Bishop of Ogdensburg January 19, 1954; first Bishop of Rockville Centre April 16, 1957; resigned May 3, 1976; died at Rockville Centre January 11, 1986. Consecrated (2) Edward Vincent Dargin, Titular Bishop of Amphipolis, Auxiliary of New York, born at New York, New York, April 25, 1898; priest September 23, 1922; named August 25, 1953; resigned as Auxiliary of New York August 11, 1973; died at New York April 20, 1981.

591. 1953, November 10, at Pittsburgh, Pennsylvania, Saint Paul Cathedral. Amleto Giovanni Cicognani, Titular Archbishop of Laodicea in Phrygia, Apostolic Delegate to the United States, assisted by John Francis Dearden, Bishop of Pittsburgh, and Michael Joseph Ready, Bishop of Columbus, consecrated Coleman Francis Carroll, Titular Bishop of Pitanae, Auxiliary of Pittsburgh, born at Pittsburgh, Pennsylvania, February 9, 1905; priest June 15, 1930; named August 25, 1953; first Bishop of Miami August 8, 1958; first Archbishop of Miami March 2, 1968; died at Miami July 26, 1977.

592. 1953, November 30, at Burlington, Vermont, Cathedral of the Immaculate Conception. Edward Francis Ryan, Bishop of Burlington, assisted by Vincent Stanislaus Waters, Bishop of Raleigh, and John Patrick Cody, Titular Bishop of Apollonia, consecrated Bernard Joseph Flanagan, first Bishop of Norwich, born at Proctor, Vermont (Burlington), March 31, 1908; priest December 8, 1931; named September 1, 1953; Bishop of Worcester August 8, 1959; resigned April 12, 1983.

593. 1953, December 29, at Chicago, Illinois, Cathedral of the Holy Name. Samuel Alphonsus Cardinal Stritch, Archbishop of Chicago, assisted by Martin Dewey McNamara, Bishop of Joliet, and William Aloysius O'Connor, Bishop of Springfield in Illinois, consecrated Raymond Peter Hillinger, Bishop of Rockford, born at Chicago, Illinois, May 2, 1904; priest April 2, 1932; named November 3, 1953; Titular Bishop of Derbe, Auxiliary of Chicago June 27, 1956; died at Chicago November 14, 1971.

594. 1954, February 24, at Baltimore, Maryland, Cathedral Basilica of the Assumption. Amleto Giovanni Cicognani, Titular Archbishop of Laodicea in Phrygia, Apostolic Delegate to the United States, assisted by John Joyce Russell, Bishop of Charleston, and Lawrence Joseph Shehan, Bishop of Bridgeport, consecrated Jerome Aloysius Daugherty Sebastian, Titular Bishop of Baris in Hellesponto, Auxiliary of Baltimore, born at Washington, District of Columbia (Baltimore), November 22, 1895; priest

May 25, 1922; named December 22, 1953; died at Baltimore October 11, 1960.

595. 1954, March 25, at Superior, Wisconsin, Cathedral of Christ the King. Albert Gregory Meyer, Archbishop of Milwaukee, assisted by William Patrick O'Connor, Bishop of Madison, and Francis Joseph Schenk, Bishop of Crookston, consecrated Joseph John Annabring, Bishop of Superior, born at Szataryliget (Csanad), Hungary, March 19, 1900; priest May 3, 1927; named January 19, 1954; died at Superior August 27, 1959.

596. 1954, May 5, at New York, New York, Saint Patrick's Cathedral. Francis Joseph Cardinal Spellman, Archbishop of New York, assisted by Joseph Francis Flannelly, Titular Bishop of Metelis, and Edward Vincent Dargin, Titular Bishop of Amphipolis, consecrated Joseph Maria Pernicone, Titular Bishop of Hadrianopolis in Honoriade, Auxiliary of New York, born at Regalbuto (Nicosia), Italy, November 4, 1903; priest December 18, 1926; named April 6, 1954; resigned as Auxiliary of New York November 28, 1978; died at the Bronx February 11, 1985.

597. 1954, May 25, at Cincinnati, Ohio, Saint Monica's Cathedral. Karl Joseph Alter, Archbishop of Cincinnati, assisted by Urban John Vehr, Archbishop of Denver, and George John Rehring, Bishop of Toledo, consecrated Clarence George Issenmann, Titular Bishop of Phytea, Auxiliary of Cincinnati, born at Hamilton, Ohio (Cincinnati), May 30, 1907; priest June 29, 1932; named March 24, 1954; Bishop of Columbus December 5, 1957; Titular Bishop of Filaca, Coadjutor and Apostolic Administrator of Cleveland October 7, 1964; succeeded to Cleveland September 22, 1966; resigned June 5, 1974; died at Cleveland July 27, 1982.

598. 1954, June 17, at Newark, New Jersey, Sacred Heart Cathedral. Thomas Aloysius Boland, Archbishop of Newark, assisted by Bartholomew Joseph Eustace, Bishop of Camden, and James Aloysius McNulty, Bishop of Paterson, consecrated Justin Joseph McCarthy, Titular Bishop of Doberus, Auxiliary of Newark, born at Sayre, Pennsylvania (Scranton), November 26, 1900; priest April 16, 1927; named March 27, 1954; Bishop of Camden January 27, 1957; died at Elizabeth, New Jersey, December 26, 1959.

599. 1954, June 29, at Saint Louis, Missouri, Saint Louis Cathedral. Joseph Elmer Ritter, Archbishop of Saint Louis, assisted by Mark Kenny Carroll, Bishop of Wichita, and John Patrick Cody, Titular Bishop of Apollonia, consecrated Leo Christopher Byrne, Titular Bishop of Sabadia, Auxiliary of Saint Louis, born at Saint Louis, Missouri, March 19, 1908; priest June 10, 1933; named May 21, 1954; Coadjutor of Wichita February

11, 1961; Apostolic Administrator of Wichita February 25, 1963; Titular Archbishop of Plestia, Coadjutor of Saint Paul and Minneapolis July 31, 1967; died at Saint Paul October 21, 1974.

600. 1954, September 8, at Boston, Massachusetts, Cathedral of the Holy Cross. Richard James Cushing, Archbishop of Boston, assisted by John Joseph Wright, Bishop of Worcester, and Vincent Stanislaus Waters, Bishop of Raleigh, consecrated Jeremiah Francis Minihan, Titular Bishop of Paphus, Auxiliary of Boston, born at Haverhill, Massachusetts (Boston), July 21, 1903; priest December 21, 1929; named May 21, 1954; died at Dublin August 14, 1973.

601. 1954, September 21, at San Francisco, California, Cathedral of Saint Mary. John Joseph Mitty, Archbishop of San Francisco, assisted by Thomas Arthur Connolly, Archbishop of Seattle, and James Joseph Sweeney, Bishop of Honolulu, consecrated John Joseph Scanlan, Titular Bishop of Cenae, Auxiliary of Honolulu, born at Iniscarra Cork (Cloyne), Ireland, May 24, 1906; priest June 22, 1930; named July 8, 1954; Apostolic Administrator of Honolulu November 10, 1967; Bishop of Honolulu March 6, 1968; resigned June 30, 1981.

602. 1954, September 21, at Washington, District of Columbia, National Shrine of the Immaculate Conception. Amleto Giovanni Cicognani, Titular Archbishop of Laodicea in Phrygia, Apostolic Delegate to the United States, assisted by Patrick Aloysius O'Boyle, Archbishop of Washington, and Henry Theophilus Klonowski, Titular Bishop of Daldis, consecrated Jerome Daniel Hannan, Bishop of Scranton, born at Pittsburgh, Pennsylvania, November 29, 1896; priest May 22, 1921; named August 17, 1954; died at Rome December 15, 1965.

603–604. 1954, October 26, at Detroit, Michigan, Cathedral of the Most Blessed Sacrament. Edward Aloysius Cardinal Mooney, Archbishop of Detroit, assisted by Allen James Babcock, Bishop of Grand Rapids, and Alexander Mieceslaus Zaleski, Titular Bishop of Lyrbe, consecrated (1) John Anthony Donovan, Titular Bishop of Rhasus, Auxiliary of Detroit, born at London, Ontario, Canada, August 5, 1911; priest December 8, 1935; named September 6, 1954; Bishop of Toledo February 25, 1967; resigned July 29, 1980. Consecrated (2) Henry Edmund Donnelly, Titular Bishop of Tymbrias, Auxiliary of Detroit, born at Hudson, Michigan (Detroit), August 28, 1904; priest August 17, 1930; named September 6, 1954; died at Detroit November 4, 1967.

605. 1954, October 28, at Burlington, Vermont, Cathedral of the Immaculate Conception. Edward Francis Ryan, Bishop of Burlington, assisted by Matthew Francis Brady, Bishop of Manchester, and Bernard

Joseph Flanagan, Bishop of Norwich, consecrated Robert Francis Joyce, Titular Bishop of Citium, Auxiliary of Burlington, born at Proctor, Vermont (Burlington), October 7, 1896; priest May 26, 1923; named July 8, 1954; Bishop of Burlington December 29, 1956; resigned December 14, 1971.

606. 1955, February 2, at Louisville, Kentucky, Cathedral of the Assumption. John Alexander Floersh, Archbishop of Louisville, assisted by Ralph Leo Hayes, Bishop of Davenport, and Clarence George Issenmann, Titular Bishop of Phytea, consecrated Charles Garrett Maloney, Titular Bishop of Capsa, Auxiliary of Louisville, born at Louisville, Kentucky, September 9, 1912; priest December 8, 1937; named December 30, 1954; resigned as Auxiliary of Louisville January 5, 1988.

607. 1955, March 6, at Rome, Vatican City, Saint Peter's Basilica. Eugene Cardinal Tisserant, Bishop of Ostia and of Porto e Santa Rufina, assisted by Pietro Sigismondi, Titular Archbishop of Neapolis in Pisidia, and Pietro Villa, Titular Bishop of Lystra, consecrated Nicholas Thomas Elko, Titular Bishop of Apollonias, Apostolic Administrator of the Exarchate of Pittsburgh of the Ruthenians, born at Donora, Pennsylvania (Pittsburgh of the Ruthenians), December 14, 1909; priest September 30, 1934; named February 5, 1955; Exarch of Pittsburgh of the Ruthenians September 5, 1955; first Bishop of Pittsburgh of the Ruthenians July 6, 1963; Titular Archbishop of Dara, Ordaining Prelate for the Byzantine Rite at Rome December 22, 1967; Auxiliary of Cincinnati August 10, 1971; resigned as Auxiliary of Cincinnati April 16, 1985.

608. 1955, March 24, at Birmingham, Alabama, Saint Paul's Co-cathedral. Thomas Joseph Toolen, Archbishop-Bishop of Mobile-Birmingham, assisted by Joseph Patrick Hurley, Archbishop-Bishop of Saint Augustine, and Richard Oliver Gerow, Bishop of Natchez-Jackson, consecrated Joseph Aloysius Durick, Titular Bishop of Cerbali, Auxiliary of Mobile-Birmingham, born at Dayton, Tennessee (Nashville), October 13, 1914; priest May 23, 1940; named December 30, 1954; Coadjutor of Nashville December 2, 1963; Apostolic Administrator of Nashville January 22, 1966; succeeded to Nashville September 4, 1969; resigned April 8, 1975.

609. 1955, June 7, at Brooklyn, New York, Our Lady of the Angels Church. Thomas Edmund Molloy, Archbishop-Bishop of Brooklyn, assisted by Raymond Augustine Kearney, Titular Bishop of Lysinia, and John Joseph Boardman, Titular Bishop of Gunela, consecrated Edmund Joseph Reilly, Titular Bishop of Nepte, Auxiliary of Brooklyn, born at New York, New York, March 25, 1897; priest April 1, 1922; named March 15, 1955; died at Brooklyn November 3, 1958.

610. 1955, September 21, at Helena, Montana, Cathedral of Saint Helena. Joseph Michael Gilmore, Bishop of Helena, assisted by Joseph Patrick Dougherty, Bishop of Yakima, and Joseph Clement Willging, Bishop of Pueblo, consecrated Bernard Joseph Topel, Titular Bishop of Binda, Coadjutor of Spokane, born at Bozeman, Montana (Helena), May 31, 1903; priest June 7, 1927; named August 9, 1955; succeeded to Spokane September 25, 1955; resigned April 11, 1978; died at Spokane October 22, 1986.

611. 1956, January 25, at New York, New York, Saint Patrick's Cathedral. Francis Joseph Cardinal Spellman, Archbishop of New York, assisted by Bryan Joseph McEntegart, Titular Bishop of Aradi, and Joseph Francis Flannelly, Titular Bishop of Metelis, consecrated Philip Joseph Furlong, Titular Bishop of Araxa, Auxiliary of New York and of the Military Vicariate of the United States, born at New York, New York, December 6, 1892; priest May 18, 1918; named December 3, 1955; resigned as Auxiliary of New York and of the Military Vicariate in 1971; died at New York April 13, 1989.

612. 1956, February 8, at Oklahoma City, Oklahoma, Cathedral of Our Lady of Perpetual Help. Eugene Joseph McGuinness, Bishop of Oklahoma City and Tulsa, assisted by Thomas Kiely Gorman, Bishop of Dallas-Fort Worth, and James Aloysius McNulty, Bishop of Paterson, consecrated Stephen Aloysius Leven, Titular Bishop of Bure, Auxiliary of San Antonio, born at Blackwell, Oklahoma (Oklahoma City), April 30, 1905; priest June 10, 1928; named December 3, 1955; Bishop of San Angelo October 20, 1969; resigned April 24, 1979; died at Oklahoma City June 28, 1983.

613. 1956, February 22, at San Antonio, Texas, Cathedral of San Fernando. Amleto Giovanni Cicognani, Titular Archbishop of Laodicea in Phrygia, Apostolic Delegate to the United States, assisted by Mariano Simon Garriga, Bishop of Corpus Christi, and Sydney Matthew Metzger, Bishop of El Paso, consecrated John Louis Morkovsky, Titular Bishop of Hieron, Auxiliary of Amarillo, born at Praha, Texas (San Antonio), August 16, 1909; priest December 5, 1933; named December 22, 1955; Bishop of Amarillo August 18, 1958; Titular Bishop of Tigava, Coadjutor of Galveston-Houston April 16, 1963; Apostolic Administrator of Galveston-Houston June 18, 1963; succeeded to Galveston-Houston April 22, 1975; resigned August 21, 1984; died at Tacoma, Washington, March 24, 1990.

614. 1956, May 1, at Harrisburg, Pennsylvania, Saint Patrick Cathedral. George Leo Leech, Bishop of Harrisburg, assisted by Michael Joseph Ready, Bishop of Columbus, and James Aloysius McNulty, Bishop of

Paterson, consecrated Lawrence Frederick Schott, Titular Bishop of Eluza, Auxiliary of Harrisburg, born at Philadelphia, Pennsylvania, July 26, 1907; priest July 15, 1935; named March 1, 1956; died at Danville, Pennsylvania, March 11, 1963.

615. 1956, May 22, at Pittsburgh, Pennsylvania, Saint Paul Cathedral. John Francis Dearden, Bishop of Pittsburgh, assisted by Jean Gay, Bishop of Basse Terre et Pointe a Pitre, and Thomas John McDonnell, Titular Bishop of Sela, consecrated Richard Henry Ackerman, CS.Sp, Titular Bishop of Lares, Auxiliary of San Diego, born at Pittsburgh, Pennsylvania, August 30, 1903; priest August 28, 1926; named April 6, 1956; Bishop of Covington April 4, 1960; resigned November 28, 1978.

616. 1956, May 31, at Seattle, Washington, Saint James Cathedral. Thomas Arthur Connolly, Archbishop of Seattle, assisted by Joseph Patrick Dougherty, Bishop of Yakima, and Hugh Aloysius Donohoe, Titular Bishop of Taium, consecrated Thomas Edward Gill, Titular Bishop of Lambaesis, Auxiliary of Seattle, born at Seattle, Washington, March 18, 1908; priest June 10, 1933; named April 8, 1956; died at Washington, District of Columbia, November 11, 1973.

617. 1956, June 4, at Los Angeles, California, Saint Vibiana's Cathedral. James Francis Aloysius Cardinal McIntyre, Archbishop of Los Angeles, assisted by Joseph Thomas McGucken, Titular Bishop of Sanavus, and Timothy Manning, Titular Bishop of Lesvi, consecrated Alden John Bell, Titular Bishop of Rhodopolis, Auxiliary of Los Angeles, born at Peterborough, Ontario, Canada, July 11, 1904; priest May 14, 1932; named April 11, 1956; Bishop of Sacramento March 30, 1962; resigned April 10, 1979; died at Sacramento August 28, 1982.

618. 1956, July 25, at Brooklyn, New York, Our Lady of Perpetual Help Church. Raymond Augustine Kearney, Titular Bishop of Lysinia, assisted by George William Ahr, Bishop of Trenton, and John Benjamin Grellinger, Titular Bishop of Syene, consecrated John Joseph Carberry, Titular Bishop of Elis, Coadjutor of Lafayette in Indiana, born at Brooklyn, New York, July 31, 1904; priest June 28, 1929; named May 3, 1956; succeeded to Lafayette in Indiana November 20, 1957; Bishop of Columbus January 16, 1965; Archbishop of Saint Louis February 17, 1968; Cardinal April 28, 1969; resigned July 31, 1979.

619. 1956, August 28, at Washington, District of Columbia, Saint Matthew's Cathedral. Amleto Giovanni Cicognani, Titular Archbishop of Laodicea in Phrygia, Apostolic Delegate to the United States, assisted by Patrick Aloysius O'Boyle, Archbishop of Washington, and John Michael McNamara, Titular Bishop of Eumenia, consecrated Philip Matthew

Hannan, Titular Bishop of Hieropolis, Auxiliary of Washington, born at Washington, District of Columbia (Baltimore), May 20, 1913; priest December 8, 1939; named June 16, 1956; Archbishop of New Orleans September 22, 1965; resigned December 6, 1988.

620. 1956, September 12, at Duluth, Minnesota, Chapel of Saint Scholastica's College. Amleto Giovanni Cicognani, Titular Archbishop of Laodicea in Phrygia, Apostolic Delegate to the United States, assisted by Thomas Anthony Welch, Bishop of Duluth, and Francis Joseph Schenk, Bishop of Crookston, consecrated Lawrence Alexander Glenn, Titular Bishop of Tuscamia, Auxiliary of Duluth, born at Bellingham, Washington (Nesqually), August 25, 1900; priest June 11, 1927; named July 13, 1956; Bishop of Crookston January 27, 1960; Titular Bishop of Blera July 24, 1968; Bishop emeritus of Crookston December 31, 1970; died at Bemidji, Minnesota, January 26, 1985.

621. 1956, October 9, at Corpus Christi, Texas, Corpus Christi Cathedral. Mariano Simon Garriga, Bishop of Corpus Christi, assisted by John Joseph Krol, Titular Bishop of Cadi, and Charles Garrett Maloney, Titular Bishop of Capsa, consecrated Adolph Marx, Titular Bishop of Citrus, Auxiliary of Corpus Christi, born at Cologne, Germany, February 18, 1915; priest May 2, 1940; named July 6, 1956; first Bishop of Brownsville July 19, 1965; died at Cologne October 31, 1965.

622. 1956, October 23, at Pittsburgh, Pennsylvania, Saint Paul Cathedral. Nicholas Thomas Elko, Titular Bishop of Apollonias, assisted by Ambrose Andrew Senyshyn, Titular Bishop of Maina, and Maxim Hermaniuk, Titular Bishop of Sinna, consecrated Stephen John Kocisko, Titular Bishop of Theveste, Auxiliary of Pittsburgh of the Ruthenians, born at Minneapolis, Minnesota (Pittsburgh of the Ruthenians), June 11, 1915; priest March 30, 1941; named July 20, 1956; first Bishop of Passaic of the Ruthenians July 6, 1963; Bishop of Pittsburgh of the Ruthenians December 22, 1967; first Archbishop of Munhall of the Ruthenians February 21, 1969; title of see changed to Pittsburgh of the Byzantines March 11, 1977.

623. 1956, October 24, at Germantown, Pennsylvania, Church of the Immaculate Conception. John Francis O'Hara, Archbishop of Philadelphia, assisted by Francis Edward Hyland, Bishop of Atlanta, and Joseph Carroll McCormick, Titular Bishop of Ruspae, consecrated Hubert James Cartwright, Titular Bishop of Neve, Coadjutor of Wilmington, born at Philadelphia, Pennsylvania, August 22, 1900; priest June 11, 1927; named August 3, 1956; died at Wilmington March 6, 1958.

624. 1956, November 8, at Philadelphia, Pennsylvania, Immaculate

Conception of the Blessed Virgin Mary Ukrainian Catholic Cathedral. Constantine Bohachevsky, Titular Archbishop of Beroe, assisted by Ambrose Andrew Senyshyn, Titular Bishop of Maina, and Nicholas Thomas Elko, Titular Bishop of Apollonias, consecrated Joseph Michael Schmondiuk, Titular Bishop of Zeugma in Syria, Auxiliary of Philadelphia of the Ukrainians, born at Wall, Pennsylvania (Philadelphia of the Ukrainians), August 6, 1912; priest March 29, 1936; named July 20, 1956; Bishop of Stamford of the Ukrainians August 14, 1961; Archbishop of Philadelphia of the Ukrainians September 20, 1977; died at Philadelphia December 25, 1978.

625. 1957, January 29, at Jackson, Mississippi, Saint Peter's Church. Richard Oliver Gerow, Bishop of Natchez-Jackson, assisted by Charles Pascal Greco, Bishop of Alexandria, and John Louis Morkovsky, Titular Bishop of Hieron, consecrated Joseph Bernard Brunini, Titular Bishop of Axomis, Auxiliary of Natchez-Jackson, born at Vicksburg, Mississippi (Natchez), July 24, 1909; priest December 5, 1933; named November 28, 1956 as Auxiliary of Natchez; title of see changed to Natchez-Jackson December 18, 1956; Apostolic Administrator of Natchez-Jackson July 11, 1966; Bishop Natchez-Jackson December 2, 1967; title of see changed to Jackson March 1, 1977; resigned January 24, 1984.

626. 1957, February 25, at Gary, Indiana, Holy Angels Cathedral. Amleto Giovanni Cicognani, Titular Archbishop of Laodicea in Phrygia, Apostolic Delegate to the United States, assisted by John Patrick Cody, Bishop of Kansas City-Saint Joseph, and Leo Aloysius Pursley, Bishop of Fort Wayne, consecrated Andrew Gregory Grutka, first Bishop of Gary, born at Joliet, Illinois (Chicago), November 17, 1908; priest December 5, 1933; named December 29, 1956; resigned July 9, 1984.

627. 1957, February 27, at Saint Paul, Minnesota, Cathedral of Saint Paul. William Otterwell Brady, Archbishop of Saint Paul, assisted by Francis Joseph Schenk, Bishop of Crookston, and James Joseph Byrne, Bishop of Boise City, consecrated Hilary Baumann Hacker, Bishop of Bismarck, born at New Ulm, Minnesota (Saint Paul), January 10, 1913; priest June 4, 1938; named December 29, 1956; resigned May 28, 1982.

628. 1957, February 27, at Fresno, California, Saint Therese Church. Aloysius Joseph Willinger, Bishop of Monterey-Fresno, assisted by Timothy Manning, Titular Bishop of Lesvi, and Merlin Joseph Guilfoyle, Titular Bishop of Bulla, consecrated Harry Anselm Clinch, Titular Bishop of Badia, Auxiliary of Monterey-Fresno, born at San Rafael, California (San Francisco), October 27, 1908; priest June 6, 1936; named November 28, 1956; Bishop of Monterey October 16, 1967; resigned January 19, 1982.

629–630. 1957, April 24, at Dubuque, Iowa, Saint Raphael's Cathedral. Amleto Giovanni Cicognani, Titular Archbishop of Laodicea in Phrygia, Apostolic Delegate to the United States, assisted by Leo Binz, Archbishop of Dubuque, and Loras Thomas Lane, Bishop of Rockford, consecrated (1) George Joseph Biskup, Titular Bishop of Hemeria, Auxiliary of Dubuque, born at Cedar Rapids, Iowa (Dubuque), August 23, 1911; priest March 19, 1937; named March 9, 1957; Bishop of Des Moines January 30, 1965; Titular Archbishop of Tamalluma, Coadjutor of Indianapolis July 20, 1967; succeeded to Indianapolis January 3, 1972; resigned March 26, 1979; died at Indianapolis October 17, 1979. Consecrated (2) James Vincent Casey, Titular Bishop of Citium, Auxiliary of Lincoln, born at Osage, Iowa (Dubuque), September 22, 1914; priest December 8, 1939; named April 5, 1957; Bishop of Lincoln June 14, 1957; Archbishop of Denver February 18, 1967; died at Denver March 14, 1986.

631. 1957, May 30, at Saint Louis, Missouri, Saint Louis. Joseph Elmer Ritter, Archbishop of Saint Louis, assisted by Charles Herman Helmsing, Bishop of Springfield-Cape Girardeau, and Leo Christopher Byrne, Titular Bishop of Sabadia, consecrated Glennon Patrick Flavin, Titular Bishop of Joannina, Auxiliary of Saint Louis, born at Saint Louis, Missouri, March 2, 1916; priest December 20, 1941; named April 17, 1957; Bishop of Lincoln May 29, 1967.

632. 1957, September 12, at Albany, New York, Cathedral of the Immaculate Conception. William Aloysius Scully, Bishop of Albany, assisted by Robert Francis Joyce, Bishop of Burlington, and Joseph Maria Pernicone, Titular Bishop of Hadrianopolis in Honoriade, consecrated Edward Joseph Maginn, Titular Bishop of Curium, Auxiliary of Albany, born at Glasgow, Scotland, January 4, 1897; priest June 10, 1922; named June 27, 1957; Apostolic Administrator of Albany January 1966 until March 13, 1969; resigned as Auxiliary of Albany July 8, 1972; died at Albany August 21, 1984.

633–634. 1957, September 24, at Newark, New Jersey, Sacred Heart Cathedral. Thomas Aloysius Boland, Archbishop of Newark, assisted by James Aloysius McNulty, Bishop of Paterson, and George William Ahr, Bishop of Trenton, consecrated (1) Walter William Curtis, Titular Bishop of Bisica, Auxiliary of Newark, born at Jersey City, New Jersey (Newark), May 3, 1913; priest December 8, 1937; named June 27, 1957; Bishop of Bridgeport September 23, 1961; resigned June 28, 1988. Consecrated (2) Martin Walter Stanton, Titular Bishop of Citium, Auxiliary of Newark, born at Jersey City, New Jersey (Newark), April 17, 1897; priest June 14, 1924; named June 27, 1957; resigned as Auxiliary of Newark April 17, 1972; died at Jersey City October 1, 1977.

635. 1957, November 30, at Rome, Italy, Chapel of the North American College.* Giuseppe Cardinal Pizzardo, assisted by Luigi Traglia, Titular Archbishop of Caesarea in Palestina, and Martin John O'Connor, Titular Bishop of Thespiae, consecrated Frederick William Freking, Bishop of Salina, born at Heron Lake, Minnesota (Winona), August 11, 1913; priest July 31, 1938; named October 10, 1957; Bishop of La Crosse December 30, 1964; resigned May 10, 1983.

Note: Bishop Freking is the first bishop to be consecrated in the chapel of the new North American College.

636. 1957, December 10, at New York, New York, Saint Patrick's Cathedral. Francis Joseph Cardinal Spellman, Archbishop of New York, assisted by Patrick Aloysius O'Boyle, Archbishop of Washington, and Edward Joseph Maginn, Titular Bishop of Curium, consecrated John Michael Fearns, Titular Bishop of Geras, Auxiliary of New York, born at New York, New York, June 25, 1897; priest February 19, 1922; named November 4, 1957; resigned as Auxiliary of New York August 12, 1972; died at New York July 4, 1977.

637. 1958, January 2, at Washington, District of Columbia, Saint Matthew's Cathedral. Amleto Giovanni Cicognani, Titular Archbishop of Laodicea in Phrygia, Apostolic Delegate to the United States, assisted by John Francis Dearden, Bishop of Pittsburgh, and Coleman Francis Carroll, Titular Bishop of Pitanae, consecrated Howard Joseph Carroll, Bishop of Altoona-Johnstown, born at Pittsburgh, Pennsylvania, August 5, 1902; priest April 2, 1927; named December 5, 1957; died at Washington March 21, 1960.

638–639. 1958, January 29, at Saint Paul, Minnesota, Cathedral of Saint Paul. William Otterwell Brady, Archbishop of Saint Paul, assisted by James Joseph Byrne, Bishop of Boise City, and Hilary Baumann Hacker, Bishop of Bismarck, consecrated (1) Alphonse James Schladweiler, first Bishop of New Ulm, born at Milwaukee, Wisconsin, July 18, 1902; priest June 9, 1929; named November 28, 1957; resigned December 23, 1975. Consecrated (2) Leonard Philip Cowley, Titular Bishop of Pertusa, Auxiliary of Saint Paul, born at Saint Paul, Minnesota, February 3, 1913; priest June 4, 1938; named November 28, 1957; Auxiliary of Saint Paul and Minneapolis July 11, 1966; died at Minneapolis August 18, 1973.

640. 1958, March 5, at Tulsa, Oklahoma, Holy Family Co-cathedral. Amleto Giovanni Cicognani, Titular Archbishop of Laodicea in Phrygia, Apostolic Delegate to the United States, assisted by Jeremiah Francis Minihan, Titular Bishop of Paphus, and Stephen Aloysius Leven, Titular Bishop of Bure, consecrated Victor Joseph Reed, Bishop of Oklahoma City and Tulsa, born at Montpelier, Indiana (Fort Wayne), December 23, 1905; priest December 21, 1929; named Titular Bishop of Limisa and Auxiliary of Oklahoma City and Tulsa December 5, 1957; Bishop of Oklahoma City and Tulsa January 21, 1958; died at Oklahoma City September 7, 1971.

641. 1958, June 17, at Cincinnati, Ohio, Cathedral of Saint Peter in Chains.* Karl Joseph Alter, Archbishop of Cincinnati, assisted by Clarence George Issenmann, Bishop of Columbus, and John Joseph Krol, Titular Bishop of Cadi, consecrated Paul Francis Leibold, Titular Bishop of Trebenna, Auxiliary of Cincinnati, born at Dayton, Ohio (Cincinnati), December 25, 1914; priest May 18, 1940; named April 10, 1958; Apostolic Administrator of Evansville in October 1965; Bishop of Evansville June 4, 1966; Archbishop of Cincinnati July 19, 1969; died at Cincinnati June 1, 1972.

---

*Note: This was the first consecration in this cathedral after its restoration.

642. 1958, September 24, at Baltimore, Maryland, Cathedral Basilica of the Assumption. Amleto Giovanni Cicognani, Titular Archbishop of Laodicea in Phrygia, Apostolic Delegate to the United States, assisted by Albert Gregory Meyer, Archbishop of Milwaukee, and Jerome Aloysius Daugherty Sebastian, Titular Bishop of Baris in Hellesponto, consecrated Michael William Hyle, Titular Bishop of Christopolis, Coadjutor of Wilmington, born at Baltimore, Maryland, October 13, 1901; priest March 12, 1927; named July 3, 1958; succeeded to Wilmington March 2, 1960; died at Wilmington December 26, 1967.

643. 1958, October 28, at Cleveland, Ohio, Cathedral of Saint John the Evangelist. Amleto Giovanni Cicognani, Titular Archbishop of Laodicea in Phrygia, Apostolic Delegate to the United States, assisted by Edward Francis Hoban, Archbishop-Bishop of Cleveland, and John Joseph Krol, Titular Bishop of Cadi, consecrated Paul John Hallinan, Bishop of Charleston, born at Painesville, Ohio (Cleveland), April 8, 1911; priest February 20, 1937; named September 9, 1958; first Archbishop of Atlanta February 19, 1962; died at Atlanta March 17, 1968.

644. 1959, March 19, at Fall River, Massachusetts, Cathedral of Saint Mary of the Assumption. James Louis Connolly, Bishop of Fall River, assisted by Russell Joseph McVinney, Bishop of Providence, and Jeremiah Francis Minihan, Titular Bishop of Paphus, consecrated James Joseph Gerrard, Titular Bishop of Forma, Auxiliary of Fall River, born at New Bedford, Massachusetts (Providence), June 9, 1897; priest May 26, 1923; named February 2, 1959; resigned as Auxiliary of Fall River in February 1976.

645. 1959, April 9, at Maryknoll, New York, Queen of the Apostles Chapel. Francis Joseph Cardinal Spellman, Archbishop of New York, assisted by Raymond Aloysius Lane, Titular Bishop of Hypaepa, and Martin Dewey McNamara, Bishop of Joliet, consecrated John William Comber, MM, Titular Bishop of Foratiana, Superior General of Maryknoll, born at Lawrence, Massachusetts (Boston), March 12, 1906; priest February 1, 1931; Superior General of Maryknoll from August 6, 1956 to August 1966; named January 13, 1959.

646–647. 1959, April 22, at Brooklyn, New York, Our Lady of Perpetual Help Church. Bryan Joseph McEntegart, Bishop of Brooklyn, assisted by James Henry Ambrose Griffiths, Titular Bishop of Gaza, and John Joseph Carberry, Bishop of Lafayette in Indiana, consecrated (1) Charles Richard Mulrooney, Titular Bishop of Valentiniana, Auxiliary of Brooklyn, born at Brooklyn, New York, January 13, 1906; priest June 10, 1930; named February 24, 1959; resigned as Auxiliary of Brooklyn January 13, 1981; died at Queens Village August 5, 1989. Consecrated (2) Joseph Peter Michael Denning, Titular Bishop of Mallus, Auxiliary of Brooklyn, born at Flushing, New York (Brooklyn), January 4, 1907; priest May 21, 1932; named February 24, 1959; resigned as Auxiliary of Brooklyn April 13, 1982; died at Elmhurst, New York, February 12, 1990.

648. 1959, May 19, at New Orleans, Louisiana, Saint Louis Cathedral. Egidio Vagnozzi, Titular Archbishop of Myra, Apostolic Delegate to the United States, assisted by Maurice Schexnayder, Bishop of Lafayette, and Louis Abel Caillouet, Titular Bishop of Setea, consecrated Robert Emmet Tracy, Titular Bishop of Sergentza, Auxiliary of Lafayette, born at New Orleans, Louisiana, September 14, 1909; priest June 12, 1932; named March 13, 1959; first Bishop of Baton Rouge August 10, 1961; resigned March 21, 1974; died at New Orleans April 4, 1980.

649. 1959, June 29, at New York, New York, Saint Patrick's Cathedral. Francis Joseph Cardinal Spellman, Archbishop of New York, assisted by Joseph Francis Flannelly, Titular Bishop of Metelis, and James Henry Ambrose Griffiths, Titular Bishop of Gaza, consecrated John Joseph Maguire, Titular Bishop of Antiphrae, Auxiliary of New York, born at New York, New York, December 11, 1904; priest December 22, 1928; named May 16, 1959; Titular Archbishop of Tabalta, Coadjutor *sedi datus* of New York September 15, 1965; resigned as Coadjutor *sedi datus* of New York January 8, 1980; died at New York July 6, 1989.

650. 1959, September 30, at Oklahoma City, Oklahoma, Cathedral of Our Lady of Perpetual Help. Victor Joseph Reed, Bishop of Oklahoma City and Tulsa, assisted by Stephen Aloysius Leven, Titular Bishop of Bure, and Glennon Patrick Flavin, Titular Bishop of Joannina, consecrated

Charles Albert Buswell, Bishop of Pueblo, born at Homestead, Oklahoma (Oklahoma), October 15, 1913; priest July 9, 1939; named August 8, 1959; resigned September 19, 1979.

651. 1959, December 21, at Boston, Massachusetts, Cathedral of the Holy Cross. Richard James Cardinal Cushing, Archbishop of Boston, assisted by Eric Francis MacKenzie, Titular Bishop of Alba, and Jeremiah Francis Minihan, Titular Bishop of Paphus, consecrated Thomas Joseph Riley, Titular Bishop of Regiae, Auxiliary of Boston, born at Waltham, Massachusetts (Boston), November 30, 1900; priest May 20, 1927; named October 31, 1959; resigned as Auxiliary of Boston June 28, 1976; died at Cambridge August 17, 1977.

652. 1960, January 1, at Alexandria, Egypt, Cathedral of the Dormition. Maximos IV Saigh, Patriarch of Antioch, of Alexandria and of Jerusalem of the Greek Melkite Catholics, assisted by Pierre Medawar, Titular Archbishop of Pelusium of the Greek Melkite Catholics, and Elias Zoghby, Titular Archbishop of Nubia, consecrated Joseph Elias Tawil, Titular Archbishop of Myra of the Greek Melkite Catholics, Greek Melkite Catholic Patriarcal Vicar at Damascus, Syria, born at Damascus, Syria, December 25, 1913; priest July 20, 1936; elected by the Greek Melkite Catholic Synod August 29, 1959; confirmed by the Holy See October 23, 1959; Apostolic Exarch for Greek Melkite Catholics in the United States October 31, 1969; first Bishop of Newton of the Greek Melkite Catholics, with the title of Archbishop *ad personam* June 28, 1976; resigned December 2, 1989.

653. 1960, February 25, at Chicago, Illinois, Cathedral of the Holy Name. Albert Gregory Cardinal Meyer, Archbishop of Chicago, assisted by Martin Dewey McNamara, Bishop of Joliet, and Raymond Peter Hillinger, Titular Bishop of Derbe, consecrated Ernest John Primeau, Bishop of Manchester, born at Chicago, Illinois, September 19, 1909; priest April 7, 1934; named November 27, 1959; resigned January 30, 1974; died at Manchester June 15, 1989.

654. 1960, February 25, at Trenton, New Jersey, Saint Mary's Cathedral. George William Ahr, Bishop of Trenton, assisted by James Aloysius McNulty, Bishop of Paterson, and James Henry Ambrose Griffiths, Titular Bishop of Gaza, consecrated James John Hogan, Titular Bishop of Philomelium, Auxiliary of Trenton, born at Philadelphia, Pennsylvania, October 17, 1911; priest December 8, 1937; named November 27, 1959; Bishop of Altoona-Johnstown May 23, 1966; resigned November 4, 1986.

655. 1960, March 17, at Norwich, Connecticut, Saint Patrick's Cathedral. Henry Joseph O'Brien, Archbishop of Hartford, assisted by Bernard

Joseph Flanagan, Bishop of Worcester, and John Francis Hackett, Titular Bishop of Helenopolis in Palestina, consecrated Vincent Joseph Hines, Bishop of Norwich, born at New Haven, Connecticut (Hartford), September 14, 1912; priest May 2, 1937; named November 27, 1959; resigned June 5, 1975.

656. 1960, March 24, at Cape Girardeau, Missouri, Cathedral of Saint Mary. Charles Herman Helmsing, Bishop of Springfield-Cape Girardeau, assisted by Mark Kenny Carroll, Bishop of Wichita, and Leo Christopher Byrne, Titular Bishop of Sabadia, consecrated Marion Francis Forst, Bishop of Dodge City, born at Saint Louis, Missouri, September 3, 1910; priest June 10, 1934; named January 2, 1960; Titular Bishop of Scala, Auxiliary of Kansas City in Kansas October 16, 1976; Bishop emeritus of Dodge City, resigning as Auxiliary of Kansas City in Kansas and from the titular see of Scala, December 23, 1986.

657. 1960, March 24, at Youngstown, Ohio, Cathedral of Saint Columba. Emmet Michael Walsh, Bishop of Youngstown, assisted by Clarence George Issenmann, Bishop of Columbus, and John Joseph Krol, Titular Bishop of Cadi, consecrated James William Malone, Titular Bishop of Alabanda, Auxiliary of Youngstown, born at Youngstown, Ohio (Cleveland), March 8, 1920; priest May 26, 1945; named January 2, 1960; Apostolic Administrator of Youngstown January 22, 1966; Bishop of Youngstown May 2, 1968.

658. 1960, May 4, at Greensburg, Pennsylvania, Blessed Sacrament Cathedral. Egidio Vagnozzi, Titular Archbishop of Myra, Apostolic Delegate to the United States, assisted by John Francis Dearden, Archbishop of Detroit, and Richard Henry Ackerman, Bishop of Covington, consecrated William Graham Connare, Bishop of Greensburg, born at Pittsburgh, Pennsylvania, December 11, 1911; priest June 14, 1936; named February 23, 1960; resigned January 20, 1987.

659. 1960, May 11, at Providence, Rhode Island, Cathedral of Saints Peter and Paul. Egidio Vagnozzi, Titular Archbishop of Myra, Apostolic Delegate to the United States, assisted by Russell Joseph McVinney, Bishop of Providence, and James Aloysius McNulty, Bishop of Paterson, consecrated Thomas Francis Maloney, Titular Bishop of Andropolis, Auxiliary of Providence, born at Providence, Rhode Island, April 17, 1903; priest July 13, 1930; named January 2, 1960; died at Providence September 10, 1962.

660. 1960, May 24, at Superior, Wisconsin, Mary E. Sawyer Civic Auditorium. Egidio Vagnozzi, Titular Archbishop of Myra, Apostolic Delegate to the United States, assisted by John Patrick Treacy, Bishop of

La Crosse, and William Patrick O'Connor, Bishop of Madison, consecrated George Albert Hammes, Bishop of Superior, born at Saint Joseph Ridge, Wisconsin (La Crosse), September 11, 1911; priest May 22, 1937; named March 28, 1960; resigned June 27, 1985.

661. 1960, October 6, at Brooklyn, New York, Our Lady of Perpetual Help Church. Bryan Joseph McEntegart, Bishop of Brooklyn, assisted by William Tiburtius McCarty, Bishop of Rapid City, and James Edward McManus, Bishop of Ponce, consecrated Edward John Harper, C.SS.R, Titular Bishop of Heraclea Pontica, Prelate of the Virgin Islands, born at Brooklyn, New York, July 23, 1910; priest June 18, 1939; named July 23, 1960; first Bishop of Saint Thomas April 20, 1977; resigned October 16, 1985.

662. 1960, October 28, at Rome, Vatican City, Saint Peter's Basilica. Pope John XXIII, assisted by Diego Venini, Titular Archbishop of Adana, and Benigno Carrara, Bishop of Imola, consecrated Edward Ernest Swanstrom, Titular Bishop of Arba, Auxiliary of New York, born at New York, New York, March 20, 1903; priest June 2, 1928; named September 14, 1960; resigned as Auxiliary of New York April 4, 1978; died at New York August 10, 1985.

663–664. 1960, December 21, at Chicago, Illinois, Cathedral of the Holy Name. Albert Gregory Cardinal Meyer, Archbishop of Chicago, assisted by William Aloysius O'Connor, Bishop of Springfield in Illinois, and Ernest John Primeau, Bishop of Manchester, consecrated (1) Cletus Francis O'Donnell, Titular Bishop of Abrittum, Auxiliary of Chicago, born at Waukon, Iowa (Dubuque), August 22, 1917; priest May 3, 1941; named October 26, 1960; Bishop of Madison February 18, 1967. Consecrated (2) Aloysius John Wycislo, Titular Bishop of Stadia, Auxiliary of Chicago, born at Chicago, Illinois, June 17, 1908; priest April 7, 1934; named October 7, 1960; Bishop of Green Bay March 4, 1968; resigned May 10, 1983.

665–666. 1960, December 22, at Philadelphia, Pennsylvania, Cathedral of Saints Peter and Paul. Egidio Vagnozzi, Titular Archbishop of Myra, Apostolic Delegate to the United States, assisted by Joseph McShea, Titular Bishop of Mina, and Joseph Carroll McCormick, Bishop of Altoona-Johnstown, consecrated (1) Francis James Furey, Titular Bishop of Temnus, Auxiliary of Philadelphia, born at Summit Hill, Pennsylvania (Philadelphia), February 22, 1905; priest March 15, 1930; named August 17, 1960; Coadjutor of San Diego July 21, 1963; Apostolic Administrator of San Diego September 12, 1963; succeeded to San Diego March 5, 1966; Archbishop of San Antonio May 23, 1969; died at San Antonio April 23, 1979. Consecrated (2) Cletus Joseph Benjamin, Titular Bishop of Binda,

Auxiliary of Philadelphia, born at Old Forge, Pennsylvania (Scranton), May 2, 1909; priest December 8, 1935; named August 17, 1960; died at Philadelphia May 15, 1961.

667. 1961, January 4, at Denver, Colorado, Cathedral of the Immaculate Conception. Egidio Vagnozzi, Titular Archbishop of Myra, Apostolic Delegate to the United States, assisted by Urban John Vehr, Archbishop of Denver, and Hubert Michael Newell, Bishop of Cheyenne, consecrated David Mono Maloney, Titular Bishop of Ruspae, Auxiliary of Denver, born at Littleton, Colorado (Denver), March 15, 1912; priest December 8, 1936; named November 5, 1960; Bishop of Wichita December 2, 1967; resigned July 16, 1982.

668. 1961, April 26, at Saint Cloud, Minnesota, Saint Mary's Cathedral. Peter William Bartholome, Bishop of Saint Cloud, assisted by Francis Joseph Schenk, Bishop of Duluth, and Joseph Maximilian Mueller, Bishop of Sioux City, consecrated Henry Joseph Soenneker, Bishop of Owensboro, born at Melrose, Minnesota (Saint Cloud), May 27, 1907; priest May 26, 1934; named March 10, 1961; resigned June 30, 1982; died at Owensboro September 24, 1987.

669. 1961, July 2, at Saint Paul, Minnesota, Cathedral of Saint Paul. William Otterwell Brady, Archbishop of Saint Paul, assisted by James Joseph Byrne, Bishop of Boise City, and Hilary Baumann Hacker, Bishop of Bismarck, consecrated Gerald Francis O'Keefe, Titular Bishop of Candyba, Auxiliary of Saint Paul, born at Saint Paul, Minnesota, March 30, 1918; priest January 29, 1944; named May 5, 1961; Auxiliary of Saint Paul and Minneapolis July 11, 1966; Bishop of Davenport October 20, 1966.

670. 1961, July 6, at Cleveland, Ohio, Cathedral of Saint John the Evangelist. Egidio Vagnozzi, Titular Archbishop of Myra, Apostolic Delegate to the United States, assisted by Paul John Hallinan, Bishop of Charleston, and Floyd Lawrence Begin, Titular Bishop of Sala, consecrated John Francis Whealon, Titular Bishop of Andrapa, Auxiliary of Cleveland, born at Barberton, Ohio (Cleveland), January 15, 1921; priest May 26, 1945; named June 5, 1961; Bishop of Erie December 9, 1966; Archbishop of Hartford December 28, 1968.

671. 1961, August 8, at Saint Louis, Missouri, Saint Louis Cathedral. Joseph Elmer Cardinal Ritter, Archbishop of Saint Louis, assisted by John Patrick Cody, Bishop of Kansas City-Saint Joseph, and Leo Christopher Byrne, Titular Bishop of Sabadia, consecrated George Joseph Gottwald, Titular Bishop of Cedamusa, Auxiliary of Saint Louis, born at Saint Louis,

Missouri, May 12, 1914; priest June 9, 1940; named June 23, 1961; resigned as Auxiliary of Saint Louis August 2, 1988.

672. 1961, October 26, at Philadelphia, Pennsylvania, Immaculate Conception of the Blessed Virgin Mary Ukrainian Catholic Cathedral. Ambrose Andrew Senyshyn, Archbishop of Philadelphia of the Ukrainians, assisted by Isidore Borecky, Bishop of Toronto of the Ukrainians, and Joseph Michael Schmondiuk, Bishop of Stamford of the Ukrainians, consecrated Jaroslav Gabro, first Bishop of Saint Nicholas of Chicago of the Ukrainians, born at Chicago, Illinois (Philadelphia of the Ukrainians), July 31, 1919; priest September 27, 1945; named August 14, 1961; died at Chicago March 28, 1980.

673. 1961, December 21, at Great Falls, Montana, Saint Anne's Cathedral. Egidio Vagnozzi, Titular Archbishop of Myra, Apostolic Delegate to the United States, assisted by William Joseph Condon, Bishop of Great Falls, and Joseph Michael Gilmore, Bishop of Helena, consecrated Eldon Bernard Schuster, Titular Bishop of Amblada, Auxiliary of Great Falls, born at Calio, North Dakota (Bismarck), March 10, 1911; priest May 27, 1937; named October 30, 1961; Bishop of Great Falls December 8, 1967; resigned December 27, 1977.

674. 1962, January 24, at San Antonio, Texas, Cathedral of the Sacred Heart. Robert Emmet Lucey, Archbishop of San Antonio, assisted by John Louis Morkovsky, Bishop of Amarillo, and Stephen Aloysius Leven, Titular Bishop of Bure, consecrated Thomas Joseph Drury, first Bishop of San Angelo, born at Ballynote (Achonry), Ireland, January 4, 1908; priest June 2, 1935; named October 30, 1961; Bishop of Corpus Christi July 19, 1965; resigned May 19, 1983.

675. 1962, February 22, at Richmond, Virginia, Cathedral of the Sacred Heart. Egidio Vagnozzi, Titular Archbishop of Myra, Apostolic Delegate to the United States, assisted by Vincent Stanislaus Waters, Bishop of Raleigh, and Joseph Howard Hodges, Titular Bishop of Rusadus, consecrated Ernest Leo Unterkoefler, Titular Bishop of Latopolis, Auxiliary of Richmond, born at Philadelphia, Pennsylvania, August 17, 1917; priest May 18, 1944; named December 11, 1961; Bishop of Charleston February 22, 1965; resigned February 22, 1990.

676. 1962, March 6, at Grand Rapids, Michigan, Saint Francis Church. Egidio Vagnozzi, Titular Archbishop of Myra, Apostolic Delegate to the United States, assisted by Allen James Babcock, Bishop of Grand Rapids, and Thomas Lawrence Noa, Bishop of Marquette, consecrated Charles Alexander Salatka, Titular Bishop of Cariana, Auxiliary of Grand Rapids, born at Grand Rapids, Michigan, February 26, 1918; priest February 24,

1945; named December 11, 1961; Bishop of Marquette January 5, 1968; Archbishop of Oklahoma City September 27, 1977.

677. 1962, April 5, at San Francisco, California, Cathedral of Saint Mary.* Egidio Vagnozzi, Titular Archbishop of Myra, Apostolic Delegate to the United States, assisted by Hugh Aloysius Donohoe, Bishop of Stockton, and Merlin Joseph Guilfoyle, Titular Bishop of Bulla, consecrated Leo Thomas Maher, first Bishop of Santa Rosa, born at Mount Union, Iowa (Davenport), July 1, 1915; priest December 18, 1943; named January 27, 1962; Bishop of San Diego August 22, 1969.

Note: This was the last consecration in this cathedral before it was destroyed by fire on September 7, 1962.

678. 1962, June 20, at Wichita, Kansas, Cathedral of the Immaculate Conception. Edward Joseph Hunkeler, Archbishop of Kansas City in Kansas, assisted by Charles Herman Helmsing, Bishop of Kansas City-Saint Joseph, and Marion Francis Forst, Bishop of Dodge City, consecrated Ignatius Jerome Strecker, Bishop of Springfield-Cape Girardeau, born at Spearville, Kansas (Wichita), November 23, 1917; priest December 19, 1942; named April 7, 1962; Archbishop of Kansas City in Kansas September 14, 1969.

679. 1962, June 29, at New York, New York, Saint Patrick's Cathedral. Francis Joseph Cardinal Spellman, Archbishop of New York, assisted by John Joseph Maguire, Titular Bishop of Antiphrae, and John Michael Fearns, Titular Bishop of Geras, consecrated Francis Frederick Reh, Bishop of Charleston, born at New York, New York, January 9, 1911; priest December 8, 1935; named June 4, 1962; Titular Bishop of Macriana in Mauritania, Rector of the North American College, Rome, September 5, 1964; Bishop of Saginaw December 11, 1968; resigned April 29, 1980.

680. 1962, July 3, at Baltimore, Maryland, Cathedral of Mary Our Queen. Egidio Vagnozzi, Titular Archbishop of Myra, Apostolic Delegate to the United States, assisted by John Joyce Russell, Bishop of Richmond, and Michael William Hyle, Bishop of Wilmington, consecrated Thomas Austin Murphy, Titular Bishop of Appiaria, Auxiliary of Baltimore, born at Baltimore, Maryland, May 11, 1911; priest June 10, 1937; named May 19, 1962; resigned as Auxiliary of Baltimore May 29, 1984.

681. 1962, July 22, at Guatemala City, Guatemala, Cathedral of Saint James (Santiago). Ambrogio Marchioni, Titular Archbishop of Severiana, Apostolic Nuncio to Guatemala, assisted by Mariano Rossell y Arellano, Archbishop of Guatemala, and Celestino Miguel Fernández Perez, Bishop of San Marcos, consecrated Hugo Mark Gerbermann, MM, Titular Bishop of Amathus in Palestina, Prelate of Huehuetenango, born at Nada, Texas (San Antonio), September 11, 1913; priest February 7, 1943; Prelate of Huehuetenango August 8, 1961; named Titular Bishop of Amathus in Palestina February 6, 1962; first Bishop of Huehuetenango December 23, 1967; Titular Bishop of Pinhel, Auxiliary of San Antonio July 22, 1975; resigned as Auxiliary of San Antonio June 30, 1982.

682. 1962, July 25, at Bismarck, North Dakota, Cathedral of the Holy Spirit. Hilary Baumann Hacker, Bishop of Bismarck, assisted by Peter William Bartholome, Bishop of Saint Cloud, and Lambert Anthony Hoch, Bishop of Sioux Falls, consecrated Sylvester William Treinen, Bishop of Boise City, born at Donnelly, Minnesota (Saint Cloud), November 19, 1917; priest June 11, 1946; named May 19, 1962; resigned August 17, 1988.

683. 1962, July 25, at Lafayette, Louisiana, Saint John Cathedral. Egidio Vagnozzi, Titular Archbishop of Myra, Apostolic Delegate to the United States, assisted by John Patrick Cody, Titular Archbishop of Bostra, and Maurice Schexnayder, Bishop of Lafayette, consecrated Warren Louis Boudreaux, Titular Bishop of Calynda, Auxiliary of Lafayette, born at Berwick, Louisiana (Lafayette), January 25, 1918; priest May 30, 1942; named May 19, 1962; Bishop of Beaumont June 4, 1971; first Bishop of Houma-Thibodaux March 2, 1977.

684. 1962, July 26, at Rockville Centre, New York, Saint Agnes Cathedral. Walter Philip Kellenberg, Bishop of Rockville Centre, assisted by James Henry Ambrose Griffiths, Titular Bishop of Gaza, and Charles Richard Mulrooney, Titular Bishop of Valentiniana, consecrated Vincent John Baldwin, Titular Bishop of Bencenna, Auxiliary of Rockville Centre, born at Brooklyn, New York, July 13, 1907; priest July 26, 1931; named June 4, 1962; resigned as Auxiliary of Rockville Centre June 5, 1979; died at West Islip, New York, September 16, 1979.

685. 1962, August 1, at Philadelphia, Pennsylvania, Cathedral of Saints Peter and Paul. Egidio Vagnozzi, Titular Archbishop of Myra, Apostolic Delegate to the United States, assisted by Joseph Carroll McCormick, Bishop of Altoona-Johnstown, and Francis James Furey, Titular Bishop of Temnus, consecrated Gerald Vincent McDevitt, Titular Bishop of Tigias, Auxiliary of Philadelphia, born at Philadelphia, Pennsylvania, February 23, 1917; priest May 30, 1942; named June 22, 1962; died at Philadelphia September 29, 1980.

686. 1962, August 5, at Dimane, Lebanon, Patriarcal Church of Our Lady of Dimane. Pierre Paul Meouchi, Patriarch of Antioch of the Maronites, assisted by Pierre Sfair, Titular Archbishop of Nisibi of the Maronites, and Abdallah Nujaim, Bishop of Baalbek of the Maronites, consecrated Francis Mansour Zayek, Titular Bishop of Callinicum of the Maronites, Auxiliary of the Ordinariate for Oriental Rites in Brazil for the Maronites, born at Manzanillo (Santiago de Cuba), Cuba, October 18, 1920; priest March 17, 1946; named May 30, 1962; first Apostolic Exarch for Maronites in the United States March 9, 1966; first Bishop of Saint Maron of Detroit of the Maronites November 29, 1971; title of see changed to Saint Maron of Brooklyn of the Maronites June 27, 1977; Archbishop *ad personam* December 10, 1982.

687. 1962, August 28, at Lansing, Michigan, Cathedral of Saint Mary. Joseph Henry Albers, Bishop of Lansing, assisted by Clarence George Issenmann, Bishop of Columbus, and Charles Alexander Salatka, Titular Bishop of Cariana, consecrated Michael Joseph Green, Titular Bishop of Trisipa, Auxiliary of Lansing, born at Saint Joseph, Michigan (Detroit), October 13, 1917; priest July 14, 1946; named June 22, 1962; Bishop of Reno March 11, 1967; resigned December 6, 1974; died at Pontiac, Michigan, August 30, 1982.

688. 1962, August 30, at Helena, Montana, Cathedral of Saint Helena. Egidio Vagnozzi, Titular Archbishop of Myra, Apostolic Delegate to the United States, assisted by Bernard Joseph Topel, Bishop of Spokane, and William Joseph Condon, Bishop of Great Falls, consecrated Raymond Gerhardt Hunthausen, Bishop of Helena, born at Anaconda, Montana (Helena), August 21, 1921; priest June 1, 1946; named July 8, 1962; Archbishop of Seattle February 13, 1975.

689. 1962, December 21, at Cleveland, Ohio, Cathedral of Saint John the Evangelist. Egidio Vagnozzi, Titular Archbishop of Myra, Apostolic Delegate to the United States, assisted by Floyd Lawrence Begin, Bishop of Oakland, and John Francis Whealon, Titular Bishop of Andrapa, consecrated Clarence Edward Elwell, Titular Bishop of Cone, Auxiliary of Cleveland, born at Cleveland, Ohio, February 4, 1904; priest March 17, 1929; named November 5, 1962; Bishop of Columbus May 24, 1968; died at Columbus February 16, 1973.

690–691. 1963, January 24, at Newark, New Jersey, Sacred Heart Cathedral. Thomas Aloysius Boland, Archbishop of Newark, assisted by James Aloysius McNulty, Bishop of Paterson, and Martin Walter Stanton, Titular Bishop of Citium, consecrated (1) John Joseph Dougherty, Titular Bishop of Cotenna, Auxiliary of Newark, born at Jersey City, New Jersey (Newark), September 16, 1907; priest July 23, 1933; named November 17, 1962; resigned as Auxiliary of Newark September 18, 1982; died at Teaneck, New Jersey, March 20, 1986. Consecrated (2) Joseph Arthur Costello, Titular Bishop of Choma, Auxiliary of Newark, born at Newark,

New Jersey, May 9, 1915; priest June 7, 1941; named November 17, 1962; died at Orange, New Jersey, September 22, 1978.

692. 1963, March 25, at Winona, Minnesota, Cathedral of the Sacred Heart. Edward Aloysius Fitzgerald, Bishop of Winona, assisted by Peter William Bartholome, Bishop of Saint Cloud, and Frederick William Freking, Bishop of Salina, consecrated George Henry Speltz, Titular Bishop of Claneus, Auxiliary of Winona, born at Winona, Minnesota, May 29, 1912; priest June 2, 1940; named February 12, 1963; Coadjutor of Saint Cloud April 4, 1966; succeeded to Saint Cloud January 21, 1968; resigned January 13, 1987.

693. 1963, May 30, at Fort Worth, Texas, Saint Patrick's Co-cathedral. Thomas Kiely Gorman, Bishop of Dallas-Fort Worth, assisted by Francis Joseph Green, Bishop of Tucson, and Albert Lewis Fletcher, Bishop of Little Rock, consecrated Lawrence Michael DeFalco, Bishop of Amarillo, born at McKeesport, Pennsylvania (Pittsburgh), August 25, 1915; priest June 11, 1942; named April 17, 1963; resigned August 28, 1979; died at Amarillo September 22, 1979.

694. 1963, September 3, at Madison, Wisconsin, Saint Raphael's Cathedral. William Patrick O'Connor, Bishop of Madison, assisted by Stanislaus Vincent Bona, Bishop of Green Bay, and John Patrick Treacy, Bishop of La Crosse, consecrated Jerome Joseph Hastrich, Titular Bishop of Gurza, Auxiliary of Madison, born at Milwaukee, Wisconsin, November 13, 1914; priest February 9, 1941; named July 25, 1963; Bishop of Gallup September 3, 1969; resigned March 20, 1990.

695. 1963, December 12, at Los Angeles, California, Saint Vibiana's Cathedral. James Francis Aloysius Cardinal McIntyre, Archbishop of Los Angeles, assisted by Joseph Thomas McGucken, Archbishop of San Francisco, and Alden John Bell, Bishop of Sacramento, consecrated John James Ward, Titular Bishop of Bria, Auxiliary of Los Angeles, born at Los Angeles, California (Monterey-Los Angeles), September 28, 1920; priest May 4, 1946; named October 10, 1963.

696–697. 1964, January 7, at Philadelphia, Pennsylvania, Cathedral of Saints Peter and Paul. John Joseph Krol, Archbishop of Philadelphia, assisted by George Leo Leech, Bishop of Harrisburg, and Gerald Vincent McDevitt, Titular Bishop of Tigias, consecrated (1) Joseph Thomas Daley, Titular Bishop of Barca, Auxiliary of Harrisburg, born at Connerton, Pennsylvania (Philadelphia), December 21, 1915; priest June 7, 1941; named November 25, 1963; Coadjutor of Harrisburg August 2, 1967; succeeded to Harrisburg October 19, 1971; died at Harrisburg September 2, 1983. Consecrated (2) John Joseph Graham, Titular Bishop of Sabrata,

Auxiliary of Philadelphia, born at Philadelphia, Pennsylvania, September 11, 1913; priest February 26, 1938; named November 25, 1963; resigned as Auxiliary of Philadelphia November 8, 1988.

698. 1964, January 30, at Providence, Rhode Island, Cathedral of Saints Peter and Paul. Russell Joseph McVinney, Bishop of Providence, assisted by Joseph McShea, Bishop of Allentown, and Gerald Vincent McDevitt, Titular Bishop of Tigias, consecrated Bernard Matthew Kelly, Titular Bishop of Tegea, Auxiliary of Providence, born at Providence, Rhode Island, May 7, 1918; priest June 3, 1944; named November 25, 1963; resigned as Auxiliary of Providence and from his titular see in June 1971.

699. 1964, March 19, at Omaha, Nebraska, Saint Cecilia's Cathedral. Gerald Thomas Bergan, Archbishop of Omaha, assisted by John Linus Paschang, Bishop of Grand Island, and James Vincent Casey, Bishop of Lincoln, consecrated Daniel Eugene Sheehan, Titular Bishop of Capsus, Auxiliary of Omaha, born at Emerson, Nebraska (Omaha), May 14, 1917; priest May 23, 1942; named January 13, 1964; Archbishop of Omaha June 18, 1969.

700. 1964, April 9, at New York, New York, Saint Patrick's Cathedral. Francis Joseph Cardinal Spellman, Archbishop of New York, assisted by Christopher Joseph Weldon, Bishop of Springfield, Massachusetts, and John Joseph Maguire, Titular Bishop of Antiphrae, consecrated Thomas Andrew Donnellan, Bishop of Ogdensburg, born at New York, New York, January 24, 1914; priest June 3, 1939; named February 28, 1964; Archbishop of Atlanta May 24, 1968; died at Atlanta October 15, 1987.

701. 1964, April 15, at Greensboro, North Carolina, Our Lady of Grace Church. Vincent Stanislaus Waters, Bishop of Raleigh, assisted by Joseph Lennox Federal, Bishop of Salt Lake City, and Albert Lewis Fletcher, Bishop of Little Rock, consecrated Charles Borromeo McLaughlin, Titular Bishop of Risinium, Auxiliary of Raleigh, born at New York, New York, September 26, 1913; priest June 7, 1941; named January 13, 1964; first Bishop of Saint Petersburg May 2, 1968; died at Saint Petersburg December 14, 1978.

702. 1964, April 21, at Pittsburgh, Pennsylvania, Saint Paul Cathedral. John Joseph Wright, Bishop of Pittsburgh, assisted by Richard Henry Ackerman, Bishop of Covington, and William Graham Connare, Bishop of Greensburg, consecrated Vincent Martin Leonard, Titular Bishop of Arsacal, Auxiliary of Pittsburgh, born at Pittsburgh, Pennsylvania, December 11, 1908; priest June 16, 1935; named February 28, 1964; Bishop of Pittsburgh June 1, 1969; resigned June 30, 1983.

703–704. 1964, May 19, at Washington, District of Columbia, National Shrine of the Immaculate Conception. Egidio Vagnozzi, Titular Archbishop of Myra, Apostolic Delegate to the United States, assisted by Patrick Aloysius O'Boyle, Archbishop of Washington, and Joseph Thomas McGucken, Archbishop of San Francisco, consecrated (1) William Joseph McDonald, Titular Bishop of Acquae Regiae, Auxiliary of Washington, born at Kilkenny (Ossory), Ireland, June 17, 1904; priest June 10, 1928; named March 17, 1964; Auxiliary of San Francisco July 26, 1967; resigned as Auxiliary of San Francisco June 5, 1979; died at San Francisco January 7, 1989. Consecrated (2) John Selby Spence, Titular Bishop of Aggersel, Auxiliary of Washington, born at Baltimore, Maryland, May 1, 1909; priest December 5, 1933; named March 17, 1964; died at Washington March 7, 1973.

705–706. 1964, June 29, at Buffalo, New York, Saint Joseph's Cathedral. James Aloysius McNulty, Bishop of Buffalo, assisted by Celestine Joseph Damiano, Archbishop-Bishop of Camden, and James Johnston Navagh, Bishop of Paterson, consecrated (1) Stanislaus Joseph Brzana, Titular Bishop of Cufruta, Auxiliary of Buffalo, born at Buffalo, New York, July 7, 1917; priest June 7, 1941; named May 14, 1964; Bishop of Ogdensburg August 19, 1968. Consecrated (2) Pius Anthony Benincasa, Titular Bishop of Buruni, Auxiliary of Buffalo, born at Niagara Falls, New York (Buffalo), July 8, 1913; priest March 27, 1937; named May 8, 1964; died at Buffalo August 12, 1986.

707. 1964, July 31, at Glennallen, Alaska, Copper Valley Mission Boarding School Chapel. Francis Joseph Cardinal Spellman, Archbishop of New York, assisted by Francis Doyle Gleeson, Bishop of Fairbanks, and Dermot Robert O'Flanagan, Bishop of Juneau, consecrated George Theodore Boileau, SJ, Titular Bishop of Ausuccura, Coadjutor of Fairbanks, born at Lathrop, Montana (Helena), September 12, 1912; priest June 13, 1948; named April 21, 1964; died at Seattle February 25, 1965.

708. 1964, November 30, at New York, New York, Saint Patrick's Cathedral. Francis Joseph Cardinal Spellman, Archbishop of New York, assisted by Christopher Joseph Weldon, Bishop of Springfield, Massachusetts, and John Joseph Maguire, Titular Bishop of Antiphrae, consecrated George Henry Guilfoyle, Titular Bishop of Marazanae, Auxiliary of New York, born at New York, New York, November 13, 1913; priest March 25, 1944; named October 17, 1964; Bishop of Camden January 2, 1968; resigned May 13, 1989.

709. 1965, January 28, at Hartford, Connecticut, Cathedral of Saint Joseph. Henry Joseph O'Brien, Archbishop of Hartford, assisted by Vincent Joseph Hines, Bishop of Norwich, and John Francis Hackett,

Titular Bishop of Helenopolis in Palestina, consecrated Joseph Francis Donnelly, Titular Bishop of Nabala, Auxiliary of Hartford, born at Norwich, Connecticut (Hartford), May 1, 1909; priest June 29, 1934; named November 9, 1964; died at New Haven June 30, 1977.

710. 1965, March 31, at Saint Paul, Minnesota, Cathedral of Saint Paul. Egidio Vagnozzi, Titular Archbishop of Myra, Apostolic Delegate to the United States, assisted by Leo Binz, Archbishop of Saint Paul, and James Joseph Byrne, Archbishop of Dubuque, consecrated James Patrick Shannon, Titular Bishop of Lacubaza, Auxiliary of Saint Paul, born at South Saint Paul, Minnesota (Saint Paul), February 16, 1921; priest June 8, 1946; named February 8, 1965; Auxiliary of Saint Paul and Minneapolis July 11, 1966; resigned as Auxiliary of Saint Paul and Minneapolis November 22, 1968; married in June 1969.

711. 1965, April 3, at Joliet, Illinois, Cathedral of Saint Raymond Nonnatus. Egidio Vagnozzi, Titular Archbishop of Myra, Apostolic Delegate to the United States, assisted by William Aloysius O'Connor, Bishop of Springfield in Illinois, and Ernest John Primeau, Bishop of Manchester, consecrated Romeo Roy Blanchette, Titular Bishop of Maxita, Auxiliary of Joliet, born at Saint George, Illinois (Chicago), January 6, 1913; priest April 3, 1937; named February 8, 1965; Bishop of Joliet July 19, 1966; resigned January 30, 1979; died at Joliet January 10, 1982.

712. 1965, May 26, at Sioux City, Iowa, Cathedral of the Epiphany. Egidio Vagnozzi, Titular Archbishop of Myra, Apostolic Delegate to the United States, assisted by James Joseph Byrne, Archbishop of Dubuque, and Joseph Maximilian Mueller, Bishop of Sioux City, consecrated Frank Henry Greteman, Titular Bishop of Vissalsa, Auxiliary of Sioux City, born at Willey, Iowa (Sioux City), December 25, 1907; priest December 8, 1932; named April 14, 1965; Bishop of Sioux City October 15, 1970; resigned January 25, 1983; died at West Palm Beach, Florida, March 21, 1987.

713. 1965, June 15, at Cincinnati, Ohio, Cathedral of Saint Peter in Chains. Karl Joseph Alter, Archbishop of Cincinnati, assisted by Clarence George Issenmann, Titular Bishop of Filaca, and John Anthony King Mussio, Bishop of Steubenville, consecrated Edward Anthony McCarthy, Titular Bishop of Tamascani, Auxiliary of Cincinnati, born at Cincinnati, Ohio, April 10, 1918; priest May 29, 1943; named April 14, 1965; first Bishop of Phoenix August 25, 1969; Coadjutor Archbishop of Miami July 5, 1976; succeeded to Miami July 26, 1977.

714. 1965, June 17, at Greensburg, Pennsylvania, Blessed Sacrament Cathedral. William Graham Connare, Bishop of Greensburg, assisted by George Leo Leech, Bishop of Harrisburg, and Vincent Martin Leonard,

Titular Bishop of Arsacal, consecrated Cyril John Vogel, Bishop of Salina, born at Pittsburgh, Pennsylvania, January 15, 1905; priest June 7, 1931; named April 14, 1965; died at Salina October 4, 1979.

715. 1965, June 29, at Erie, Pennsylvania, Saint Peter's Cathedral. John Joseph Krol, Archbishop of Philadelphia, assisted by John Selby Spence, Titular Bishop of Aggersel, and Joseph Francis Donnelly, Titular Bishop of Nabala, consecrated Alfred Michael Watson, Titular Bishop of Nationa, Auxiliary of Erie, born at Erie, Pennsylvania, July 11, 1907; priest May 10, 1934; named May 17, 1965; Bishop of Erie March 17, 1969; resigned July 16, 1982; died at Erie January 4, 1990.

716. 1965, August 5, at Chicago, Illinois, Cathedral of the Holy Name. Cletus Francis O'Donnell, Titular Bishop of Abrittum, assisted by Bernard Joseph Flanagan, Bishop of Worcester, and William Graham Connare, Bishop of Greensburg, consecrated Nevin William Hayes, O.Carm., Titular Bishop of Novasinna, Prelate of Sicuani, Peru, born at Chicago, Illinois, February 17, 1922; priest June 8, 1946; Prelate of Sicuani January 10, 1959; named Titular Bishop of Novasinna May 5, 1965; resigned as Prelate of Sicuani November 7, 1970; Auxiliary of Chicago February 2, 1971; died at Chicago July 12, 1988.

717. 1965, August 11, at Cleveland, Ohio, Cathedral of Saint John the Evangelist. Egidio Vagnozzi, Titular Archbishop of Myra, Apostolic Delegate to the United States, assisted by Leo Christopher Byrne, Titular Bishop of Sabadia, and Clarence George Issenmann, Titular Bishop of Filaca, consecrated Raymond Joseph Gallagher, Bishop of Lafayette in Indiana, born at Cleveland, Ohio, November 19, 1912; priest March 25, 1939; named June 21, 1965; resigned October 26, 1982.

718. 1965, August 26, at Dubuque, Iowa, Saint Raphael's Cathedral. Egidio Vagnozzi, Titular Archbishop of Myra, Apostolic Delegate to the United States, assisted by James Joseph Byrne, Archbishop of Dubuque, and James Vincent Casey, Bishop of Lincoln, consecrated Loras Joseph Watters, Titular Bishop of Fidoloma, Auxiliary of Dubuque, born at Dubuque, Iowa, October 14, 1915; priest June 7, 1941; named June 21, 1965; Bishop of Winona January 8, 1969; resigned October 14, 1986.

719–720. 1965, December 13, at New York, New York, Saint Patrick's Cathedral. Francis Joseph Cardinal Spellman, Archbishop of New York, assisted by Joseph Thomas McGucken, Archbishop of San Francisco, and John Joseph Maguire, Titular Archbishop of Tabalta, consecrated (1) William Joseph Moran, Titular Bishop of Centuria, Auxiliary of the Military Vicar of the United States, born at San Francisco, California, January 15, 1906; priest June 20, 1931; named September 15, 1965; resigned as Auxiliary of the Military Vicar January 15, 1981. Consecrated (2) Terence James Cooke, Titular Bishop of Summa, Auxiliary of New York, born at New York, New York, May 1, 1921; priest December 1, 1945; named September 15, 1965; Archbishop of New York March 2, 1968; Military Vicar of the United States April 4, 1968; Cardinal April 28, 1969; died at New York October 6, 1983.

721. 1965, December 20, at Detroit, Michigan, Cathedral of the Most Blessed Sacrament. John Francis Dearden, Archbishop of Detroit, assisted by John Anthony Donovan, Titular Bishop of Rhasus, and Gerald Vincent McDevitt, Titular Bishop of Tigias, consecrated Joseph Matthew Breitenbeck, Titular Bishop of Tepelta, Auxiliary of Detroit, born at Detroit, Michigan, August 3, 1914; priest May 30, 1942; named October 18, 1965; Bishop of Grand Rapids October 6, 1969; resigned June 24, 1989.

722. 1965, December 21, at Washington, District of Columbia, National Shrine of the Immaculate Conception. Egidio Vagnozzi, Titular Archbishop of Myra, Apostolic Delegate to the United States, assisted by William Edward Cousins, Archbishop of Milwaukee, and Patrick Aloysius O'Boyle, Archbishop of Washington, consecrated Paul Francis Tanner, Titular Bishop of Lamasba, General Secretary of the National Catholic Welfare Conference (now the United States Catholic Conference), born at Peoria, Illinois, January 15, 1905; priest May 30, 1931; named October 18, 1965; Bishop of Saint Augustine February 15, 1968; resigned April 21, 1979.

723. 1966, January 6, at New Orleans, Louisiana, Cathedral Basilica of Saint Louis. Egidio Vagnozzi, Titular Archbishop of Myra, Apostolic Delegate to the United States, assisted by Philip Matthew Hannan, Archbishop of New Orleans, and John Patrick Cody, Archbishop of Chicago, consecrated Harold Robert Perry, SVD, Titular Bishop of Mons in Mauritania, Auxiliary of New Orleans, born at Lake Charles, Louisiana (New Orleans), October 9, 1916; priest June 6, 1944; named September 29, 1965.

724. 1966, January 25, at Altoona, Pennsylvania, Cathedral of the Blessed Sacrament. Joseph Carroll McCormick, Bishop of Altoona-Johnstown, assisted by John Anthony King Mussio, Bishop of Steubenville, and John Joseph Boardman, Titular Bishop of Gunela, consecrated Jerome Arthur Pechillo, TOR, Titular Bishop of Novasparsa, Prelate of Coronel Oviedo, Paraguay, born at Brooklyn, New York, May 16, 1919; priest June 10, 1947; Prelate of Coronel Oviedo September 10, 1961; named Titular Bishop of Novasparsa October 20, 1965; resigned as Prelate of Coronel Oviedo and named Auxiliary of Newark March 6, 1976.

725. 1966, March 9, at Dallas, Texas, Sacred Heart Cathedral. Thomas Kiely Gorman, Bishop of Dallas-Fort Worth, assisted by Leo Aloysius Pursley, Bishop of Fort Wayne-South Bend, and Lawrence Michael DeFalco, Bishop of Amarillo, consecrated Thomas Ambrose Tschoepe, Bishop of San Angelo, born at Pilot Point, Texas (Dallas), December 17, 1915; priest May 30, 1943; named January 7, 1966; Bishop of Dallas August 22, 1969.

726. 1966, March 25, at Albany, New York, Cathedral of the Immaculate Conception. Francis Joseph Cardinal Spellman, Archbishop of New York, assisted by Edward Joseph Maginn, Titular Bishop of Curium, and Edward Ernest Swanstrom, Titular Bishop of Arba, consecrated John Joseph Thomas Ryan, first Archbishop of Anchorage, born at Albany, New York, November 1, 1913; priest June 3, 1939; named February 7, 1966; Apostolic Administrator of Juneau from June 19, 1968 to September 8, 1971; Titular Archbishop of Gabi, Coadjutor *sedi datus* of the Military Vicariate November 4, 1975; Military Ordinary of the United States March 16, 1985.

727. 1966, April 14, at Saint Paul, Minnesota, Cathedral of Saint Paul. Leo Binz, Archbishop of Saint Paul, assisted by Harold William Henry, Archbishop of Kwang Ju, and William Aloysius O'Connor, Bishop of Springfield in Illinois, consecrated James Edward Michaels, SSC, Titular Bishop of Verbe, Auxiliary of Kwang Ju, South Korea, born at Chicago, Illinois, May 30, 1926; priest December 21, 1951; named February 15, 1966; Auxiliary of Wheeling April 3, 1973; Auxiliary of Wheeling-Charleston August 21, 1974; resigned as Auxiliary of Wheeling-Charleston September 22, 1987 and became a Trappist.

728. 1966, April 26, at Washington, District of Columbia, Saint Matthew's Cathedral. Patrick Aloysius O'Boyle, Archbishop of Washington, assisted by Philip Matthew Hannan, Archbishop of New Orleans, and William Joseph McDonald, Titular Bishop of Acquae Regiae, consecrated Edward John Herrmann, Titular Bishop of Lamzella, Auxiliary of Washington, born at Baltimore, Maryland, November 6, 1913; priest June 12, 1947; named March 4, 1966; Bishop of Columbus June 26, 1973; resigned September 18, 1982.

729. 1966, April 26, at Charleston, South Carolina, Cathedral of Saint John the Baptist. Paul John Hallinan, Archbishop of Atlanta, assisted by Ernest Leo Unterkoefler, Bishop of Charleston, and Francis Frederick Reh, Titular Bishop of Macriana in Mauritania, consecrated Joseph Louis Bernardin, Titular Bishop of Lugura, Auxiliary of Atlanta, born at Columbia, South Carolina (Charleston), April 2, 1928; priest April 26, 1952; named March 4, 1966; resigned as Auxiliary of Atlanta April 5, 1968 upon appointment as General Secretary of the National Conference of Catholic Bishops; Archbishop of Cincinnati November 21, 1972; Archbishop of Chicago July 8, 1982; Cardinal February 2, 1983.

730. 1966, May 26, at New Orleans, Louisiana, Cathedral Basilica of Saint Louis. Egidio Vagnozzi, Titular Archbishop of Myra, Apostolic Delegate to the United States, assisted by Charles Pascal Greco, Bishop of Alexandria, and Louis Abel Caillouet, Titular Bishop of Setea, consecrated Joseph Gregory Vath, Titular Bishop of Novaliciana, Auxiliary of Mobile-Birmingham, born at New Orleans, Louisiana, March 12, 1918; priest June 7, 1941; named March 4, 1966; first Bishop of Birmingham September 29, 1969; died at Birmingham July 14, 1987.

731. 1966, May 29, at Boston, Massachusetts, Cathedral of the Holy Cross. Athanasios Toutoungi, Archbishop of Aleppo of the Greek Melkite Catholics, assisted by George Hakim, Archbishop of Akka of the Greek Melkite Catholics, and Paul Achkar, Archbishop of Laodicea de Syria of the Greek Melkite Catholics, consecrated Justin Abraham Najmy, BA, Titular Bishop of Augustopolis in Phrygia, first Apostolic Exarch for the Greek Melkite Catholics of the United States, born at Aleppo, Syria, April 23, 1898; priest December 25, 1926; named January 27, 1966; died at Manchester, New Hampshire, June 11, 1968.

732. 1966, June 1, at Hartford, Connecticut, Cathedral of Saint Joseph. Henry Joseph O'Brien, Archbishop of Hartford, assisted by Daniel Joseph Feeney, Bishop of Portland, and John Francis Hackett, Titular Bishop of Helenopolis in Palestina, consecrated Peter Leo Gerety, Titular Bishop of Crepedula, Coadjutor of Portland, born at Shelton, Connecticut (Hartford), July 19, 1912; priest June 29, 1939; named March 4, 1966; Apostolic Administrator of Portland February 2, 1967; succeeded to Portland September 15, 1969; Archbishop of Newark March 25, 1974; resigned May 30, 1986.

733. 1966, June 9, at Fall River, Massachusetts, Cathedral of Saint Mary of the Assumption. James Louis Connolly, Bishop of Fall River, assisted by James Joseph Gerrard, Titular Bishop of Forma, and Gerald Vincent McDevitt, Titular Bishop of Tigias, consecrated Humberto Sousa Medeiros, Bishop of Brownsville, born at Arrifes Sao Miguel (Angra), Azores, Portugal, October 6, 1915; priest June 15, 1946; named April 14, 1966; Archbishop of Boston September 8, 1970; Cardinal March 5, 1973; died at Boston September 17, 1983.

734. 1966, July 25, at Baltimore, Maryland, Cathedral of Mary Our Queen. Lawrence Joseph Cardinal Shehan, Archbishop of Baltimore, assisted by Sante Portalupi, Titular Archbishop of Christopolis, Apostolic

Nuncio to Honduras, and Bernardino Mazzarella, Bishop of Comayagua, consecrated Nicholas D'Antonio Salza, OFM, Titular Bishop of Giufi Salaria, Prelate of Olancho, Honduras, born at Rochester, New York, July 10, 1916; priest June 7, 1942; Prelate of Olancho December 28, 1963; named Titular Bishop of Giufi Salaria April 19, 1966; resigned as Prelate of Olancho August 6, 1977; Vicar General of New Orleans August 22, 1977.

735. 1966, September 8, at Pittsburgh, Pennsylvania, Saint Paul Cathedral. John Joseph Wright, Bishop of Pittsburgh, assisted by William Graham Connare, Bishop of Greensburg, and Vincent Martin Leonard, Titular Bishop of Arsacal, consecrated John Bernard McDowell, Titular Bishop of Tamazuca, Auxiliary of Pittsburgh, born at New Castle, Pennsylvania (Pittsburgh), July 17, 1921; priest November 4, 1945; named July 19, 1966.

736. 1966, September 28, at Houston, Texas, Saint Vincent de Paul Church. John Louis Morkovsky, Titular Bishop of Tigava, assisted by Leo Christopher Byrne, Titular Bishop of Sabadia, and James John Hogan, Bishop of Altoona-Johnstown, consecrated Vincent Medeley Harris, first Bishop of Beaumont, born at Conroe, Texas (Galveston), October 14, 1913; priest March 19, 1938; named July 4, 1966; Titular Bishop of Rotaria, Coadjutor of Austin April 21, 1971; succeeded to Austin November 15, 1971; resigned December 19, 1985; died at Houston March 31, 1988.

737. 1966, October 5, at Richmond, Virginia, Cathedral of the Sacred Heart. John Joyce Russell, Bishop of Richmond, assisted by Vincent Stanislaus Waters, Bishop of Raleigh, and Joseph Howard Hodges, Bishop of Wheeling, consecrated James Louis Flaherty, Titular Bishop of Tabuda, Auxiliary of Richmond, born at Norfolk, Virginia (Richmond), May 13, 1910; priest December 8, 1936; named August 8, 1966; died at Norfolk July 28, 1975.

738. 1966, December 8, at Camden, New Jersey, Saint Joseph's Procathedral. Celestine Joseph Damiano, Archbishop-Bishop of Camden, assisted by James John Hogan, Bishop of Altoona-Johnstown, and Pius Anthony Benincasa, Titular Bishop of Buruni, consecrated James Louis Schad, Titular Bishop of Panatoria, Auxiliary of Camden, born at Philadelphia, Pennsylvania, July 20, 1917; priest April 10, 1943; named October 18, 1966.

739. 1967, January 25, at Baltimore, Maryland, Cathedral of Mary Our Queen. Lawrence Joseph Cardinal Shehan, Archbishop of Baltimore, assisted by John Joyce Russell, Bishop of Richmond, and Thomas Austin Murphy, Titular Bishop of Appiaria, consecrated Thomas Joseph

Mardaga, Titular Bishop of Mutugenna, Auxiliary of Baltimore, born at Baltimore, Maryland, May 14, 1913; priest May 14, 1940; named December 9, 1966; Bishop of Wilmington March 9, 1968; died at Wilmington May 28, 1984.

740. 1967, April 3, at Kansas City, Missouri, Cathedral of the Immaculate Conception. Charles Herman Helmsing, Bishop of Kansas City-Saint Joseph, assisted by John Patrick Cody, Archbishop of Chicago, and Joseph Mary Marling, Bishop of Jefferson City, consecrated Joseph Vincent Sullivan, Titular Bishop of Thagamuta, Auxiliary of Kansas City-Saint Joseph, born at Kansas City, Missouri, August 15, 1919; priest June 1, 1946; named March 4, 1967; Bishop of Baton Rouge August 8, 1974; died at Baton Rouge September 4, 1982.

741. 1967, April 14, at Saginaw, Michigan, Saint Mary Cathedral. John Francis Dearden, Archbishop of Detroit, assisted by Stephen Stanislaus Woznicki, Bishop of Saginaw, and Stephen Aloysius Leven, Titular Bishop of Bure, consecrated James Aloysius Hickey, Titular Bishop of Taraqua, Auxiliary of Saginaw, born at Midland, Michigan (Detroit), October 11, 1920; priest June 15, 1946; named February 18, 1967; Rector of the North American College, Rome, in March 1969; Bishop of Cleveland June 5, 1974; Archbishop of Washington August 17, 1980; Cardinal June 28, 1988.

742. 1967, April 21, at New York, New York, Saint Patrick's Cathedral. Francis Joseph Cardinal Spellman, Archbishop of New York, assisted by Terence James Cooke, Titular Bishop of Summa, and George Henry Guilfoyle, Titular Bishop of Marazanae, consecrated Edwin Bernard Broderick, Titular Bishop of Thizica, Auxiliary of New York, born at New York, New York, January 16, 1917; priest May 30, 1942; named March 4, 1967; Bishop of Albany March 13, 1969; resigned June 3, 1976.

743. 1967, May 25, at Boston, Massachusetts, Cathedral of the Holy Cross. Richard James Cardinal Cushing, Archbishop of Boston, assisted by Walter William Curtis, Bishop of Bridgeport, and Edward Ernest Swanstrom, Titular Bishop of Arba, consecrated James Edward Charles Burke, OP, Titular Bishop of Lamiggiga, Prelate of Chimbote, Peru, born at Philadelphia, Pennsylvania, November 30, 1926; priest June 8, 1956; Prelate of Chimbote March 8, 1965; named Titular Bishop of Lamiggiga April 8, 1967; resigned as Prelate of Chimbote June 2, 1978; Episcopal Vicar of Wilmington August 31, 1978.

744. 1967, August 8, at New Orleans, Louisiana, Cathedral Basilica of Saint Louis. Philip Matthew Hannan, Archbishop of New Orleans, assisted by Charles Pascal Greco, Bishop of Alexandria, and Robert Emmet

151

Tracy, Bishop of Baton Rouge, consecrated Gerard Louis Frey, Bishop of Savannah, born at New Orleans, Louisiana, May 10, 1914; priest April 2, 1938; named May 29, 1967; Bishop of Lafayette November 7, 1972; resigned May 13, 1989.

745–747. 1967, August 24, at Chicago, Illinois, Cathedral of the Holy Name. John Patrick Cardinal Cody, Archbishop of Chicago, assisted by Cletus Francis O'Donnell, Bishop of Madison, and Aloysius John Wycislo, Titular Bishop of Stadia, consecrated (1) Thomas Joseph Grady, Titular Bishop of Vamalla, Auxiliary of Chicago, born at Chicago, Illinois, October 9, 1914; priest April 23, 1938; named June 16, 1967; Bishop of Orlando November 6, 1974; resigned December 12, 1989. Consecrated (2) William Edward McManus, Titular Bishop of Mesarfelta, Auxiliary of Chicago, born at Chicago, Illinois, January 27, 1914; priest April 15, 1939; named June 16, 1967; Bishop of Fort Wayne-South Bend August 24, 1976; resigned February 18, 1985. Consecrated (3) John Lawrence May, Titular Bishop of Tagarbala, Auxiliary of Chicago, born at Evanston, Illinois (Chicago), March 31, 1922; priest May 3, 1947; named June 16, 1967; Bishop of Mobile October 8, 1969; Archbishop of Saint Louis January 24, 1980.

748. 1967, December 12, at San Diego, California, Saint Joseph Cathedral. Luigi Raimondi, Titular Archbishop of Tarsus, Apostolic Delegate to the United States, assisted by Francis James Furey, Bishop of San Diego, and Frederick William Freking, Bishop of La Crosse, consecrated John Raphael Quinn, Titular Bishop of Thisiduo, Auxiliary of San Diego, born at Riverside, California (Los Angeles-San Diego), March 28, 1929; priest July 19, 1953; named October 21, 1967; Bishop of Oklahoma City and Tulsa November 18, 1971; first Archbishop of Oklahoma City December 13, 1972; Archbishop of San Francisco February 16, 1977.

749. 1967, December 12, at Trenton, New Jersey, Saint Mary's Cathedral. George William Ahr, Bishop of Trenton, assisted by Walter William Curtis, Bishop of Bridgeport, and James John Hogan, Bishop of Altoona-Johnstown, consecrated John Charles Reiss, Titular Bishop of Simidicca, Auxiliary of Trenton, born at Red Bank, New Jersey (Trenton), May 13, 1922; priest May 31, 1947; named October 21, 1967; Bishop of Trenton March 5, 1980.

750. 1968, January 4, at San Francisco, California, Saint Ignatius Church. Joseph Thomas McGucken, Archbishop of San Francisco, assisted by Hugh Aloysius Donohoe, Bishop of Stockton, and Ernest John Primeau, Bishop of Manchester, consecrated Mark Joseph Hurley, Titular Bishop of Thunusuda, Auxiliary of San Francisco, born at San Francisco, California, December 13, 1919; priest September 23, 1944; named November 21, 1967;

Bishop of Santa Rosa November 12, 1969; resigned April 15, 1986.

751. 1968, January 6, at Guatemala City, Guatemala, Cathedral of Saint James (Santiago). Bruno Torpigliani, Titular Archbishop of Malliana, Apostolic Nuncio to Guatemala, assisted by Mario Casariego, Archbishop of Guatemala, and Rafael González Estrada, Titular Bishop of Matrega, consecrated Richard James Ham, MM, Titular Bishop of Puzia in Numidia, Auxiliary of Guatemala, born at Chicago, Illinois, July 11, 1921; priest June 12, 1948; named November 28, 1967; resigned as Auxiliary of Guatemala in February 1979; Episcopal Vicar of Saint Paul and Minneapolis in January 1980; Auxiliary of Saint Paul and Minneapolis October 7, 1980.

752. 1968, February 22, at Fairbanks, Alaska, Sacred Heart Cathedral. Luigi Raimondi, Titular Archbishop of Tarsus, Apostolic Delegate to the United States, assisted by John Joseph Thomas Ryan, Archbishop of Anchorage, and Francis Doyle Gleeson, Bishop of Fairbanks, consecrated Robert Louis Whelan, SJ, Titular Bishop of Sicilibba, Coadjutor of Fairbanks, born at Wallace, Idaho (Boise City), April 16, 1912; priest June 17, 1944; named November 29, 1967; succeeded to Fairbanks November 15, 1968; resigned June 1, 1985.

753–754. 1968, March 14, at Rochester, New York, Sacred Heart Cathedral. Luigi Raimondi, Titular Archbishop of Tarsus, Apostolic Delegate to the United States, assisted by Fulton John Sheen, Bishop of Rochester, and James Edward Kearney, Titular Bishop of Tabaicara, consecrated (1) Dennis Walter Hickey, Titular Bishop of Rusucurru, Auxiliary of Rochester, born at Danville, New York (Rochester), October 28, 1914; priest June 7, 1941; named January 5, 1968; resigned as Auxiliary of Rochester January 16, 1990. Consecrated (2) John Edgar McCafferty, Titular Bishop of Tanudaia, Auxiliary of Rochester, born at New York, New York, January 6, 1920; priest March 17, 1945; named January 5, 1968; died at Rochester April 29, 1980.

755. 1968, April 3, at Joliet, Illinois, Cathedral of Saint Raymond Nonnatus. John Patrick Cardinal Cody, Archbishop of Chicago, assisted by Romeo Roy Blanchette, Bishop of Joliet, and Cletus Francis O'Donnell, Bishop of Madison, consecrated Raymond James Vonesh, Titular Bishop of Vanariona, Auxiliary of Joliet, born at Chicago, Illinois, January 25, 1916; priest May 3, 1941; named January 5, 1968.

756–757. 1968, May 1, at Detroit, Michigan, Cathedral of the Most Blessed Sacrament. John Francis Dearden, Archbishop of Detroit, assisted by Alexander Mieceslaus Zaleski, Bishop of Lansing, and Joseph Matthew Breitenbeck, Titular Bishop of Tepelta, consecrated (1) Walter

Joseph Schoenherr, Titular Bishop of Timidana, Auxiliary of Detroit, born at Center Line, Michigan (Detroit), February 28, 1920; priest October 27, 1945; named March 4, 1968. Consecrated (2) Thomas John Gumbleton, Titular Bishop of Ululi, Auxiliary of Detroit, born at Detroit, Michigan, January 26, 1930; priest June 2, 1956; named March 4, 1968.

758. 1968, June 5, at Houston, Texas, Sacred Heart Co-cathedral. Thomas Kiely Gorman, Bishop of Dallas-Fort Worth, assisted by John Louis Morkovsky, Titular Bishop of Tigava, and Frank Henry Greteman, Titular Bishop of Vissalsa, consecrated John Joseph Cassata, Titular Bishop of Bida, Auxiliary of Dallas-Fort Worth, born at Galveston, Texas, November 8, 1908; priest December 8, 1932; named March 12, 1968; first Bishop of Fort Worth August 22, 1969; resigned September 16, 1980; died at Houston September 8, 1989.

759–760. 1968, June 13, at Chicago, Illinois, Quigley Seminary South, Sacred Heart Chapel. John Patrick Cardinal Cody, Archbishop of Chicago, assisted by Ernest John Primeau, Bishop of Manchester, and Cletus Francis O'Donnell, Bishop of Madison, consecrated (1) Alfred Leo Abramowicz, Titular Bishop of Pesto, Auxiliary of Chicago, born at Chicago, Illinois, January 27, 1919; priest May 1, 1943; named May 2, 1968. Consecrated (2) Michael Ryan Patrick Dempsey, Titular Bishop of Tronto, Auxiliary of Chicago, born at Chicago, Illinois, September 10, 1918; priest May 1, 1943; named May 2, 1968; died at Chicago January 8, 1974.

761. 1968, June 14, at Baton Rouge, Louisiana, Saint Joseph Cathedral. Luigi Raimondi, Titular Archbishop of Tarsus, Apostolic Delegate to the United States, assisted by Robert Emmet Tracy, Bishop of Baton Rouge, and Louis Abel Caillouet, Titular Bishop of Setea, consecrated William Donald Borders, first Bishop of Orlando, born at Washington, Indiana (Indianapolis), October 9, 1913; priest May 18, 1940; named May 2, 1968; Archbishop of Baltimore March 25, 1974; resigned April 6, 1989.

762. 1968, June 19, at Davenport, Iowa, Sacred Heart Cathedral. Luigi Raimondi, Titular Archbishop of Tarsus, Apostolic Delegate to the United States, assisted by Ralph Leo Hayes, Titular Bishop of Naraggara, and Gerald Francis O'Keefe, Bishop of Davenport, consecrated Maurice John Dingman, Bishop of Des Moines, born at West Point, Iowa (Davenport), January 20, 1914; priest December 8, 1939; named April 2, 1968; resigned October 14, 1986.

763. 1968, July 2, at Worcester, Massachusetts, Saint Paul's Cathedral. Bernard Joseph Flanagan, Bishop of Worcester, assisted by John Joseph Wright, Bishop of Pittsburgh, and Christopher Joseph Weldon, Bishop of

Springfield, consecrated Timothy Joseph Harrington, Titular Bishop of Rusuca, Auxiliary of Worcester, born at Holyoke, Massachusetts (Springfield), December 19, 1918; priest June 19, 1946; named April 2, 1968; Bishop of Worcester September 1, 1983.

764. 1968, August 28, at Miami, Florida, Saint Mary's Cathedral. Coleman Francis Carroll, Archbishop of Miami, assisted by Joseph Aloysius Durick, Titular Bishop of Cerbali, and Joseph Louis Bernardin, Titular Bishop of Lugura, consecrated John Joseph Fitzpatrick, Titular Bishop of Cenae, Auxiliary of Miami, born at Trenton, Ontario (Kingston), Canada, October 12, 1918; priest December 13, 1942; named June 24, 1968; Bishop of Brownsville April 21, 1971.

765. 1968, September 3, at Cleveland, Ohio, Cathedral of Saint John the Evangelist. Clarence George Issenmann, Bishop of Cleveland, assisted by John Francis Whealon, Bishop of Erie, and Harold Robert Perry, Titular Bishop of Mons in Mauritania, consecrated William Michael Cosgrove, Titular Bishop of Trisipa, Auxiliary of Cleveland, born at Canton, Ohio (Cleveland), November 26, 1916; priest December 18, 1943; named June 12, 1968; Bishop of Belleville August 30, 1976; resigned May 19, 1981.

766. 1968, September 11, at Baltimore, Maryland, Cathedral of Mary Our Queen. Lawrence Joseph Cardinal Shehan, Archbishop of Baltimore, assisted by Thomas Austin Murphy, Titular Bishop of Appiaria, and Thomas Joseph Mardaga, Bishop of Wilmington, consecrated Francis Joseph Gossman, Titular Bishop of Agunto, Auxiliary of Baltimore, born at Baltimore, Maryland, April 1, 1930; priest December 17, 1955; named July 15, 1968; Bishop of Raleigh April 2, 1975.

767. 1968, September 12, at Boston, Massachusetts, Cathedral of the Holy Cross. Richard James Cardinal Cushing, Archbishop of Boston, assisted by Jeremiah Francis Minihan, Titular Bishop of Paphus, and Thomas Joseph Riley, Titular Bishop of Regiae, consecrated Daniel Anthony Cronin, Titular Bishop of Egnatia, Auxiliary of Boston, born at Boston, Massachusetts, November 14, 1927; priest December 20, 1952; named June 10, 1968; Bishop of Fall River October 30, 1970.

768. 1968, September 12, at Brooklyn, New York, Our Lady of Perpetual Help Church. Luigi Raimondi, Titular Archbishop of Tarsus, Apostolic Delegate to the United States, assisted by Terence James Cooke, Archbishop of New York, and John Joseph Boardman, Titular Bishop of Gunela, consecrated Francis John Mugavero, Bishop of Brooklyn, born at Brooklyn, New York, June 8, 1914; priest May 18, 1940; named July 15, 1968; resigned February 10, 1990.

769. 1968, September 26, at Grand Rapids, Michigan, Saint Andrew's Cathedral. John Francis Dearden, Archbishop of Detroit, assisted by Allen James Babcock, Bishop of Grand Rapids, and Charles Alexander Salatka, Bishop of Marquette, consecrated Joseph Crescent McKinney, Titular Bishop of Lentini, Auxiliary of Grand Rapids, born at Grand Rapids, Michigan, September 10, 1928; priest December 20, 1953; named July 19, 1968.

770. 1968, October 11, at Rockford, Illinois, Saint Peter's Cathedral. Luigi Raimondi, Titular Archbishop of Tarsus, Apostolic Delegate to the United States, assisted by Leo Binz, Archbishop of Saint Paul and Minneapolis, and James Joseph Byrne, Archbishop of Dubuque, consecrated Arthur Joseph O'Neill, Bishop of Rockford, born at East Dubuque, Illinois (Rockford), December 14, 1917; priest March 27, 1943; named August 19, 1968.

771. 1968, October 17, at Huron, South Dakota, The Huron Arena. Lambert Anthony Hoch, Bishop of Sioux Falls, assisted by Francis Joseph Schenk, Bishop of Duluth, and Thomas Joseph Riley, Titular Bishop of Regiae, consecrated Paul Francis Anderson, Titular Bishop of Polignano, Coadjutor of Duluth, born at Roslindale, Massachusetts (Boston), April 20, 1917; priest January 6, 1943; named July 19, 1968; succeeded to Duluth April 30, 1969; resigned and named Auxiliary of Sioux Falls August 17, 1982; died at Rochester, Minnesota, January 4, 1987.

772. 1968, October 24, at Passaic, New Jersey, Saint Michael the Archangel Cathedral. Stephen John Kocisko, Bishop of Pittsburgh of the Ruthenians, assisted by Augustine Eugene Hornyak, Titular Bishop of Hermonthis, and Michael Rusnak, Titular Bishop of Tzernicus, consecrated Michael Joseph Dudick, Bishop of Passaic of the Ruthenians, born at Saint Clair, Pennsylvania (Pittsburgh of the Ruthenians), February 24, 1916; priest November 13, 1945; named July 29, 1968.

773. 1969, January 6, at Rome, Vatican City, Saint Peter's Basilica. Pope Paul VI, assisted by Sergio Pignedoli, Titular Archbishop of Iconium, and Ernesto Civardi, Titular Archbishop of Sardica, consecrated Bernard Joseph McLaughlin, Titular Bishop of Mottola, Auxiliary of Buffalo, born at Buffalo, New York, November 19, 1912; priest December 21, 1935; named December 28, 1968; resigned as Auxiliary of Buffalo January 5, 1988.

774. 1969, March 25, at Saint Louis, Missouri, Saint Louis Cathedral. John Joseph Carberry, Archbishop of Saint Louis, assisted by Leo Byrne, Titular Archbishop of Plestia, and Charles Herman Helmsing, Bishop of Kansas City-Saint Joseph, consecrated Joseph Alphonsus McNicholas,

Titular Bishop of Scala, Auxiliary of Saint Louis, born at Saint Louis, Missouri, January 13, 1923; priest June 7, 1949; named January 31, 1969; Bishop of Springfield in Illinois July 22, 1975; died at Springfield April 17, 1983.

775. 1969, April 23, at Denver, Colorado, Cathedral of the Immaculate Conception. Luigi Raimondi, Titular Archbishop of Tarsus, Apostolic Delegate to the United States, assisted by James Vincent Casey, Archbishop of Denver, and Hubert Michael Newell, Bishop of Cheyenne, consecrated George Roche Evans, Titular Bishop of Tubyza, Auxiliary of Denver, born at Denver, Colorado, September 25, 1922; priest May 31, 1947; named February 24, 1969; died at Denver September 13, 1985.

776. 1969, April 25, at Little Rock, Arkansas, Cathedral of Saint Andrew. Albert Lewis Fletcher, Bishop of Little Rock, assisted by Lawrence Michael DeFalco, Bishop of Amarillo, and Warren Louis Boudreaux, Titular Bishop of Calynda, consecrated Lawrence Preston Joseph Graves, Titular Bishop of Vina, Auxiliary of Little Rock, born at Texarkana, Arkansas (Little Rock), May 4, 1916; priest June 11, 1942; named February 24, 1969; Bishop of Alexandria May 10, 1973; Bishop of Alexandria-Shreveport October 18, 1976; resigned July 20, 1982.

777. 1969, May 1, at Seattle, Washington, Saint James Cathedral. Thomas Arthur Connolly, Archbishop of Seattle, assisted by Thomas Edward Gill, Titular Bishop of Lambaesis, and Joseph Patrick Dougherty, Titular Bishop of Altino, consecrated Cornelius Michael Power, Bishop of Yakima, born at Seattle, Washington, December 18, 1913; priest June 3, 1939; named February 5, 1969; Archbishop of Portland in Oregon January 15, 1974; resigned July 1, 1986; Apostolic Administrator of Portland in Oregon from July 1, 1986 until September 21, 1986.

778. 1969, June 12, at Parma, Ohio, Saint John the Baptist Cathedral. Stephen John Kocisko, Archbishop of Munhall of the Ruthenians, assisted by Michael Joseph Dudick, Bishop of Passaic of the Ruthenians, and Michael Rusnak, Titular Bishop of Tzernicus, consecrated Emil John Mihalik, first Bishop of Parma of the Ruthenians, born at Pittsburgh, Pennsylvania, February 7, 1920; priest September 21, 1945; named March 22, 1969; died at Cleveland January 27, 1984.

779. 1969, August 18, at Jefferson City, Missouri, Saint Joseph Cathedral. Luigi Raimondi, Titular Archbishop of Tarsus, Apostolic Delegate to the United States, assisted by Charles Herman Helmsing, Bishop of Kansas City-Saint Joseph, and Joseph Mary Marling, Titular Bishop of Lesina, consecrated Michael Francis McAuliffe, Bishop of

Jefferson City, born at Kansas City, Missouri, November 22, 1920; priest May 31, 1945; named July 2, 1969.

780. 1969, August 27, at Dubuque, Iowa, Saint Raphael's Cathedral. James Joseph Byrne, Archbishop of Dubuque, assisted by Leo Binz, Archbishop of Saint Paul and Minneapolis, and Edward Aloysius Fitzgerald, Titular Bishop of Zerta, consecrated Francis John Dunn, Titular Bishop of Turris Tamalleni, Auxiliary of Dubuque, born at Elkader, Iowa (Dubuque), March 22, 1922; priest January 11, 1948; named June 1, 1969; died at Cedar Rapids November 17, 1989.

781. 1969, October 16, at Milwaukee, Wisconsin, Saint John Cathedral. William Edward Cousins, Archbishop of Milwaukee, assisted by Jerome Joseph Hastrich, Bishop of Gallup, and John Benjamin Grellinger, Titular Bishop of Syene, consecrated Leo Joseph Brust, Titular Bishop of Suelli, Auxiliary of Milwaukee, born at Saint Francis, Wisconsin (Milwaukee), January 7, 1916; priest May 30, 1942; named August 22, 1969.

782. 1969, October 30, at Rapid City, South Dakota, Cathedral of Our Lady of Perpetual Help. George Henry Speltz, Bishop of Saint Cloud, assisted by Peter William Bartholome, Titular Bishop of Tanaramusa, and William Tiburtius McCarty, Titular Bishop of Rotdon, consecrated Harold Joseph Dimmerling, Bishop of Rapid City, born at Braddock, Pennsylvania (Pittsburgh), September 23, 1914; priest May 2, 1940; named September 11, 1969; died at Rapid City December 13, 1987.

783. 1969, November 28, at Rochester, New York, Sacred Heart Cathedral. Luigi Raimondi, Titular Archbishop of Tarsus, Apostolic Delegate to the United States, assisted by Fulton John Sheen, Titular Archbishop of Newport, and Lawrence Bernard Brennan Casey, Bishop of Paterson, consecrated Joseph Lloyd Hogan, Bishop of Rochester, born at Lima, New York (Rochester), March 11, 1916; priest June 6, 1942; named October 6, 1969; resigned November 28, 1978.

784. 1970, January 6, at the Bronx, New York, Saint Barnabas Church. Vincent Stanislaus Waters, Bishop of Raleigh, assisted by Joseph Lennox Federal, Bishop of Salt Lake City, and Charles Borromeo McLaughlin, Bishop of Saint Petersburg, consecrated George Edward Lynch, Titular Bishop of Satafi, Auxiliary of Raleigh, born at New York, New York, March 4, 1917; priest May 29, 1943; named October 20, 1969; resigned as Auxiliary of Raleigh April 16, 1985.

785. 1970, February 3, at Evansville, Indiana, Saint Benedict's Church. Luigi Raimondi, Titular Archbishop of Tarsus, Apostolic Delegate to the United States, assisted by George Joseph Biskup, Archbishop of

Indianapolis, and Joseph Aloysius Durick, Bishop of Nashville, consecrated Francis Raymond Shea, Bishop of Evansville, born at Knoxville, Tennessee (Nashville), December 4, 1913; priest March 19, 1939; named December 1, 1969; resigned March 11, 1989.

786. 1970, March 19, at San Francisco, California, Holy Name of Jesus Church. Mark Joseph Hurley, Bishop of Santa Rosa, assisted by William Edward McManus, Titular Bishop of Mesarfelta, and Joseph Louis Bernardin, Titular Bishop of Lugura, consecrated Francis Thomas Hurley, Titular Bishop of Daimlaig, Auxiliary of Juneau, born at San Francisco, California, February 6, 1927; priest June 16, 1951; named January 27, 1970; Bishop of Juneau July 13, 1971; Archbishop of Anchorage April 29, 1976.

787–788. 1970, March 19, at New York, New York, Saint Patrick's Cathedral. Terence James Cardinal Cooke, Archbishop of New York, assisted by John Joseph Maguire, Titular Archbishop of Tabalta, and Edwin Bernard Broderick, Bishop of Albany, consecrated (1) Patrick Vincent Ahern, Titular Bishop of Naiera, Auxiliary of New York, born at New York, New York, March 8, 1919; priest January 27, 1945; named January 27, 1970. Consecrated (2) Edward Dennis Head, Titular Bishop of Ard Sratha, Auxiliary of New York, born at White Plains, New York (New York), August 15, 1919; priest January 27, 1945; named January 27, 1970; Bishop of Buffalo January 17, 1973.

789–790. 1970, April 2, at Philadelphia, Pennsylvania, Cathedral of Saints Peter and Paul. John Joseph Cardinal Krol, Archbishop of Philadelphia, assisted by Gerald Vincent McDevitt, Titular Bishop of Tigias, and John Joseph Graham, Titular Bishop of Sabrata, consecrated (1) Martin Nicholas Lohmuller, Titular Bishop of Ramsbiria, Auxiliary of Philadelphia, born at Philadelphia, Pennsylvania, August 21, 1919; priest June 3, 1944; named February 12, 1970. Consecrated (2) Thomas Jerome Welsh, Titular Bishop of Inis Cathaig, Auxiliary of Philadelphia, born at Weatherley, Pennsylvania (Philadelphia), December 20, 1920; priest May 30, 1946; named February 12, 1970; first Bishop of Arlington May 28, 1974; Bishop of Allentown February 3, 1983.

791. 1970, April 6, at Springfield, Missouri, Cathedral of Saint Agnes. John Joseph Cardinal Carberry, Archbishop of Saint Louis, assisted by Charles Herman Helmsing, Bishop of Kansas City-Saint Joseph, and Joseph Vincent Sullivan, Titular Bishop of Thagamuta, consecrated William Wakefield Baum, Bishop of Springfield-Cape Girardeau, born at Dallas, Texas, November 21, 1926; priest May 12, 1951; named February 18, 1970; Archbishop of Washington March 5, 1973; Cardinal May 24, 1976; Prefect of the Congregation for Catholic Education January 15, 1980; resigned as Archbishop of Washington March 18, 1980.

792. 1970, May 5, at San Antonio, Texas, Cathedral of San Fernando. Luigi Raimondi, Titular Archbishop of Tarsus, Apostolic Delegate to the United States, assisted by Francis James Furey, Archbishop of San Antonio, and John Louis Morkovsky, Titular Bishop of Tigava, consecrated Patrick Fernández Flores, Titular Bishop of Italica, Auxiliary of San Antonio, born at Ganado, Texas (San Antonio), July 26, 1929; priest May 26, 1956; named March 9, 1970; Bishop of El Paso March 17, 1978; Archbishop of San Antonio August 23, 1979.

793. 1970, June 24, at Green Bay, Wisconsin, Veterans Memorial Arena. Aloysius John Wycislo, Bishop of Green Bay, assisted by John Benjamin Grellinger, Titular Bishop of Syene, and Frederick William Freking, Bishop of La Crosse, consecrated Mark Francis Schmitt, Titular Bishop of Ceanannus Mor, Auxiliary of Green Bay, born at Algoma, Wisconsin (Green Bay), February 14, 1923; priest May 22, 1948; named April 30, 1970; Bishop of Marquette March 15, 1978.

794. 1970, June 30, at Pittsburgh, Pennsylvania, Saint Paul Cathedral. John Joseph Cardinal Wright, Prefect of the Congregation for the Clergy, assisted by Vincent Martin Leonard, Bishop of Pittsburgh, and John Bernard McDowell, Titular Bishop of Tamazuca, consecrated Anthony Gerald Bosco, Titular Bishop of Labico, Auxiliary of Pittsburgh, born at New Castle, Pennsylvania (Pittsburgh), August 1, 1927; priest June 7, 1952; named May 14, 1970; Bishop of Greensburg April 2, 1987.

795. 1970, September 8, at San Francisco, California, Holy Name of Jesus Church. Joseph Thomas McGucken, Archbishop of San Francisco, assisted by Hugh Aloysius Donohoe, Bishop of Fresno, and Merlin Joseph Guilfoyle, Bishop of Stockton, consecrated Norman Francis McFarland, Titular Bishop of Bida, Auxiliary of San Francisco, born at Martinez, California (San Francisco), February 21, 1922; priest June 15, 1946; named June 5, 1970; Bishop of Reno February 4, 1976; title of see changed to Reno-Las Vegas October 13, 1976; Bishop of Orange December 18, 1986.

796. 1970, September 29, at Crookston, Minnesota, Cathedral of the Immaculate Conception. Luigi Raimondi, Titular Archbishop of Tarsus, Apostolic Delegate to the United States, assisted by Francis Frederick Reh, Bishop of Saginaw, and James Aloysius Hickey, Titular Bishop of Taraqua, consecrated Kenneth Joseph Povish, Bishop of Crookston, born at Alpena, Michigan (Detroit), April 19, 1924; priest January 3, 1950; named July 24, 1970; Bishop of Lansing October 8, 1975.

797. 1970, October 28, at Dubuque, Iowa, Saint Raphael's Cathedral. Luigi Raimondi, Titular Archbishop of Tarsus, Apostolic Delegate to the

United States, assisted by Leo Binz, Archbishop of Saint Paul, and Minneapolis and James Joseph Byrne, Archbishop of Dubuque, consecrated Justin Albert Driscoll, Bishop of Fargo, born at Dubuque, Iowa, September 30, 1920; priest July 28, 1945; named September 8, 1970; died at Bismarck November 19, 1984.

798. 1970, December 1, at Richmond, Virginia, Cathedral of the Sacred Heart. John Joyce Russell, Bishop of Richmond, assisted by Ernest Leo Unterkoefler, Bishop of Charleston, and Joseph Howard Hodges, Bishop of Wheeling, consecrated Walter Francis Sullivan, Titular Bishop of Selsea, Auxiliary of Richmond, born at Washington, District of Columbia (Baltimore), June 10, 1928; priest May 9, 1953; named October 15, 1970; Apostolic Administrator of Richmond April 28, 1973; Bishop of Richmond May 28, 1974.

799. 1971, January 6, at Memphis, Tennessee, Mid South Coliseum. John Joseph Cardinal Wright, Prefect of the Congregation for the Clergy, assisted by Luigi Raimondi, Titular Archbishop of Tarsus, and Thomas Joseph McDonough, Archbishop of Louisville, consecrated Carroll Thomas Dozier, first Bishop of Memphis, born at Richmond, Virginia, August 18, 1911; priest March 19, 1937; named November 12, 1970; resigned July 27, 1982; died at Memphis December 7, 1985.

800. 1971, January 7, at Rockville Centre, New York, Saint Agnes Cathedral. Walter Philip Kellenberg, Bishop of Rockville Centre, assisted by Vincent John Baldwin, Titular Bishop of Bencenna, and Charles Richard Mulrooney, Titular Bishop of Valentiniana, consecrated John Raymond McGann, Titular Bishop of Morosbisdus, Auxiliary of Rockville Centre, born at Brooklyn, New York, December 2, 1924; priest June 3, 1950; named November 12, 1970; Bishop of Rockville Centre May 3, 1976.

801. 1971, January 25, at Portland, Maine, Cathedral of the Immaculate Conception. Peter Leo Gerety, Bishop of Portland, assisted by Bernard Joseph Flanagan, Bishop of Worcester, and Lawrence Preston Joseph Graves, Titular Bishop of Vina, consecrated Edward Cornelius O'Leary, Titular Bishop of Moglena, Auxiliary of Portland, born at Bangor, Maine (Portland), August 21, 1920; priest June 15, 1946; named November 12, 1970; Bishop of Portland October 22, 1974; resigned September 27, 1988.

802. 1971, February 11, at Saint Louis, Missouri, Saint Louis Cathedral. John Joseph Cardinal Carberry, Archbishop of Saint Louis, assisted by Glennon Patrick Flavin, Bishop of Lincoln, and Lawrence Preston Joseph Graves, Titular Bishop of Vina, consecrated Charles Roman Koester, Titular Bishop of Suacia, Auxiliary of Saint Louis, born at Jefferson City,

Missouri (Saint Louis), September 16, 1915; priest December 20, 1941; named January 2, 1971.

803–804. 1971, March 25, at Los Angeles, California, Saint Vibiana's Cathedral. Timothy Manning, Archbishop of Los Angeles, assisted by Joseph Thomas McGucken, Archbishop of San Francisco, and Alden John Bell, Bishop of Sacramento, consecrated (1) Juan Alfredo Arzube, Titular Bishop of Civitate, Auxiliary of Los Angeles, born at Guayaquil, Ecuador, June 1, 1918; priest May 5, 1954; named February 19, 1971. Consecrated (2) William Robert Johnson, Titular Bishop of Blera, Auxiliary of Los Angeles, born at Tonopah, Nevada (Sacramento), November 19, 1918; priest May 28, 1944; named February 19, 1971; first Bishop of Orange March 24, 1976; died at Orange July 28, 1986.

805. 1971, April 22, at Syracuse, New York, Cathedral of the Immaculate Conception. David Frederick Cunningham, Bishop of Syracuse, assisted by Stanislaus Joseph Brzana, Bishop of Ogdensburg, and Joseph Lloyd Hogan, Bishop of Rochester, consecrated Frank James Harrison, Titular Bishop of Aquae in Numidia, Auxiliary of Syracuse, born at Syracuse, New York, August 20, 1912; priest June 4, 1937; named March 1, 1971; Bishop of Syracuse November 9, 1976; resigned June 10, 1987.

806–807. 1971, May 25, at Philadelphia, Pennsylvania, Immaculate Conception of the Blessed Virgin Mary Ukrainian Catholic Cathedral. Ambrose Andrew Senyshyn, Archbishop of Philadelphia of the Ukrainians, assisted by Jaroslav Gabro, Bishop of Saint Nicholas of Chicago of the Ukrainians, and Michael Joseph Dudick, Bishop of Passaic of the Ruthenians, consecrated (1) John Stock, Titular Bishop of Pergamum, Auxiliary of Philadelphia of the Ukrainians, born at Saint Clair, Pennsylvania (Philadelphia of the Ukrainians), July 5, 1918; priest December 4, 1943; named January 11, 1971; died in an automobile accident June 29, 1972, near Mount Holly, New Jersey. Consecrated (2) Basil Harry Losten, Titular Bishop of Arcadiopolis in Asia, Auxiliary of Philadelphia of the Ukrainians, born at Chesapeake, Maryland (Philadelphia of the Ukrainians), May 11, 1930; priest June 10, 1957; named March 15, 1971; Apostolic Administrator of Philadelphia of the Ukrainians June 8, 1976; Bishop of Stamford of the Ukrainians September 20, 1977.

808. 1971, June 30, at Baker, Oregon, Cathedral of Saint Francis de Sales. Robert Joseph Dwyer, Archbishop of Portland in Oregon, assisted by Thomas Kiely Gorman, Bishop emeritus of Dallas-Fort Worth, and Michael Joseph Green, Bishop of Reno, consecrated Thomas John Connolly, Bishop of Baker, born at Tonopah, Nevada (Sacramento), July 18, 1922; priest April 8, 1947; named April 26, 1971.

809. 1971, July 15, at Peoria, Illinois, Saint Mary's Cathedral. John Patrick Cardinal Cody, Archbishop of Chicago, assisted by John Baptist Franz, Bishop emeritus of Peoria, and George Henry Speltz, Bishop of Saint Cloud, consecrated Edward William O'Rourke, Bishop of Peoria, born at Downs, Illinois (Peoria), October 31, 1917; priest May 28, 1944; named May 24, 1971; resigned January 23, 1990.

810. 1971, July 20, at Gaylord, Michigan, Our Lady of Mount Carmel Cathedral. John Francis Cardinal Dearden, Archbishop of Detroit, assisted by Charles Alexander Salatka, Bishop of Marquette, and Joseph Crescent McKinney, Titular Bishop of Lentini, consecrated Edmund Casimir Szoka, first Bishop of Gaylord, born at Grand Rapids, Michigan, September 14, 1927; priest June 4, 1954; named June 11, 1971; Archbishop of Detroit March 21, 1981; Cardinal June 28, 1988; President of the Prefecture of Economic Affairs of the Holy See January 22, 1990.

811. 1971, July 21, at Kalamazoo, Michigan, Saint Augustine Cathedral. John Francis Cardinal Dearden, Archbishop of Detroit, assisted by Alexander Mieceslaus Zaleski, Bishop of Lansing, and Michael Joseph Green, Bishop of Reno, consecrated Paul Vincent Donovan, first Bishop of Kalamazoo, born at Bernard, Iowa (Dubuque), September 1, 1924; priest May 20, 1950; named June 11, 1971.

812. 1971, August 24, at South Bend, Indiana, Saint Matthew Co-cathedral. George Joseph Biskup, Archbishop of Indianapolis, assisted by Leo Aloysius Pursley, Bishop of Fort Wayne-South Bend, and Andrew Gregory Grutka, Bishop of Gary, consecrated Joseph Robert Crowley, Titular Bishop of Maraguia, Auxiliary of Fort Wayne-South Bend, born at Fort Wayne, Indiana, January 12, 1915; priest May 1, 1953; named June 8, 1971.

813–814. 1971, September 8, at Saint Paul, Minnesota, Cathedral of Saint Paul. Luigi Raimondi, Titular Archbishop of Tarsus, Apostolic Delegate to the United States, assisted by Leo Binz, Archbishop of Saint Paul and Minneapolis, and Leo Christopher Byrne, Titular Archbishop of Plestia, consecrated (1) John Robert Roach, Titular Bishop of Cenae, Auxiliary of Saint Paul and Minneapolis, born at Prior Lake, Minnesota (Saint Paul), July 31, 1921; priest June 8, 1946; named July 12, 1971; Archbishop of Saint Paul and Minneapolis May 21, 1975. Consecrated (2) Raymond Alphonse Lucker, Titular Bishop of Meta, Auxiliary of Saint Paul and Minneapolis, born at Saint Paul, Minnesota, February 24, 1927; priest June 7, 1952; named July 12, 1971; Bishop of New Ulm December 23, 1975.

815. 1972, January 12, at Charlotte, North Carolina, Saint Patrick's

Cathedral. Luigi Raimondi, Titular Archbishop of Tarsus, Apostolic Delegate to the United States, assisted by Vincent Stanislaus Waters, Bishop of Raleigh, and George Edward Lynch, Titular Bishop of Satafi, consecrated Michael Joseph Begley, first Bishop of Charlotte, born at Mattineague, Massachusetts (Springfield), March 12, 1909; priest May 26, 1934; named November 25, 1971; resigned May 29, 1984.

816. 1972, January 25, at Burlington, Vermont, Cathedral of the Immaculate Conception. Robert Francis Joyce, Bishop emeritus of Burlington, assisted by Bernard Joseph Flanagan, Bishop of Worcester, and James Aloysius Hickey, Titular Bishop of Taraqua, consecrated John Aloysius Marshall, Bishop of Burlington, born at Worcester, Massachusetts (Springfield), April 26, 1928; priest December 19, 1953; named December 14, 1971.

817. 1972, January 25, at Miami, Florida, Saint Mary's Cathedral. John Francis Cardinal Dearden, Archbishop of Detroit, assisted by Coleman Francis Carroll, Archbishop of Miami, and Paul Francis Tanner, Bishop of Saint Augustine, consecrated Rene Henry Gracida, Titular Bishop of Masuccaba, Auxiliary of Miami, born at New Orleans, Louisiana, June 9, 1923; priest May 23, 1959; named December 6, 1971; first Bishop of Pensacola-Tallahassee October 7, 1975; Bishop of Corpus Christi May 19, 1983.

818. 1972, January 26, at Providence, Rhode Island, Cathedral of Saints Peter and Paul. Robert Francis Joyce, Bishop emeritus of Burlington, assisted by Bernard Joseph Flanagan, Bishop of Worcester, and Edward Cornelius O'Leary, Titular Bishop of Moglena, consecrated Louis Edward Gelineau, Bishop of Providence, born at Burlington, Vermont, May 3, 1928; priest June 5, 1954; named December 6, 1971.

819–820. 1972, February 2, at Boston, Massachusetts, Cathedral of the Holy Cross. Humberto Sousa Medeiros, Archbishop of Boston, assisted by Jeremiah Francis Minihan, Titular Bishop of Paphus, and Thomas Joseph Riley, Titular Bishop of Regiae, consecrated (1) Lawrence Joseph Riley, Titular Bishop of Daimlaig, Auxiliary of Boston, born at Boston, Massachusetts, September 6, 1914; priest September 21, 1940; named December 1, 1971; resigned as Auxiliary of Boston January 16, 1990. Consecrated (2) Joseph Francis Maguire, Titular Bishop of Mactaris, Auxiliary of Boston, born at Boston, Massachusetts, September 4, 1919; priest June 29, 1945; named December 1, 1971; Coadjutor of Springfield April 3, 1976; succeeded to Springfield October 15, 1977.

821. 1972, February 13, at Rome, Vatican City, Saint Peter's Basilica. Pope Paul VI, assisted by Bernhard Jan Cardinal Alfrink, Archbishop of

Utrecht, and William Cardinal Conway, Archbishop of Armagh, consecrated Edward Thomas O'Meara, Titular Bishop of Tisiduo, Auxiliary of Saint Louis, born at Saint Louis, Missouri, August 3, 1921; priest December 21, 1946; named January 28, 1972; Archbishop of Indianapolis November 21, 1979.

822. 1972, September 5, at Savannah, Georgia, Cathedral of Saint John the Baptist. Thomas Joseph McDonough, Archbishop of Louisville, assisted by Philip Matthew Hannan, Archbishop of New Orleans, and Gerard Louis Frey, Bishop of Savannah, consecrated Andrew Joseph McDonald, Bishop of Little Rock, born at Savannah, Georgia, October 24, 1923; priest May 8, 1948; named July 4, 1972.

823. 1972, September 15, at New York, New York, Saint Patrick's Cathedral. Terence James Cardinal Cooke, Archbishop of New York, assisted by John Joseph Maguire, Titular Archbishop of Tabalta, and Patrick Vincent Ahern, Titular Bishop of Naiera, consecrated James Patrick Mahoney, Titular Bishop of Ipagro, Auxiliary of New York, born at Kingston, New York (New York), August 16, 1925; priest May 19, 1951; named July 25, 1972.

824. 1972, September 19, at Tulsa, Oklahoma, The Civic Center. John Raphael Quinn, Archbishop of Oklahoma City, assisted by John Lawrence May, Bishop of Mobile, and Charles Albert Buswell, Bishop of Pueblo, consecrated John Joseph Sullivan, Bishop of Grand Island, born at Horton, Kansas (Leavenworth), July 5, 1920; priest September 23, 1944; named July 25, 1972; Bishop of Kansas City-Saint Joseph June 21, 1977.

825. 1972, September 21, at Lansing, Michigan, Saint Mary Cathedral. Alexander Mieceslaus Zaleski, Bishop of Lansing, assisted by Michael Joseph Green, Bishop of Reno, and Paul Vincent Donovan, Bishop of Kalamazoo, consecrated James Stephen Sullivan, Titular Bishop of Siccesi, Auxiliary of Lansing, born at Kalamazoo, Michigan (Detroit), July 23, 1929; priest June 4, 1955; named July 25, 1972; Bishop of Fargo March 29, 1985.

826. 1973, January 28, at Jackson, Mississippi, Municipal Stadium. Luigi Raimondi, Titular Archbishop of Tarsus, Apostolic Delegate to the United States, assisted by Harold Robert Perry, Titular Bishop of Mons in Mauritania, and Joseph Bernard Brunini, Bishop of Natchez-Jackson, consecrated Joseph Lawson Howze, Titular Bishop of Maxita, Auxiliary of Natchez-Jackson, born at Daphne, Alabama (Mobile), August 30, 1923; priest May 7, 1959; named November 8, 1972; first Bishop of Biloxi March 1, 1977.

827. 1973, February 2, at Brooklyn, New York, Basilica of Our Lady of Perpetual Help. Francis John Mugavero, Bishop of Brooklyn, assisted by John Joseph Boardman, Titular Bishop of Gunela, and Paul Leonard Hagarty, Bishop of Nassau, consecrated John Joseph Snyder, Titular Bishop of Forlimpopoli, Auxiliary of Brooklyn, born at New York, New York, October 25, 1925; priest June 9, 1951; named December 13, 1972; Bishop of Saint Augustine October 2, 1979.

828. 1973, February 7, at Tulsa, Oklahoma, Holy Family Cathedral. Luigi Raimondi, Titular Archbishop of Tarsus, Apostolic Delegate to the United States, assisted by Wendelin Joseph Nold, Bishop of Galveston-Houston, and John Louis Morkovsky, Titular Bishop of Tigava, consecrated Bernard James Ganter, first Bishop of Tulsa, born at Galveston, Texas, July 17, 1928; priest May 22, 1952; named December 13, 1972; Bishop of Beaumont October 3, 1977.

829–830. 1973, April 3, at Detroit, Michigan, Cathedral of the Most Blessed Sacrament. John Francis Cardinal Dearden, Archbishop of Detroit, assisted by Walter Joseph Schoenherr, Titular Bishop of Timidana, and Thomas John Gumbleton, Titular Bishop of Ululi, consecrated (1) Joseph Leopold Imesch, Titular Bishop of Pomaria, Auxiliary of Detroit, born at Grosse Pointe Farms, Michigan (Detroit), June 21, 1931; priest December 16, 1956; named February 8, 1973; Bishop of Joliet June 30, 1979. Consecrated (2) Arthur Henry Krawczak, Titular Bishop of Subbar, Auxiliary of Detroit, born at Detroit, Michigan, February 2, 1913; priest May 18, 1940; named February 8, 1973; resigned as Auxiliary of Detroit August 17, 1982.

831. 1973, April 26, at Collegeville, Minnesota, Saint John's Abbey Church. John Joseph Cardinal Krol, Archbishop of Philadelphia, assisted by Joseph Louis Bernardin, Archbishop of Cincinnati, and George Henry Speltz, Bishop of Saint Cloud, consecrated James Steven Rausch, Titular Bishop of Summa, Auxiliary of Saint Cloud, born at Albany, Minnesota (Saint Cloud), September 4, 1928; priest June 2, 1956; named March 5, 1973; Bishop of Phoenix January 17, 1977; died at Phoenix May 18, 1981.

832. 1973, April 27, at New York, New York, Saint Patrick's Cathedral. Terence James Cardinal Cooke, Archbishop of New York, assisted by John Joseph Maguire, Titular Archbishop of Tabalta, and Joseph Maria Pernicone, Titular Bishop of Hadrianopolis in Honoriade, consecrated Anthony Francis Mestice, Titular Bishop of Villa Nova, Auxiliary of New York, born at New York, New York, December 6, 1923; priest June 4, 1949; named March 5, 1973.

833. 1973, April 27, at Savannah, Georgia, Cathedral of Saint John the

Baptist. Thomas Andrew Donnellan, Archbishop of Atlanta, assisted by Justin Albert Driscoll, Bishop of Fargo, and Francis Joseph Gossman, Titular Bishop of Agunto, consecrated Raymond William Lessard, Bishop of Savannah, born at Grafton, North Dakota (Fargo), December 21, 1930; priest December 16, 1956; named March 5, 1973.

834. 1973, May 15, at Oakland, Pittsburgh, Pennsylvania, Holy Spirit Church. Stephen John Kocisko, Archbishop of Munhall of the Ruthenians, assisted by Michael Joseph Dudick, Bishop of Passaic of the Ruthenians, and Emil John Mihalik, Bishop of Parma of the Ruthenians, consecrated John Michael Bilock, Titular Bishop of Pergamus, Auxiliary of Munhall of the Ruthenians, born at McAdoo, Pennsylvania (Pittsburgh of the Ruthenians), June 20, 1916; priest February 3, 1946; named March 1, 1973; title of see changed to Pittsburgh of the Byzantines March 11, 1977.

835. 1973, December 5, at Springfield, Missouri, Cathedral of Saint Agnes. Joseph Bernard Brunini, Bishop of Natchez-Jackson, assisted by William Wakefield Baum, Archbishop of Washington, and Joseph Louis Bernardin, Archbishop of Cincinnati, consecrated Bernard Francis Law, Bishop of Springfield-Cape Girardeau, born at Torreon (Saltillo), Mexico, November 4, 1931; priest May 21, 1961; named October 22, 1973; Archbishop of Boston January 11, 1984; Cardinal May 25, 1985.

836. 1974, May 16, at Sacramento, California, Memorial Auditorium. Alden John Bell, Bishop of Sacramento, assisted by Floyd Lawrence Begin, Bishop of Oakland, and Hugh Aloysius Donohoe, Bishop of Fresno, consecrated John Stephen Cummins, Titular Bishop of Lambaesis, Auxiliary of Sacramento, born at Oakland, California (San Francisco), March 3, 1928; priest January 24, 1953; named February 12, 1974; Bishop of Oakland May 3, 1977.

837. 1974, May 29, at Toledo, Ohio, Queen of the Most Holy Rosary Cathedral. John Anthony Donovan, Bishop of Toledo, assisted by Joseph Louis Bernardin, Archbishop of Cincinnati, and William Michael Cosgrove, Titular Bishop of Trisipa, consecrated Albert Henry Ottenweller, Titular Bishop of Perdices, Auxiliary of Toledo, born at Stanford, Montana (Great Falls), April 15, 1916; priest June 19, 1943; named April 17, 1974; Bishop of Steubenville September 27, 1977.

838. 1974, June 21, at San Diego, California, Golden Hall. Leo Thomas Maher, Bishop of San Diego, assisted by John Raphael Quinn, Archbishop of Oklahoma City, and Patrick Fernández Flores, Titular Bishop of Italica, consecrated Gilbert Espinosa Chavez, Titular Bishop of Magarmel, Auxiliary of San Diego, born at Ontario, California (Los Angeles-San Diego), May 9, 1932; priest March 19, 1960; named April 9, 1974.

839. 1974, July 25, at Albuquerque, New Mexico, New Mexico State University Sports Stadium. Jean Jadot, Titular Archbishop of Zuri, Apostolic Delegate to the United States, assisted by James Peter Davis, Archbishop emeritus of Santa Fe, and Patrick Fernández Flores, Titular Bishop of Italica, consecrated Robert Fortune Sanchez, Archbishop of Santa Fe, born at Socorro, New Mexico (Santa Fe), March 20, 1934; priest December 20, 1959; named June 1, 1974.

840–841. 1974, September 12, at Washington, District of Columbia, National Shrine of the Immaculate Conception. William Wakefield Baum, Archbishop of Washington, assisted by Harold Robert Perry, Titular Bishop of Mons in Mauritania, and Edward John Herrmann, Bishop of Columbus, consecrated (1) Thomas William Lyons, Titular Bishop of Mortlach, Auxiliary of Washington, born at Washington, District of Columbia (Baltimore), September 26, 1923; priest May 22, 1948; named July 12, 1974; died at Baltimore March 25, 1988. Consecrated (2) Eugene Antonio Marino, SSJ, Titular Bishop of Walla Walla, Auxiliary of Washington, born at Biloxi, Mississippi (Natchez), May 29, 1934; priest June 9, 1962; named July 12, 1974; Archbishop of Atlanta March 10, 1988.

842. 1974, September 12, at Youngstown, Ohio, Cathedral of Saint Columba. James William Malone, Bishop of Youngstown, assisted by Joseph Louis Bernardin, Archbishop of Cincinnati, and William Michael Cosgrove, Titular Bishop of Trisipa, consecrated William Anthony Hughes, Titular Bishop of Inis Cathaig, Auxiliary of Youngstown, born at Youngstown, Ohio (Cleveland), September 23, 1921; priest April 6, 1946; named July 17, 1974; Bishop of Covington March 8, 1979.

843. 1974, September 20, at Denver, Colorado, Cathedral of the Immaculate Conception. James Vincent Casey, Archbishop of Denver, assisted by George Roche Evans, Titular Bishop of Tubyza, and Charles Albert Buswell, Bishop of Pueblo, consecrated Richard Charles Patrick Hanifen, Titular Bishop of Abercorn, Auxiliary of Denver, born at Denver, Colorado, June 15, 1931; priest June 6, 1959; named July 23, 1974; first Bishop of Colorado Springs November 10, 1983.

844. 1974, October 7, at Providence, Rhode Island, Cathedral of Saints Peter and Paul. Louis Edward Gelineau, Bishop of Providence, assisted by John Francis Whealon, Archbishop of Hartford, and John Francis Hackett, Titular Bishop of Helenopolis in Palestina, consecrated Kenneth Anthony Angell, Titular Bishop of Septimunicia, Auxiliary of Providence, born at Providence, Rhode Island, August 3, 1930; priest May 26, 1956; named August 9, 1974.

845. 1974, October 28, at Boise, Idaho, Cathedral of Saint John the

Evangelist. Sylvester William Treinen, Bishop of Boise City, assisted by James Joseph Byrne, Archbishop of Dubuque, and Alberto Uribe Urdaneta, Archbishop of Cali, consecrated Nicholas Eugene Walsh, Bishop of Yakima, born at Burnsville, Minnesota (Saint Paul), October 20, 1916; priest June 6, 1942; named September 10, 1974; Titular Bishop of Bolsena, Auxiliary of Seattle August 10, 1976; resigned as Auxiliary of Seattle and from the titular see of Bolsena, assuming the title of Bishop emeritus of Yakima, September 6, 1983.

846. 1974, December 20, at Cincinnati, Ohio, Cathedral of Saint Peter in Chains. Joseph Louis Bernardin, Archbishop of Cincinnati, assisted by Nicholas Thomas Elko, Titular Archbishop of Dara, and James William Malone, Bishop of Youngstown, consecrated Daniel Edward Pilarczyk, Titular Bishop of Holdem, Auxiliary of Cincinnati, born at Dayton (Cincinnati), August 12, 1934; priest December 20, 1959; named November 12, 1974; Archbishop of Cincinnati October 30, 1982.

847. 1975, February 3, at Manchester, New Hampshire, Saint Joseph Cathedral. Ernest John Primeau, Bishop emeritus of Manchester, assisted by Edward Cornelius O'Leary, Bishop of Portland, and Timothy Joseph Harrington, Titular Bishop of Rusuca, consecrated Odore Joseph Gendron, Bishop of Manchester, born at Manchester, New Hampshire, September 13, 1921; priest June 7, 1947; named December 12, 1974.

848–851. 1975, February 11, at Boston, Massachusetts, Cathedral of the Holy Cross. Humberto Sousa Cardinal Medeiros, Archbishop of Boston, assisted by Thomas Joseph Riley, Titular Bishop of Regiae, and Lawrence Joseph Riley, Titular Bishop of Daimlaig, consecrated (1) Thomas Vose Daily, Titular Bishop of Bladia, Auxiliary of Boston, born at Belmont, Massachusetts (Boston), September 23, 1927; priest January 10, 1952; named December 28, 1974; first Bishop of Palm Beach June 16, 1984; Bishop of Brooklyn February 10, 1990. Consecrated (2) John Michael D'Arcy, Titular Bishop of Mediana, Auxiliary of Boston, born at Brighton, Massachusetts (Boston), August 18, 1932; priest February 2, 1957; named December 28, 1974; Bishop of Fort Wayne-South Bend February 18, 1985. Consecrated (3) Joseph John Ruocco, Titular Bishop of Polignano, Auxiliary of Boston, born at Boston, Massachusetts, April 21, 1922; priest May 6, 1948; named December 28, 1974; died at Lowell, Massachusetts, July 26, 1980. Consecrated (4) John Joseph Mulcahy, Titular Bishop of Penafiel, Auxiliary of Boston, born at Dorchester, Massachusetts (Boston), June 26, 1922; priest May 1, 1947; named December 28, 1974.

852. 1975, March 19, at Fresno, California, Fresno Convention Center. Hugh Aloysius Donohoe, Bishop of Fresno, assisted by William Robert Johnson, Titular Bishop of Blera, and John Stephen Cummins, Titular

Bishop of Lambaesis, consecrated Roger Michael Mahony, Titular Bishop of Tamascani, Auxiliary of Fresno, born at Hollywood, California (Los Angeles-San Diego), February 27, 1936; priest May 1, 1962; named January 7, 1975; Bishop of Stockton February 15, 1980; Archbishop of Los Angeles July 12, 1985.

853. 1975, May 20, at Nashville, Tennessee, Opryland Auditorium. Thomas Joseph McDonough, Archbishop of Louisville, assisted by Joseph Aloysius Durick, Bishop emeritus of Nashville, and Francis Raymond Shea, Bishop of Evansville, consecrated James Daniel Niedergeses, Bishop of Nashville, born at Lawrenceburg, Tennessee (Nashville), February 2, 1917; priest May 20, 1944; named April 8, 1975.

854. 1975, June 26, at Greensburg, Pennsylvania, Blessed Sacrament Cathedral. William Graham Connare, Bishop of Greensburg, assisted by Cyril John Vogel, Bishop of Salina, and John Bernard McDowell, Titular Bishop of Tamazuca, consecrated Norbert Felix Gaughan, Titular Bishop of Taraqua, Auxiliary of Greensburg, born at Pittsburgh, Pennsylvania, May 30, 1921; priest November 4, 1945; named April 2, 1975; Bishop of Gary July 9, 1984.

855. 1975, July 3, at Kansas City, Missouri, Cathedral of the Immaculate Conception. Charles Herman Helmsing, Bishop of Kansas City-Saint Joseph, assisted by William Wakefield Baum, Archbishop of Washington, and Joseph Vincent Sullivan, Bishop of Baton Rouge, consecrated George Kinsey Fitzsimons, Titular Bishop of Pertusa, Auxiliary of Kansas City-Saint Joseph, born at Kansas City, Missouri, September 4, 1928; priest March 18, 1961; named May 20, 1975; Bishop of Salina March 28, 1984.

856. 1975, August 6, at Norwich, Connecticut, Saint Patrick's Cathedral. John Francis Whealon, Archbishop of Hartford, assisted by Vincent Joseph Hines, Bishop emeritus of Norwich, and Louis Edward Gelineau, Bishop of Providence, consecrated Daniel Patrick Reilly, Bishop of Norwich, born at Providence, Rhode Island, May 12, 1928; priest May 30, 1953; named June 5, 1975.

857. 1975, November 12, at Portland, Maine, Cathedral of the Immaculate Conception. Edward Cornelius O'Leary, Bishop of Portland, assisted by Timothy Joseph Harrington, Titular Bishop of Rusuca, and Odore Joseph Gendron, Bishop of Manchester, consecrated Amedee Wilfrid Proulx, Titular Bishop of Clipia, Auxiliary of Portland, born at Sanford, Maine (Portland), August 31, 1932; priest May 31, 1958; named September 16, 1975.

858. 1975, December 13, at New York, New York, Saint Patrick's

Cathedral. Terence James Cardinal Cooke, Archbishop of New York, assisted by John Joseph Thomas Ryan, Titular Archbishop of Gabi, and William Joseph Moran, Titular Bishop of Centuria, consecrated James Jerome Killeen, Titular Bishop of Vamalla, Auxiliary of the Military Vicar of the United States, born at New York, New York, July 17, 1917; priest May 30, 1942; named November 4, 1975; died at New York September 8, 1978.

859–860. 1976, February 29, at Baltimore, Maryland, Cathedral of Mary Our Queen. William Donald Borders, Archbishop of Baltimore, assisted by Cardinal Lawrence Joseph Shehan, Archbishop emeritus of Baltimore, and Thomas Austin Murphy, Titular Bishop of Appiaria, consecrated (1) Philip Francis Murphy, Titular Bishop of Tacarata, Auxiliary of Baltimore, born at Cumberland, Maryland (Baltimore), March 25, 1933; priest December 20, 1958; named January 19, 1976. Consecrated (2) James Francis Stafford, Titular Bishop of Respecta, Auxiliary of Baltimore, born at Baltimore, Maryland, July 26, 1932; priest December 15, 1957; named January 19, 1976; Bishop of Memphis November 17, 1982; Archbishop of Denver May 30, 1986.

861. 1976, April 28, at Helena, Montana, Carroll College Center. Cornelius Michael Power, Archbishop of Portland in Oregon, assisted by Thomas John Connolly, Bishop of Baker, and Francis Peter Leipzig, Bishop emeritus of Baker, consecrated Elden Francis Curtiss, Bishop of Helena, born at Baker, Oregon, July 16, 1932; priest May 24, 1958; named March 4, 1976.

862–863. 1976, June 11, at Cleveland, Ohio, Cathedral of Saint John the Evangelist. James Aloysius Hickey, Bishop of Cleveland, assisted by Joseph Louis Bernardin, Archbishop of Cincinnati, and Clarence George Issenmann, Bishop emeritus of Cleveland, consecrated (1) Michael Joseph Murphy, Titular Bishop of Arindela, Auxiliary of Cleveland, born at Cleveland, Ohio, July 1, 1915; priest February 28, 1942; named April 12, 1976; Coadjutor Bishop of Erie November 20, 1978; succeeded to Erie July 16, 1982. Consecrated (2) Gilbert Ignatius Sheldon, Titular Bishop of Taparura, Auxiliary of Cleveland, born at Cleveland, Ohio, September 20, 1926; priest February 28, 1953; named April 12, 1976.

864–866. 1976, June 25, at Newark, New Jersey, Sacred Heart Cathedral. Peter Leo Gerety, Archbishop of Newark, assisted by Thomas Aloysius Boland, Archbishop emeritus of Newark, and Harold Robert Perry, Titular Bishop of Mons in Mauritania, consecrated (1) Robert Francis Garner, Titular Bishop of Blera, Auxiliary of Newark, born at Jersey City, New Jersey (Newark), April 27, 1920; priest June 15, 1946; named May 3, 1976. Consecrated (2) Joseph Abel Francis, SVD, Titular Bishop of

Valliposita, Auxiliary of Newark, born at Lafayette, Louisiana, September 30, 1923; priest October 7, 1950; named May 3, 1976. Consecrated (3) Dominic Anthony Marconi, Titular Bishop of Bure, Auxiliary of Newark, born at Newark, New Jersey, March 13, 1927; priest May 30, 1953; named May 3, 1976.

867. 1976, June 29, at New Orleans, Louisiana, Cathedral Basilica of Saint Louis. Philip Matthew Hannan, Archbishop of New Orleans, assisted by William Donald Borders, Archbishop of Baltimore, and Joseph Vincent Sullivan, Bishop of Baton Rouge, consecrated Stanley Joseph Ott, Titular Bishop of Nicives, Auxiliary of New Orleans, born at Gretna, Louisiana (New Orleans), June 29, 1927; priest December 8, 1951; named May 24, 1976; Bishop of Baton Rouge January 13, 1983.

868. 1976, July 18, at Columbus, Ohio, Saint Joseph Cathedral. Edward John Herrmann, Bishop of Columbus, assisted by Joseph Louis Bernardin, Archbishop of Cincinnati, and James Aloysius Hickey, Bishop of Cleveland, consecrated George Avis Fulcher, Titular Bishop of Morosbisdus, Auxiliary of Columbus, born at Columbus, Ohio January 30, 1922; priest February 28, 1948; named May 24, 1976; Bishop of Lafayette in Indiana February 4, 1983; died in an automobile accident near Rockville, Indiana, January 25, 1984.

869. 1976, July 21, at Philadelphia, Pennsylvania, Cathedral of Saints Peter and Paul. John Joseph Cardinal Krol, Archbishop of Philadelphia, assisted by Gerald Vincent McDevitt, Titular Bishop of Tigias, John Joseph Graham, Titular Bishop of Sabrata, and Martin Nicholas Lohmuller, Titular Bishop of Ramsbiria, consecrated Edward Thomas Hughes, Titular Bishop of Segia, Auxiliary of Philadelphia, born at Lansdowne, Pennsylvania (Philadelphia), November 13, 1920; priest May 31, 1947; named June 14, 1976; Bishop of Metuchen December 11, 1986.

870. 1976, August 17, at Saint Louis, Missouri, Saint Louis Cathedral. John Joseph Cardinal Carberry, Archbishop of Saint Louis, assisted by Joseph Alphonsus McNicholas, Bishop of Springfield in Illinois, and Charles Herman Helmsing, Bishop of Kansas City-Saint Joseph, consecrated John Nicholas Wurm, Titular Bishop of Plestia, Auxiliary of Saint Louis, born at Saint Louis, Missouri, December 6, 1927; priest April 3, 1954; named June 25, 1976; Bishop of Belleville September 21, 1981; died at Belleville April 27, 1984.

871. 1976, August 31, at Cheyenne, Wyoming, Saint Mary's Cathedral. Hubert Michael Newell, Bishop of Cheyenne, assisted by Charles Herman Helmsing, Bishop of Kansas City-Saint Joseph, and Michael Francis McAuliffe, Bishop of Jefferson City, consecrated Joseph Hubert

Hart, Titular Bishop of Thimida Regia, Auxiliary of Cheyenne, born at Kansas City, Missouri, September 26, 1931; priest May 1, 1956; named July 1, 1976; Bishop of Cheyenne April 25, 1978.

872. 1976, September 2, at Crookston, Minnesota, Cathedral of the Immaculate Conception. John Robert Roach, Archbishop of Saint Paul and Minneapolis, assisted by Joseph Alphonsus McNicholas, Bishop of Springfield in Illinois, and William Aloysius O'Connor, Bishop emeritus of Springfield in Illinois, consecrated Victor Herman Balke, Bishop of Crookston, born at Meppen, Illinois (Springfield in Illinois), September 29, 1931; priest May 24, 1958; named July 3, 1976.

873. 1976, September 21, at Scranton, Pennsylvania, Saint Peter's Cathedral. Joseph Carroll McCormick, Bishop of Scranton, assisted by John Raphael Quinn, Archbishop of Oklahoma City, and Stanley Joseph Ott, Titular Bishop of Nicives, consecrated James Clifford Timlin, Titular Bishop of Gunugus, Auxiliary of Scranton, born at Scranton, Pennsylvania, August 5, 1927; priest December 16, 1951; named July 26, 1976; Bishop of Scranton April 11, 1984.

874. 1976, October 18, at Boston, Massachusetts, Cathedral of the Holy Cross. Humberto Sousa Cardinal Medeiros, Archbishop of Boston, assisted by Thomas Joseph Riley, Titular Bishop of Regiae, and Lawrence Joseph Riley, Titular Bishop of Daimlaig, consecrated Daniel Anthony Hart, Titular Bishop of Tepelta, Auxiliary of Boston, born at Lawrence, Massachusetts (Boston), August 24, 1927; priest February 2, 1953; named August 24, 1976.

875. 1976, November 23, at Scranton, Pennsylvania, Saint Peter's Cathedral. Stephen John Kocisko, Archbishop of Munhall of the Ruthenians, assisted by Michael Joseph Dudick, Bishop of Passaic of the Ruthenians, and Emil John Mihalik, Bishop of Parma of the Ruthenians, consecrated Thomas Victor Dolinay, Titular Bishop of Thyatira, Auxiliary of Passaic of the Ruthenians, born at Uniontown, Pennsylvania (Pittsburgh of the Ruthenians), July 24, 1923; priest May 16, 1948; named June 28, 1976; first Bishop of Van Nuys of the Ruthenians December 3, 1981; Coadjutor Archbishop of Pittsburgh of the Byzantines February 19, 1990.

876. 1976, December 13, at San Antonio, Texas, San Antonio Convention Center Arena. Francis James Furey, Archbishop of San Antonio, assisted by Patrick Fernández Flores, Titular Bishop of Italica, and Thomas Joseph Drury, Bishop of Corpus Christi, consecrated Raymundo Joseph Peña, Titular Bishop of Trisipa, Auxiliary of San Antonio, born at Corpus

Christi, Texas, February 19, 1934; priest May 25, 1957; named October 16, 1976; Bishop of El Paso April 24, 1980.

877. 1976, December 14, at Wichita, Kansas, Cathedral of the Immaculate Conception. David Mono Maloney, Bishop of Wichita, assisted by Marion Francis Forst, Titular Bishop of Scala, and Richard Charles Patrick Hanifen, Titular Bishop of Abercorn, consecrated Eugene John Gerber, Bishop of Dodge City, born at Kingman, Kansas (Wichita), April 30, 1931; priest May 19, 1959; named October 16, 1976; Bishop of Wichita November 17, 1982.

878–879. 1977, January 25, at Saint Paul, Minnesota, Cathedral of Saint Paul. John Robert Roach, Archbishop of Saint Paul and Minneapolis, assisted by Leo Binz, Archbishop emeritus of Saint Paul, and James Richard Ham, Titular Bishop of Puzia in Numidia, consecrated (1) Paul Vincent Dudley, Titular Bishop of Ursona, Auxiliary of Saint Paul and Minneapolis, born at Northfield, Minnesota (Saint Paul), November 29, 1926; priest June 2, 1951; named November 9, 1976; Bishop of Sioux Falls November 6, 1978. Consecrated (2) John Francis Kinney, Titular Bishop of Caorle, Auxiliary of Saint Paul and Minneapolis, born at Oelwein, Iowa (Dubuque), June 11, 1937; priest February 2 1963; named November 9, 1976; Bishop of Bismarck May 28, 1982.

880–881. 1977, February 19, at Los Angeles, California, Saint Vibiana's Cathedral. Timothy Cardinal Manning, Archbishop of Los Angeles, assisted by John James Ward, Titular Bishop of Bria, and Juan Alfredo Arzube, Titular Bishop of Civitate, consecrated (1) Manuel Duran Moreno, Titular Bishop of Tamagrista, Auxiliary of Los Angeles, born at Placentia, California (Los Angeles-San Diego), November 27, 1930; priest April 25, 1961; named December 20, 1976; Bishop of Tucson January 9, 1982. Consecrated (2) Thaddeus Anthony Shubsda, Titular Bishop of Trau, Auxiliary of Los Angeles, born at Los Angeles, California (Los Angeles-San Diego), April 2, 1925; priest April 26, 1950; named December 20, 1976; Bishop of Monterey May 26, 1982.

882. 1977, March 27, at Loudonville, New York, Siena College. Terence James Cardinal Cooke, Archbishop of New York, assisted by Edwin Bernard Broderick, Bishop emeritus of Albany, and Edward Joseph Maginn, Titular Bishop of Curium, consecrated Howard James Hubbard, Bishop of Albany, born at Troy, New York (Albany), October 31, 1938; priest December 18, 1963; named January 24, 1977.

883. 1977, April 14, at Manchester, New Hampshire, Saint Joseph Cathedral. Odore Joseph Gendron, Bishop of Manchester, assisted by Ernest John Primeau, Bishop emeritus of Manchester, and John Francis

Hackett, Titular Bishop of Helenopolis in Palestina, consecrated Robert Edward Mulvee, Titular Bishop of Summa, Auxiliary of Manchester, born at Boston, Massachusetts, February 15, 1930; priest June 30, 1957; named February 15, 1977; Bishop of Wilmington February 16, 1985.

884–885. 1977, May 9, at Rockville Centre, New York, Saint Agnes Cathedral. John Raymond McGann, Bishop of Rockville Centre, assisted by Walter Philip Kellenberg, Bishop emeritus of Rockville Centre, and Vincent John Baldwin, Titular Bishop of Bencenna, consecrated (1) Gerald Augustine John Ryan, Titular Bishop of Munatiana, Auxiliary of Rockville Centre, born at Brooklyn, New York, August 24, 1923; priest June 3, 1950; named February 28, 1977; died at Brentwood, New York, June 4, 1985. Consecrated (2) James Joseph Daly, Titular Bishop of Castra Nova, Auxiliary of Rockville Centre, born at New York, New York, August 14, 1921; priest May 22, 1948; named February 28, 1977.

886. 1977, May 12, at Yakima, Washington, Holy Family Church. Raymond Gerhardt Hunthausen, Archbishop of Seattle, assisted by Bernard Joseph Topel, Bishop of Spokane, and Bernard Francis Law, Bishop of Springfield-Cape Girardeau, consecrated William Stephen Skylstad, Bishop of Yakima, born at Methow, Washington (Spokane), March 2, 1934; priest May 21, 1960; named February 16, 1977.

887–889. 1977, June 29, at New York, New York, Saint Patrick's Cathedral. Terence James Cardinal Cooke, Archbishop of New York, assisted by John Joseph Maguire, Titular Archbishop of Tabalta, and Patrick Vincent Ahern, Titular Bishop of Naiera, consecrated (1) Theodore Edgar McCarrick, Titular Bishop of Rusubisir, Auxiliary of New York, born at New York, New York, July 7, 1930; priest May 31, 1958; named May 24, 1977; first Bishop of Metuchen November 19, 1981; Archbishop of Newark May 30, 1986. Consecrated (2) Austin Bernard Vaughan, Titular Bishop of Cluain Iraird, Auxiliary of New York, born at New York, New York, September 27, 1927; priest December 8, 1951; named May 24, 1977. Consecrated (3) Francisco Garmendia, Titular Bishop of Limisa, Auxiliary of New York, born at Lazcano (San Sebastian), Spain, November 6, 1924; priest June 29, 1947; named May 24, 1977.

890. 1977, July 21, at Joliet, Illinois, Cathedral of Saint Raymond Nonnatus. Romeo Roy Blanchette, Bishop of Joliet, assisted by Andrew Gregory Grutka, Bishop of Gary, and Raymond James Vonesh, Titular Bishop of Vanariona, consecrated Daniel William Kucera, OSB, Titular Bishop of Natchez, Auxiliary of Joliet, born at Chicago, Illinois, May 7, 1923; priest May 26, 1949; named May 30, 1977; Bishop of Salina March 5, 1980; Archbishop of Dubuque December 16, 1983.

891. 1977, August 4, at La Crosse, Wisconsin, Cathedral of Saint Joseph the Workman. Frederick William Freking, Bishop of La Crosse, assisted by Arthur Joseph O'Neill, Bishop of Rockford, and Mark Francis Schmitt, Titular Bishop of Ceanannus Mor, consecrated John Joseph Paul, Titular Bishop of Lambaesis, Auxiliary of La Crosse, born at La Crosse, Wisconsin, August 17, 1918; priest January 24, 1943; named May 10, 1977; Bishop of La Crosse October 14, 1983.

892. 1977, August 15, at Washington, District of Columbia, National Shrine of the Immaculate Conception. Joseph Louis Bernardin, Archbishop of Cincinnati, assisted by James Steven Rausch, Bishop of Phoenix, and Eugene Antonio Marino, Titular Bishop of Walla Walla, consecrated Thomas Cajetan Kelly, OP, Titular Bishop of Tusuros, Auxiliary of Washington, born at Rochester, New York, July 14, 1931; priest June 5, 1958; named July 2, 1977; Archbishop of Louisville December 28, 1981.

893. 1977, November 8, at Milwaukee, Wisconsin, Saint John Cathedral. Jean Jadot, Titular Archbishop of Zuri, Apostolic Delegate to the United States, assisted by William Edward Cousins, Archbishop emeritus of Milwaukee, and William Graham Connare, Bishop of Greensburg, consecrated Rembert George Weakland, OSB, Archbishop of Milwaukee, born at Patton, Pennsylvania (Altoona), April 2, 1927; priest June 24, 1951; named September 17, 1977.

894. 1978, January 13, at Honolulu, Hawaii, Exhibition Hall of the Neal Blaisdell Center. John Joseph Scanlan, Bishop of Honolulu, assisted by John Raphael Quinn, Archbishop of San Francisco, and James Clifford Timlin, Titular Bishop of Gunugus, consecrated Joseph Anthony Ferrario, Titular Bishop of Cuse, Auxiliary of Honolulu, born at Scranton, Pennsylvania, March 3, 1926; priest May 19, 1951; named November 3, 1977; Bishop of Honolulu May 13, 1982.

895. 1978, February 28, at Paterson, New Jersey, Cathedral of Saint John the Baptist. Peter Leo Gerety, Archbishop of Newark, assisted by Joseph Louis Bernardin, Archbishop of Cincinnati, and Peter Poreku Dery, Archbishop of Tamale, Ghana, consecrated Frank Joseph Rodimer, Bishop of Paterson, born at Rockaway, New Jersey (Newark), October 25, 1927; priest May 19, 1951; named December 5, 1977.

896–897. 1978, March 2, at Portland, Oregon, Civic Auditorium. Cornelius Michael Power, Archbishop of Portland in Oregon, assisted by Elden Francis Curtiss, Bishop of Helena, and Alfredo Francisco Mendez, Bishop of Arecibo, consecrated (1) Paul Edward Waldschmidt, CSC, Titular Bishop of Citium, Auxiliary of Portland in Oregon, born at Evansville, Indiana (Indianapolis), January 7, 1920; priest June 24, 1946;

named November 28, 1977; resigned as Auxiliary of Portland in Oregon January 8, 1990. Consecrated (2) Kenneth Donald Steiner, Titular Bishop of Avensa, Auxiliary of Portland in Oregon, born at David City, Nebraska (Lincoln), November 25, 1936; priest May 19, 1962; named November 28, 1977.

898. 1978, March 9, at Madison, Wisconsin, Saint Raphael Cathedral. Cletus Francis O'Donnell, Bishop of Madison, assisted by Jerome Joseph Hastrich, Bishop of Gallup, and Rembert George Weakland, Archbishop of Milwaukee, consecrated George Otto Wirz, Titular Bishop of Municipa, Auxiliary of Madison, born at Monroe, Wisconsin (Milwaukee), January 17, 1929; priest May 31, 1952; named December 13, 1977.

899. 1978, March 13, at Syracuse, New York, Cathedral of the Immaculate Conception. Frank James Harrison, Bishop of Syracuse, assisted by David Frederick Cunningham, Bishop emeritus of Syracuse, and Francis John Mugavero, Bishop of Brooklyn, consecrated Thomas Joseph Costello, Titular Bishop of Perdices, Auxiliary of Syracuse, born at Camden, New York (Syracuse), February 23, 1929; priest June 5, 1954; named January 2, 1978.

900. 1978, March 28, at Grand Island, Nebraska, Cathedral of the Nativity of the Blessed Virgin Mary. Daniel Eugene Sheehan, Archbishop of Omaha, assisted by Charles Herman Helmsing, Bishop emeritus of Kansas City-Saint Joseph, and John Joseph Sullivan, Bishop of Kansas City-Saint Joseph, consecrated Lawrence James McNamara, Bishop of Grand Island, born at Chicago, Illinois, August 5, 1928; priest May 30, 1953; named January 2, 1978.

901. 1978, April 20, at Tulsa, Oklahoma, Holy Family Cathedral. Charles Alexander Salatka, Archbishop of Oklahoma City, assisted by Thomas Andrew Donnellan, Archbishop of Atlanta, and Andrew Joseph McDonald, Bishop of Little Rock, consecrated Eusebius Joseph Beltran, Bishop of Tulsa, born at Ashley, Pennsylvania (Scranton), August 31, 1934; priest May 14, 1960; named February 17, 1978.

902. 1978, June 23, at Toledo, Ohio, Queen of the Most Holy Rosary Cathedral. John Anthony Donovan, Bishop of Toledo, assisted by Joseph Louis Bernardin, Archbishop of Cincinnati, and Albert Henry Ottenweller, Bishop of Steubenville, consecrated James Robert Hoffman, Titular Bishop of Italica, Auxiliary of Toledo, born at Fremont, Ohio (Toledo), June 12, 1932; priest July 28, 1957; named April 18, 1978; Bishop of Toledo December 12, 1980.

903. 1978, June 24, at Hartford, Connecticut, Cathedral of Saint Joseph.

John Francis Whealon, Archbishop of Hartford, assisted by John Francis Hackett, Titular Bishop of Helenopolis in Palestina, and Ulises Aurelio Casiano Vargas, Bishop of Mayaguez, consecrated Peter Anthony Rosazza, Titular Bishop of Oppidum Novum, Auxiliary of Hartford, born at New Haven, Connecticut (Hartford), February 13, 1935; priest June 29, 1961; named February 17, 1978.

904–905. 1978, June 29, at San Francisco, California, Cathedral of Saint Mary. John Raphael Quinn, Archbishop of San Francisco, assisted by Joseph Thomas McGucken, Archbishop emeritus of San Francisco, and William Joseph McDonald, Titular Bishop of Aquae Regiae, consecrated (1) Francis Anthony Quinn, Titular Bishop of Numana, Auxiliary of San Francisco, born at Los Angeles, California (Monterey-Los Angeles), September 11, 1921; priest June 15, 1946; named April 24, 1978; Bishop of Sacramento December 12, 1979. Consecrated (2) Roland Pierre DuMaine, Titular Bishop of Sarda, Auxiliary of San Francisco, born at Paducah, Kentucky (Louisville), August 2, 1931; priest June 15, 1957; named April 24, 1978; first Bishop of San Jose in California January 27, 1981.

906. 1978, August 21, at Great Falls, Montana, College of Great Falls. Cornelius Michael Power, Archbishop of Portland in Oregon, assisted by Eldon Bernard Schuster, Bishop emeritus of Great Falls, and Alfred Leo Abramowicz, Titular Bishop of Pesto, consecrated Thomas Joseph Murphy, Bishop of Great Falls, born at Chicago, Illinois, October 3, 1932; priest April 12, 1958; named July 5, 1978; title of see changed to Great Falls-Billings February 14, 1980; Coadjutor Archbishop of Seattle May 26, 1987.

907. 1978, November 6, at Riverside, California, Raincross Square. Timothy Cardinal Manning, Archbishop of Los Angeles, assisted by John Raphael Quinn, Archbishop of San Francisco, and Leo Thomas Maher, Bishop of San Diego, consecrated Philip Francis Straling, first Bishop of San Bernardino, born at San Bernardino, California (Los Angeles-San Diego), April 25, 1933; priest March 19, 1959; named July 14, 1978.

908. 1978, December 14, at Spokane, Washington, Cathedral of Our Lady of Lourdes. Raymond Gerhardt Hunthausen, Archbishop of Seattle, assisted by Harold Joseph Dimmerling, Bishop of Rapid City, and Bernard Joseph Topel, Bishop emeritus of Spokane, consecrated Lawrence Harold Welsh, Bishop of Spokane, born at Winton, Wyoming (Cheyenne), February 1, 1935; priest May 26, 1962; named November 6, 1978.

909. 1979, February 22, at Green Bay, Wisconsin, Saint Francis Xavier Cathedral. Aloysius John Wycislo, Bishop of Green Bay, assisted by Mark Francis Schmitt, Bishop of Marquette, and John Benjamin Grellinger,

Titular Bishop of Syene, consecrated Robert Fealey Morneau, Titular Bishop of Massa Lubrense, Auxiliary of Green Bay, born at New London, Wisconsin (Green Bay), September 10, 1938; priest May 28, 1966; named December 11, 1978.

910. 1979, March 14, at Houston, Texas, Saint Theresa's Church. John Louis Morkovsky, Bishop of Galveston-Houston, assisted by Lawrence Michael DeFalco, Bishop of Amarillo, and Patrick Fernández Flores, Bishop of El Paso, consecrated John Edward McCarthy, Titular Bishop of Pedena, Auxiliary of Galveston-Houston, born at Houston, Texas (Galveston), June 21, 1930; priest May 26, 1956; named January 15, 1979; Bishop of Austin December 19, 1985.

911–912. 1979, March 24, at Miami Beach, Florida, Miami Beach Convention Hall. Edward Anthony McCarthy, Archbishop of Miami, assisted by Rene Henry Gracida, Bishop of Pensacola-Tallahassee, and John Joseph Fitzpatrick, Bishop of Brownsville, consecrated (1) Agustín Alejo Román, Titular Bishop of Sertei, Auxiliary of Miami, born at San Antonio de los Baños (San Cristobal de la Habana), Cuba, May 5, 1928; priest July 5, 1959; named January 25, 1979. Consecrated (2) John Joseph Nevins, Titular Bishop of Rusticiana, Auxiliary of Miami, born at New Rochelle, New York (New York), January 19, 1932; priest June 6, 1959; named January 25, 1979; first Bishop of Venice June 16, 1984.

913. 1979, May 14, at Belleville, Illinois, Cathedral of Saint Peter. William Michael Cosgrove, Bishop of Belleville, assisted by Albert Rudolph Zuroweste, Bishop emeritus of Belleville, and Philip Francis Murphy, Titular Bishop of Tacarata, consecrated Stanley Girard Schlarman, Titular Bishop of Capri, Auxiliary of Belleville, born at Belleville, Illinois, July 27, 1933; priest July 13, 1958; named March 8, 1979; Bishop of Dodge City February 25, 1983.

914–918. 1979, May 27, at Rome, Vatican City, Saint Peter's Basilica. Pope John Paul II, assisted by Duraisamy Simon Lourdusamy, Archbishop emeritus of Bangalore, and Eduardo Martínez Somalo, Titular Archbishop of Thagora, consecrated (1) Michael Hughes Kenny, Bishop of Juneau, born at Hollywood, California (Los Angeles), June 26, 1937; priest March 30, 1963; named March 22, 1979. Consecrated (2) William Russell Houck, Titular Bishop of Alessano, Auxiliary of Jackson, born at Mobile, Alabama, June 26, 1926; priest May 19, 1951; named March 28, 1979; Bishop of Jackson April 11, 1984. Consecrated (3) William Thomas Larkin, Bishop of Saint Petersburg, born at Mount Morris, New York (Rochester), March 31, 1923; priest May 15, 1947; named April 18, 1979; resigned November 29, 1988. Consecrated (4) John Joseph O'Connor, Titular Bishop of Curzola, Auxiliary of the Military Vicar of the United States, born at Philadelphia, Pennsylvania, January 15, 1920; priest December 15, 1945; named April 18, 1979; Bishop of Scranton May 6, 1983; Archbishop of New York and Apostolic Administrator of the Military Vicariate of the United States January 26, 1984; ceased his duties as Apostolic Administrator of the Military Vicariate of the United States on March 25, 1985; Cardinal May 25, 1985. Consecrated (5) Matthew Harvey Clark, Bishop of Rochester, born at Troy, New York (Albany), July 15, 1937; priest December 19, 1962; named April 23, 1979.

919–921. 1979, August 1, at Cleveland, Ohio, Cathedral of Saint John the Evangelist. James Aloysius Hickey, Bishop of Cleveland, assisted by Clarence George Issenmann, Bishop emeritus of Cleveland, and Joseph Abel Francis, Titular Bishop of Valliposita, consecrated (1) Anthony Michael Pilla, Titular Bishop of Scardona, Auxiliary of Cleveland, born at Cleveland, Ohio, November 12, 1932; priest May 23, 1959; named June 30, 1979; Bishop of Cleveland November 13, 1980. Consecrated (2) James Anthony Griffin, Titular Bishop of Holar, Auxiliary of Cleveland, born at Fairview Park, Ohio (Cleveland), June 13, 1934; priest May 28, 1960; named June 30, 1979; Bishop of Columbus February 4, 1983. Consecrated (3) James Patterson Lyke, OFM, Titular Bishop of Furnos Major, Auxiliary of Cleveland, born at Chicago, Illinois, February 18, 1939; priest June 24, 1966; named June 30, 1979.

922. 1979, September 21, at Harrisburg, Pennsylvania, Saint Patrick's Cathedral. Joseph Thomas Daley, Bishop of Harrisburg, assisted by Francis Joseph Gossman, Bishop of Raleigh, and Martin Nicholas Lohmuller, Titular Bishop of Ramsbiria, consecrated William Henry Keeler, Titular Bishop of Ulcinium, Auxiliary of Harrisburg, born at San Antonio, Texas, March 4, 1931; priest July 17, 1955; named July 24, 1979; Bishop of Harrisburg November 10, 1983; Archbishop of Baltimore April 6, 1989.

923. 1979, October 25, at San Angelo, Texas, Cathedral of the Sacred Heart. Patrick Fernández Flores, Archbishop of San Antonio, assisted by John Louis Morkovsky, Bishop of Galveston-Houston, and John Edward McCarthy, Titular Bishop of Pedena, consecrated Joseph Anthony Fiorenza, Bishop of San Angelo, born at Beaumont, Texas (Galveston), January 25, 1931; priest May 29, 1954; named August 20, 1979; Bishop of Galveston-Houston December 6, 1984.

924. 1979, October 30, at Mobile, Alabama, Cathedral Basilica of the Immaculate Conception. Philip Matthew Hannan, Archbishop of New Orleans, assisted by John Lawrence May, Bishop of Mobile, and Lawrence Preston Joseph Graves, Bishop of Alexandria-Shreveport, consecrated William Benedict Friend, Titular Bishop of Pomaria, Auxiliary of

Alexandria-Shreveport, born at Miami, Florida (Saint Augustine), October 22, 1931; priest May 7, 1959; named August 31, 1979; Bishop of Alexandria-Shreveport November 17, 1982; first Bishop of Shreveport June 16, 1986.

925. 1979, November 12, at Rome, Vatican City, Sistine Chapel. Pope John Paul II, assisted by Josyp Cardinal Slipyj, Major Archbishop of Lviv of the Ukrainians, and Maxim Hermaniuk, Archbishop of Winnipeg of the Ukrainians, consecrated Myroslav Ivan Lubachivsky, Archbishop of Philadelphia of the Ukrainians, born at Dolyna (Lviv), Ukraine, June 24, 1914; priest September 21, 1938; named September 13, 1979; Coadjutor Archbishop of Lviv of the Ukrainians March 27, 1980; succeeded to the Major Archiepiscopal see of Lviv of the Ukrainians September 7, 1984; Cardinal May 25, 1985.

926. 1979, December 19, at Milwaukee, Wisconsin, Saint John Cathedral. Rembert George Weakland, Archbishop of Milwaukee, assisted by William Edward Cousins, Archbishop emeritus of Milwaukee, and Robert Fortune Sanchez, Archbishop of Santa Fe, consecrated Richard John Sklba, Titular Bishop of Castro di Puglia, Auxiliary of Milwaukee, born at Racine, Wisconsin (Milwaukee), September 11, 1935; priest December 20, 1959; named November 5, 1979.

927. 1979, December 20, at Superior, Wisconsin, Cathedral of Christ the King. George Albert Hammes, Bishop of Superior, assisted by Rembert George Weakland, Archbishop of Milwaukee, and William Edward Cousins, Archbishop emeritus of Milwaukee, consecrated Raphael Michael Fliss, Coadjutor Bishop of Superior, born at Milwaukee, Wisconsin, October 25, 1930; priest May 26, 1956; named November 5, 1979; succeeded to Superior June 27, 1985.

928. 1980, March 4, at Fresno, California, Selland Arena of the Fresno Convention Center. Hugh Aloysius Donohoe, Bishop of Fresno, assisted by Roger Michael Mahony, Bishop of Stockton, and Juan Alfredo Arzube, Titular Bishop of Civitate, consecrated José de Jesús Madera Uribe, M.Sp.S, Coadjutor Bishop of Fresno, born at San Francisco, California, November 27, 1927; priest June 15, 1957; named December 12, 1979; succeeded to Fresno July 1, 1980.

929. 1980, April 25, at Lake Charles, Louisiana, Civic Center. Gerard Louis Frey, Bishop of Lafayette, assisted by Maurice Schexnayder, Bishop emeritus of Lafayette, and Harold Robert Perry, Titular Bishop of Mons in Mauritania, consecrated Jude Speyrer, first Bishop of Lake Charles, born at Leonville, Louisiana (Lafayette), April 14, 1929; priest July 25, 1953; named January 29, 1980.

930. 1980, May 30, at Amarillo, Texas, Civic Center. Patrick Fernández Flores, Archbishop of San Antonio, assisted by John Louis Morkovsky, Bishop of Galveston-Houston, and Thomas Joseph Drury, Bishop of Corpus Christi, consecrated Leroy Theodore Matthiesen, Bishop of Amarillo, born at Olfen, Texas (San Antonio), June 2, 1921; priest March 10, 1946; named March 18, 1980.

931. 1980, August 12, at Saint Paul, Minnesota, Cathedral of Saint Paul. John Robert Roach, Archbishop of Saint Paul and Minneapolis, assisted by Paul Vincent Dudley, Bishop of Sioux Falls, and Raymond Alphonse Lucker, Bishop of New Ulm, consecrated William Henry Bullock, Titular Bishop of Natchez, Auxiliary of Saint Paul and Minneapolis, born at Maple Lake, Minnesota (Saint Paul), April 13, 1927; priest June 7, 1952; named June 3, 1980; Bishop of Des Moines February 5, 1987.

932. 1980, August 22, at Springfield, Massachusetts, Saint Michael's Cathedral. Joseph Francis Maguire, Bishop of Springfield, assisted by Thomas Robert Manning, Bishop-Prelate of Coroico, and Timothy Joseph Harrington, Titular Bishop of Rusuca, consecrated Leo Edward O'Neil, Titular Bishop of Bencenna, Auxiliary of Springfield, born at Holyoke, Massachusetts (Springfield), January 31, 1928; priest June 4, 1955; named June 3, 1980; Coadjutor Bishop of Manchester September 30, 1989.

933. 1980, September 4, at Youngstown, Ohio, Cathedral of Saint Columba. James William Malone, Bishop of Youngstown, assisted by Joseph Louis Bernardin, Archbishop of Cincinnati, and William Anthony Hughes, Bishop of Covington, consecrated Benedict Charles Franzetta, Titular Bishop of Oderzo, Auxiliary of Youngstown, born at East Liverpool, Ohio (Cleveland), August 1, 1921; priest April 29, 1950; named July 26, 1980.

934. 1980, September 10, at Pueblo, Colorado, Massari Gymnasium. James Vincent Casey, Archbishop of Denver, assisted by Robert Fortune Sanchez, Archbishop of Santa Fe, and Charles Albert Buswell, Bishop emeritus of Pueblo, consecrated Arthur Nicholas Tafoya, Bishop of Pueblo, born at Alameda, New Mexico (Santa Fe), March 2, 1933; priest May 12, 1962; named July 1, 1980.

935. 1980, November 16, at Mobile, Alabama, Mobile Municipal Auditorium. John Lawrence May, Archbishop of Saint Louis, assisted by William Benedict Friend, Titular Bishop of Pomaria, and Raymond William Lessard, Bishop of Savannah, consecrated Oscar Hugh Lipscomb, first Archbishop of Mobile, born at Mobile, Alabama, September 21, 1931; priest July 15, 1956; named July 29, 1980.

936. 1980, November 17, at Salt Lake City, Utah, Salt Palace. John Raphael Quinn, Archbishop of San Francisco, assisted by Sylvester William Treinen, Bishop of Boise City, and Joseph Lennox Federal, Bishop emeritus of Salt Lake City, consecrated William Kenneth Weigand, Bishop of Salt Lake City, born at Bend, Oregon (Baker), May 23, 1937; priest May 25, 1963; named September 3, 1980.

937–939. 1980, November 24, at Brooklyn, New York, Basilica of Our Lady of Perpetual Help. Francis John Mugavero, Bishop of Brooklyn, assisted by John Joseph Snyder, Bishop of Saint Augustine, and Charles Richard Mulrooney, Titular Bishop of Valentiniana, consecrated (1) Anthony Joseph Bevilacqua, Titular Bishop of Aquae Albae in Byzacena, Auxiliary of Brooklyn, born at Brooklyn, New York, June 17, 1923; priest June 11, 1949; named October 4, 1980; Bishop of Pittsburgh October 10, 1983; Archbishop of Philadelphia February 11, 1988. Consecrated (2) Joseph Michael Sullivan, Titular Bishop of Suliana, Auxiliary of Brooklyn, born at Brooklyn, New York, March 23, 1930; priest June 2, 1956; named October 4, 1980. Consecrated (3) Rene Arnold Valero, Titular Bishop of Vicus Turris, Auxiliary of Brooklyn, born at New York, New York, August 15, 1930; priest June 2, 1956; named October 4, 1980.

940. 1980, November 24, at Saginaw, Michigan, Saginaw Civic Center. John Francis Cardinal Dearden, Archbishop emeritus of Detroit, assisted by Francis Frederick Reh, Bishop emeritus of Saginaw, and Thomas John Gumbleton, Titular Bishop of Ululi, consecrated Kenneth Edward Untener, Bishop of Saginaw, born at Detroit, Michigan, August 3, 1937; priest June 1, 1963; named October 4, 1980.

941. 1981, January 25, at Bkerké, Lebanon, Patriarcal Church of Our Lady of the Assumption. Antoine Pierre Khoraiche, Patriarch of Antioch of the Maronites, assisted by Francis Mansour Zayek, Bishop of Saint Maron of Brooklyn of the Maronites, and Nasrallah Sfeir, Titular Bishop of Tarsus of the Maronites, consecrated John George Chedid, Titular Bishop of Callinicum of the Maronites, Auxiliary of Saint Maron of Brooklyn of the Maronites, born at Eddid (Gibail et Batrun), Lebanon, July 4, 1923; priest December 21, 1951; named October 13, 1980.

942–943. 1981, March 1, at Rome, Italy, Church of Santa Sofia. Josyp Cardinal Slipyj, Major Archbishop of Lviv of the Ukrainians, assisted by Basil Harry Losten, Bishop of Stamford of the Ukrainians, and Nile Nicholas Savaryn, Bishop of Edmonton of the Ukrainians, consecrated (1) Stephen Sulyk, Archbishop of Philadelphia of the Ukrainians, born at Balnycia (Przemysl of the Ukrainians), Ukraine, October 2, 1924; priest June 14, 1952; named December 29, 1980. Consecrated (2) Innocent Hilarion Lotocky, OSBM, Bishop of Saint Nicholas of Chicago of the

Ukrainians, born at Petlykiwci (Stanislaviv of the Ukrainians), Ukraine, November 3, 1915; priest November 24, 1940; named December 29, 1980.

944. 1981, March 19, at Saint Petersburg, Florida, Cathedral of Saint Jude the Apostle. William Thomas Larkin, Bishop of Saint Petersburg, assisted by Edward Anthony McCarthy, Archbishop of Miami, and Thomas Joseph McDonough, Archbishop of Louisville, consecrated Joseph Keith Symons, Titular Bishop of Sigus, Auxiliary of Saint Petersburg, born at Champion, Illinois (Sault Sainte Marie and Marquette), October 14, 1932; priest May 18, 1958; named January 16, 1981; Bishop of Pensacola-Tallahassee September 29, 1983.

945–946. 1981, August 12, at Philadelphia, Pennsylvania, Cathedral Basilica of Saints Peter and Paul. John Joseph Cardinal Krol, Archbishop of Philadelphia, assisted by John Joseph Graham, Titular Bishop of Sabrata, and Martin Nicholas Lohmuller, Titular Bishop of Ramsbiria, consecrated (1) Louis Anthony DeSimone, Titular Bishop of Cillium, Auxiliary of Philadelphia, born at Philadelphia, Pennsylvania, February 21, 1922; priest May 10, 1952; named June 27, 1981. Consecrated (2) Francis Bible Schulte, Titular Bishop of Afufenia, Auxiliary of Philadelphia, born at Philadelphia, Pennsylvania, December 23, 1926; priest May 10, 1952; named June 27, 1981; Bishop of Wheeling-Charleston May 31, 1985; Archbishop of New Orleans December 6, 1988.

947. 1981, August 20, at San Antonio, Texas, Villita Assembly Hall. Patrick Fernández Flores, Archbishop of San Antonio, assisted by Sydney Matthew Metzger, Bishop emeritus of El Paso, and John Louis Morkovsky, Bishop of Galveston-Houston, consecrated Charles Victor Grahmann, Titular Bishop of Equilium, Auxiliary of San Antonio, born at Hallettsville, Texas (San Antonio), July 15, 1931; priest March 17, 1956; named June 27, 1981; first Bishop of Victoria in Texas April 13, 1982; Coadjutor Bishop of Dallas December 9, 1989.

948. 1981, September 13, at Fort Worth, Texas, Tarrant County Convention Center. Patrick Fernández Flores, Archbishop of San Antonio, assisted by John Joseph Cassata, Bishop emeritus of Fort Worth, and John Joseph Fitzpatrick, Bishop of Brownsville, consecrated Joseph Patrick Delaney, Bishop of Fort Worth, born at Fall River, Massachusetts, August 29, 1934; priest December 18, 1960; named July 10, 1981.

949. 1981, September 14, at Boston, Massachusetts, Cathedral of the Holy Cross. Humberto Sousa Cardinal Medeiros, Archbishop of Boston, assisted by Thomas Vose Daily, Titular Bishop of Bladia, and John Michael D'Arcy, Titular Bishop of Mediana, consecrated Alfred Clifton Hughes, Titular Bishop of Maximiana in Byzacena, Auxiliary of Boston, born at Boston, Massachusetts, December 2, 1932; priest December 15, 1957; named July 21, 1981.

950. 1981, September 24, at San Francisco, California, Cathedral of Saint Mary. John Raphael Quinn, Archbishop of San Francisco, assisted by Michael Hughes Kenny, Bishop of Juneau, and Joseph Anthony Ferrario, Titular Bishop of Cuse, consecrated Daniel Francis Walsh, Titular Bishop of Tigias, Auxiliary of San Francisco, born at San Francisco, California, October 2, 1937; priest March 30, 1963; named June 30, 1981; Bishop of Reno-Las Vegas June 3, 1987.

951. 1981, September 30, at Joliet, Illinois, Cathedral of Saint Raymond Nonnatus. Joseph Leopold Imesch, Bishop of Joliet, assisted by Raymond James Vonesh, Titular Bishop of Vanariona, and Daniel William Kucera, Bishop of Salina, consecrated Daniel Leo Ryan, Titular Bishop of Surista, Auxiliary of Joliet, born at Mankato, Minnesota (Winona), September 28, 1930; priest May 3, 1956; named August 13, 1981; Bishop of Springfield in Illinois November 19, 1983.

952. 1981, October 13, at Philadelphia, Pennsylvania, Immaculate Conception of the Blessed Virgin Mary Ukrainian Catholic Cathedral. Stephen Sulyk, Archbishop of Philadelphia of the Ukrainians, assisted by Basil Harry Losten, Bishop of Stamford of the Ukrainians, and Innocent Hilarion Lotocky, Bishop of Saint Nicholas of Chicago of the Ukrainians, consecrated Robert Mikhail Moskal, Titular Bishop of Agathopolis, Auxiliary of Philadelphia of the Ukrainians, born at Carnegie, Pennsylvania (Philadelphia of the Ukrainians), October 24, 1937; priest March 25, 1963; named August 3, 1981; first Bishop of Saint Josaphat in Parma of the Ukrainians December 5, 1983.

953. 1981, November 4, at Sacramento, California, Cathedral of the Blessed Sacrament. Francis Anthony Quinn, Bishop of Sacramento, assisted by John Raphael Quinn, Archbishop of San Francisco, and Robert Fortune Sanchez, Archbishop of Santa Fe, consecrated Alphonse Gallegos, OAR, Titular Bishop of Sasabe, Auxiliary of Sacramento, born at Albuquerque, New Mexico (Santa Fe), February 20, 1931; priest May 24, 1958; named August 24, 1981.

954. 1981, December 5, at Philadelphia, Pennsylvania, Cathedral Basilica of Saints Peter and Paul. Hemaiagh Pierre XVII Ghedighian, Patriarch of Cilicia of the Armenians, assisted by Paul Coussa, Titular Archbishop of Colonia in Armenia, and Andre Bedoglouyan, Titular Bishop of Comana Armeniae, consecrated Mikail Nerses Setian, Titular Bishop of Ancyra of the Armenians, Apostolic Exarch for Armenian Catholics in the United States and Canada, born at Sivas (Istanbul),

Turkey, November 18, 1918; priest April 13, 1941; named July 3, 1981.

955. 1981, December 6, at Gaylord, Michigan, Saint Mary Cathedral. Edmund Casimir Szoka, Archbishop of Detroit, assisted by Joseph Matthew Breitenbeck, Bishop of Grand Rapids, and Joseph Crescent McKinney, Titular Bishop of Lentini, consecrated Robert John Rose, Bishop of Gaylord, born at Grand Rapids, Michigan, February 28, 1930; priest December 21, 1955; named October 8, 1981; Bishop of Grand Rapids June 24, 1989.

956. 1981, December 6, at San Antonio, Texas, San Antonio Convention Center. Patrick Fernández Flores, Archbishop of San Antonio, assisted by John Louis Morkovsky, Bishop of Galveston-Houston, and Rafael Ayala y Ayala, Bishop of Tehuacan, consecrated Ricardo Ramirez, CSB, Titular Bishop of Vatarba, Auxiliary of San Antonio, born at Bay City, Texas (Galveston), September 12, 1936; priest December 10, 1966; named October 26, 1981; first Bishop of Las Cruces August 17, 1982.

957–958. 1982, January 6, at Rome, Vatican City, Saint Peter's Basilica. Pope John Paul II, assisted by Eduardo Martínez Somalo, Titular Archbishop of Thagora, and Lucas Moreira Neves, Titular Archbishop of Feradi Major, consecrated (1) Thomas Joseph O'Brien, Bishop of Phoenix, born at Indianapolis, Indiana, November 29, 1935; priest May 7, 1961; named November 19, 1981. Consecrated (2) Anthony Michael Milone, Titular Bishop of Plestia, Auxiliary of Omaha, born at Omaha, Nebraska, September 24, 1932; priest December 15, 1957; named November 9, 1981; Bishop of Great Falls-Billings December 12, 1987.

959. 1982, March 7, at Bagdad, Iraq, Chaldean Cathedral. Paul II Cheikho, Patriarch of Babylon of the Chaldeans, assisted by Emmanuel-Karim Delly, Titular Archbishop of Kaskar of the Chaldeans, Georges Garmo, Archbishop of Mossul of the Chaldeans, Stephane Babaca, Archbishop of Arbil of the Chaldeans, Stephane Katcho, Archbishop of Bassorah of the Chaldeans, Abdul-Ahad Sana, Bishop of Alquoch of the Chaldeans, and Abdul-Ahad Rabban, Bishop of Aqra of the Chaldeans, consecrated Ibrahim Namo Ibrahim, Titular Bishop of Anbar of the Chaldeans, Apostolic Exarch for Chaldean Catholics in the United States, born at Telkaif (Mossul), Iraq, October 10, 1937; priest December 30, 1962; named January 11, 1982; first Bishop of Saint Thomas Apostle of Detroit of the Chaldeans August 3, 1985.

960. 1982, July 2, at Cleveland, Ohio, Cathedral of Saint John the Evangelist. Anthony Michael Pilla, Bishop of Cleveland, assisted by Joseph Louis Bernardin, Archbishop of Cincinnati, and William Michael Cosgrove, Bishop emeritus of Belleville, consecrated Edward Anthony

Pevec, Titular Bishop of Mercia, Auxiliary of Cleveland, born at Cleveland, Ohio, April 16, 1925; priest April 29, 1950; named April 2, 1982.

961–962. 1982, September 8, at New York, New York, Saint Patrick's Cathedral. Terence James Cardinal Cooke, Archbishop of New York, assisted by John Joseph Maguire, Titular Archbishop of Tabalta, and Harold Robert Perry, Titular Bishop of Mons in Mauritania, consecrated (1) Joseph Thomas O'Keefe, Titular Bishop of Tre Taverne, Auxiliary of New York, born at New York, New York, March 12, 1919; priest April 17, 1948; named July 3, 1982; Bishop of Syracuse June 10, 1987. Consecrated (2) Emerson John Moore, Titular Bishop of Curubis, Auxiliary of New York, born at New York, New York, May 16, 1938; priest May 30, 1964; named July 3, 1982.

963. 1982, November 3, at Trenton, New Jersey, Saint Mary's Cathedral. John Charles Reiss, Bishop of Trenton, assisted by George William Ahr, Bishop emeritus of Trenton, and James John Hogan, Bishop of Altoona-Johnstown, consecrated Edward Urban Kmiec, Titular Bishop of Simiddica, Auxiliary of Trenton, born at Trenton, New Jersey, June 4, 1936; priest December 20, 1961; named August 27, 1982.

964. 1982, December 15, at Owensboro, Kentucky, Sports Center. Thomas Cajetan Kelly, Archbishop of Louisville, assisted by Henry Joseph Soenneker, Bishop emeritus of Owensboro, and Raymond Alphonse Lucker, Bishop of New Ulm, consecrated John Jeremiah McRaith, Bishop of Owensboro, born at Hutchinson, Minnesota (Saint Paul), December 6, 1934; priest February 21, 1960; named October 23, 1982.

965–967. 1983, January 27, at Detroit, Michigan, Cathedral of the Most Blessed Sacrament. Edmund Casimir Szoka, Archbishop of Detroit, assisted by Harold Robert Perry, Titular Bishop of Mons in Mauritania, and Arthur Henry Krawczak, Titular Bishop of Subbar, consecrated (1) Moses Bosco Anderson, SSE, Titular Bishop of Vatarba, Auxiliary of Detroit, born at Selma, Alabama (Mobile), September 9, 1928; priest May 30, 1958; named December 3, 1982. Consecrated (2) Patrick Ronald Cooney, Titular Bishop of Hodelm, Auxiliary of Detroit, born at Detroit, Michigan, March 10, 1934; priest December 20, 1959; named December 3, 1982; Bishop of Gaylord November 6, 1989. Consecrated (3) Dale Joseph Melczek, Titular Bishop of Trau, Auxiliary of Detroit, born at Detroit, Michigan, November 9, 1938; priest June 6, 1964; named December 3, 1982.

968. 1983, April 7, at Newark, New Jersey, Sacred Heart Cathedral. Peter Leo Gerety, Archbishop of Newark, assisted by Joseph Thomas

O'Keefe, Titular Bishop of Tre Taverne, and Alphonse Gallegos, Titular Bishop of Sasabe, consecrated David Arias, OAR, Titular Bishop of Badiae, Auxiliary of Newark, born at Mataluenga (Leon), Spain, July 22, 1929; priest May 31, 1952; named January 20, 1983.

969–971. 1983, May 10, at New York, New York, Saint Patrick's Cathedral. Terence James Cardinal Cooke, Archbishop of New York, assisted by John Joseph Thomas Ryan, Titular Archbishop of Gabi, and Louis Edward Gelineau, Bishop of Providence, consecrated (1) Joseph Thomas Dimino, Titular Bishop of Carini, Auxiliary of the Military Vicariate of the United States, born at New York, New York, January 7, 1923; priest June 4, 1949; named March 25, 1983. Consecrated (2) Francis Xavier Roque, Titular Bishop of Bagai, Auxiliary of the Military Vicariate of the United States, born at Providence, Rhode Island, October 9, 1928; priest September 19, 1953; named March 25, 1983. Consecrated (3) Lawrence James Kenney, Titular Bishop of Holar, Auxiliary of the Military Vicariate of the United States, born at New Rochelle, New York (New York), August 30, 1930; priest June 2, 1956; named March 25, 1983.

972–973. 1983, May 12, at Los Angeles, California, Saint Vibiana's Cathedral. Timothy Caridnal Manning, Archbishop of Los Angeles, assisted by John James Ward, Titular Bishop of Bria, and Juan Alfredo Arzube, Titular Bishop of Civitate, consecrated (1) Donald William Montrose, Titular Bishop of Vescovio, Auxiliary of Los Angeles, born at Denver, Colorado, May 13, 1923; priest May 7, 1949; named March 25, 1983; Bishop of Stockton December 17, 1985. Consecrated (2) William Joseph Levada, Titular Bishop of Capri, Auxiliary of Los Angeles, born at Long Beach, California (Los Angeles-San Diego), June 15, 1936; priest December 20, 1971; named March 25, 1983; Archbishop of Portland in Oregon July 1, 1986.

974. 1983, May 23, at Duluth, Minnesota, Cathedral of Our Lady of the Rosary. John Robert Roach, Archbishop of Saint Paul and Minneapolis, assisted by Loras Joseph Watters, Bishop of Winona, and Paul Francis Anderson, Bishop emeritus of Duluth, consecrated Robert Henry Brom, Bishop of Duluth, born at Arcadia, Wisconsin (La Crosse), September 18, 1938; priest December 18, 1963; named March 25, 1983; Coadjutor Bishop of San Diego April 22, 1989.

975. 1983, June 17, at Lubbock, Texas, Lubbock Memorial Civic Center. Patrick Fernández Flores, Archbishop of San Antonio, assisted by Leroy Theodore Matthiesen, Bishop of Amarillo, and Thomas Ambrose Tschoepe, Bishop of Dallas, consecrated Michael Jarboe Sheehan, first Bishop of Lubbock, born at Wichita, Texas (Dallas), July 9, 1939; priest July 19, 1964; named March 25, 1983.

976. 1983, June 26, at Detroit, Michigan, Saint John's Church. Traian Crisan, Titular Archbishop of Drivastum, Secretary of the Congregation for the Causes of the Saints, assisted by Emil John Mihalik, Bishop of Parma of the Ruthenians, and Michael Joseph Dudick, Bishop of Passaic of the Ruthenians, consecrated Vasile Louis Puscas, Titular Bishop of Leuce, Apostolic Exarch for Romanian Catholics of the Byzantine Rite in the United States, born at Aurora, Illinois (Rockford), September 13, 1915; priest May 14, 1942; named December 4, 1982; first Bishop of Saint George in Canton of the Romanians March 26, 1987.

977. 1983, July 25, at San Antonio, Texas, Cathedral of San Fernando. Patrick Fernández Flores, Archbishop of San Antonio, assisted by John Louis Morkovsky, Bishop of Galveston-Houston, and Hugo Mark Gerbermann, Titular Bishop of Pinhel, consecrated Bernard Ferdinand Popp, Titular Bishop of Capsus, Auxiliary of San Antonio, born at Nada, Texas (San Antonio), December 6, 1917; priest February 24, 1943; named June 3, 1983.

978. 1983, July 27, at Washington, District of Columbia, National Shrine of the Immaculate Conception. Pio Laghi, Titular Archbishop of Mauriana, Apostolic Delegate to the United States, assisted by Edward John Herrmann, Bishop emeritus of Columbus, and Francis Bible Schulte, Titular Bishop of Afufenia, consecrated Laszlo Anthony Iranyi, Sch.P., Titular Bishop of Castel Mediano, charged with the spiritual assistance of Catholic Hungarians in the diaspora, born at Szeged, Hungary, April 9, 1923; priest March 13, 1948; named May 20, 1983; died at Cologne, West Germany, March 6, 1987.

979. 1983, August 4, at Arlington, Virginia, Cathedral of Saint Thomas More. Pio Laghi, Titular Archbishop of Mauriana, Apostolic Delegate to the United States, assisted by Thomas Joseph Murphy, Bishop of Great Falls-Billings, and Thomas Jerome Welsh, Bishop of Allentown, consecrated John Richard Keating, Bishop of Arlington, born at Chicago, Illinois, July 20, 1934; priest December 20, 1958; named June 3, 1983.

980. 1983, August 17, at Sioux City, Iowa, Cathedral of the Epiphany. James Joseph Byrne, Archbishop of Dubuque, assisted by Gerald Francis O'Keefe, Bishop of Davenport, and Frank Henry Greteman, Bishop emeritus of Sioux City, consecrated Lawrence Donald Soens, Bishop of Sioux City, born at Iowa City, Iowa (Davenport), August 26, 1926; priest May 6, 1950; named June 15, 1983.

981. 1983, August 23, at Scranton, Pennsylvania, Saint Peter's Cathedral. Stephen John Kocisko, Archbishop of Pittsburgh of the Byzantines, assisted by Michael Joseph Dudick, Bishop of Passaic of the

Ruthenians, and John Michael Bilock, Titular Bishop of Pergamus, consecrated Andrew Pataki, Titular Bishop of Telmissus, Auxiliary of Passaic of the Ruthenians born at Palmerton, Pennsylvania (Pittsburgh of the Ruthenians), August 30, 1927; priest February 24, 1952; named May 30, 1983; Bishop of Parma of the Ruthenians June 19, 1984.

982. 1983, September 8, at Chicago, Illinois, Ukrainian Cathedral of Saint Nicholas. Innocent Hilarion Lotocky, Bishop of Saint Nicholas of Chicago of the Ukrainians, assisted by Daniel William Kucera, Bishop of Salina, and Emil John Mihalik, Bishop of Parma of the Ruthenians, consecrated Vladimir Ladislas Tarasevitch, OSB, Titular Bishop of Mariamme, Apostolic Visitor for Catholic Byelorussians of the diaspora, born at Kleshniaki (Vilnius), Byelorussia, November 27, 1921; priest May 26, 1949; named July 1, 1983; died at Chicago January 2, 1986.

983. 1983, November 29, at New York, New York, Saint Patrick's Cathedral. John Joseph Thomas Ryan, Titular Archbishop of Gabi, assisted by Joseph Thomas Dimino, Titular Bishop of Carini, and Francis Xavier Roque, Titular Bishop of Bagai, consecrated Angelo Thomas Acerra, OSB, Titular Bishop of Lete, Auxiliary of the Military Vicariate of the United States, born at Memphis, Tennessee (Nashville), November 7, 1925; priest May 20, 1950; named September 29, 1983.

984. 1983, December 5, at Cleveland, Ohio, Cathedral of Saint John the Evangelist. Anthony Michael Pilla, Bishop of Cleveland, assisted by Daniel Edward Pilarczyk, Archbishop of Cincinnati, and Gilbert Ignatius Sheldon, Titular Bishop of Taparura, consecrated Alexander James Quinn, Titular Bishop of Socia, Auxiliary of Cleveland, born at Cleveland, Ohio, April 8, 1932; priest May 24, 1958; named October 14, 1983.

985–988. 1983, December 13, at Chicago, Illinois, Cathedral of the Holy Name. Joseph Louis Cardinal Bernardin, Archbishop of Chicago, assisted by Alfred Leo Abramowicz, Titular Bishop of Pesto, and Nevin William Hayes, Titular Bishop of Novasinna, consecrated (1) Timothy Joseph Lyne, Titular Bishop of Vamalla, Auxiliary of Chicago, born at Chicago, Illinois, March 21, 1919; priest May 1, 1943; named October 18, 1983. Consecrated (2) John George Vlazny, Titular Bishop of Stagnum, Auxiliary of Chicago, born at Chicago, Illinois, February 22, 1937; priest December 20, 1961; named October 18, 1983; Bishop of Winona May 13, 1987. Consecrated (3) Placido Rodríguez, CMF, Titular Bishop of Fuerteventura, Auxiliary of Chicago, born at Celaya (Morelia), Mexico, October 11, 1940; priest May 23, 1968; named October 18, 1983. Consecrated (4) Wilton Daniel Gregory, Titular Bishop of Oliva, Auxiliary of Chicago, born at Chicago, Illinois, December 7, 1947; priest May 9, 1973; named October 18, 1983.

989. 1984, January 11, at Saint Paul, Minnesota, Cathedral of Saint Paul. John Robert Roach, Archbishop of Saint Paul and Minneapolis, assisted by John Francis Kinney, Bishop of Bismarck, and Paul Vincent Dudley, Bishop of Sioux Falls, consecrated Robert James Carlson, Titular Bishop of Avioccala, Auxiliary of Saint Paul and Minneapolis, born at Minneapolis, Minnesota (Saint Paul), June 30, 1944; priest May 23, 1970; named November 19, 1983.

990. 1984, January 25, at Green Bay, Wisconsin, Saint Francis Xavier Cathedral. Pio Laghi, Titular Archbishop of Mauriana, Apostolic Delegate to the United States, assisted by Aloysius John Wycislo, Bishop emeritus of Green Bay, and Vincent Martin Leonard, Bishop emeritus of Pittsburgh, consecrated Adam Joseph Maida, Bishop of Green Bay, born at East Vandergrift, Pennsylvania (Pittsburgh), March 18, 1930; priest May 26, 1956; named November 7, 1983.

991–992. 1984, February 10, at Saint Louis, Missouri, Saint Louis Cathedral. John Lawrence May, Archbishop of Saint Louis, assisted by George Joseph Gottwald, Titular Bishop of Cedamussa, and Charles Roman Koester, Titular Bishop of Suacia, consecrated (1) Edward Joseph O'Donnell, Titular Bishop of Britonia, Auxiliary of Saint Louis, born at Saint Louis, Missouri, July 4, 1931; priest April 6, 1957; named December 1, 1983. Consecrated (2) James Terry Steib, SVD, Titular Bishop of Fallaba, Auxiliary of Saint Louis, born at Vacherie, Louisiana (New Orleans), May 17, 1940; priest January 6, 1967; named December 1, 1983.

993. 1984, May 1, at Fairbanks, Alaska, Sacred Heart Cathedral. Robert Louis Whelan, Bishop of Fairbanks, assisted by Francis Thomas Hurley, Archbishop of Anchorage, and Michael Hughes Kenny, Bishop of Juneau, consecrated Michael Joseph Kaniecki, SJ, Coadjutor Bishop of Fairbanks, born at Detroit, Michigan, April 13, 1935; priest June 5, 1965; named March 8, 1984; succeeded to Fairbanks June 1, 1985.

994. 1984, May 3, at Toledo, Ohio, Queen of the Most Holy Rosary Cathedral. James Robert Hoffman, Bishop of Toledo, assisted by Daniel Edward Pilarczyk, Archbishop of Cincinnati, and John Anthony Donovan, Bishop emeritus of Toledo, consecrated Robert William Donnelly, Titular Bishop of Garba, Auxiliary of Toledo, born at Toledo, Ohio, March 22, 1931; priest May 25, 1957; named March 14, 1984.

995. 1984, June 6, at Lafayette, Indiana, Cathedral of Saint Mary of the Immaculate Conception. Edward Thomas O'Meara, Archbishop of Indianapolis, assisted by Raymond Joseph Gallagher, Bishop emeritus of Lafayette in Indiana and Joseph Robert Crowley, Titular Bishop of Maraguia consecrated William Leo Higi, Bishop of Lafayette in Indiana, born at Anderson, Indiana (Indianapolis), August 29, 1933; priest May 30, 1959; named April 7, 1984.

996. 1984, June 19, at Covington, Kentucky, Cathedral Basilica of the Assumption. William Anthony Hughes, Bishop of Covington, assisted by Thomas Cajetan Kelly, Archbishop of Louisville, and Richard Henry Ackerman, Bishop emeritus of Covington, consecrated James Kendrick Williams, Titular Bishop of Catula, Auxiliary of Covington, born at Athertonville, Kentucky (Louisville), September 5, 1936; priest May 25, 1963; named April 25, 1984; first Bishop of Lexington January 14, 1988.

997–998. 1984, July 2, at Baltimore, Maryland, Cathedral of Mary Our Queen. William Donald Borders, Archbishop of Baltimore, assisted by Eugene Antonio Marino, Titular Bishop of Walla Walla, and Thomas Austin Murphy, Titular Bishop of Appiaria, consecrated (1) William Clifford Newman, Titular Bishop of Numluli, Auxiliary of Baltimore, born at Baltimore, Maryland, August 16, 1928; priest May 20, 1954; named May 25, 1984. Consecrated (2) John Huston Ricard, SSJ, Titular Bishop of Rucuma, Auxiliary of Baltimore, born at New Roads, Louisiana (New Orleans), February 29, 1940; priest May 25, 1968; named May 25, 1984.

999. 1984, July 14, at Garden Grove, California, Saint Columban's Church. Timothy Cardinal Manning, Archbishop of Los Angeles, assisted by William Robert Johnson, Bishop of Orange, and Manuel Duran Moreno, Bishop of Tucson, consecrated John Thomas Steinbock, Titular Bishop of Midila, Auxiliary of Orange, born at Los Angeles, California, July 16, 1937; priest May 10, 1963; named May 25, 1984; Bishop of Santa Rosa January 17, 1987.

1000. 1984, July 25, at Cincinnati, Ohio, Cathedral of Saint Peter in Chains. Daniel Edward Pilarczyk, Archbishop of Cincinnati, assisted by Nicholas Thomas Elko, Titular Archbishop of Dara, and Edward Anthony McCarthy, Archbishop of Miami, consecrated James Henry Garland, Titular Bishop of Garriana, Auxiliary of Cincinnati, born at Wilmington, Ohio (Cincinnati), December 31, 1931; priest August 15, 1959; named June 2, 1984.

1001. 1984, August 2, at Saint Thomas, Virgin Islands, Cathedral of Saints Peter and Paul. Edward John Harper, Bishop of Saint Thomas, assisted by James Aloysius Hickey, Archbishop of Washington, and Eugene Antonio Marino, Titular Bishop of Walla Walla, consecrated Sean Patrick O'Malley, OFM.Cap, Coadjutor Bishop of Saint Thomas, born at Lakewood, Ohio (Cleveland), June 29, 1944; priest August 29, 1970; named June 2, 1984; succeeded to Saint Thomas October 16, 1985.

1002. 1984, September 14, at Portland, Maine, Cathedral of the Immaculate Conception. Pio Laghi, Titular Archbishop of Mauriana, Apostolic Pro-Nuncio to the United States, assisted by Edward Cornelius O'Leary, Bishop of Portland, and Vincentas Brizgys, Titular Bishop of Bosana, consecrated Paulius Antanas Baltakis, OFM, Titular Bishop of Egara, charged with the spiritual assistance of Lithuanian Catholics in the diaspora, born at Troskunai (Panevezys), Lithuania, January 1, 1925; priest August 24, 1952; named June 1, 1984.

1003. 1984, December 11, at Belleville, Illinois, Cathedral of Saint Peter. Joseph Louis Cardinal Bernardin, Archbishop of Chicago, assisted by William Michael Cosgrove, Bishop emeritus of Belleville, and Thomas Joseph Murphy, Bishop of Great Falls-Billings, consecrated James Patrick Keleher, Bishop of Belleville, born at Chicago, Illinois, July 31, 1931; priest April 12, 1958; named October 20, 1984.

1004. 1984, December 12, at Springfield, Missouri, Immaculate Conception Church. John Lawrence May, Archbishop of Saint Louis, assisted by Bernard Francis Law, Archbishop of Boston, and Glennon Patrick Flavin, Bishop of Lincoln, consecrated John Joseph Leibrecht, Bishop of Springfield-Cape Girardeau, born at Overland, Missouri (Saint Louis), August 18, 1930; priest March 17, 1956; named October 20, 1984.

1005. 1984, December 18, at Charlotte, North Carolina, Charlotte Convention Center. Michael Joseph Begley, Bishop emeritus of Charlotte, assisted by James Aloysius Hickey, Archbishop of Washington, and Thomas William Lyons, Titular Bishop of Mortlach, consecrated John Francis Donoghue, Bishop of Charlotte, born at Washington, District of Columbia (Baltimore), August 9, 1928; priest June 4, 1955; named November 3, 1984.

1006. 1985, April 16, at Buffalo, New York, Saint Joseph's Cathedral. Edward Dennis Head, Bishop of Buffalo, assisted by Bernard Joseph McLaughlin, Titular Bishop of Mottola, and Stanislaus Joseph Brzana, Bishop of Ogdensburg, consecrated Donald Walter Trautman, Titular Bishop of Sassura, Auxiliary of Buffalo, born at Buffalo, New York, June 24, 1936; priest April 7, 1962; named February 27, 1985.

1007. 1985, May 22, at Rome, Italy, Church of Saints John and Paul. Bernardin Cardinal Gantin, Prefect of the Congregation for Bishops, assisted by John Joseph O'Connor, Archbishop of New York, and John Richard Keating, Bishop of Arlington, consecrated Edward Michael Egan, Titular Bishop of Allegheny, Auxiliary of New York, born at Oak Park, Illinois (Chicago), April 2, 1932; priest December 15, 1957; named April 1, 1985; Bishop of Bridgeport November 5, 1988.

1008. 1985, June 26, at Joliet, Illinois, Cathedral of Saint Raymond Nonnatus. Joseph Leopold Imesch, Bishop of Joliet, assisted by Raymond James Vonesh, Titular Bishop of Vanariona, and Daniel Leo Ryan, Bishop of Springfield in Illinois, consecrated Roger Louis Kaffer, Titular Bishop of Dusa, Auxiliary of Joliet, born at Joliet, Illinois (Chicago), August 14, 1927; priest May 1, 1954; named April 25, 1985.

1009. 1985, July 26, at San Angelo, Texas, San Angelo Coliseum. Patrick Fernández Flores, Archbishop of San Antonio, assisted by Joseph Anthony Fiorenza, Bishop of Galveston-Houston, and John Joseph Fitzpatrick, Bishop of Brownsville, consecrated Michael David Pfeifer, OMI, Bishop of San Angelo, born at Alamo, Texas (Corpus Christi), May 18, 1937; priest December 21, 1964; named May 31, 1985.

1010. 1985, August 4, at Washington, District of Columbia, National Shrine of the Immaculate Conception. James Aloysius Hickey, Archbishop of Washington, assisted by Thomas William Lyons, Titular Bishop of Mortlach, and Eugene Antonio Marino, Titular Bishop of Walla Walla, consecrated Alvaro Corrada del Rio, SJ, Titular Bishop of Rusticiana, Auxiliary of Washington, born at Santurce, Puerto Rico (San Juan de Puerto Rico), May 13, 1942; priest July 6, 1974; named May 31, 1985.

1011. 1985, September 19, at Boston, Massachusetts, Cathedral of the Holy Cross. Bernard Francis Cardinal Law, Archbishop of Boston, assisted by Daniel Anthony Cronin, Bishop of Fall River, and John Aloysius Marshall, Bishop of Burlington, consecrated Robert Joseph Banks, Titular Bishop of Taraqua, Auxiliary of Boston, born at Winthrop, Massachusetts (Boston), February 26, 1928; priest December 20, 1952; named June 26, 1985.

1012. 1986, January 6, at Rome, Vatican City, Saint Peter's Basilica. Pope John Paul II, assisted by Agostino Cardinal Casaroli, Secretary of State, and Bernardin Cardinal Gantin, Prefect of the Congregation for Bishops, consecrated Donald William Wuerl, Titular Bishop of Rosemarkie, Auxiliary of Seattle, born at Pittsburgh, Pennsylvania, November 12, 1940; priest December 17, 1966; named November 30, 1985; resigned as Auxiliary of Seattle May 26, 1987; Bishop of Pittsburgh February 12, 1988.

1013. 1986, March 19, at Miami, Florida, Saint Mary's Cathedral. Edward Anthony McCarthy, Archbishop of Miami, assisted by Joseph Francis Maguire, Bishop of Springfield, Massachusetts, and Reginald Edward Vincent Arliss, Bishop-Prelate emeritus of Marbel, consecrated Norbert Leonard Dorsey, CP, Titular Bishop of Mactaris, Auxiliary of Miami, born at Springfield, Massachusetts, December 14, 1929; priest

April 28, 1956; named January 10, 1986; Bishop of Orlando March 10, 1990.

1014. 1986, April 21, at Manchester, New Hampshire, Saint Joseph Cathedral. Odore Joseph Gendron, Bishop of Manchester, assisted by Ernest John Primeau, Bishop emeritus of Manchester, and Robert Edward Mulvee, Bishop of Wilmington, consecrated Joseph John Gerry, OSB, Titular Bishop of Praecausa, Auxiliary of Manchester, born at Millinocket, Maine (Portland), September 12, 1928; priest June 12, 1954; named February 4, 1986; Bishop of Portland December 21, 1988.

1015. 1986, May 6, at Gallup, New Mexico, Red Rock State Park Arena. Robert Fortune Sanchez, Archbishop of Santa Fe, assisted by Jerome Joseph Hastrich, Bishop of Gallup, and Anthony Michael Pilla, Bishop of Cleveland, consecrated Donald Edmond Pelotte, SSS, Coadjutor Bishop of Gallup, born at Waterville, Maine (Portland), April 13, 1945; priest September 2, 1972; named February 24, 1986; succeeded to Gallup March 20, 1990.

1016. 1986, June 24, at Albany, New York, Cathedral of the Immaculate Conception. Howard James Hubbard, Bishop of Albany, assisted by Philip Matthew Hannan, Archbishop of New Orleans, and Gerard Louis Frey, Bishop of Lafayette, consecrated Harry Joseph Flynn, Coadjutor Bishop of Lafayette, born at Schenectady, New York (Albany), May 2, 1933; priest May 28, 1960; named April 19, 1986; succeeded to Lafayette May 13, 1989.

1017. 1986, June 27, at Richmond, Virginia, Cathedral of the Sacred Heart. Walter Francis Sullivan, Bishop of Richmond, assisted by John Francis Donoghue, Bishop of Charlotte, and James Aloysius Hickey, Archbishop of Washington, consecrated David Edward Foley, Titular Bishop of Ottaba, Auxiliary of Richmond, born at Worcester, Massachusetts (Springfield), February 3, 1930; priest May 26, 1956; named May 3, 1986.

1018. 1986, June 29, at Roslindale, Massachusetts, Our Lady of the Annunciation Cathedral. Maximos V Hakim, Patriarch of Antioch, of Alexandria and of Jerusalem of the Greek Melkite Catholics, assisted by Joseph Elias Tawil, Archbishop-Bishop of Newton of the Greek Melkite Catholics, and Michel Hakim, Archbishop-Bishop of Saint Sauveur de Montréal of the Greek Melkite Catholics, consecrated John Adel Elya, BS, Titular Bishop of Abila in Lysinia, Auxiliary of Newton of the Greek Melkite Catholics, born at Magdouche (Saida), Lebanon, September 16, 1928; priest February 17, 1952; named March 21, 1986.

1019.   1986, June 29, at Houston, Texas, Albert Thomas Convention Center. Joseph Anthony Fiorenza, Bishop of Galveston-Houston, assisted by Edward Anthony McCarthy, Archbishop of Miami, and Agustín Alejo Román, Titular Bishop of Sertei, consecrated Enrique San Pedro, SJ, Titular Bishop of Siccesi, Auxiliary of Galveston-Houston, born at Havana, Cuba, March 9, 1926; priest March 18, 1957; named April 1, 1986.

1020.   1986, July 29, at Alexandria, Louisiana, Saint Francis Xavier Cathedral. Pio Laghi, Titular Archbishop of Mauriana, Apostolic Pro-Nuncio to the United States, assisted by Philip Matthew Hannan, Archbishop of New Orleans, and William Benedict Friend, Bishop of Shreveport, consecrated John Clement Favalora, Bishop of Alexandria, born at New Orleans, Louisiana, December 5, 1935; priest December 20, 1961; named June 16, 1986; Bishop of Saint Petersburg March 12, 1989.

1021.   1986, September 17, at Rockville Centre, New York, Saint Agnes Cathedral. John Raymond McGann, Bishop of Rockville Centre, assisted by James Joseph Daly, Titular Bishop of Castra Nova, and Rene Arnold Valero, Titular Bishop of Vicus Turris, consecrated Alfred John Markiewicz, Titular Bishop of Afufenia, Auxiliary of Rockville Centre, born at Brooklyn, New York, May 17, 1928; priest June 6, 1953; named July 1, 1986.

1022.   1987, January 6, at Rome, Vatican City, Saint Peter's Basilica. Pope John Paul II, assisted by Eduardo Martínez Somalo, Titular Archbishop of Thagora, and José T. Sanchez, Archbishop emeritus of Nueva Segovia, consecrated William Jerome McCormack, Titular Bishop of Nicives, Auxiliary of New York, born at New York, New York, January 24, 1924; priest February 21, 1959; named December 18, 1986.

1023.   1987, February 4, at Passaic, New Jersey, Saint Michael's Cathedral. Stephen John Kocisko, Archbishop of Pittsburgh of the Byzantines, assisted by Michael Joseph Dudick, Bishop of Passaic of the Ruthenians, and Thomas Victor Dolinay, Bishop of Van Nuys of the Ruthenians, consecrated George Martin Kuzma, Titular Bishop of Telmissus, Auxiliary of Passaic of the Ruthenians, born at Windber, Pennsylvania (Pittsburgh of the Ruthenians), July 24, 1925; priest May 29, 1955; named November 11, 1986.

1024-1026.   1987, February 23, at Los Angeles, California, Los Angeles Sports Arena. Roger Michael Mahony, Archbishop of Los Angeles, assisted by John James Ward, Titular Bishop of Bria, and Juan Alfredo Arzube, Titular Bishop of Civitate, consecrated (1) George Patrick Ziemann, Titular Bishop of Obba, Auxiliary of Los Angeles, born at Pasadena, California (Los Angeles), September 13, 1941; priest May 29,

1967; named December 23, 1986. Consecrated (2) Armando Xavier Ochoa, Titular Bishop of Sitifis, Auxiliary of Los Angeles, born at Oxnard, California (Los Angeles), April 9, 1943; priest May 23, 1970; named December 23, 1986. Consecrated (3) Carl Anthony Fisher, SSJ, Titular Bishop of Tlos, Auxiliary of Los Angeles, born at Pascagoula, Mississippi (Natchez), November 24, 1945; priest June 2, 1973; named December 23, 1986.

1027. 1987, February 24, at Tyler, Texas, Oil Palace. Patrick Fernández Flores, Archbishop of San Antonio, assisted by Thomas Ambrose Tschoepe, Bishop of Dallas, and Michael Jarboe Sheehan, Bishop of Lubbock, consecrated Charles Edwin Herzig, first Bishop of Tyler, born at San Antonio, Texas, August 14, 1929; priest May 31, 1955; named December 12, 1986.

1028. 1987, February 27, at Worcester, Massachusetts, Saint Paul's Cathedral. Timothy Joseph Harrington, Bishop of Worcester, assisted by Bernard Joseph Flanagan, Bishop emeritus of Worcester, and John Aloysius Marshall, Bishop of Burlington, consecrated George Edward Rueger, Titular Bishop of Maronana, Auxiliary of Worcester, born at Worcester, Massachusetts (Springfield), September 23, 1929; priest January 6, 1958; named January 16, 1987.

1029. 1987, March 2, at Memphis, Tennessee, Cathedral of the Immaculate Conception. Thomas Cajetan Kelly, Archbishop of Louisville, assisted by James Francis Stafford, Archbishop of Denver, and Edward Thomas O'Meara, Archbishop of Indianapolis, consecrated Daniel Mark Buechlein, OSB, Bishop of Memphis, born at Jasper, Indiana (Indianapolis), April 20, 1938; priest May 3, 1964; named January 16, 1987.

1030. 1987, April 1, at Dubuque, Iowa, Saint Raphael's Cathedral. Daniel William Kucera, Archbishop of Dubuque, assisted by James Joseph Byrne, Archbishop emeritus of Dubuque, and Francis John Dunn, Titular Bishop of Turris Tamalleni, consecrated William Edwin Franklin, Titular Bishop of Surista, Auxiliary of Dubuque, born at Parnell, Iowa (Davenport), May 3, 1930; priest February 4, 1956; named January 29, 1987.

1031. 1987, May 20, at Altoona, Pennsylvania, Cathedral of the Blessed Sacrament. Jozef Cardinal Tomko, assisted by James John Hogan, Bishop emeritus of Altoona-Johnstown, and Francis Frederick Reh, Bishop emeritus of Saginaw, consecrated Joseph Victor Adamec, Bishop of Altoona-Johnstown, born at Bannister, Michigan (Saginaw), August 13, 1935; priest July 3, 1960; named March 12, 1987.

1032. 1987, August 24, at Collegeville, Minnesota, Saint John's Abbey Church. John Robert Roach, Archbishop of Saint Paul and Minneapolis, assisted by John Joseph Sullivan, Bishop of Kansas City-Saint Joseph, and George Henry Speltz, Bishop emeritus of Saint Cloud, consecrated Jerome George Hanus, OSB, Bishop of Saint Cloud, born at Brainard, Nebraska (Lincoln), May 26, 1940; priest July 30, 1966; named July 6, 1987.

1033. 1987, September 3, at Peoria, Illinois, Saint Mary's Cathedral. Edward William O'Rourke, Bishop of Peoria, assisted by Thomas Cajetan Kelly, Archbishop of Louisville, and Donald William Wuerl, Titular Bishop of Rosemarkie, consecrated John Joseph Myers, Coadjutor Bishop of Peoria, born at Ottawa, Illinois (Peoria), July 26, 1941; priest December 17, 1966; named July 7, 1987; succeeded to Peoria January 23, 1990.

1034. 1988, January 6, at Rome, Vatican City, Saint Peter's Basilica. Pope John Paul II, assisted by Eduardo Martínez Somalo, Titular Archbishop of Thagora, and Giovanni Battista Re, Titular Archbishop of Vescovio, consecrated John Gavin Nolan, Titular Bishop of Natchez, Auxiliary of the Military Ordinariate of the United States, born at Mechanicville, New York (Albany), March 15, 1924; priest June 11, 1949; named December 12, 1987.

1035–1036. 1988, January 25, at Newark, New Jersey, Sacred Heart Cathedral. Theodore Edgar McCarrick, Archbishop of Newark, assisted by Peter Leo Gerety, Archbishop emeritus of Newark, and Walter William Curtis, Bishop of Bridgeport, consecrated (1) James Thomas McHugh, Titular Bishop of Morosbisdus, Auxiliary of Newark, born at Orange, New Jersey (Newark), January 3, 1932; priest May 25, 1957; named November 20, 1987; Bishop of Camden May 13, 1989. Consecrated (2) John Mortimer Smith, Titular Bishop of Tre Taverne, Auxiliary of Newark, born at Orange, New Jersey (Newark), June 23, 1935; priest May 27, 1961; named November 20, 1987.

1037. 1988, February 19, at Houston, Texas, Sam Houston Coliseum. Joseph Anthony Fiorenza, Bishop of Galveston-Houston, assisted by Philip Matthew Hannan, Archbishop of New Orleans, and James Terry Steib, Titular Bishop of Fallaba, consecrated Curtis John Guillory, SVD, Titular Bishop of Stagnum, Auxiliary of Galveston-Houston, born at Lafayette, Louisiana, September 18, 1943; priest December 16, 1972; named December 28, 1987.

1038. 1988, March 8, at Scranton, Pennsylvania, Saint Peter's Cathedral. James Clifford Timlin, Bishop of Scranton, assisted by Anthony John Bevilacqua, Archbishop of Philadelphia, and Joseph Carroll McCormick, Bishop emeritus of Scranton, consecrated Francis Xavier DiLorenzo,

Titular Bishop of Tigias, Auxiliary of Scranton, born at Philadelphia, Pennsylvania, April 15, 1942; priest May 18, 1968; named January 21, 1988.

1039. 1988, March 25, at Birmingham, Alabama, Saint Paul's Cathedral. Oscar Hugh Lipscomb, Archbishop of Mobile, assisted by James Aloysius Hickey, Archbishop of Washington, and Eugene Antonio Marino, Archbishop of Atlanta, consecrated Raymond James Boland, Bishop of Birmingham, born at Tipperary Town (Cashel), Ireland, February 8, 1932; priest July 16, 1957; named January 28, 1988.

1040–1041. 1988, April 11, at Chicago, Illinois, Cathedral of the Holy Name. Joseph Louis Cardinal Bernardin, Archbishop of Chicago, assisted by Alfred Leo Abramowicz, Titular Bishop of Pesto, and Nevin William Hayes, Titular Bishop of Novasinna, consecrated (1) Thaddeus Joseph Jakubowski, Titular Bishop of Plestia, Auxiliary of Chicago, born at Chicago, Illinois, April 5, 1924; priest May 3, 1950; named February 12, 1988. Consecrated (2) John Robert Gorman, Titular Bishop of Catula, Auxiliary of Chicago, born at Chicago, Illinois, December 11, 1925; priest May 1, 1952; named February 12, 1988.

1042. 1988, April 12, at Hartford, Connecticut, Cathedral of Saint Joseph. John Francis Whealon, Archbishop of Hartford, assisted by Daniel Patrick Reilly, Bishop of Norwich, and Francis Frederick Reh, Bishop emeritus of Saginaw, consecrated Paul Stephen Loverde, Titular Bishop of Ottabia, Auxiliary of Hartford, born at Framingham, Massachusetts (Boston), September 3, 1940; priest December 18, 1965; named February 3, 1988.

1043. 1988, April 27, at Philadelphia, Pennsylvania, Immaculate Conception of the Blessed Virgin Mary Ukrainian Catholic Cathedral. Stephen Sulyk, Archbishop of Philadelphia of the Ukrainians, assisted by Maxim Hermaniuk, Archbishop of Winnipeg of the Ukrainians, and Innocent Hilarion Lotocky, Bishop of Saint Nicholas of Chicago of the Ukrainians, consecrated Michael Kuchmiak, C.SS.R, Titular Bishop of Agathopolis, Auxiliary of Philadelphia of the Ukrainians, born at Obertyn (Stanislaviv of the Ukrainians), Ukraine, February 5, 1923; priest May 13, 1956; named February 27, 1988; Apostolic Exarch for Ukrainian Catholics in Great Britain June 24, 1989.

1044. 1988, July 26, at Rapid City, South Dakota, Rushmore Plaza Civic Center. Pio Laghi, Titular Archbishop of Mauriana, Apostolic Pro-Nuncio to the United States, assisted by John Robert Roach, Archbishop of Saint Paul and Minneapolis, and James Francis Stafford, Archbishop of Denver, consecrated Charles Joseph Chaput, OFM.Cap, Bishop of Rapid City, born at Concordia, Kansas, September 26, 1944; priest August 30, 1970; named April 29, 1988.

1045. 1988, August 1, at Wheeling, West Virginia, Saint Joseph's Cathedral. Francis Bible Schulte, Bishop of Wheeling-Charleston, assisted by William Donald Borders, Archbishop of Baltimore, and Donald William Wuerl, Bishop of Pittsburgh, consecrated Bernard William Schmitt, Titular Bishop of Walla Walla, Auxiliary of Wheeling-Charleston, born at Wheeling, West Virginia, August 17, 1928; priest May 28, 1955; named May 27, 1988; Bishop of Wheeling-Charleston March 29, 1989.

1046. 1988, September 8, at Knoxville, Tennessee, Holiday Inn Convention Center. Pio Laghi, Titular Archbishop of Mauriana, Apostolic Pro-Nuncio to the United States, assisted by James Daniel Niedergeses, Bishop of Nashville, and Michael Francis McAuliffe, Bishop of Jefferson City, consecrated Anthony Joseph O'Connell, first Bishop of Knoxville, born at Lisheen (Killaloe), Ireland, May 5, 1938; priest March 30, 1963; named May 27, 1988.

1047. 1988, October 3, at Boston, Massachusetts, Cathedral of the Holy Cross. Bernard Francis Cardinal Law, Archbishop of Boston, assisted by John Joseph Cardinal O'Connor, Archbishop of New York, and Luis Cardinal Aponte Martínez, Archbishop of San Juan de Puerto Rico, consecrated Roberto Octavio González Nieves, OFM, Titular Bishop of Ursona, Auxiliary of Boston, born at Elizabeth, New Jersey (Newark), June 2, 1950; priest May 8, 1977; named July 19, 1988.

1048–1049. 1988, December 13, at Rockville Centre, New York, Saint Agnes Cathedral. John Raymond McGann, Bishop of Rockville Centre, assisted by James Joseph Daly, Titular Bishop of Castra Nova, and Alfred John Markiewicz, Titular Bishop of Afufenia, consecrated (1) Emil Aloysius Wcela, Titular Bishop of Filaca, Auxiliary of Rockville Centre, born at Bay Shore, New York (Brooklyn), May 1, 1931; priest June 2, 1956; named October 21, 1988. Consecrated (2) John Charles Dunne, Titular Bishop of Abercorn, Auxiliary of Rockville Centre, born at Brooklyn, New York, October 30, 1937; priest June 1, 1963; named October 21, 1988.

1050. 1988, December 15, at San Antonio, Texas, Saint Matthew's Church. Patrick Fernández Flores, Archbishop of San Antonio, assisted by Charles Victor Grahmann, Bishop of Victoria in Texas, and Charles Edwin Herzig, Bishop of Tyler, consecrated Edmond Carmody, Titular Bishop of Mortlach, Auxiliary of San Antonio, born at Alahana, New Townsandes (Kerry), Ireland, January 12, 1934; priest June 8, 1957; named November 5, 1988.

1051–1052. 1988, December 20, at Washington, District of Columbia, National Shrine of the Immaculate Conception. James Aloysius Cardinal Hickey, Archbishop of Washington, assisted by Eugene Antonio Marino, Archbishop of Atlanta, and Alvaro Corrada del Rio, Titular Bishop of Rusticiana, consecrated (1) Leonard James Olivier, SVD, Titular Bishop of Legia, Auxiliary of Washington, born at Lake Charles, Louisiana (New Orleans), October 12, 1923; priest June 29, 1951; named November 10, 1988. Consecrated (2) William George Curlin, Titular Bishop of Rosemarkie, Auxiliary of Washington, born at Portsmouth, Virginia (Richmond), August 30, 1927; priest May 25, 1957; named November 10, 1988.

1053–1054. 1989, January 25, at San Francisco, California, Cathedral of Saint Mary. John Raphael Quinn, Archbishop of San Francisco, assisted by Mark Joseph Hurley, Bishop emeritus of Santa Rosa, and Michael Joseph Kaniecki, Bishop of Fairbanks, consecrated (1) Carlos Arthur Sevilla, SJ, Titular Bishop of Mina, Auxiliary of San Francisco, born at San Francisco, California, August 9, 1935; priest June 3, 1966; named December 6, 1988. Consecrated (2) Patrick Joseph McGrath, Titular Bishop of Allegheny, Auxiliary of San Francisco, born at Dublin, Ireland July 11, 1945; priest June 7, 1970; named December 6, 1988.

1055. 1989, February 13, at Pittsburgh, Pennsylvania, Saint Paul Cathedral. Donald William Wuerl, Bishop of Pittsburgh, assisted by Anthony Gerald Bosco, Bishop of Greensburg, and John Bernard McDowell, Titular Bishop of Tamazuca, consecrated William Joseph Winter, Titular Bishop of Uthina, Auxiliary of Pittsburgh, born at Pittsburgh, Pennsylvania, May 20, 1930; priest December 17, 1955; named December 21, 1988.

1056. 1989, April 3, at Boise, Idaho, Pavillion of Boise Stadium. William Joseph Levada, Archbishop of Portland in Oregon, assisted by Sylvester William Treinen, Bishop emeritus of Boise City, and Thaddeus Anthony Shubsda, Bishop of Monterey, consecrated Tod David Brown, Bishop of Boise City, born at San Francisco, California, November 15, 1936; priest May 1, 1963; named December 21, 1988.

1057. 1989, April 11, at Evansville, Indiana, Saint Benedict's Church. Edward Thomas O'Meara, Archbishop of Indianapolis, assisted by Thomas Joseph O'Brien, Bishop of Phoenix, and Daniel Mark Buechlein, Bishop of Memphis, consecrated Gerald Andrew Gettelfinger, Bishop of Evansville, born at Ramsey, Indiana (Indianapolis), October 27, 1935; priest May 7, 1961; named March 11, 1989.

1058. 1989, May 24, at Charleston, South Carolina, Cathedral of Saint

John the Baptist. Pio Laghi, Titular Archbishop of Mauriana, Apostolic Pro-Nuncio to the United States, assisted by Eugene Antonio Marino, Archbishop of Atlanta, and Norbert Felix Gaughan, Bishop of Gary, consecrated David Bernard Thompson, Coadjutor Bishop of Charleston, born at Philadelphia, Pennsylvania, May 29, 1923; priest May 27, 1950; named April 22, 1989; succeeded to Charleston February 22, 1990.

1059. 1989, June 29, at Saint Louis, Missouri, Saint Louis Cathedral. John Lawrence May, Archbishop of Saint Louis, assisted by Edward Joseph O'Donnell, Titular Bishop of Britonia, and James Terry Steib, Titular Bishop of Fallaba, consecrated Paul Albert Zipfel, Titular Bishop of Walla Walla, Auxiliary of Saint Louis, born at Saint Louis, Missouri, September 22, 1935; priest March 18, 1961; named May 13, 1989.

1060. 1989, July 6, at West Paterson, New Jersey, Saint Ann's Melkite Church. Joseph Elias Tawil, Archbishop-Bishop of Newton of the Greek Melkite Catholics assisted by Michel Hakim, Archbishop-Bishop of Saint Sauveur de Montreal of the Greek Melkite Catholics, and Pedro Rai, Archbishop-Bishop of Nuestra Senora del Paraiso en Mexico of the Greek Melkite Catholics, consecrated Nicholas Samra, Titular Bishop of Gerasa, Auxiliary of Newton of the Greek Melkite Catholics, born at Patterson, New Jersey, August 18, 1944; priest May 10, 1970; named April 22, 1989.

1061. 1989, August 24, at Alexandria, Louisiana, Rapides Parish Coliseum. Francis Bible Schulte, Archbishop of New Orleans, assisted by Warren Louis Boudreaux, Bishop of Houma-Thibodaux, and Jude Speyrer, Bishop of Lake Charles, consecrated Sam Galip Jacobs, Bishop of Alexandria, born at Greenwood, Mississippi (Natchez), March 4, 1938; priest June 6, 1964; named July 1, 1989.

Appendix A

Americans Consecrated for Service to the Holy See (Exclusive of Those Prelates Who Exercised Episcopal Ministry in the United States)

1. 1903, July 5, at Rome, Italy, Chapel of the North American College. Sebastiano Cardinal Martinelli, OSA, assisted by Edmond Stonor, Titular Archbishop of Trapezus, and Diomede Panici, Titular Archbishop of Laodicea in Syria, consecrated Robert John Seton, Titular Archbishop of Heliopolis, born at Livorno, Italy, August 28, 1839; priest April 15, 1865; named June 22, 1903; died at Convent Station, New Jersey, March 22, 1927.

2. 1921, October 28, at Rome, Italy, Capranica College. Antonio Cardinal Vico, assisted by Clemente Micara, Titular Archbishop of Apamea, and Giovanni Zonchi, Titular Archbishop of Colosses, consecrated George Joseph Caruana, Bishop of Puerto Rico, born at Sliema (Malta), Malta, April 23, 1882; priest October 28, 1905; named August 5, 1921; title of see changed to San Juan November 21, 1924; Titular Archbishop of Sebastea in Armenia, and Apostolic Delegate to Mexico and the Antilles December 23, 1925; Apostolic Inter-Nuncio to Haiti January 28, 1927; Apostolic Nuncio to Cuba September 15, 1935; resigned as Nuncio to Cuba May 1, 1947; died at Philadelphia March 25, 1951.

3. 1949, June 14, at Seoul, South Korea, Cathedral of the Immaculate Conception. Thomas John McDonnell, Titular Bishop of Sela, assisted by Paul Kinam Ro, Titular Bishop of Colbasa, and Adrien Larribeau, Titular Bishop of Dusa, consecrated Patrick James Byrne, MM, Titular Bishop of Gazera, Apostolic Delegate to Korea, born at Washington, District of Columbia (Baltimore), October 26, 1888; priest June 23, 1915; Prefect Apostolic of Pyong Yang, Korea June 21, 1927; resigned August 12, 1929; Prefect Apostolic of Kyoto, Japan March 19, 1937; resigned in 1941; Apostolic Visitor to Korea July 17, 1947; named Titular Bishop of Gazera and Apostolic Delegate April 7, 1949; died in prison at Hachangri, North Korea, November 25, 1950.

4. 1960, October 28, at Rome, Vatican City, Saint Peter's Basilica. Pope

John XXIII, assisted by Diego Venini, Titular Archbishop of Adana, and Benigno Carrara, Bishop of Imola, consecrated Joseph Francis McGeough, Titular Archbishop of Hemesa, Apostolic Delegate to South Africa, born at New York, New York, August 29, 1903; priest December 20, 1930; Apostolic Inter-Nuncio to Ethiopia May 9, 1957; named Titular Archbishop of Hemesa September 17, 1960; Apostolic Delegate to South Africa September 20, 1960; Apostolic Nuncio to Ireland July 8, 1967; resigned in March 1969; died at New York October 12, 1970.

5.   1967, June 25, at Rome, Italy, Church of San Anselmo. Eugene Cardinal Tisserant, Titular Bishop of Ostia and of Porto e Santa Rufina, assisted by Joseph Carroll McCormick, Bishop of Scranton, and Luigi Faveri, Bishop of Tivoli, consecrated Francis John Brennan, Titular Archbishop of Tubunae in Mauritania, Dean of the Sacred Roman Rota, born at Shenandoah, Pennsylvania (Philadelphia), May 7, 1894; priest April 3, 1920; Auditor of the Sacred Roman Rota August 1, 1940; Dean December 14, 1959; named June 10, 1967; Cardinal June 26, 1967; Prefect of the Sacred Congregation for the Discipline of the Sacraments January 15, 1968; died at Philadelphia July 2, 1968.

6–7.   1969, January 6, at Rome, Vatican City, Saint Peter's Basilica. Pope Paul VI, assisted by Sergio Pignedoli, Titular Archbishop of Iconium, and Ernesto Civardi, Titular Archbishop of Sardica, consecrated (1) Raymond Philip Etteldorf, Titular Archbishop of Tindari, Apostolic Delegate to New Zealand, born at Ossian, Iowa (Dubuque), August 18, 1911; priest December 8, 1937; named December 21, 1968; Apostolic Pro-Nuncio to Ethiopia June 22, 1974; resigned in October 1982; resigned from service to the Holy See December 27, 1984; died at Dubuque March 15, 1986. Consecrated (2) Paul Casimir Marcinkus, Titular Bishop of Horta, Secretary of the Institute for the Works of Religion, born at Cicero, Illinois (Chicago), January 15, 1922; priest May 3, 1947; named December 24, 1968; President of the Institute for the Works of Religion in 1972; Titular Archbishop of Horta, Pro-President of the Pontifical Commission for the State of Vatican City September 26, 1981.

8.   1969, June 15, at Belleville, Illinois, Cathedral of Saint Peter. Luigi Raimondi, Titular Archbishop of Tarsus, Apostolic Delegate to the United States, assisted by Albert Rudolph Zuroweste, Bishop of Belleville, and Vincentas Brizgys, Titular Bishop of Bosana, consecrated Antanas Louis Deksnys, Titular Bishop of Lavello, charged with providing spiritual assistance to Lithuanian Catholics living outside Lithuania in Europe, born at Butaniskiai (Panevezys), Lithuania, May 9, 1906; priest May 30, 1931; named April 12, 1969; resigned June 7, 1984.

9.   1972, February 13, at Rome, Vatican City, Saint Peter's Basilica. Pope

Paul VI, assisted by Bernhard Jan Cardinal Alfrink, Archbishop of Utrecht, and William Cardinal Conway, Archbishop of Armagh, consecrated Edward Louis Heston, CSC, Titular Archbishop of Numida, President of the Pontifical Commission for Social Communications, born at Ravenna, Ohio (Cleveland), September 9, 1907; priest December 22, 1934; named January 6, 1972; died at Denver May 2, 1973.

10. 1983, November 20, at Miami, Florida, Saint Mary's Cathedral. Agostino Cardinal Casaroli, Secretary of State, assisted by Edward Anthony McCarthy, Archbishop of Miami, and John Joseph Nevins, Titular Bishop of Rusticiana, consecrated Ambrose Battista DePaoli, Titular Archbishop of Lares, Apostolic Pro-Nuncio to Sri Lanka, born at Jeannette, Pennsylvania (Pittsburgh), August 19, 1934; priest December 18, 1960; named September 23, 1983; Apostolic Pro-Nuncio to Lesotho and Apostolic Delegate to South Africa February 6, 1988.

11. 1984, May 8, at Philadelphia, Pennsylvania, Cathedral Basilica of Saints Peter and Paul. John Joseph Cardinal Krol, Archbishop of Philadelphia, assisted by Martin Nicholas Lohmuller, Titular Bishop of Ramsbiria, and Thomas Jerome Welsh, Bishop of Allentown, consecrated John Patrick Foley, Titular Archbishop of Neapolis in Proconsulari, President of the Pontifical Commission for Social Communications, born at Darby, Pennsylvania (Philadelphia), November 11, 1935; priest May 19, 1962; named April 5, 1984.

12. 1985, September 14, at Albano, Italy, Cathedral of San Pancrazio Martire. Pope John Paul II, assisted by Eduardo Martinez Somalo, Titular Archbishop of Thagora, and Achille Silvestrini, Titular Archbishop of Novaliciana, consecrated Justin Francis Rigali, Titular Archbishop of Bolsena, President of the Pontifical Ecclesiastical Academy, born at Los Angeles, California (Los Angeles-San Diego), April 19, 1935; priest April 25, 1961; named June 8, 1985; Secretary of the Congregation for Bishops December 21, 1989; Secretary of the College of Cardinals January 20, 1990.

Appendix B

Apostolic Delegates and the Apostolic Pro-Nuncio

1. 1888, June 10, at Rome, Italy, Church of San Alfonso. Raffaele Cardinal Monaco La Valletta, Bishop of Albano, assisted by Angelo Bianchi, Titular Bishop of Tanis, and Raffaele Sirolli, Bishop of Aquino Sora e Pontecorvo, consecrated Francesco Satolli, Titular Archbishop of Naupactus, Rector of the Pontifical Academy of Noble Ecclesiastics, born at Marsciano (Perugia), Italy, July 21, 1839; priest June 14, 1862; named June 1, 1888; Apostolic Delegate to the United States of America January 14, 1893; Cardinal November 29, 1895; Bishop of Frascati June 22, 1903; died at Rome January 8, 1910.

2. 1892, July 17, at Rome, Italy, San Antonio in Via Merulana. Raffaele Cardinal Monaco La Valletta, Bishop of Ostia e Velletri, assisted by Antonio Grasselli, Titular Archbishop of Colosses, and Tancrede Fausti, Titular Archbishop of Seleucia, consecrated Angelo Raffaele Gennaro Falconio, OFM.Ref, Bishop of Lacedonia, born at Pescocostanzo (Monte Cassino), Italy, September 20, 1842; priest January 3, 1866; named July 11, 1892; Archbishop of Acerenza e Matera November 29, 1895; Titular Archbishop of Larissa and Apostolic Delegate to Canada September 30, 1899; Apostolic Delegate to the United States of America September 30, 1902; Cardinal November 27, 1911; Bishop of Velletri May 25, 1914; Prefect of the Sacred Congregation for Religious February 26, 1916; died at Rome February 7, 1917.

3. 1896, August 30, at Rome, Italy, Church of San Agostino. Mariano Cardinal Rampolla del Tindaro, assisted by Guglielmo Pifferi, Titular Bishop of Porfireone, and Vincenzo Giuseppe Veneri, Bishop of Amelia, consecrated Sebastiano Martinelli, OSA, Titular Archbishop of Ephesus, Apostolic Delegate to the United States of America, born at Borgo Sant'Anna (Lucca), Italy, August 20, 1848; priest March 4, 1871; named August 18, 1896; Cardinal April 15, 1901; Prefect of the Sacred Congregation of Rites February 8, 1909; died at Rome July 4, 1918.

4. 1912, March 3, at Rome, Italy, College de Propaganda Fide. Rafael Cardinal Merry del Val, Secretary of State, assisted by Pietro Berruti,

Bishop of Vigevano, and Thomas Francis Kennedy, Titular Bishop of Hadrianopolis, consecrated Giovanni Vincenzo Bonzano, Titular Archbishop of Melitene, Apostolic Delegate to the United States of America, born at Castelletto Scazzoso (Alessandria), Italy, September 27, 1867; priest May 21, 1890; Apostolic Delegate to the United States of America February 1, 1912; named Titular Archbishop of Melitene February 3, 1912; Cardinal December 14, 1922; died at Rome November 25, 1927.

5. 1916, December 10, at Rome, Italy, College de Propaganda Fide. Domenico Cardinal Serafini, assisted by Joseph Amand Legrand, Bishop of Dacca, and Agostino Zampini, Titular Bishop of Porfireone, consecrated Pietro Fumasoni-Biondi, Titular Archbishop of Dioclea, Apostolic Delegate to the East Indies, born at Rome, Italy, September 4, 1872; priest April 17, 1897; named November 14, 1916; Apostolic Delegate to Japan December 6, 1919 to March 1921; Secretary of the Sacred Congregation of the Propagation of the Faith June 16, 1921; Apostolic Delegate to the United States of America December 14, 1922; Cardinal March 13, 1933; Prefect of the Sacred Congregation of the Propagation of the Faith March 16, 1933; died at Rome July 12, 1960.

6. 1933, April 23, at Rome, Italy, Church of Santa Susanna. Raffaele Carlo Cardinal Rossi, OCD, assisted by Giuseppe Pizzardo, Titular Archbishop of Nicea, and Carlo Salotti, Titular Archbishop of Philippopolis, consecrated Amleto Giovanni Cicognani, Titular Archbishop of Laodicea in Phrygia, Apostolic Delegate to the United States of America, born at Brigishella (Faenza), Italy, February 24, 1883; priest September 23, 1905; named March 17, 1933; Cardinal December 15, 1958; Secretary of State August 14, 1961; Titular Bishop of Frascati May 23, 1962; resigned as Secretary of State May 1, 1969; Titular Bishop of Ostia, retaining the title of Frascati, and Dean of the Sacred College of Cardinals March 24, 1972; died at the Vatican December 17, 1973.

7. 1949, May 22, at Rome, Italy, Church of Santa Maria sopra Minerva. Adeodato Giovanni Cardinal Piazza, OCD, assisted by Francesco Borgongini-Duca, Titular Archbishop of Heraclea in Europa, and Roberto Ronca, Titular Archbishop of Naupactus, consecrated Egidio Vagnozzi, Titular Archbishop of Myra, Apostolic Delegate to the Philippines, born at Rome, Italy, February 2, 1906; priest December 22, 1928; named March 14, 1949; Apostolic Nuncio to the Philippines August 9, 1951; Apostolic Delegate to the United States of America December 18, 1958; Cardinal June 26, 1967; President of the Prefecture for the Economic Affairs of the Holy See in January 1968; died at Rome December 26, 1980.

8. 1954, January 31, at Rome, Italy, Church of San Carlo al Corso.

Adeodato Giovanni Cardinal Piazza, OCD, Bishop of Sabina e Poggio Mirteto, assisted by Antonio Samore, Titular Archbishop of Ternobus, and Giuseppe Dell'Omo, Bishop of Acqui, consecrated Luigi Raimondi, Titular Archbishop of Tarsus, Apostolic Nuncio to Haiti, born at Acqui-Lussito, Italy, October 25, 1912; priest June 6, 1936; named December 24, 1953; Apostolic Delegate to Mexico December 15, 1956; Apostolic Delegate to the United States of America June 30, 1967; Cardinal March 5, 1973; Prefect of the Sacred Congregation of the Saints March 21, 1973; died at the Vatican June 24, 1975.

9. 1968, May 1, at Woluwe-Saint-Pierre (Brussels 15), Belgium, Church of Notre-Dame des Graces. Leon Joseph Cardinal Suenens, Archbishop of Mechelen-Bruxelles, assisted by Silvio Oddi, Titular Archbishop of Mesembria, Apostolic Nuncio to Belgium and Luxembourg, and Andre Marie Charue, Bishop of Namur consecrated Jean Jadot, Titular Archbishop of Zuri, Apostolic Pro-Nuncio to Thailand, Apostolic Delegate to Laos, Malaysia and Singapore, born at Brussels (Mechelen-Bruxelles), Belgium, November 23, 1909; priest February 11, 1934; named February 23, 1968; Apostolic Pro-Nuncio to Cameroun and Gabon, Apostolic Delegate to Equatorial Guinea May 15, 1971; Apostolic Delegate to the United States of America May 23, 1973; Pro-President of the Secretariat for Non-Christians June 27, 1980; resigned April 8, 1984.

10. 1969, June 22, at Faenza, Italy, Cathedral of San Pietro. Amleto Giovanni Cardinal Cicognani, assisted by Agostino Casaroli, Titular Archbishop of Carthage, and Giuseppe Battaglia, Bishop of Faenza, consecrated Pio Laghi, Titular Archbishop of Mauriana, Apostolic Delegate to Jerusalem and Palestine, born at Castiglione (Faenza), Italy, May 21, 1922; priest April 20, 1946; named May 24, 1969; Apostolic Pro-Nuncio to Cyprus May 28, 1973, remaining Apostolic Delegate to Jerusalem and Palestine; Apostolic Nuncio to Argentina April 22, 1974; Apostolic Delegate to the United States of America and Permanent Observer of the Holy See to the Organization of American States with the personal title of Apostolic Nuncio December 10, 1980; Apostolic Pro-Nuncio to the United States of America March 26, 1984.

Part II

Ordinations of U.S. Catholic Bishops by Place of Consecration

Part II presents an overview of American consecrations, using the place of consecration as its point of reference, and is divided into two sections.

The first section is devoted to those consecrations that have taken place within the territory of the United States, including the District of Columbia and the U.S. Virgin Islands.

The framework of this section is an alphabetical list of all contemporary American dioceses in which consecrations have taken place. Each diocesan list will be subdivided, where necessary, between consecrations that took place in the episcopal see and those that occurred elsewhere within the diocese. In several instances, consecrations took place in cities that are now found in a diocese other than that to which they pertained at the time of the ceremony. These consecrations are listed under the present dioceses to which they pertain, with their former dioceses noted in the text.

Each entry will give the date of consecration, the name of the bishop, and his diocese at the time of his consecration. Auxiliaries will be noted by the letter "A" in parentheses after their dioceses, coadjutors with "C," vicars apostolic with "VA," patriarchal vicars with "VP," and administrators with "AD."

The second section lists American consecrations that have taken place in other countries. Its format will be similar to the first section. Countries are listed in alphabetical order, subdivided by their episcopal sees.

Section One

Diocese of Albany

Albany

1865, October 15	John Conroy	Albany
1872, May 5	Edgar Wadhams	Ogdensburg
1892, May 5	Henry Gabriels	Ogdensburg
1894, July 1	Thomas Burke	Albany
1957, September 12	Edward Maginn	Albany (A)
1966, March 25	John Joseph Ryan	Anchorage
1986, June 24	Harry Flynn	Lafayette (C)

Loudonville

1977, March 27	Howard Hubbard	Albany

Diocese of Alexandria

Alexandria

1986, July 29	John Favalora	Alexandria
1989, August 24	Sam Jacobs	Alexandria

Diocese of Altoona–Johnstown

Altoona

1966, January 25	Jerome Pechillo	Coronel Oviedo
1987, May 20	Joseph Adamec	Altoona-Johnstown

Diocese of Amarillo

Amarillo

1980, May 30	Leroy Matthiesen	Amarillo

Archdiocese of Anchorage

Anchorage
1951, October 3   Dermot O'Flanagan   Juneau*

At this time, Anchorage was part of the Diocese of Juneau.

Diocese of Arlington

Arlington
1983, August 4   John Keating   Arlington

Archdiocese of Atlanta

Atlanta
1911, August 29   John Gunn   Natchez*

At this time, Atlanta was part of the Diocese of Savannah.

Diocese of Baker

Baker
1928, March 6   Edward Kelly   Boise City
1971, June 30   Thomas Connolly   Baker

Archdiocese of Baltimore

Baltimore
1800, December 7   Leonard Neale   Baltimore (C)
1810, October 28   Michael Egan   Philadelphia
1810, November 1   Jean Cheverus   Boston
1817, December 14   Ambrose Maréchal   Baltimore
1825, November 1   Benedict Fenwick   Boston
1826, October 29   John Dubois   New York
1828, May 25   James Whitfield   Baltimore
1833, October 13   John Purcell   Cincinnati
1834, September 14   Samuel Eccleston   Baltimore (C)

1841, March 14	John Chanche	Natchez
1841, March 21	Richard Whelan	Richmond
1844, March 17	William Tyler	Hartford
1852, March 28	John Neumann	Philadelphia
1857, May 3	William Elder	Natchez
1857, August 2	John Barry	Savannah
1858, April 25	John Verot	Florida (VA)
1868, August 16	James Gibbons	No. Carolina (VA)
1868, August 16	Thomas Becker	Wilmington
1870, February 27	Thomas Foley	Chicago (C)
1873, April 17	William Gross	Savannah
1882, January 8	Henry Northrop	No. Carolina (VA)
1885, April 19	Alphonse Glorieux	Idaho (VA)
1886, November 14	Alfred Curtis	Wilmington
1888, July 1	Leo Haid	No. Carolina (VA)
1888, November 4	John Foley	Detroit
1891, November 1	Placide Chapelle	Santa Fe (C)
1894, April 8	Patrick Donahue	Wheeling
1897, May 16	Edward Allen	Mobile
1900, June 17	Henry Granjon	Tucson
1901, November 24	Thomas Conaty	CUA, Rector
1908, May 3	Denis O'Connell	CUA, Rector
1909, January 10	Owen Corrigan	Baltimore (A)
1914, November 15	Thomas Shahan	CUA, Rector
1917, March 15	William Russell	Charleston
1925, June 24	William Hafey	Raleigh
1927, May 4	Thomas Toolen	Mobile
1928, March 29	John McNamara	Baltimore (A)
1935, October 23	Peter Ireton	Richmond (C)
1954, February 24	Jerome Sebastian	Baltimore (A)
1958, September 24	Michael Hyle	Wilmington (C)
1962, July 3	Thomas Murphy	Baltimore (A)
1966, July 25	Nicholas D'Antonio	Olancho
1967, January 25	Thomas Mardaga	Baltimore (A)
1968, September 11	Francis Gossman	Baltimore (A)
1976, February 29	Philip Murphy	Baltimore (A)
1976, February 29	James Stafford	Baltimore (A)
1984, July 2	William Newman	Baltimore (A)
1984, July 2	John Ricard	Baltimore (A)

Fell's Point
1810, November 4   Benedict Flaget   Bardstown

Diocese of Baton Rouge

Baton Rouge
1968, June 14   William Borders   Orlando

Donaldsonville
1824, March 25   Joseph Rosati   New Orleans (C)*

---

*At this time, Donaldsonville was part of the Archdiocese of New Orleans.

Diocese of Belleville

Belleville
1870, January 23	Peter Baltes	Alton*
1888, April 25	John Janssen	Belleville
1914, February 24	Henry Althoff	Belleville
1930, June 17	Joseph Schlarman	Peoria
1947, October 16	Joseph Mueller	Sioux City (C)
1948, January 29	Albert Zuroweste	Belleville
1969, June 15	Antanas Deksnys	Lithuanians
1979, May 14	Stanley Schlarman	Belleville (A)
1984, December 11	James Keleher	Belleville

---

*At this time, Belleville was part of the Diocese of Alton.

Diocese of Biloxi

Bay Saint Louis
1948, May 26   Leo Fahey   Baker City (C)*

---

*At this date, Bay Saint Louis was part of the Diocese of Natchez.

Diocese of Birmingham

Birmingham

1955, March 24	Joseph Durick	Mobile-Birmingham (A)*
1988, March 25	Raymond Boland	Birmingham

At this time, Birmingham was part of the Diocese of Mobile-Birmingham.

Diocese of Bismarck

Bismarck

1962, July 25	Sylvester Treinen	Boise City

Diocese of Boise City

Boise

1974, October 28	Nicholas Walsh	Yakima
1989, April 3	Tod Brown	Boise City

Archdiocese of Boston

Boston

1866, March 11	John Williams	Boston
1891, August 5	John Brady	Boston (A)
1909, July 25	Joseph Anderson	Boston (A)
1927, November 10	John Peterson	Boston (A)
1933, January 5	Daniel Desmond	Alexandria
1939, June 29	Richard Cushing	Boston (A)
1945, January 3	Edward Ryan	Burlington
1945, June 8	Louis Kelleher	Boston (A)
1947, June 30	John Wright	Boston (A)
1950, September 14	Eric MacKenzie	Boston (A)
1950, September 14	Thomas Markham	Boston (A)
1954, September 8	Jeremiah Minihan	Boston (A)
1959, December 21	Thomas Riley	Boston (A)
1967, May 25	James Burke	Chimbote
1968, September 12	Daniel Cronin	Boston (A)
1972, February 2	Lawrence Riley	Boston (A)

1972, February 2	Joseph Maguire	Boston (A)
1975, February 11	Thomas Daily	Boston (A)
1975, February 11	John D'Arcy	Boston (A)
1975, February 11	Joseph Ruocco	Boston (A)
1975, February 11	John Mulcahy	Boston (A)
1976, October 18	Daniel Hart	Boston (A)
1981, September 14	Alfred Hughes	Boston (A)
1985, September 19	Robert Banks	Boston (A)
1988, October 3	Roberto González	Boston (A)

Lawrence

1940, June 11	Raymond Lane	Fushun (VA)

Diocese of Brooklyn

Brooklyn

1909, September 21	George Mundelein	Brooklyn (A)
1920, October 3	Thomas Molloy	Brooklyn (A)
1929, October 28	Aloysius Willinger	Ponce
1935, February 25	Raymond Kearney	Brooklyn (A)
1947, July 1	James McManus	Ponce
1952, June 11	John Boardman	Brooklyn (A)
1955, June 7	Edmund Reilly	Brooklyn (A)
1956, July 25	John Carberry	Lafayette, Ind. (C)
1959, April 22	Charles Mulrooney	Brooklyn (A)
1959, April 22	Joseph Denning	Brooklyn (A)
1960, October 6	Edward Harper	Virgin Islands
1968, September 12	Francis Mugavero	Brooklyn
1973, February 2	John Snyder	Brooklyn (A)
1980, November 24	Anthony Bevilacqua	Brooklyn (A)
1980, November 24	Joseph Sullivan	Brooklyn (A)
1980, November 24	Rene Valero	Brooklyn (A)

Diocese of Buffalo

Buffalo

1868, November 8	Stephen Ryan	Buffalo
1897, February 24	James Quigley	Buffalo
1918, July 25	Thomas Walsh	Trenton

1919, March 25	Edmund Gibbons	Albany
1928, April 26	John McMahon	Trenton
1943, June 29	Joseph Burke	Buffalo (A)
1952, September 24	James Navagh	Raleigh (A)
1952, September 24	Leo Smith	Buffalo (A)
1953, February 11	Celestine Damiano	Papal Diplomat
1964, June 29	Stanislaus Brzana	Buffalo (A)
1964, June 29	Pius Benincasa	Buffalo (A)
1985, April 16	Donald Trautman	Buffalo (A)

Diocese of Burlington

Burlington

1892, June 29	John Michaud	Burlington (C)
1910, April 14	Joseph Rice	Burlington
1938, October 26	Matthew Brady	Burlington
1953, November 30	Bernard Flanagan	Norwich
1954, October 28	Robert Joyce	Burlington (A)
1972, January 25	John Marshall	Burlington

Diocese of Camden

Camden

| 1966, December 8 | James Schad | Camden (A) |

Diocese of Charleston

Charleston

1858, March 14	Patrick Lynch	Charleston
1877, May 13	John Moore	Saint Augustine
1966, April 26	Joseph Bernardin	Atlanta (A)
1989, May 24	David Thompson	Charleston (C)

Diocese of Charlotte

Charlotte

1972, January 12	Michael Begley	Charlotte
1984, December 18	John Donoghue	Charlotte

Greensboro

1964, April 15	Charles McLaughlin	Raleigh (A)

Diocese of Cheyenne

Cheyenne

1913, April 16	James Duffy	Kearney
1976, August 31	Joseph Hart	Cheyenne (A)

Archdiocese of Chicago

Chicago

1871, June 11	Michael Fink	Kansas (VA)
1881, July 25	John McMullen	Davenport
1883, September 16	Patrick Riordan	San Francisco (C)
1887, October 28	Maurice Burke	Cheyenne
1893, November 30	Edward Dunne	Dallas
1899, May 1	Alexander McGavick	Chicago (A)
1901, July 25	Peter Muldoon	Chicago (A)
1908, July 29	Paul Rhode	Chicago (A)
1909, September 1	Edmund Dunne	Peoria
1921, December 21	Edward Hoban	Chicago (A)
1924, February 25	James Griffin	Springfield, Ill.
1924, October 2	Francis Kelley	Oklahoma
1928, May 1	Bernard Sheil	Chicago (A)
1932, February 25	Stanislaus Bona	Grand Island
1934, April 25	William O'Brien	Chicago (A)
1935, May 1	William Griffin	La Crosse (A)
1941, February 24	Francis Magner	Marquette
1949, March 7	Martin McNamara	Joliet
1949, March 7	William Cousins	Chicago (A)
1949, March 7	William O'Connor	Springfield, Ill.
1953, December 29	Raymond Hillinger	Rockford

1960, February 25	Ernest Primeau	Manchester
1960, December 21	Cletus O'Donnell	Chicago (A)
1960, December 21	Aloysius Wycislo	Chicago (A)
1965, August 5	Nevin Hayes	Sicuani
1967, August 24	Thomas Grady	Chicago (A)
1967, August 24	William McManus	Chicago (A)
1967, August 24	John May	Chicago (A)
1968, June 13	Alfred Abramowicz	Chicago (A)
1968, June 13	Michael Dempsey	Chicago (A)
1983, December 13	Timothy Lyne	Chicago (A)
1983, December 13	John Vlazny	Chicago (A)
1983, December 13	Placido Rodríguez	Chicago (A)
1983, December 13	Wilton Gregory	Chicago (A)
1988, April 11	Thaddeus Jakubowski	Chicago (A)
1988, April 11	John Gorman	Chicago (A)

Archdiocese of Cincinnati

Cincinnati

1833, October 6	Frederick Résé	Detroit
1844, March 19	Ignatius Reynolds	Charleston
1844, March 19	John Henni	Milwaukee
1847, October 10	Louis Rappe	Cleveland
1850, November 24	John Lamy	New Mexico (VA)
1853, November 1	George Carrell	Covington
1853, November 1	Ireneus Baraga	Upper Michigan (VA)
1854, April 23	Joshua Young	Erie
1857, April 26	James Wood	Philadelphia (C)
1857, April 26	Henry Juncker	Alton
1858, January 10	John Luers	Fort Wayne
1862, March 25	Sylvester Rosecrans	Cincinnati (A)
1868, August 16	Joseph Macheboeuf	Colorado (VA)
1869, February 7	Ignatius Mrak	Sault Sainte Marie and Marquette
1870, January 9	Augustus Toebbe	Covington
1870, April 24	Caspar Borgess	Detroit (C)
1872, April 14	Joseph Dwenger	Fort Wayne
1872, April 14	Richard Gilmour	Cleveland
1900, August 25	Henry Moeller	Columbus
1924, May 1	Francis Beckman	Lincoln

1929, December 27	Joseph Albers	Cincinnati (A)
1931, June 10	Urban Vehr	Denver
1937, October 7	George Rehring	Cincinnati (A)
1938, October 28	Francis Thill	Concordia
1940, October 9	Bernard Espelage	Gallup
1945, May 1	John Mussio	Steubenville
1947, August 6	Joseph Marling	Kansas City (A)
1954, May 25	Clarence Issenmann	Cincinnati (A)
1958, June 17	Paul Leibold	Cincinnati (A)
1965, June 15	Edward McCarthy	Cincinnati (A)
1974, December 20	Daniel Pilarczyk	Cincinnati (A)
1984, July 25	James Garland	Cincinnati (A)

Diocese of Cleveland

Cleveland

1908, February 25	Joseph Koudelka	Cleveland (A)
1928, February 16	Thomas O'Reilly	Scranton
1932, September 8	James McFadden	Cleveland (A)
1933, September 21	Charles LeBlond	Saint Joseph
1945, October 2	John Treacy	La Crosse (C)
1946, May 28	John Hagan	Cleveland (A)
1947, May 1	Floyd Begin	Cleveland (A)
1948, May 18	John Dearden	Pittsburgh (C)
1953, September 2	John Krol	Cleveland (A)
1958, October 28	Paul Hallinan	Charleston
1961, July 6	John Whealon	Cleveland (A)
1962, December 21	Clarence Elwell	Cleveland (A)
1965, August 11	Raymond Gallagher	Lafayette, Ind.
1968, September 3	William Cosgrove	Cleveland (A)
1976, June 11	Michael Murphy	Cleveland (A)
1976, June 11	Gilbert Sheldon	Cleveland (A)
1979, August 1	Anthony Pilla	Cleveland (A)
1979, August 1	James Griffin	Cleveland (A)
1979, August 1	James Lyke	Cleveland (A)
1982, July 2	Edward Pevec	Cleveland (A)
1983, December 5	Alexander Quinn	Cleveland (A)

Diocese of Columbus

Columbus

1867, February 3	Edward Fitzgerald	Little Rock*
1881, August 8	John Watterson	Columbus
1942, February 24	Edward Hettinger	Columbus (A)
1976, July 18	George Fulcher	Columbus (A)

At this date, Columbus was part of the Archdiocese of Cincinnati.

Worthington

1944, December 21	Henry Grimmelsman	Evansville

Diocese of Corpus Christi

Corpus Christi

1956, October 9	Adolph Marx	Corpus Christi (A)

Diocese of Covington

Covington

1885, January 25	Camillus Maes	Covington
1916, January 25	Ferdinand Brossart	Covington
1923, July 25	Francis Howard	Covington
1984, June 19	James Williams	Covington (A)

Diocese of Crookston

Crookston

1970, September 29	Kenneth Povish	Crookston
1976, September 2	Victor Balke	Crookston

Diocese of Dallas

Dallas

1911, July 12	Joseph Lynch	Dallas
1927, April 26	Rudolph Gerken	Amarillo

1942, October 7	Augustine Danglmayr	Dallas (A)
1948, February 25	Wendelin Nold	Galveston (C)
1966, March 9	Thomas Tschoepe	San Angelo

Diocese of Davenport

Davenport

1884, September 14	Henry Cosgrove	Davenport
1904, November 30	James Davis	Davenport (C)
1936, April 16	William Adrian	Nashville
1968, June 19	Maurice Dingman	Des Moines

Archdiocese of Denver

Denver

1887, October 28	Nicholas Matz	Denver (C)
1915, October 28	Anthony Schuler	El Paso
1947, September 24	Hubert Newell	Cheyenne (C)
1961, January 4	David Maloney	Denver (A)
1969, April 23	George Evans	Denver (A)
1974, September 20	Richard Hanifen	Denver (A)

Diocese of Des Moine

Des Moines

| 1943, February 17 | John Boylan | Rockford |
| 1948, May 13 | Edward Daly | Des Moines |

Archdiocese of Detroit

Detroit

1924, September 30	Joseph Plagens	Detroit (A)
1938, January 25	Stephen Woznicki	Detroit (A)
1947, March 25	Allen Babcock	Detroit (A)
1950, May 23	Alexander Zaleski	Detroit (A)
1954, October 26	John Donovan	Detroit (A)
1954, October 26	Henry Donnelly	Detroit (A)

1965, December 20	Joseph Breitenbeck	Detroit (A)
1968, May 1	Walter Schoenherr	Detroit (A)
1968, May 1	Thomas Gumbleton	Detroit (A)
1973, April 3	Joseph Imesch	Detroit (A)
1973, April 3	Arthur Krawczak	Detroit (A)
1983, January 27	Moses Anderson	Detroit (A)
1983, January 27	Patrick Cooney	Detroit (A)
1983, January 27	Dale Melczek	Detroit (A)

Archdiocese of Dubuque

Dubuque

1866, September 30	John Hennessy	Dubuque
1897, February 24	Thomas Lenihan	Cheyenne
1904, September 21	Mathias Lenihan	Great Falls
1904, December 21	John Carroll	Helena
1918, May 1	Daniel Gorman	Boise City
1919, May 21	Thomas Drumm	Des Moines
1924, April 8	Edward Howard	Davenport (A)
1927, July 25	Henry Rohlman	Davenport
1930, October 28	Louis Kucera	Lincoln
1946, September 12	Edward Fitzgerald	Dubuque (A)
1951, August 20	Loras Lane	Dubuque (A)
1957, April 24	George Biskup	Dubuque (A)
1957, April 24	James Casey	Lincoln (A)
1965, August 26	Loras Watters	Dubuque (A)
1969, August 27	Francis Dunn	Dubuque (A)
1970, October 28	Justin Driscoll	Fargo
1987, April 1	William Franklin	Dubuque (A)

Diocese of Duluth

Duluth

1956, September 12	Lawrence Glenn	Duluth (A)
1983, May 23	Robert Brom	Duluth

Diocese of Erie

Erie

1891, April 5	Thomas Brennan	Dallas
1918, February 6	John Gannon	Erie (A)
1936, November 30	Richard Guilfoyle	Altoona
1948, October 28	Edward McManaman	Erie (A)
1965, June 29	Alfred Watson	Erie (A)

Diocese of Evansville

Evansville

1970, February 3	Francis Shea	Evansville
1989, April 11	Gerald Gettelfinger	Evansville

Ferdinand

1880, February 1	Martin Marty	Dakota (VA)*

---

*At this date, Ferdinand was part of the Diocese of Vincennes.

Vincennes

1847, October 24	John Bazin	Vincennes*
1849, January 14	James de Saint-Palais	Vincennes*

---

*At this date, Vincennes was the diocesan seat of what is now the Archdiocese of Indianapolis. In 1944, Vincennes became part of the newly established Diocese of Evansville.

Diocese of Fairbanks

Fairbanks

1968, February 22	Robert Whelan	Fairbanks (C)
1984, May 1	Michael Kaniecki	Fairbanks (C)

Glennallen

1964, July 31	George Boileau	Fairbanks (C)

Diocese of Fall River

Fall River

1907, September 19	Daniel Feehan	Fall River
1930, May 27	James Cassidy	Fall River (A)
1959, March 19	James Gerrard	Fall River (A)
1966, June 9	Humberto Medeiros	Brownsville

Diocese of Fargo

Fargo

1940, May 28	Vincent Ryan	Bismarck
1945, January 10	William Mulloy	Covington
1946, August 22	Leo Dworschak	Rapid City (C)

Diocese of Fort Wayne–South Bend

Fort Wayne

1900, November 30	Herman Alerding	Fort Wayne
1925, June 30	John Noll	Fort Wayne
1945, January 10	John Bennett	Lafayette, Ind.
1950, September 19	Leo Pursley	Fort Wayne (A)

South Bend

1971, August 24	Joseph Crowley	Ft. Wayne-South Bend (A)

Notre Dame

1927, August 1	George Finnegan	Helena
1940, January 15	John O'Hara	Military (A)

Diocese of Fort Worth

Fort Worth

1963, May 30	Lawrence DeFalco	Amarillo*
1981, September 13	Joseph Delaney	Fort Worth

---

*At this date, Fort Worth was part of the Diocese of Dallas-Fort Worth.

Diocese of Fresno

Fresno

1933, June 29	Philip Scher	Monterey-Fresno*
1957, February 27	Harry Clinch	Monterey-Fresno (A)*
1975, March 19	Roger Mahony	Fresno (A)
1980, March 4	José Madera	Fresno (C)

*At these dates, Fresno was part of the Diocese of Monterey-Fresno.

Diocese of Gallup

Gallup

1986, May 6	Donald Pelotte	Gallup (C)

Diocese of Galveston–Houston

Galveston

1882, April 30	Nicholas Gallagher	Galveston (C)
1948, April 14	Louis Reicher	Austin

Houston

1966, September 28	Vincent Harris	Beaumont
1968, June 5	John Cassata	Dallas-Fort Worth (A)
1979, March 14	John McCarthy	Galveston-Houston (A)
1986, June 29	Enrique San Pedro	Galveston-Houston (A)
1988, February 19	Curtis Guillory	Galveston-Houston (A)

Diocese of Gary

Gary

1957, February 25	Andrew Grutka	Gary

Diocese of Gaylord

Gaylord

1971, July 20	Edmund Szoka	Gaylord
1981, December 6	Robert Rose	Gaylord

Diocese of Grand Island

Grand Island

1978, March 28	Lawrence McNamara	Grand Island

Diocese of Grand Rapids

Grand Rapids

1883, April 22	Henry Richter	Grand Rapids
1911, February 22	Joseph Schrembs	Grand Rapids (A)
1915, September 8	Michael Gallagher	Grand Rapids (C)
1927, February 24	Charles White	Spokane
1943, November 18	Francis Haas	Grand Rapids
1946, March 19	Thomas Noa	Sioux City (C)
1962, March 6	Charles Salatka	Grand Rapids (A)
1968, September 26	Joseph McKinney	Grand Rapids (A)

Diocese of Great Falls–Billings

Great Falls

1961, December 21	Eldon Schuster	Great Falls (A)
1978, August 21	Thomas Murphy	Great Falls

Diocese of Green Bay

Green Bay

1886, September 21	Frederick Katzer	Green Bay
1904, July 25	Joseph Fox	Green Bay
1970, June 24	Mark Schmitt	Green Bay (A)
1979, February 22	Robert Morneau	Green Bay (A)
1984, January 25	Adam Maida	Green Bay

Diocese of Greensburg

Greensburg

1960, May 4	William Connare	Greensburg
1965, June 17	Cyril Vogel	Salina
1975, June 26	Norbert Gaughan	Greensburg (A)

Diocese of Harrisburg

Harrisburg

1888, March 11	Thomas McGovern	Harrisburg
1956, May 1	Lawrence Schott	Harrisburg (A)
1979, September 21	William Keeler	Harrisburg (A)

Archdiocese of Hartford

Hartford

1876, March 19	Thomas Galberry	Hartford
1879, August 10	Lawrence McMahon	Hartford
1894, February 22	Michael Tierney	Hartford
1910, April 10	John Nilan	Hartford
1920, April 28	John Murray	Hartford (A)
1926, April 28	Maurice McAuliffe	Hartford (A)
1940, May 14	Henry O'Brien	Hartford (A)
1953, March 19	John Hackett	Hartford (A)
1965, January 28	Joseph Donnelly	Hartford (A)
1966, June 1	Peter Gerety	Portland, Maine (C)
1978, June 24	Peter Rosazza	Hartford (A)
1988, April 12	Paul Loverde	Hartford (A)

Diocese of Helena

Helena

1936, February 19	Joseph Gilmore	Helena
1942, February 24	Joseph Willging	Pueblo
1955, September 21	Bernard Topel	Spokane (C)
1962, August 30	Raymond Hunthausen	Helena
1976, April 28	Elden Curtiss	Helena

Diocese of Honolulu

Honolulu
1978, January 13   Joseph Ferrario   Honolulu (A)

Archdiocese of Indianapolis

Indianapolis
1900, April 25   Denis O'Donaghue   Indianapolis (A)
1910, September 15   Joseph Chartrand   Indianapolis (C)
1924, March 25   Alphonse Smith   Nashville
1933, March 28   Joseph Ritter   Indianapolis (A)

Saint-Mary-of-the-Woods
1921, June 14   Emmanuel Ledvina   Corpus Christi

Diocese of Jackson

Jackson
1957, January 29   Joseph Brunini   Natchez-Jackson (A)
1973, January 28   Joseph Howze   Natchez-Jackson (A)

Natchez
1891, September 8   Theophile Meerschaert   Oklahoma (VA)

Diocese of Jefferson City

Jefferson City
1969, August 18   Michael McAuliffe   Jefferson City

Diocese of Joliet

Joliet
1965, April 3   Romeo Blanchette   Joliet (A)
1968, April 3   Raymond Vonesh   Joliet (A)
1977, July 21   Daniel Kucera   Joliet (A)

| 1981, September 30 | Daniel Ryan | Joliet (A) |
| 1985, June 26 | Roger Kaffer | Joliet (A) |

Diocese of Kalamazoo

Kalamazoo

| 1971, July 21 | Paul Donovan | Kalamazoo |

Archdiocese of Kansas City in Kansas

Leavenworth

| 1898, September 21 | John Cunningham | Concordia |
| 1911, February 22 | John Ward | Leavenworth |

Diocese of Kansas City–Saint Joseph

Kansas City

1896, June 29	John Glennon	Kansas City (C)
1904, December 27	Thomas Lillis	Leavenworth
1921, March 30	Francis Tief	Concordia
1967, April 3	Joseph Sullivan	Kansas City-Saint Joseph (A)
1975, July 3	George Fitzsimons	Kansas City-Saint Joseph (A)

Saint Joseph*

| 1928, May 1 | Francis Johannes | Leavenworth (C) |
| 1936, December 21 | Charles Buddy | San Diego |

---

*At the dates of these consecrations, Saint Joseph was a separate diocese.

Diocese of Knoxville

Knoxville

| 1988, September 8 | Anthony O'Connell | Knoxville |

Diocese of La Crosse

La Crosse
1892, February 25   James Schwebach   La Crosse
1977, August 4   John Paul   La Crosse (A)

Diocese of Lafayette in Indiana

Lafayette
1984, June 6   William Higi   Lafayette, Ind.

Diocese of Lafayette

Lafayette
1962, July 25   Warren Boudreaux   Lafayette (A)

Diocese of Lake Charles

Lake Charles
1980, April 25   Jude Speyrer   Lake Charles

Diocese of Lansing

Lansing
1962, August 28   Michael Green   Lansing (A)
1972, September 21   James Sullivan   Lansing (A)

Ann Arbor
1911, January 26   Edward Kelly   Detroit (A)*

---

*At this date, Ann Arbor pertained to the Diocese of Detroit.

Diocese of Little Rock

Little Rock

1940, April 25	Albert Fletcher	Little Rock (A)
1969, April 25	Lawrence Graves	Little Rock (A)

Archdiocese of Los Angeles

Los Angeles

1873, August 3	Francis Mora	Monterey-Los Angeles (C)
1915, August 24	Joseph Glass	Salt Lake City
1924, August 24	Stephen Alencastre	Hawaii (C-VA)
1931, July 22	Thomas Gorman	Reno
1934, May 1	Robert Lucey	Amarillo
1941, March 19	Joseph McGucken	Los Angeles (A)
1946, October 15	Timothy Manning	Los Angeles (A)
1956, June 4	Alden Bell	Los Angeles (A)
1963, December 12	John Ward	Los Angeles (A)
1971, March 25	Juan Arzube	Los Angeles (A)
1971, March 25	William Johnson	Los Angeles (A)
1977, February 19	Manuel Moreno	Los Angeles (A)
1977, February 19	Thaddeus Shubsda	Los Angeles (A)
1983, May 12	Donald Montrose	Los Angeles (A)
1983, May 12	William Levada	Los Angeles (A)
1987, February 23	George Ziemann	Los Angeles (A)
1987, February 23	Armando Ochoa	Los Angeles (A)
1987, February 23	Carl Fisher	Los Angeles (A)

Archdiocese of Louisville

Louisville

1848, September 10	Martin Spalding	Louisville (C)
1865, September 24	Peter Lavialle	Louisville
1926, November 30	Theodore Reverman	Superior
1938, February 24	Francis Cotton	Owensboro
1955, February 2	Charles Maloney	Louisville (A)

Bardstown

1819, August 15	John David	Bardstown (C)
1830, June 6	Francis Kenrick	Philadelphia (C)
1834, July 20	Guy Chabrat	Bardstown (C)
1838, September 16	Richard Miles	Nashville
1850, November 10	John McGill	Richmond

Springfield

1822, January 13	Edward Fenwick	Cincinnati

Diocese of Lubbock

Lubbock

1983, June 17	Michael Sheehan	Lubbock

Diocese of Madison

Madison

1963, September 3	Jerome Hastrich	Madison (A)
1978, March 9	George Wirz	Madison (A)

Diocese of Manchester

Manchester

1884, June 11	Denis Bradley	Manchester
1904, September 8	John Delaney	Manchester
1907, March 19	George Guertin	Manchester
1975, February 3	Odore Gendron	Manchester
1977, April 14	Robert Mulvee	Manchester (A)
1986, April 21	Joseph Gerry	Manchester (A)

Diocese of Marquette

Marquette

1899, August 24	Frederick Eis	Sault Sainte Marie and Marquette
1922, May 3	Joseph Pinten	Superior

Negaunee
1879, September 14   John Vertin   Sault Sainte Marie
and Marquette

Diocese of Memphis

Memphis
1971, January 6   Carroll Dozier   Memphis
1987, March 2   Daniel Buechlein   Memphis

Archdiocese of Miami

Miami
1968, August 28   John Fitzpatrick   Miami (A)
1972, January 25   Rene Gracida   Miami (A)
1983, November 20   Ambrose DePaoli   Papal Diplomat
1986, March 19   Norbert Dorsey   Miami (A)

Miami Beach
1979, March 24   Agustín Román   Miami (A)
1979, March 24   John Nevins   Miami (A)

Archdiocese of Milwaukee

Milwaukee
1868, September 6   Michael Heiss   La Crosse
1875, June 29   Francis Krautbauer   Green Bay
1881, August 24   Kilian Flasch   La Crosse
1905, July 25   Augustine Schinner   Superior
1914, January 14   Edward Kozlowski   Milwaukee (A)
1935, October 15   Aloisius Muench   Fargo
1942, March 7   William O'Connor   Superior
1946, April 11   Albert Meyer   Superior
1947, August 28   Roman Atkielski   Milwaukee (A)
1949, July 24   John Grellinger   Green Bay (A)
1969, October 16   Leo Brust   Milwaukee (A)
1977, November 8   Rembert Weakland   Milwaukee
1979, December 19   Richard Sklba   Milwaukee (A)

Archdiocese of Mobile

Mobile

1837, December 10	John Loras	Dubuque
1874, December 8	Anthony Pellicer	San Antonio
1874, December 8	Dominic Manucy	Brownsville (VA)
1910, April 14	John Shaw	San Antonio (C)
1924, October 15	Richard Gerow	Natchez
1979, October 30	William Friend	Alexandria-Shreveport (A)
1980, November 16	Oscar Lipscomb	Mobile

Diocese of Nashville

Nashville

1883, June 24	Joseph Rademacher	Nashville
1887, November 30	Richard Scannell	Concordia
1894, July 25	Thomas Byrne	Nashville
1906, June 11	John Morris	Little Rock (C)
1975, May 20	James Niedergeses	Nashville

Archdiocese of Newark

Newark

1873, May 4	Michael Corrigan	Newark
1881, October 18	Winand Wigger	Newark
1892, March 27	Sebastian Messmer	Green Bay
1901, July 25	John O'Connor	Newark
1933, June 29	John Duffy	Syracuse
1935, July 25	Thomas McLaughlin	Newark (A)
1936, June 29	Francis Monaghan	Ogdensburg (C)
1938, May 1	William Griffin	Newark (A)
1940, July 25	Thomas Boland	Newark (A)
1947, October 7	James McNulty	Newark (A)
1954, June 17	Justin McCarthy	Newark (A)
1957, September 24	Walter Curtis	Newark (A)
1957, September 24	Martin Stanton	Newark (A)
1963, January 24	John Dougherty	Newark (A)
1963, January 24	Joseph Costello	Newark (A)

1976, June 25	Robert Garner	Newark (A)
1976, June 25	Joseph Francis	Newark (A)
1976, June 25	Dominic Marconi	Newark (A)
1983, April 7	David Arias	Newark (A)
1988, January 25	James McHugh	Newark (A)
1988, January 25	John Smith	Newark (A)

Union City

1913, May 20	Henry Nussbaum	Corpus Christi

Archdiocese of New Orleans

New Orleans

1830, June 24	Leo DeNeckère	New Orleans
1835, November 22	Anthony Blanc	New Orleans
1842, March 6	John Odin	Texas (VA)
1853, November 30	Augustus Martin	Natchitoches
1859, December 4	John Quinlan	Mobile
1870, May 1	Napoleon Perché	New Orleans (C)
1885, March 19	Anthony Durier	Natchitoches
1889, June 18	Thomas Heslin	Natchez
1899, April 9	Gustave Rouxel	New Orleans (A)
1899, July 2	James Blenk	Puerto Rico
1904, November 30	Cornelius Van de Ven	Natchitoches
1911, November 29	John Laval	New Orleans (A)
1918, December 8	Arthur Drossaerts	San Antonio
1918, December 8	Jules Jeanmard	Lafayette, La.
1946, February 25	Charles Greco	Alexandria
1947, October 28	Louis Caillouet	New Orleans (A)
1951, February 22	Maurice Schexnayder	Lafayette, La. (A)
1959, May 19	Robert Tracy	Lafayette, La. (A)
1966, January 6	Harold Perry	New Orleans (A)
1966, May 26	Joseph Vath	Mobile-Birmingham (A)
1967, August 8	Gerard Frey	Savannah
1976, June 29	Stanley Ott	New Orleans (A)

Diocese of Newton—Greek Melkite Catholics

Boston
1966, May 29   Justin Najmy   Melkite Exarch

Roslindale
1986, June 29   John Elya   Newton (A)

West Paterson
1989, July 6   Nicholas Samra   Newton (A)

Archdiocese of New York

New York

1838, January 7	John Hughes	New York (C)
1844, March 10	John McCloskey	New York (C)
1844, March 10	William Quarter	Chicago
1844, March 10	Andrew Byrne	Little Rock
1847, October 17	John Timon	Buffalo
1853, October 30	James Bayley	Newark
1853, October 30	John Loughlin	Brooklyn
1853, October 30	Louis de Goesbriand	Burlington
1855, April 22	David Bacon	Portland, Maine
1868, July 12	Bernard McQuaid	Rochester
1872, April 21	Francis McNeirny	Albany (C)
1877, May 1	John Spalding	Peoria
1881, November 1	Michael O'Farrell	Trenton
1892, April 25	Charles McDonnell	Brooklyn
1895, December 21	John Farley	New York (A)
1903, August 24	Charles Colton	Buffalo
1904, April 25	Thomas Cusack	New York (A)
1914, October 28	Patrick Hayes	New York (A)
1921, October 28	John Dunn	New York (A)
1923, May 1	Daniel Curley	Syracuse
1926, September 8	John Mitty	Salt Lake City
1928, May 29	Joseph Rummel	Omaha
1932, October 28	James Kearney	Salt Lake City
1934, May 1	Stephen Donahue	New York (A)
1938, March 25	Bartholomew Eustace	Camden
1941, January 8	James McIntyre	New York (A)

236

1943, January 25	William McCarty	Military (A)
1943, August 3	Bryan McEntegart	Ogdensburg
1945, March 19	Joseph Donahue	New York (A)
1945, October 11	William Arnold	Military (A)
1945, October 24	William Scully	Albany (C)
1947, September 15	Thomas McDonnell	New York (A)
1948, January 14	Patrick O'Boyle	Washington
1948, December 16	Joseph Flannelly	New York (A)
1950, January 18	James Griffiths	Military (A)
1950, March 24	Christopher Weldon	Springfield, Mass.
1953, October 5	Walter Kellenberg	New York (A)
1953, October 5	Edward Dargin	New York (A)
1954, May 5	Joseph Pernicone	New York (A)
1956, January 25	Philip Furlong	Military (A)
1957, December 10	John Fearns	New York (A)
1959, June 29	John Maguire	New York (A)
1962, June 29	Francis Reh	Charleston
1964, April 9	Thomas Donnellan	Ogdensburg
1964, November 30	George Guilfoyle	New York (A)
1965, December 13	William Moran	Military (A)
1965, December 13	Terence Cooke	New York (A)
1967, April 21	Edwin Broderick	New York (A)
1970, March 19	Patrick Ahern	New York (A)
1970, March 19	Edward Head	New York (A)
1972, September 15	James Mahoney	New York (A)
1973, April 27	Anthony Mestice	New York (A)
1975, December 13	James Killeen	Military (A)
1977, June 29	Theodore McCarrick	New York (A)
1977, June 29	Austin Vaughan	New York (A)
1977, June 29	Francisco Garmendia	New York (A)
1982, September 8	Joseph O'Keefe	New York (A)
1982, September 8	Emerson Moore	New York (A)
1983, May 10	Joseph Dimino	Military (A)
1983, May 10	Francis Roque	Military (A)
1983, May 10	Lawrence Kenney	Military (A)
1983, November 29	Angelo Acerra	Military (A)

Bronx

1970, January 6	George Lynch	Raleigh (A)

Maryknoll

| 1959, April 9 | John Comber | Maryknoll Superior |

Diocese of Norwich

Norwich

| 1960, March 17 | Vincent Hines | Norwich |
| 1975, August 6 | Daniel Reilly | Norwich |

Diocese of Ogdensburg

Ogdensburg

| 1912, May 1 | Joseph Conroy | Ogdensburg (A) |

Archdiocese of Oklahoma City

Oklahoma City

| 1956, February 8 | Stephen Leven | San Antonio (A) |
| 1959, September 30 | Charles Buswell | Pueblo |

Archdiocese of Omaha

Omaha

1912, April 11	Patrick McGovern	Cheyenne
1945, May 1	Edward Hunkeler	Grand Island
1951, October 9	John Paschang	Grand Island
1964, March 19	Daniel Sheehan	Omaha (A)

Diocese of Orange

Garden Grove

| 1984, July 14 | John Steinbock | Orange (A) |

Diocese of Owensboro

Owensboro
1982, December 15   John McRaith   Owensboro

Diocese of Parma—Ruthenians

Parma
1969, June 12   Emil Mihalik   Parma

Diocese of Passaic—Ruthenians

Passaic
1968, October 24   Michael Dudick   Passaic
1987, February 4   George Kuzma   Passaic (A)

Scranton
1976, November 23   Thomas Dolinay   Passaic (A)
1983, August 23   Andrew Pataki   Passaic (A)

Diocese of Paterson

Paterson
1978, February 28   Frank Rodimer   Paterson

Diocese of Peoria

Peoria
1900, September 21   Peter O'Reilly   Peoria (A)
1934, June 13   Gerald Bergan   Des Moines
1971, July 15   Edward O'Rourke   Peoria
1987, September 3   John Myers   Peoria (C)

Archdiocese of Philadelphia

Philadelphia

1841, November 21	Peter Lefevere	Detroit (C)
1841, November 30	Peter Kenrick	Saint Louis (C)
1850, November 10	Francis Gartland	Savannah
1868, July 12	Jeremiah Shanahan	Harrisburg
1868, July 12	William O'Hara	Scranton
1876, August 20	James O'Connor	Nebraska (VA)
1892, February 25	John Horstmann	Cleveland
1897, February 24	Edmond Prendergast	Philadelphia (A)
1898, February 24	John Fitzmaurice	Erie (C)
1899, May 1	John Shanahan	Harrisburg
1910, May 10	John MacGinley	Caceres
1912, September 17	John McCort	Philadelphia (A)
1916, September 21	Philip McDevitt	Harrisburg
1921, September 19	Michael Crane	Philadelphia (A)
1923, November 6	Daniel Gercke	Tucson
1925, November 30	Edmond Fitzmaurice	Wilmington
1925, November 30	Edwin Byrne	Ponce
1929, May 20	Gerald O'Hara	Philadelphia (A)
1935, October 17	George Leech	Harrisburg (A)
1936, March 19	Hugh Lamb	Philadelphia (A)
1937, December 21	Eugene McGuinness	Raleigh
1947, April 23	Joseph McCormick	Philadelphia (A)
1949, December 21	Francis Hyland	Savannah-Atlanta (A)
1952, March 19	Joseph McShea	Philadelphia (A)
1960, December 22	Francis Furey	Philadelphia (A)
1960, December 22	Cletus Benjamin	Philadelphia (A)
1962, August 1	Gerald McDevitt	Philadelphia (A)
1964, January 7	Joseph Daley	Harrisburg (A)
1964, January 7	John Graham	Philadelphia (A)
1970, April 2	Martin Lohmuller	Philadelphia (A)
1970, April 2	Thomas Welsh	Philadelphia (A)
1976, July 21	Edward Hughes	Philadelphia (A)
1981, August 12	Louis DeSimone	Philadelphia (A)
1981, August 12	Francis Schulte	Philadelphia (A)
1984, May 8	John Foley	Roman Curia

Germantown

1956, October 24	Hubert Cartwright	Wilmington (C)

Archdiocese of Philadelphia—Ukrainians

Philadelphia

1956, November 8	Joseph Schmondiuk	Philadelphia (A)
1961, October 26	Jaroslav Gabro	Saint Nicholas
1971, May 25	John Stock	Philadelphia (A)
1971, May 25	Basil Losten	Philadelphia (A)
1981, October 13	Robert Moskal	Philadelphia (A)
1988, April 27	Michael Kuchmiak	Philadelphia (A)

Archdiocese of Pittsburgh—Byzantines

Pittsburgh

1946, November 5	Daniel Ivancho	Pittsburgh (C)
1956, October 23	Stephen Kocisko	Pittsburgh (A)
1973, May 15	John Bilock	Pittsburgh (A)

Diocese of Pittsburgh

Pittsburgh

1860, December 9	Michael Domenec	Pittsburgh
1868, August 2	Tobias Mullen	Erie
1876, March 19	John Tuigg	Pittsburgh
1885, August 2	Richard Phelan	Pittsburgh (C)
1903, February 24	John Canevin	Pittsburgh (C)
1921, June 29	Hugh Boyle	Pittsburgh
1933, September 21	Ralph Hayes	Helena
1953, November 10	Coleman Carroll	Pittsburgh (A)
1956, May 22	Richard Ackerman	San Diego (A)
1964, April 21	Vincent Leonard	Pittsburgh (A)
1966, September 8	John McDowell	Pittsburgh (A)
1970, June 30	Anthony Bosco	Pittsburgh (A)
1989, February 13	William Winter	Pittsburgh (A)

Diocese of Portland

Portland, Maine

1875, June 2	James Healy	Portland
1906, October 18	Louis Walsh	Portland
1932, August 24	Joseph McCarthy	Portland
1946, September 12	Daniel Feeney	Portland (A)
1971, January 25	Edward O'Leary	Portland (A)
1975, November 12	Amedee Proulx	Portland (A)
1984, September 14	Paulius Baltakis	Lithuanians

Archdiocese of Portland in Oregon

Portland, Oregon

1903, August 25	Charles O'Reilly	Baker City
1930, October 28	Edwin O'Hara	Great Falls
1950, September 12	Francis Leipzig	Baker City
1978, March 2	Paul Waldschmidt	Portland (A)
1978, March 2	Kenneth Steiner	Portland (A)

Diocese of Providence

Providence

1858, March 14	Francis MacFarland	Hartford*
1872, April 28	Thomas Hendricken	Providence
1887, April 14	Matthew Harkins	Providence
1904, May 1	William Stang	Fall River
1912, April 25	Austin Dowling	Des Moines
1915, April 28	Thomas Doran	Providence (A)
1917, October 23	Denis Lowney	Providence (A)
1919, April 10	William Hickey	Providence (C)
1934, May 22	Francis Keough	Providence
1948, July 14	Russell McVinney	Providence
1960, May 11	Thomas Maloney	Providence (A)
1964, January 30	Bernard Kelly	Providence (A)
1972, January 26	Louis Gelineau	Providence
1974, October 7	Kenneth Angell	Providence (A)

*At this date, Providence was part of the Diocese of Hartford.

Diocese of Pueblo

Pueblo
1980, September 10   Arthur Tafoya   Pueblo

Diocese of Raleigh

Raleigh
1951, April 11   Joseph Federal   Salt Lake City (A)

Diocese of Rapid City

Rapid City
1969, October 30   Harold Dimmerling   Rapid City
1988, July 26   Charles Chaput   Rapid City

Diocese of Richmond

Richmond
1878, August 25   John Keane   Richmond
1881, May 1   Francis Janssens   Natchez
1889, October 20   Augustine Van de Vyver Richmond
1900, June 3   Benjamin Keiley   Savannah
1945, May 15   Vincent Waters   Raleigh
1952, October 15   Joseph Hodges   Richmond (A)
1962, February 22   Ernest Unterkoefler   Richmond (A)
1966, October 5   James Flaherty   Richmond (A)
1970, December 1   Walter Sullivan   Richmond (A)
1986, June 27   David Foley   Richmond (A)

Diocese of Rochester

Rochester
1850, November 10   Bernard O'Reilly   Hartford*
1905, May 24   Thomas Hickey   Rochester (C)
1912, December 4   Edward Hanna   San Francisco (A)
1929, March 19   John O'Hern   Rochester

1937, August 18	Walter Foery	Syracuse
1953, May 5	Lawrence Casey	Rochester (A)
1968, March 14	Dennis Hickey	Rochester (A)
1968, March 14	John McCafferty	Rochester (A)
1969, November 28	Joseph Hogan	Rochester

At this date, Rochester was part of the Diocese of Buffalo.

Diocese of Rockford

Rockford

1942, December 21	Leo Binz	Winona (C)
1968, October 11	Arthur O'Neill	Rockford

Diocese of Rockville Centre

Rockville Centre

1962, July 26	Vincent Baldwin	Rockville Centre (A)
1971, January 7	John McGann	Rockville Centre (A)
1977, May 9	Gerald Ryan	Rockville Centre (A)
1977, May 9	James Daly	Rockville Centre (A)
1986, September 17	Alfred Markiewicz	Rockville Centre (A)
1988, December 13	Emil Wcela	Rockville Centre (A)
1988, December 13	John Dunne	Rockville Centre (A)

Diocese of Sacramento

Sacramento

1896, June 16	Thomas Grace	Sacramento
1974, May 16	John Cummins	Sacramento (A)
1981, November 4	Alphonse Gallegos	Sacramento (A)

Diocese of Saginaw

Saginaw

1938, May 17	William Murphy	Saginaw

| 1967, April 14 | James Hickey | Saginaw (A) |
| 1980, November 24 | Kenneth Untener | Saginaw |

Diocese of Saint Augustine

Saint Augustine

1902, May 18	William Kenny	Saint Augustine
1914, June 30	Michael Curley	Saint Augustine
1922, May 3	Patrick Barry	Saint Augustine
1947, April 30	Thomas McDonough	Saint Augustine (A)

Diocese of Saint Cloud

Saint Cloud

| 1875, May 30 | Rupert Seidenbusch | No. Minnesota (VA) |
| 1961, April 26 | Henry Soenneker | Owensboro |

Collegeville

| 1973, April 26 | James Rausch | Saint Cloud (A) |
| 1987, August 24 | Jerome Hanus | Saint Cloud |

Diocese of Saint George in Canton—Romanians

Detroit

| 1983, June 26 | Vasile Puscas | Romanian Exarch |

Archdiocese of Saint Louis

Saint Louis

1826, November 5	Michael Portier	Florida (VA)
1834, October 28	Simon Brute de Remur	Vincennes
1849, February 11	John Van de Velde	Chicago
1851, March 25	John Miège	Kansas (VA)
1854, July 25	Anthony O'Regan	Chicago
1857, May 3	Timothy Smyth	Dubuque (C)
1857, May 3	James Duggan	Saint Louis (C)
1859, May 8	James O'Gorman	Nebraska (VA)

1859, May 8	James Whelan	Nashville (C)
1859, July 24	Thomas Grace	Saint Paul
1865, November 1	Patrick Feehan	Nashville
1868, July 12	Joseph Melcher	Green Bay
1868, September 13	John Hogan	Saint Joseph
1872, April 14	Patrick Ryan	Saint Louis (C)
1887, November 30	Thomas Bonacum	Lincoln
1888, November 30	John Hennessy	Wichita
1918, November 10	Christopher Byrne	Galveston
1922, November 8	Francis Gilfillan	Saint Joseph (C)
1933, November 30	Christian Winkelmann	Saint Louis (A)
1937, September 21	Paul Schulte	Leavenworth
1940, April 23	George Donnelly	Saint Louis (A)
1947, April 23	Mark Carroll	Wichita
1947, July 2	John Cody	Saint Louis (A)
1948, May 20	Leo Steck	Salt Lake City (A)
1949, April 19	Charles Helmsing	Saint Louis (A)
1954, June 29	Leo Byrne	Saint Louis (A)
1957, May 30	Glennon Flavin	Saint Louis (A)
1961, August 8	George Gottwald	Saint Louis (A)
1969, March 25	Joseph McNicholas	Saint Louis (A)
1971, February 11	Charles Koester	Saint Louis (A)
1976, August 17	John Wurm	Saint Louis (A)
1984, February 10	Edward O'Donnell	Saint Louis (A)
1984, February 10	James Steib	Saint Louis (A)
1989, June 29	Paul Zipfel	Saint Louis (A)

Diocese of Saint Nicholas in Chicago—Ukrainians

Chicago
1942, October 22	Ambrose Senyshyn	Philadelphia (A)*
1983, September 8	Vladimir Tarasevitch	Byelorussians

*At this date, Chicago was part of the Ukrainian Exarchate of Philadelphia.

Archdiocese of Saint Paul and Minneapolis

Saint Paul
1875, December 21	John Ireland	Saint Paul (C)

1889, December 27	Joseph Cotter	Winona
1889, December 27	James McGolrick	Duluth
1889, December 27	John Shanley	Jamestown
1897, September 21	James Trobec	Sault Sainte Marie and Marquette
1898, June 29	Alexander Christie	Vancouver Island
1902, October 28	John Stariha	Lead
1902, October 28	James Keane	Cheyenne
1910, May 19	James O'Reilly	Fargo
1910, May 19	John Lawler	Saint Paul (A)
1910, May 19	Patrick Heffron	Winona
1910, May 19	Joseph Busch	Lead
1910, May 19	John Wehrle	Bismarck
1910, May 19	Timothy Corbett	Crookston
1926, February 3	Thomas Welch	Duluth
1939, August 24	William Brady	Sioux Falls
1945, May 24	James Connolly	Fall River (C)
1945, May 24	Francis Schenk	Crookston
1947, July 2	James Byrne	Saint Paul (A)
1957, February 27	Hilary Hacker	Bismarck
1958, January 29	Alphonse Schladweiler	New Ulm
1958, January 29	Leonard Cowley	Saint Paul (A)
1961, July 2	Gerald O'Keefe	Saint Paul (A)
1965, March 31	James Shannon	Saint Paul (A)
1966, April 14	James Michaels	Kwang Ju (A)
1971, September 8	John Roach	Saint Paul (A)
1971, September 8	Raymond Lucker	Saint Paul (A)
1977, January 25	Paul Dudley	Saint Paul (A)
1977, January 25	John Kinney	Saint Paul (A)
1980, August 12	William Bullock	Saint Paul (A)
1984, January 11	Robert Carlson	Saint Paul (A)

Diocese of Saint Petersburg

Saint Petersburg

1981, March 19	Joseph Symons	Saint Petersburg (A)

Diocese of Saint Thomas

Saint Thomas
1984, August 2   Sean O'Malley   Saint Thomas (C)

Diocese of Salt Lake City

Salt Lake City
1937, October 28   Duane Hunt   Salt Lake City
1952, August 5   Robert Dwyer   Reno
1980, November 17   William Weigand   Salt Lake City

Diocese of San Angelo

San Angelo
1962, January 24   Thomas Drury   San Angelo
1979, October 25   Joseph Fiorenza   San Angelo
1985, July 26   Michael Pfeifer   San Angelo

Archdiocese of San Antonio

San Antonio
1881, May 8   John Neraz   San Antonio
1895, October 28   John Forest   San Antonio
1936, September 21   Mariano Garriga   Corpus Christi (C)
1940, April 10   Sidney Metzger   Santa Fe (A)
1941, October 22   Lawrence FitzSimon   Amarillo
1956, February 22   John Morkovsky   Amarillo (A)
1970, May 5   Patrick Flores   San Antonio (A)
1976, December 13   Raymundo Peña   San Antonio (A)
1981, August 20   Charles Grahmann   San Antonio (A)
1981, December 6   Ricardo Ramirez   San Antonio (A)
1983, July 25   Bernard Popp   San Antonio (A)
1988, December 15   Edmond Carmody   San Antonio (A)

Diocese of San Bernardino

Riverside

1978, November 6	Philip Straling	San Bernardino

Diocese of San Diego

San Diego

1967, December 12	John Quinn	San Diego (A)
1974, June 21	Gilbert Chavez	San Diego (A)

Archdiocese of San Francisco

San Francisco

1868, August 9	Louis Lootens	Idaho and Montana (VA)
1881, January 16	Patrick Manogue	Grass Valley (C)
1881, August 21	Bernard Koeckemann	Hawaii (C, VA)
1887, June 29	Lawrence Scanlan	Utah (VA)
1892, September 25	Francis Ropert	Hawaii (VA)
1894, April 8	George Montgomery	Monterey-Los Angeles (C)
1903, July 25	Libert Boeynaems	Hawaii (VA)
1917, December 5	John Cantwell	Monterey-Los Angeles
1920, December 4	Patrick Keane	Sacramento (A)
1939, August 24	Thomas Connolly	San Francisco (A)
1941, July 25	James Sweeney	Honolulu
1947, October 7	Hugh Donohoe	San Francisco (A)
1948, June 29	James O'Dowd	San Francisco (A)
1950, September 21	Merlin Guilfoyle	San Francisco (A)
1954, September 21	John Scanlan	Honolulu (A)
1962, April 5	Leo Maher	Santa Rosa
1968, January 4	Mark Hurley	San Francisco (A)
1970, March 19	Francis Hurley	Juneau (A)
1970, September 8	Norman McFarland	San Francisco (A)
1978, June 29	Francis Quinn	San Francisco (A)
1978, June 29	Roland DuMaine	San Francisco (A)
1981, September 24	Daniel Walsh	San Francisco (A)
1989, January 25	Carlos Sevilla	San Francisco (A)
1989, January 25	Patrick McGrath	San Francisco (A)

Archdiocese of Santa Fe

Santa Fe

1885, May 1	Peter Bourgade	Arizona (VA)
1902, July 25	John Pitaval	Santa Fe (A)
1919, May 7	Albert Daeger	Santa Fe

Albuquerque

1974, July 25	Robert Sanchez	Santa Fe

Diocese of Savannah

Savannah

1922, October 18	Michael Keyes	Savannah
1927, September 8	Emmet Walsh	Charleston
1972, September 5	Andrew McDonald	Little Rock
1973, April 27	Raymond Lessard	Savannah

Diocese of Scranton

Scranton

1896, March 22	Michael Hoban	Scranton (C)
1901, September 8	Eugene Garvey	Altoona
1923, April 5	Andrew Brennan	Scranton (A)
1943, January 27	Martin O'Connor	Scranton (A)
1947, July 2	Henry Klonowski	Scranton (A)
1976, September 21	James Timlin	Scranton (A)
1988, March 8	Francis DiLorenzo	Scranton (A)

Archdiocese of Seattle

Seattle

1917, July 25	Joseph Crimont	Alaska (VA)
1919, March 25	Joseph McGrath	Baker City
1929, March 12	Robert Armstrong	Sacramento
1951, September 26	Joseph Dougherty	Yakima
1956, May 31	Thomas Gill	Seattle (A)
1969, May 1	Cornelius Power	Yakima

Vancouver

1879, October 28	Egidius Junger	Nesqually
1896, September 8	Edward O'Dea	Nesqually

Diocese of Sioux City

Sioux City

1919, April 8	Edmond Heelan	Sioux City (A)
1965, May 26	Frank Greteman	Sioux City (A)
1983, August 17	Lawrence Soens	Sioux City

Diocese of Sioux Falls

Sioux Falls

1952, March 25	Lambert Hoch	Bismarck

Huron

1968, October 17	Paul Anderson	Duluth (C)

Diocese of Spokane

Spokane

1939, February 24	Walter Fitzgerald	Alaska (C, VA)
1939, October 18	William Condon	Great Falls
1948, April 5	Francis Gleeson	Alaska (VA)
1978, December 14	Lawrence Welsh	Spokane

Diocese of Springfield–Cape Girardeau

Springfield

1970, April 6	William Baum	Springfield-Cape Girardeau
1973, December 5	Bernard Law	Springfield-Cape Girardeau
1984, December 12	John Leibrecht	Springfield-Cape Girardeau

Cape Girardeau
1960, March 24   Marion Forst   Dodge City

Diocese of Springfield in Illinois

Springfield
1951, August 29   John Franz   Dodge City

Alton
1888, May 1   James Ryan   Alton

Diocese of Springfield

Springfield, Massachusetts
1870, September 25   Patrick O'Reilly   Springfield
1892, October 18   Thomas Beaven   Springfield
1902, May 25   Philip Garrigan   Sioux City
1921, September 8   Thomas O'Leary   Springfield
1980, August 22   Leo O'Neil   Springfield (A)

Diocese of Steubenville

Steubenville
1904, February 25   James Hartley   Columbus*

---

*At this date, Steubenville was part of the Diocese of Columbus.

Diocese of Superior

Superior
1954, March 25   Joseph Annabring   Superior
1960, May 24   George Hammes   Superior
1979, December 20   Raphael Fliss   Superior (C)

Diocese of Syracuse

Syracuse

1887, May 1	Patrick Ludden	Syracuse
1909, May 16	John Grimes	Syracuse (C)
1950, June 8	David Cunningham	Syracuse (A)
1971, April 22	Frank Harrison	Syracuse (A)
1978, March 13	Thomas Costello	Syracuse (A)

Diocese of Toledo

Toledo

1921, June 10	August Schwertner	Wichita
1921, November 30	Samuel Stritch	Toledo
1931, June 17	Karl Alter	Toledo
1974, May 29	Albert Ottenweller	Toledo (A)
1978, June 23	James Hoffman	Toledo (A)
1984, May 3	Robert Donnelly	Toledo (A)

Diocese of Trenton

Trenton

1894, October 18	James McFaul	Trenton
1950, March 20	George Ahr	Trenton
1960, February 25	James Hogan	Trenton (A)
1967, December 12	John Reiss	Trenton (A)
1982, November 3	Edward Kmiec	Trenton (A)

Diocese of Tucson

Tucson

1943, October 6	James Davis	San Juan
1953, September 17	Francis Green	Tucson (A)

Diocese of Tulsa

Tulsa

1958, March 5	Victor Reed	Oklahoma City and Tulsa*
1972, September 19	John Sullivan	Grand Island
1973, February 7	Bernard Ganter	Tulsa
1978, April 20	Eusebius Beltran	Tulsa

At this date, Tulsa was part of the Diocese of Oklahoma City and Tulsa.

Diocese of Tyler

Tyler

1987, February 24	Charles Herzig	Tyler

Archdiocese of Washington

Washington

1885, September 20	Jeremiah O'Sullivan	Mobile*
1896, April 19	Thomas O'Gorman	Sioux Falls*
1919, March 30	William Turner	Buffalo*
1933, September 19	Gerald Shaughnessy	Seattle*
1933, October 25	James Ryan	CUA Rector*
1940, April 2	Joseph Corrigan	CUA Rector**
1944, December 14	Michael Ready	Columbus**
1945, December 12	Lawrence Shehan	Baltimore and Washington (A)**
1950, March 14	John Russell	Charleston
1950, September 21	Patrick McCormick	Washington (A)
1954, September 21	Jerome Hannan	Scranton
1956, August 28	Philip Hannan	Washington (A)
1958, January 2	Howard Carroll	Altoona-Johnstown
1964, May 19	William McDonald	Washington (A)
1964, May 19	John Spence	Washington (A)
1965, December 21	Paul Tanner	NCWC Secretary
1966, April 26	Edward Herrmann	Washington (A)
1974, September 12	Thomas Lyons	Washington (A)
1974, September 12	Eugene Marino	Washington (A)

1977, August 15	Thomas Kelly	Washington (A)
1983, July 27	Laszlo Iranyi	Hungarians
1985, August 4	Alvaro Corrada del Rio	Washington (A)
1988, December 20	Leonard Olivier	Washington (A)
1988, December 20	William Curlin	Washington (A)

*At this date, Washington was part of the Archdiocese of Baltimore.
**At this date, Washington was part of the Archdiocese of Baltimore and Washington.

Georgetown
| 1844, March 24 | John Fitzpatrick | Boston (C)* |

*At this date, Georgetown was a town within the District of Columbia and was part of the Archdiocese of Baltimore.

Diocese of Wheeling–Charleston

Wheeling
1875, May 23	John Kain	Wheeling
1922, May 11	John Swint	Wheeling (A)
1988, August 1	Bernard Schmitt	Wheeling-Charleston (A)

Diocese of Wichita

Wichita
1911, July 6	John Tihen	Lincoln
1962, June 20	Ignatius Strecker	Springfield-Cape Girardeau
1976, December 14	Eugene Gerber	Dodge City

Diocese of Wilmington

Wilmington
| 1897, May 9 | John Monaghan | Wilmington |

Diocese of Winona

Winona
1926, June 9	Francis Kelly	Winona (A)
1938, November 9	John Peschges	Crookston
1963, March 25	George Speltz	Winona (A)

Rochester
1942, March 3	Peter Bartholome	Saint Cloud (C)

Diocese of Worcester

Worcester
1968, July 2	Timothy Harrington	Worcester (A)
1987, February 27	George Rueger	Worcester (A)

Diocese of Yakima

Yakima
1977, May 12	William Skylstad	Yakima

Diocese of Youngtown

Youngstown
1960, March 24	James Malone	Youngstown (A)
1974, September 12	William Hughes	Youngstown (A)
1980, September 4	Benedict Franzetta	Youngstown (A)

Apostolic Exarchate—Armenians

Philadelphia
1981, December 5	Mikail Setian	Armenian Exarch

Section Two

Belgium

Archdiocese of Mechelen-Bruxelles

Woluwe-Saint Pierre
1968, May 1   Jean Jadot   Papal Diplomat

Canada

Archdiocese of Montréal

Montréal
1845, July 25   Francis Blanchet   Oregon (VA)
1846, September 27   Augustin Blanchet   Walla Walla

Diocese of Victoria

Victoria
1873, June 29   Charles Seghers   Vancouver Island
1879, December 14   John Brondel   Vancouver Island

Chile

Archdiocese of Santiago de Chile

Santiago
1847, November 28   Louis Maigret   Hawaii (VA)

China

Archdiocese of Canton

Sancian Island
1927, May 22   James E. Walsh   Kongmoon (VA)

Cuba

Archdiocese of San Cristobal de la Habana

Havana
1795, April 26   Luis Peñalver   New Orleans
1903, October 28   Bonaventure Broderick   Havana (A)

Egypt

Patriarchate of Alexandria of the Greek Melkite Catholics

Cairo
1960, January 1   Joseph Tawil   Damascus (VP)

England

Diocese of Plymouth

Lulworth Castle
1790, August 15   John Carroll   Baltimore

Archdiocese of Westminster

London
1820, September 24   Henry Conwell   Philadelphia

France

Diocese of Belley

Belley
1851, January 26   Joseph Cretin   Saint Paul

Diocese of Clermont

Clermont
1869, June 20   John Salpointe   Arizona (VA)

Diocese of Le Mans

Le Mans
1860, November 25   Peter Dufal   East Bengal (VA)

Archdiocese of Lyons

Lyons
1862, November 23   Claude Dubuis   Galveston

Archdiocese of Paris

Paris
1839, August 18   Celestin de La   Vincennes
                         Hailandière

Archdiocese of Rennes

Rennes
1877, April 22   Francis Leray   Natchitoches

Guatemala

Archdiocese of Guatemala

Guatemala City
1962, July 22   Hugo Gerbermann   Huehuetenango
1968, January 6   Richard Ham   Guatemala (A)

India

Archdiocese of Bombay

Bombay
1854, June 4   Ignatius Persico   Bombay (C, VA)

Iraq

Patriarchate of Babylon of the Chaldeans

Bagdad
1982, March 7   Ibrahim Ibrahim   Chaldean Exarch

Ireland

Diocese of Cork

Cork
1820, September 21   John England   Charleston

Archdiocese of Dublin

Dublin
1861, February 3   Eugene O'Connell   Marysville (VA)

Diocese of Kildare and Leighlin

Carlow
1834, December 21   William Clancy   Charleston (C)

Diocese of Ossory

Kilkenny
1820, August 24   Patrick Kelly   Richmond

Italy

Diocese of Albano

Albano

1985, September 14	Justin Rigali	Roman Curia

Diocese of Faenza

Faenza

1969, June 22	Pio Laghi	Papal Diplomat

Diocese of Rome

Rome

1801, November 15	Francisco Porro	New Orleans
1808, April 24	Richard Concanen	New York
1814, November 6	John Connolly	New York
1815, September 24	Louis DuBourg	New Orleans
1843, August 15	Michael O'Connor	Pittsburgh
1850, June 30	Joseph Alemany	Monterey
1854, March 12	Thaddeus Amat	Monterey
1868, May 24	William McCloskey	Louisville
1878, May 12	Francis Chatard	Vincennes
1888, June 10	Francesco Satolli	Papal Diplomat
1892, July 17	Angelo Falconio	Lacedonia
1896, August 30	Sebastiano Martinelli	Papal Diplomat
1901, May 19	William O'Connell	Portland, Maine
1903, June 14	Dennis Dougherty	Nueva Segovia
1903, July 5	Robert Seton	Roman Curia
1903, August 15	Jeremiah Harty	Manila
1907, December 29	Thomas Kennedy	North American College Rector
1909, May 1	John Farrelly	Cleveland
1912, March 3	Giovanni Bonzano	Papal Diplomat
1916, December 10	Pietro Fumasoni-Biondi	Papal Diplomat
1918, September 8	John McNicholas	Duluth
1921, October 28	George Caruana	Puerto Rico
1922, June 29	Bernard Mahoney	Sioux Falls
1923, April 8	John Floersh	Louisville (C)

1924, June 15	Constantine Bohachevskyj	Ukrainian Exarch
1924, June 15	Basil Takacs	Ruthenian Exarch
1926, January 31	Edward Mooney	Papal Diplomat
1929, October 20	Ivan Bucko	Lviv (A)
1932, September 8	Francis Spellman	Boston (A)
1933, April 23	Amleto Cicognani	Papal Diplomat
1933, June 29	James Walsh	Maryknoll Superior
1934, March 17	Moses Kiley	Trenton
1940, October 6	Joseph Hurley	Saint Augustine
1949, May 22	Egidio Vagnozzi	Papal Diplomat
1951, June 11	Fulton Sheen	New York (A)
1954, January 31	Luigi Raimondi	Papal Diplomat
1955, March 6	Nicholas Elko	Pittsburgh, Ruthenians (AD)
1957, November 30	Frederick Freking	Salina
1962, October 28	Joseph McGeough	Papal Diplomat
1962, October 28	Edward Swanstrom	New York (A)
1967, June 25	Francis Brennan	Roman Curia
1969, January 6	Raymond Etteldorf	Papal Diplomat
1969, January 6	Paul Marcinkus	Roman Curia
1969, January 6	Bernard McLaughlin	Buffalo (A)
1972, February 13	Edward Heston	Roman Curia
1972, February 13	Edward O'Meara	Saint Louis (A)
1979, May 27	Michael Kenny	Juneau
1979, May 27	William Houck	Jackson (A)
1979, May 27	William Larkin	Saint Petersburg
1979, May 27	John O'Connor	Military (A)
1979, May 27	Matthew Clark	Rochester
1979, November 12	Myroslav Lubachivsky	Philadelphia, Ukrainians
1981, March 1	Stephen Sulyk	Philadelphia, Ukrainians
1981, March 1	Innocent Lotocky	Saint Nicholas of Chicago
1982, January 6	Thomas O'Brien	Phoenix
1982, January 6	Anthony Milone	Omaha (A)
1985, May 22	Edward Egan	New York (A)
1986, January 6	Donald Wuerl	Seattle (A)
1987, January 6	William McCormack	New York (A)
1988, January 6	John Nolan	Military (A)

Lebanon

Patriarchate of Antioch of the Maronites

Bkerké
1981, January 25   John Chedid   Saint Maron (A)

Dimane
1962, August 5   Francis Zayek   Maronites, Brazil (A)

Mexico

Diocese of Zacatecas

Guadalupe, Zacatecas
1840, October 4   Francisco Garcia Diego   California

South Korea

Archdiocese of Seoul

Seoul
1949, June 14   Patrick Byrne   Papal Diplomat

Spain

Archdiocese of Barcelona

Barcelona
1890, November 9   Peter Verdaguer   Brownsville (VA)

Switzerland

Territorial Abbey of Maria Einsiedeln

Einsiedeln
1889, October 20   John Zardetti   Saint Cloud

Ukraine

Major Archdiocese of Lviv of the Ukrainians

Lviv

1907, May 12	Soter Ortynsky	Ukrainian and Ruthenian Exarch

Index

Brady, John / 199
Brady, Matthew Francis / 457
Brady, William Otterwell / 463
Breitenbeck, Joseph Matthew / 721
Brennan, Andrew James Louis / 361
Brennan, Francis John / 5-A
Brennan, Thomas Francis / 198
Broderick, Bonaventure Finbarr / 260
Broderick, Edwin Bernard / 742
Brom, Robert H. / 974
Brondel, John Baptist / 152
Brossart, Ferdinand / 322
Brown, Tod David / 1056
Brunini, Joseph Bernard / 625
Brust, Leo Joseph / 781
Brute de Remur, Simon / 28
Brzana, Stanislaus Joseph / 705
Bucko, Ivan / 403
Buddy, Charles Francis / 446
Buechlein, Daniel Mark / 1029
Bullock, William H. / 931
Burke, James Edward Charles / 743
Burke, Joseph Aloysius / 491
Burke, Maurice Francis / 181
Burke, Thomas Martin A. / 214
Busch, Joseph Francis / 295
Buswell, Charles Albert / 650
Byrne, Andrew / 44
Byrne, Christopher Edward / 332
Byrne, Edwin Vincent / 378
Byrne, James Joseph / 528
Byrne, Leo Christopher / 599
Byrne, Patrick James / 3-A
Byrne, Thomas Sebastian / 215

Caillouet, Louis Abel / 537
Canevin, John Francis Regis / 254
Cantwell, John Joseph / 327
Carberry, John Joseph / 618
Carlson, Robert James / 989
Carmody, Edmond / 1050
Carrell, George Aloysius / 69
Carroll, Coleman Francis / 591
Carroll, Howard Joseph / 637
Carroll, John / 1

Carroll, John Patrick / 269
Carroll, Mark Kenny / 522
Cartwright, Hubert James / 623
Caruana, George Joseph / 2-A
Casey, James Vincent / 630
Casey, Lawrence Bernard / 586
Cassata, John Joseph / 758
Cassidy, James Edwin / 406
Chabrat, Guy Ignatius / 26
Chanche, John Joseph Mary / 36
Chapelle, Placide Louis / 201
Chaput, Charles Joseph / 1044
Chartrand, Joseph / 298
Chatard, Francis Silas / 147
Chavez, Gilbert Espinosa / 838
Chedid, John George / 941
Christie, Alexander / 231
Cicognani, Amleto Giovanni / 6-B
Clancy, William / 29
Clark, Matthew H. / 918
Clinch, Harry Anselm / 628
Cody, John Patrick / 527
Colton, Charles Henry / 258
Comber, John William / 645
Conaty, Thomas James / 248
Concanen, Richard Luke / 5
Condon, William Joseph / 464
Connare, William Graham / 658
Connolly, James Louis / 504
Connolly, John / 9
Connolly, Thomas Arthur / 462
Connolly, Thomas John / 808
Conroy, John Joseph / 97
Conroy, Joseph Henry / 308
Conwell, Henry / 15
Cooke, Terence James / 720
Cooney, Patrick R. / 966
Corbett, Timothy / 297
Corrada del Rio, Alvaro / 1010
Corrigan, Joseph Moran / 466
Corrigan, Michael Augustine / 131
Corrigan, Owen Patrick / 282
Cosgrove, Henry / 169
Cosgrove, William Michael / 765
Costello, Joseph Arthur / 691

Garriga, Mariano Simon / 444
Garrigan, Philip Joseph / 250
Gartland, Francis Xavier / 60
Garvey, Eugene Augustine / 247
Gaughan, Norbert Felix / 854
Gelineau, Louis Edward / 818
Gendron, Odore Joseph / 847
Gerber, Eugene John / 877
Gerbermann, Hugo Mark / 681
Gercke, Daniel James / 364
Gerety, Peter Leo / 732
Gerken, Rudolph Aloysius / 386
Gerow, Richard Oliver / 374
Gerrard, James Joseph / 644
Gerry, Joseph John / 1014
Gettelfinger, Gerald A. / 1057
Gibbons, Edmund Francis / 335
Gibbons, James / 109
Gilfillan, Francis / 359
Gill, Thomas Edward / 616
Gilmour, Richard / 126
Glass, Joseph Sarsfield / 319
Gleeson, Francis Doyle / 541
Glenn, Lawrence Alexander / 620
Glennon, John Joseph / 222
Glorieux, Alphonse Joseph / 172
Goesbriand, Louis de / 68
González Nieves, Robert O. / 1047
Gorman, Daniel Mary / 329
Gorman, John Robert / 1041
Gorman, Thomas Kiely / 412
Gossman, Francis Joseph / 766
Gottwald, George Joseph / 671
Grace, Thomas / 221
Grace, Thomas Langton / 89
Gracida, Rene Henry / 817
Grady, Thomas Joseph / 745
Graham, John Joseph / 697
Grahmann, Charles Victor / 947
Granjon, Henry / 240
Graves, Lawrence Preston J. / 776
Greco, Charles Pascal / 511
Green, Francis Joseph / 588
Green, Michael Joseph / 687
Gregory, Wilton Daniel / 988

Grellinger, John Benjamin / 555
Greteman, Frank Henry / 712
Griffin, James Aloysius / 365
Griffin, James Anthony / 920
Griffin, William Aloysius / 455
Griffin, William Richard / 435
Griffiths, James Henry Ambrose / 557
Grimes, John / 284
Grimmelsman, Henry Joseph / 496
Gross, William Hickley / 130
Grutka, Andrew Gregory / 626
Guertin, George Albert / 275
Guilfoyle, George Henry / 708
Guilfoyle, Merlin Joseph / 567
Guilfoyle, Richard Thomas / 445
Guillory, Curtis John / 1037
Gumbleton, Thomas John / 757
Gunn, John Edward / 304

Haas, Francis Joseph / 494
Hacker, Hilary Baumann / 627
Hackett, John Francis / 585
Hafey, William Joseph / 375
Hagan, John Raphael / 514
Haid, Leo Michael / 188
Hallinan, Paul John / 643
Ham, Richard James / 751
Hammes, George Albert / 660
Hanifen, Richard Charles Patrick / 843
Hanna, Edward Joseph / 310
Hannan, Jerome Daniel / 602
Hannan, Philip Matthew / 619
Hanus, Jerome George / 1032
Harkins, Matthew / 178
Harper, Edward John / 661
Harrington, Timothy Joseph / 763
Harris, Vincent Medeley / 736
Harrison, Frank James / 805
Hart, Daniel Anthony / 874
Hart, Joseph Hubert / 871
Hartley, James Joseph / 261
Harty, Jeremiah James / 257
Hastrich, Jerome Joseph / 694
Hayes, Nevin William / 716
Hayes, Patrick Joseph / 316

Kelly, Patrick / 13
Kelly, Thomas Cajetan / 892
Kennedy, Thomas Francis / 278
Kenney, Lawrence James / 971
Kenny, Michael Hughes / 914
Kenny, William John / 249
Kenrick, Francis Patrick / 22
Kenrick, Peter Richard / 39
Keough, Francis Patrick / 432
Keyes, Michael Joseph / 358
Kiley, Moses Elias / 428
Killeen, James Jerome / 858
Kinney, John F. / 879
Klonowski, Henry Theophilus / 529
Kmiec, Edward Urban / 963
Kocisko, Stephen John / 622
Koeckemann, Bernard H. / 159
Koester, Charles Roman / 802
Koudelka, Joseph Maria / 279
Kozlowski, Edward / 313
Krautbauer, Francis Xavier / 139
Krawczak, Arthur Henry / 830
Krol, John Joseph / 587
Kucera, Daniel William / 890
Kucera, Louis Benedict / 408
Kuchmiak, Michael / 1043
Kuzma, George Martin / 1023

Laghi, Pio / 10-B
La Hailandière, Celestin de / 34
Lamb, Hugh Louis / 441
Lamy, John Baptist / 62
Lane, Loras Thomas / 572
Lane, Raymond Aloysius / 472
Larkin, William Thomas / 916
Laval, John Marius / 305
Lavialle, Peter Joseph / 96
Law, Bernard Francis / 835
Lawler, John Jeremiah / 293
LeBlond, Charles Hubert / 424
Ledvina, Emmanuel Boleslaus / 347
Leech, George Leo / 438
Lefebvre de Cheverus, Jean / 7
Lefevère, Peter Paul / 38
Leibold, Paul Francis / 641

Leibrecht, John Joseph / 1004
Leipzig, Francis Peter / 563
Lenihan, Mathias Clement / 266
Lenihan, Thomas Mathias / 226
Leonard, Vincent Martin / 702
Leray, Francis Xavier / 144
Lessard, Raymond William / 833
Levada, William Joseph / 973
Leven, Stephen Aloysius / 612
Lillis, Thomas Francis / 270
Lipscomb, Oscar Hugh / 935
Lohmuller, Martin Nicholas / 789
Lootens, Louis / 108
Loras, John Mathias / 31
Losten, Basil Harry / 807
Lotocky, Innocent Hilarion / 943
Loughlin, John / 67
Loverde, Paul Stephen / 1042
Lowney, Denis Matthew / 326
Lubachivsky, Myroslav Ivan / 925
Lucey, Robert Emmet / 431
Lucker, Raymond Alphonse / 814
Ludden, Patrick Anthony / 179
Luers, John Henry / 83
Lyke, James Patterson / 921
Lynch, George Edward / 784
Lynch, Joseph Patrick / 303
Lynch, Patrick Neeson / 85
Lyne, Timothy Joseph / 985
Lyons, Thomas William / 840

MacFarland, Francis Patrick / 84
MacGinley, John Bernard / 291
Macheboeuf, Joseph Projectus / 111
MacKenzie, Eric Francis / 564
Madera Uribe, José de Jesús / 928
Maes, Camillus Paul / 170
Maginn, Edward Joseph / 632
Magner, Francis Joseph / 477
Maguire, John Joseph / 649
Maguire, Joseph Francis / 820
Maher, Leo Thomas / 677
Mahoney, Bernard Joseph / 357
Mahoney, James Patrick / 823
Mahony, Roger Michael / 852

Maida, Adam Joseph / 990
Maigret, Louis Désiré / 54
Malone, James William / 657
Maloney, Charles Garrett / 606
Maloney, David Mono / 667
Maloney, Thomas Francis / 659
Manning, Timothy / 518
Manogue, Patrick / 155
Manucy, Dominic / 135
Marcinkus, Paul Casimir / 7-A
Marconi, Dominic Anthony / 866
Mardaga, Thomas Joseph / 739
Maréchal, Ambrose / 11
Marino, Eugene Antonio / 841
Markham, Thomas Francis / 565
Markiewicz, Alfred John / 1021
Marling Joseph Mary / 530
Marshall, John Aloysius / 816
Martin, Augustus Mary / 71
Martinelli, Sebastiano / 3-B
Marty, Martin / 153
Marx, Adolph / 621
Matthiesen, Leroy Theodore / 930
Matz, Nicholas Chrysostom / 182
May, John Lawrence / 747
McAuliffe, Maurice Francis / 381
McAuliffe, Michael Francis / 779
McCafferty, John Edgar / 754
McCarrick, Theodore Edgar / 887
McCarthy, Edward Anthony / 713
McCarthy, John Edward / 910
McCarthy, Joseph Edward / 414
McCarthy, Justin Joseph / 598
McCarty, William Tiburtius / 488
McCloskey, John / 42
McCloskey, William George / 102
McCormack, William J. / 1022
McCormick, Joseph Carroll / 521
McCormick, Patrick Joseph / 568
McCort, John Joseph / 309
McDevitt, Gerald Vincent / 685
McDevitt, Philip Richard / 323
McDonald, Andrew Joseph / 822
McDonald, William Joseph / 703
McDonnell, Charles Edward / 205

McDonnell, Thomas John / 532
McDonough, Thomas Joseph / 523
McDowell, John Bernard / 735
McEntegart, Bryan Joseph / 492
McFadden, James Augustine / 416
McFarland, Norman Francis / 795
McFaul, James Augustine / 216
McGann, John Raymond / 800
McGavick, Alexander Joseph / 235
McGeough, Joseph Francis / 4-A
McGill, John / 61
McGolrick, James / 195
McGovern, Patrick Aloysius / 306
McGovern, Thomas / 185
McGrath, Joseph Francis / 336
McGrath, Joseph Michael / 440
McGrath, Patrick Joseph / 1054
McGucken, Joseph Thomas / 478
McGuinness, Eugene Joseph / 451
McHugh, James Thomas / 1035
McIntyre, James Francis / 476
McKinney, Joseph Crescent / 769
McLaughlin, Bernard Joseph / 773
McLaughlin, Charles Borromeo / 701
McLaughlin, Thomas Henry / 436
McMahon, John Joseph / 396
McMahon, Lawrence Stephen / 149
McManaman, Edward Peter / 549
McManus, James Edward / 526
McManus, William Edward / 746
McMullen, John / 158
McNamara, John Michael / 395
McNamara, Lawrence J. / 900
McNamara, Martin Dewey / 551
McNeirny, Francis / 127
McNicholas, John Timothy / 331
McNicholas, Joseph Alphonsus / 774
McNulty, James Aloysius / 534
McQuaid, Bernard Joseph / 103
McRaith, John Jeremiah / 964
McShea, Joseph / 577
McVinney, Russell Joseph / 548
Medeiros, Humberto Sousa / 733
Meerschaert, Theophile / 200
Melcher, Joseph / 104

Smyth, Timothy Clement / 80
Snyder, John Joseph / 827
Soenneker, Henry Joseph / 668
Soens, Lawrence Donald / 980
Spalding, John Lancaster / 145
Spalding, Martin John / 55
Spellman, Francis Joseph / 415
Speltz, George Henry / 692
Spence, John Selby / 704
Speyrer, Jude / 929
Stafford, James Francis / 860
Stang, William / 263
Stanton, Martin Walter / 634
Stariha, John / 252
Steck, Leo John / 545
Steib, James Terry / 992
Steinbock, John Thomas / 999
Steiner, Kenneth Donald / 897
Stock, John / 806
Straling, Philip Francis / 907
Strecker, Ignatius Jerome / 678
Stritch, Samuel Alphonsus / 352
Sullivan, James Stephen / 825
Sullivan, John Joseph / 824
Sullivan, Joseph M. / 938
Sullivan, Joseph Vincent / 740
Sullivan, Walter Francis / 798
Sulyk, Stephen / 942
Swanstrom, Edward Ernest / 662
Sweeney, James Joseph / 479
Swint, John Joseph / 356
Symons, Joseph Keith / 944
Szoka, Edmund Casimir / 810

Tafoya, Arthur Nicholas / 934
Takacs, Basil / 370
Tanner, Paul Francis / 722
Tarasevitch, Vladimir L. / 982
Tawil, Joseph Elias / 652
Thill, Francis Augustine / 458
Thompson, David Bernard / 1058
Tief, Francis Joseph / 345
Tierney, Michael / 211
Tihen, John Henry / 302
Timlin, James Clifford / 873

Timon, John / 52
Toebbe, Augustus Maria / 117
Toolen, Thomas Joseph / 387
Topel, Bernard Joseph / 610
Tracy, Robert Emmet / 648
Trautman, Donald W. / 1006
Treacy, John Patrick / 507
Treinen, Sylvester William / 682
Trobec, James / 229
Tschoepe, Thomas Ambrose / 725
Tuigg, John / 142
Turner, William / 337
Tyler, William Barber / 45

Untener, Kenneth E. / 940
Unterkoefler, Ernest Leo / 675

Vagnozzi, Egidio / 7-B
Valero, Rene A. / 939
Van de Velde, John Oliver / 57
Van de Ven, Cornelius / 268
Van de Vyver, Augustine / 193
Vath, Joseph Gregory / 730
Vaughan, Austin B. / 888
Vehr, Urban John / 410
Verdaguer, Peter / 197
Verot, John Marcel / 86
Vertin, John / 150
Vlazny, John George / 986
Vogel, Cyril John / 714
Vonesh, Raymond James / 755

Wadhams, Edgar Philip / 129
Waldschmidt, Paul Edward / 896
Walsh, Daniel Francis / 950
Walsh, Emmet Michael / 391
Walsh, James Anthony / 422
Walsh, James Edward / 388
Walsh, Louis Sebastian / 274
Walsh, Nicholas E. / 845
Walsh, Thomas Joseph / 330
Ward, John / 301
Ward, John James / 695
Waters, Vincent Stanislaus / 503
Watson, Alfred Michael / 715

276

Watters, Loras Joseph / 718
Watterson, John Ambrose / 154
Wcela, Emil Aloysius / 1048
Weakland, Rembert George / 893
Wehrle, Vincent John Baptist / 296
Weigand, William Kenneth / 936
Welch, Thomas Anthony / 380
Weldon, Christopher Joseph / 560
Welsh, Lawrence Harold / 908
Welsh, Thomas Jerome / 790
Whealon, John Francis / 670
Whelan, James / 88
Whelan, Richard Vincent / 37
Whelan, Robert Louis / 752
White, Charles Daniel / 385
Whitfield, James / 21
Wigger, Winand Michael / 161
Willging, Joseph Clement / 481
Williams, James Kendrick / 996
Williams, John Joseph / 99
Willinger, Aloysius Joseph / 404
Winkelmann, Christian / 427
Winter, William Joseph / 1055
Wirz, George Otto / 898
Wood, James Frederick / 77
Woznicki, Stephen Stanislaus / 452
Wright, John Joseph / 525
Wuerl, Donald William / 1012
Wurm, John Nicholas / 870
Wycislo, Aloysius John / 664

Young, Joshua Mary / 73

Zaleski, Alexander Mieceslaus / 561
Zardetti, John Joseph Otto / 192
Zayek, Francis Mansour / 686
Ziemann, George Patrick / 1024
Zipfel, Paul A. / 1059
Zuroweste, Albert Rudolph / 539